Empire of Extinction

Empire of Extinction

*Russians and the North Pacific's Strange
Beasts of the Sea, 1741–1867*

RYAN TUCKER JONES
SENIOR LECTURER
DEPARTMENT OF HISTORY
UNIVERSITY OF AUCKLAND

OXFORD
UNIVERSITY PRESS

OXFORD

UNIVERSITY PRESS

Oxford University Press is a department of the University of Oxford.
It furthers the University's objective of excellence in research, scholarship,
and education by publishing worldwide.

Oxford   New York
Auckland   Cape Town   Dar es Salaam   Hong Kong   Karachi
Kuala Lumpur   Madrid   Melbourne   Mexico City   Nairobi
New Delhi   Shanghai   Taipei   Toronto

With offices in
Argentina   Austria   Brazil   Chile   Czech Republic   France   Greece
Guatemala   Hungary   Italy   Japan   Poland   Portugal   Singapore
South Korea   Switzerland   Thailand   Turkey   Ukraine   Vietnam

Oxford is a registered trademark of Oxford University Press
in the UK and certain other countries.

Published in the United States of America by
Oxford University Press
198 Madison Avenue, New York, NY 10016

Library of Congress Cataloging-in-Publication Data
Jones, Ryan Tucker, author.
Empire of extinction : Russians and the North Pacific's strange beasts of the sea, 1741–1867 /
Ryan Tucker Jones.
pages cm
Includes bibliographical references and index.
ISBN 978–0–19–934341–6 (hardback); 978–0–19–067081–8 (paperback)
1. Extinct animals—North Pacific Region.   2. Steller's sea cow Effect of human beings on—North
Pacific Ocean.   3. Fur trade—North Pacific Region.   4. Nature—Effect of human beings on—North
Pacific Region—History.   5. Natural history—North Pacific Region.   6. North Pacific Region—
Colonization—Environmental aspects.   7. North Pacific Ocean—Environmental conditions.
8. Russia—Colonies—North Pacific Region.   I. Title.
QL88.15.N69J66 2014
591.6809182′3—dc23
2013047262

To my father, Helmuth Jones, and my grandfather,
the late Everett Jones.

They inspired this work in many ways, by teaching me
the value of history, the pleasure of hard work,
the importance of travel, and the locations of home.

CONTENTS

ACKNOWLEDGMENTS

The trajectory of researching and writing this book mirrored, in some ways, that of its subject. I began studying the history of the Russian Empire while living in New York City. In 2005, I moved to St. Petersburg, Russia, to conduct research. After freezing through one of the city's coldest winters in recent history, it became clear that I needed to experience firsthand the empire's furthest reaches. In the early summer of 2006, I spent a month in Siberia and Kamchatka, exiting the archives and moving into the fields and mountains. That experience convinced me I had chosen the right subject; the lands and seas I had previously encountered only in old documents came alive before my eyes, and forever changed me with their beauty and wildness. The following year, I went to Kodiak Island, and with two old friends kayaked among whales and sea otters, camping on some of the loneliest shores in North America. While I was revising my dissertation, my father traveled with me to Sitka and Unalaska—the latter being a place where both of my grandfathers spent part of World War II. Last year, as I finished this manuscript, my beautiful wife joined me on the pilgrimage of St. Herman on Spruce Island, in Alaska. There we received the generous hospitality of the Alutiit, who shared their stories and their salmon. At some point, I realized that, while the Russians had left the Pacific and gone back to Europe, I had come home.

The debts incurred along this path are enormous. David Armitage taught me to be an historian, helped me to think big, and opened innumerable doors I hardly knew existed. He has been both a mentor and friend for the last nine years. John McNeill introduced me to the field of environmental history, and made it so exciting that I still cannot imagine writing about anything else. Richard Wortman instructed me in the nuts and bolts of Russian imperial history, and steered me clear of the big mistakes. Doug Weiner did a little of all of the above, while also giving generously of his immense knowledge of Russian environmental history.

In St. Petersburg, Tatiana Fedorovna at the Russian State Archive of the Navy saved this book by generously taking time to introduce me to eighteenth-century Russian handwriting. She is a shining example of the best side of Russian archival culture. In the United States, Anastasia Tarmann-Lynch at the Alaska State Library provided invaluable guidance, suggestions, and ideas. Her colleagues there also deserves thanks, as do librarians and archivists at the St. Petersburg Academy of Sciences Archive, the Russian State Historical Archive, the Krasheninnikov Library in Kamchatka, the Staatsbibliothek zu Berlin, the John Carter Brown Library, the Bancroft Library at the University of California Berkeley, and the University of Washington Special Collections. At Oxford University Press, Susan Ferber has continually streamlined my prose; I wish she had been there from the start. The publisher's anonymous readers also sharpened my arguments and gave the book new directions.

Along the way, this book has also benefitted from generous financial support. The Fulbright Program funded research in St. Petersburg and Moscow, and the American Council of Learned Societies provided support during the writing process. Appalachian State University and Idaho State University both contributed travel and research support at various points along the way. The Alaska Historical Society both alerted me to the importance of local history and kindly awarded me a travel fellowship to present my research in Unalaska. Many thanks to all.

Less tangibly, but just as importantly, a number of friends and colleagues have given support and intelligence. At Columbia University, Jason Governale, Kevin Murphy, and Giovanni Ruffini shared expertise and sometimes loaned spare couches. In Russia (and beyond), Stephen Brain inspired me with his archival tenacity and environmental acumen. Julia Lajus has been a warm friend and facilitator in St. Petersburg and in many unlikely parts of the world, from Kolding to Perth. At Appalachian State University, Ed Behrend-Martinez and Judkin Browning initiated me into a different kind of foreign culture and helped me navigate the early stages of book contracts. My excellent department at Idaho State University, and in particular Kevin Marsh, has given me more support and encouragement than I could have ever expected. In Alaska, Jenya Anichenko and Jason Rogers linked me much more directly to the places (and boats) I write about in this book. Katherine Arndt, at the University of Alaska-Fairbanks, shared with me her unrivaled knowledge of Russian America's primary sources. Along the way, at multiple points and places, I was also fortunate to become friends with Ilya Vinkovetsky and Andrei Znamenski.

When I began this research, I was living by myself in a small apartment on 113th Street in Manhattan. While the housing space remains small, it is now filled with the wonderful, ever-supportive Hannah Cutting-Jones and the ever-wonderful and sometimes supportive Genevieve and Everett. Hannah read every chapter of this book at various stages, providing the eye for detail and sense of style I often lack. Though she came to this book halfway through its creation, she is its Katharine the Great. Thank you, beyond measure, for coming with me to St. Petersburg, Trier, Alaska, and places even more remote. My mother, Janie Jones, also helped nourish this book. She was with me the first time I saw Russia and her house was always my second library. Though I'm sure she wishes I had chosen a warmer field of research, it meant a lot to me, and to this book, that she always supported me.

Empire of Extinction

Introduction

The Meanings of Steller and His Sea Cow

… as with the individual, so with the species, the hour of life has run its course, and is spent.

—Charles Darwin, *The Voyage of the Beagle*

On an unrecorded day in the 1760s, the last Steller's sea cow (*hydrodamalis gigas*) died. Before eighteenth-century human hunters began killing it, this gigantic manatee—up to thirty feet long and covered with thick layers of fat—had lived in the shallow bays of two small islands in the North Pacific, and nowhere else. Its ancestors had once inhabited the seas from Baja California, Mexico, to Kamchatka, Russia—but with climate change and human predation, its numbers had dwindled to several thousand by the middle of the eighteenth century.[1] Despite this decline, on isolated, uninhabited Bering and Copper Islands the last members of the species might have survived indefinitely had a floodtide of empire not suddenly swept them away. Russian explorers discovered the sea cow in 1741, and in less than thirty years the fur traders who followed up on this discovery had hunted the animal to extinction. By the nineteenth century, the descendants of the sea cow's killers were wondering what animal could have left behind the gigantic bones lying on the shoreline. Even the memory of the sea cow had vanished. (See Figures 0.1 and 0.2 for renderings of Steller's sea cow.)

Though the sea cow's murderers soon forgot its very existence, I do not think the animal should be brushed so easily over the cliff of oblivion. Nor did Rudyard Kipling. In his story "The White Seal," he imagined a last herd of Steller's sea cows still living around the now-abandoned islands where the Russians had first encountered them. Kotick, a white seal and the hero of the story, discovers the sea cows while looking for a place to escape from the Russian sealers on the Pribylof Islands. Kipling writes that the sea cows "were like no walrus, sea lion, seal, bear, whale, shark, fish, squid, or scallop that Kotick had ever seen. They were between twenty and thirty feet long, and they had no hind

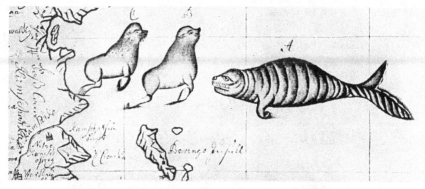

Figure 0.1 Steller's Sea Cow from a 1742 Drawing (Detail). From Waxell's chart of Bering's voyages, 1741 in Frank Alfred Golder's *Bering's Voyages* (New York, 1922). Courtesy of Alaska State Library.

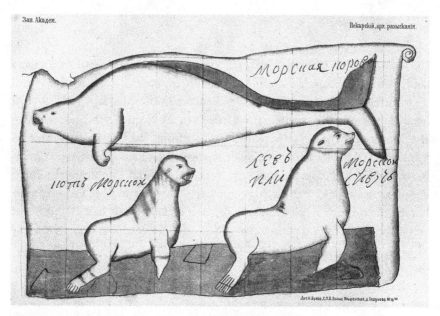

Figure 0.2 Steller's sea cow, a fur seal, and a sea lion (detail). From *Zapiski Imperatorskoi Akademii Nauk* (1895). Courtesy of Alaska State Library.

flippers." Like other lost creatures, such as the dodo, the sea cows seemed comically mish-mashed, doomed by their absurdity to extinction: "Their heads were the most foolish-looking things you ever saw, and they balanced on the ends of their tails in deep water when they weren't grazing, bowing solemnly to each other and waving their front flippers as a fat man waves his arm." As Kotick mutters in disgust, "People who are such idiots as these are would have been killed long ago if they hadn't found out some safe island."[2] True to the seal's intuition, the forgotten beasts, all slobber and seaweed, lead Kotick northward to a secret island enclosing a hidden lagoon which is safe from all human attack. There, Kotick's herd of seals finds a perfect breeding ground, and escape from human hunters, "away and away in the Bering Sea." As the seal mother sings:

> Where billow meets billow, then soft be thy pillow,
> Ah, weary wee flipperling, curl at thy ease!
> The storm shall not wake thee, nor shark overtake thee,
> Asleep in the arms of the slow-swinging seas![3]

Kipling's remarkable, poignant look at empire from the sea cow's and fur seal's perspectives expresses the haunting sense of loss that extinction has left on colonial landscapes and seascapes. It sits ill at ease with his well-known praise of the "White Man's Burden" and ultimate sanction of the British Raj's authority over humans and animals in India.[4] Like Herman Melville, perhaps, he could see the paradoxes provoked by the violence necessary to civilization. And like Melville—whose great white whale, Moby Dick, ultimately survives Ahab's relentless global hunt—Kipling indulged in the hope that empire's effects on animals were reversible. Possibly the fact that it was Russians and Americans—and not the British—who were killing these animals made imagining the alternatives to empire easier for Kipling. If so, he would not have been the first for whom Russians' barbarity laid bare the cruelties of colonial expansion. As early as the 1780s, Europeans were already using the Russian North Pacific as an example of empire's havoc and wastage, with the sea cow, fur seal, and sea otter at the center.

The death of the last sea cow in a lonely corner of the North Pacific in the 1760s was precisely the event that provoked discussions of extinction beginning in the 1780s, at a time when the dodo was still commonly thought to be either imaginary or still extant. Marine biologist and historian Richard Ellis has called the disappearance of Steller's sea cow "the paradigm of anthropogenic extinction," [5] and the scientific literature recognizes it as one of only three known megafaunal extinctions to occur in the modern era before 1800.[6] Yet, historians have had little to say about the loss of the sea cow. When mentioned at all, its extinction stands either as an ironic consequence of European scientific study,[7] or a reminder that human degradation of the environment is not a recent or new phenomenon.[8] A recent study of the environmental history of the early modern world assesses the ecological effects of the Russian fur trade while ignoring the sea cow's extinction altogether.[9] Nor have historians or scientists credited eighteenth- and early-nineteenth-century natural historians with understanding the significance of the extinction. Ellis claims that, into the 1820s, "the concept of extinction was completely alien."[10] However, in 1812 the German scientist

Georg Heinrich von Langsdorff had written that Steller's sea cow "...must now be ranked among the list of beings lost from the animal kingdom, like the dudu, the mammoth, the carnivorous elephant of Ohio, and others."[11] Before him, the Englishman Martin Sauer had learned as early as the 1790s of the animal's disappearance, and wrote about it in an unheralded description of his travels that ushered in the modern understanding of extinction.[12]

Empire of Extinction uses the death of the last sea cow to explore the shape and magnitude of colonial environmental change, as well as Europeans' responses to those changes. The sea cow, along with other animals such as the sea otter and fur seal (creatures the German naturalist Georg Wilhelm Steller in 1742 termed "strange beasts of the sea") are also crucial for understanding Russia's expansion into the North Pacific—the imperial movement responsible for their extinction. Marine mammals were central players in this history, as objects of the hunt, as symbols of a larger natural world, and as unpredictable historical actors in their own right. The ocean and its inhabitants also shaped the often tragic relationship between Russians, Kamchadals, Aleuts, and other indigenous peoples. Understanding how and why Russians thrust themselves into Eastern Siberia and Alaska, and what consequences these actions held, also requires understanding the sea cow and its brethren. However, environmental change in the North Pacific did not present ready lessons. Natural historians, who provided the most detailed accounts of the region, also were the first to try to make sense of the sea cow's disappearance. They observed the rapid changes brought to the ocean, interpreted them with help from prevailing scientific ideas, drew some surprising new conclusions, and publicized news of the sea cow's extinction throughout Europe.

In 1973, Victor B. Scheffer, American wildlife biologist and author of the then very popular books *The Year of the Seal* (1972) and *The Year of the Whale* (1969), imagined, like Kipling, a remnant sea cow population. In Scheffer's story, a fourteen-year-old Russian named Nikita sails to Bering Island and is astounded by the number of bones on the beach. As he examines a bashed-in skull from the presumably extinct animals, a "strangled snort" sounds in the lagoon. A gigantic sea cow surfaces, raises its head, and pauses, "as though listening for lost companions."

> The boy watched in fascination, afraid to shift his cramped and chilled position, while tears dripped from his nose. He sneezed—and when he looked up the animal was gone. It reappeared quietly, offshore. As it stared toward the land, the boy was brushed with a feeling he could not understand, as though he had heard a door closing in an empty house. He shivered, and walked slowly toward camp. He never told anyone what he had seen until he was a full-grown man with a small boy on his knee.[13]

Scheffer understood the sea cow's extinction as a lesson for modern humans. "The message of the sea cow is undiminished with the passing of 200 years," he wrote. "The sea cow is gone and Earth is a lonelier place.... The wisdom, goodness, and greatness of Man will be measured not wholly by his technical power over the wild things of Earth but also by his moral strength in letting them be."[14]

There is a close connection between Kipliing and Scheffer's lament for lost species and Russia's colonial experience. Historian Alexander Etkind has described Russia's colonial past as a process of "loss, splitting, and reconfiguration," to a degree perhaps unique among Western empires.[15] Loss came from both the process of Russia's outward imperial expansion, as other peoples were subjugated, and through Russia's internal colonization by an exploitative, brutalizing state and intellectual subservience to Western Europe. The loss in ecological diversity that accompanied Russian (and other) imperial expansion should be added as well. This loss was felt not only by those like the biologist Scheffer and the novelist Kipling, but also, much earlier, by Russians and Europeans who experienced the Empire in the eighteenth and early nineteenth centuries. And, like the loss Etkind describes, perceptions of ecological change were closely related to Western critiques of the Russian Empire.

Conceptions and realities of empire and extinction thus provide the fundamental tension in this book. They are encapsulated by two different statements of humans' relationships with the natural world: one French, one Russian. One of the era's most influential naturalists, the Frenchman Georges-Louis Leclerc, Comte du Buffon, wrote in 1792 that the ability to subjugate animals was consequence and proof of humanity's civility, for "the empire over animals, like all other empires, could not be established previous to the institution of society." As Europeans reached the pinnacle of enlightenment, their dominion over animals became unassailable. The observable decrease in wild animals everywhere further proved the progress of European civilization:

> But when the human race multiplied, and spread over the earth, and when, by the aid of the arts and society, man was able to conquer the universe, he, by degrees, lessened the number of ferocious beasts, he purged the earth of those gigantic animals of which we sometimes still find the enormous bones; he destroyed, or reduced to a small number every hurtful and voracious species; he opposed one animal to another, and conquered some by fraud, others by force; and attacking them by every rational method he arrived at a means of safety, and has established an empire which is only bounded by inaccessible solitudes, burning sands, frozen mountains, and obscure caverns, which now serve as retreats for the small number of species of ferocious animals that remains.[16]

Despite Buffon's sometimes rueful attitude toward the destruction of species, empire—both over animals and other humans—seemed to him and others the highest expression and best test of civilization in the eighteenth century. Europeans traveling in the North Pacific often made the same calculation. In recounting Russia's conquest of the Aleutian Islands, the German poet-scientist Adelbert von Chamisso wrote "before they were discovered by the Russians [they were] the peaceable abode of the waterfowl and seals." Now, however, "the animals are subdued as well as the people."[17] Mastery over animal populations served as a powerful metaphor for human empire in the eighteenth century.

Buffon's test of civilization was precisely what many Europeans (and some Russians) thought the Russian Empire failed. Russians could never completely master North Pacific nature, just as they never could master their own empire. Mastery, in fact, was a complex concept. The uncontrolled destruction of animals could, paradoxically, weaken imperial claims. Environmental degradation reshaped the fur trade and drew reprimands from European naturalists. The North Pacific experience also prompted some Europeans to think beyond Buffon's simple equation of civilization and domination, and to reevaluate humanity's relationship with the natural world. The sea cow's extinction represents at once both the flattening effects that early modern imperial expansion had on biological diversity and the eroding of the confidence that Europeans had in the rightness of this expansion.

An alternative understanding of humanity's relationship with nature was formulated by the Russian fur trader Aleksandr Baranov. In a few ragged verses he had set to song, Baranov insisted that:

> Building the union of communities,
> we do not need the fulsome Hellenic muse.
> Simple nature alone
> teaches us to follow the rules and honor her law.
> Buildings be erected in the New World parts!
> Rus' presses forward: Nootka is her goal![18]

Instead of humanity proving its civilization (represented here by the "fulsome Hellenic muse") through conquering nature, Baranov wrote of following the law implicit in the non-human world surrounding him. "Building the union" of Russians and Native Americans ("our numerous friends"), Baranov would win for Russia a permanent place in the New World. His song captures important aspects of Russian colonization in the North Pacific—namely, cooperation and accommodation with colonial peoples and environments—that challenge the notion that Russians thought only in terms of subduing nature and native. And yet, the melody of domination and destruction can be heard in Baranov's song nearly as clearly as in Buffon's definition of civilization; Baranov called on Russia to reshape the North Pacific's environment through building and to claim the ocean's space as her own by removing the British and Spanish from Nootka Sound, south of the Russian colonies. Considering the end results of such actions, Baranov's doggerel ultimately had no more space in it for the sea cow than did Buffon's manicured prose.

By examining Russian activity in the North Pacific from 1741 to 1867, *Empire of Extinction* illuminates the motivations, contradictions, and results of Baranov's task—how to build a profitable, secure, and justifiable empire on the basis of exploiting marine mammals and indigenous people. Chapter 1 examines the Second Kamchatka Expedition (1725–1745), when natural historians from all around Europe—but primarily Russia and Germany—actively shaped Russian policy toward the region and formulated European ideas of nature there. The often contentious relationship between Steller and his Russian colleague Stepan Krasheninnikov demonstrates the ways in which North Pacific nature was being presented to a European public, as well as the ways naturalists could sometimes work against imperial interests. Steller, along with all his pioneering work in marine biology, also chafed against Russian oppression of Kamchatka's indigenous peoples, and he began to paint a picture of the natural world in decline. Chapter 2 relates how these premonitions came horrifyingly true when, after 1742, *promyshlenniki* (fur traders) spread through the Aleutian Islands and forced the native Aleuts to hunt sea otters, in the process exterminating the sea cow and nearly doing the same to sea otters. Though some scholars have contended that the Russians did not destroy Alaska's fur resources, archival records provide a remarkably detailed record of this decline and also reveal the unique visibility of this decline taking place among limited populations of animals confined to isolated islands. However, environmental change was not a simple story of overhunting; rather, the extinction of the sea cow and near-extinction of the sea otter were part of longer precolonial and non-human histories as well. Chapter 3 examines the relationship between natural historians and imperial power in St. Petersburg, and naturalists' evolving understanding of Russian colonialism during a time when few actually visited the North Pacific. While many fur traders and scientists still claimed that sea otters had simply migrated elsewhere, there was a dawning realization that the fur trade was wreaking unprecedented environmental havoc.

Chapter 4 relates how, from the 1790s through the 1820s, St. Petersburg launched a new era of state exploration in the North Pacific. Naturalists on board government voyages revolutionized European comprehension of the region and also helped guide the Russian Empire towards new conservationist policies. They published (sometimes without permission) scathing critiques of Russian environmental policies, establishing connections between Russian colonial mismanagement and the extirpation of fur-bearing animals. It was within this context that Sauer and Langsdorff made their startling claims of the sea cow's extinction. Still, many naturalists and others resisted the idea, and Chapter 5 examines the case of Peter Simon Pallas—by 1800 the empire's most famous scientist—and the reasons why his massive survey of Russia's fauna avoided discussing extinction entirely. That Pallas missed this signal event in natural history was testimony to the powerful structures that empires imposed on human minds. The interconnected history of Thomas Pennant's *Arctic Zoology* (1785–1787) reveals the close, ongoing connection between nature and empire, as well as the surprising consequences of the American Revolution on ideas about extinction. Chapter 6 relates how, even as naturalists tempered their criticisms of Russian colonialism after 1820, imperial officials confronted the problem of extinction head on, instituting impressive conservation measures that built in strength until the 1867 sale of the colony. American and British fur traders replaced the Russians as environmental villains in imperial accounts—evidence that the Russian empire had absorbed the concerns of natural historians even as it left them with less to complain about. This was no easy story of enlightened triumph, for ideas of conservation became a principal justification for keeping management of the fur trade out of supposedly irresponsible indigenous hands.

The history of the Russian North Pacific reshapes understandings of environmental and imperial history in several ways. *Empire of Extinction* illustrates the rapid ecological change that took place in the preindustrial era and relates the conjuncture of human and non-human forces involved in this change. It also demonstrates the powerful impact colonial environments had on European conceptions of the natural world—an idea articulated most thoroughly by the British historian Richard Grove.[19] Such insights place Siberia and Alaska firmly within a global history of colonialism, rather than only Russian and American national histories. Focusing on naturalists reveals the points of tension and cooperation between scientists and empires in this era of flourishing natural history. This topic has produced much controversy, with the majority of scholars depicting naturalists as lackeys of growing imperial states. *Empire of Extinction* shows that there were many reasons for scientists to back European imperialism, but that sometimes direct, disturbing experiences with colonialism changed men's minds. These naturalists did not normally criticize imperialism in general, but saved their harshest words specifically for Russian imperialism. It mattered that Russians were killing sea cows and sea otters, and Russians' persistent fixation with the vast size of the territory and recurrent insecurities in the face of Western scrutiny shaped environmental outcomes in the North Pacific. As Russia's only maritime territory, the North Pacific presented different challenges, and was conceived in different terms. Thus, though emblematic of a larger history of early-modern imperial degradation of the natural world, environmental change and changing environmental conceptions in the North Pacific were both uniquely traumatic and uniquely creative. *Empire of Extinction* is thus a testament to both the brutality and the surprising flexibility of Russian imperial institutions so far from the tsar and so close to the ocean.

The North Pacific Ocean

The land, water, and animals of the North Pacific Ocean are leading characters in this history, alongside Russians, Aleuts, Germans, and other members of the human species. As many environmental historians have shown, the natural world has not been a static backdrop for human actions, but is rather made up of elements and creatures with their own complex histories, which have intertwined with people's affairs. The North Pacific is no exception; indeed, the region has exhibited frequent volcanic activity and high volatility in short- and long-term weather patterns, number of animals and mixture of species, and its human history.

Historical ecologists recognize the ocean between Kamchatka and British Columbia as one of the world's richest in nutrients and speciation. Despite the frequent storms, ever-present fogs, and long winters, the region has been home to diverse and numerous life-forms. As the American naturalist John Muir put it during his 1881 trip to the Aleutian Islands, "there is no lack of warm, eager life even here."[20] Even in the wake of 140 years of Russian and American exploitation, Muir might have left out his "even here." In fact, along with the tropical Indo-Pacific, the North Pacific has been one of the world's greatest engines for marine evolution. Most of the world's pinnipeds (literally, "fin-feet," i.e., walrus, seals, and sea lions) evolved in the area, and it remains their most abundant location.[21] Sea cows did not originate in the North Pacific, but are thought to have extended their range northward in a warmer era. Their vegetarian diet proved to be an untrustworthy source of nutrition in such cold seas. On the other hand, those species that eat plankton (fish and whales) and those who eat the plankton-fed fish (pinnipeds, more fish and whales) have found the North Pacific to be among the richest seas in the world, and the region's herring, salmon, sea otter, and whale populations remain among the highest anywhere. Humans have, for at least 16,000 years, inserted themselves into this food web, tying themselves to the fate of plankton, whales, and every organism in between.

Despite the North Pacific's unrelenting cold, humans discovered many opportunities here. From Kamchatka to Southeast Alaska, Kamchadals, Aleuts, Alutiit, Tlingit (see Figure 0.3 for their pre-contact territories), and others found the ocean environment to provide the best nutrition as well as cultural inspiration. As in most high-latitude locations, the ocean contains a much higher

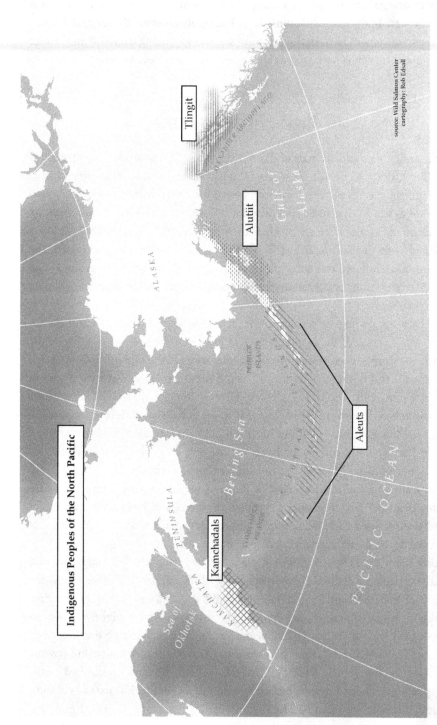

Figure 0.3 Indigenous Peoples of the North Pacific discussed most frequently in the book.

biomass than the land.[22] Additionally, the land has proved fickle and danger-ous, given the North Pacific's frequent volcanic and seismic activity. Volcanic eruptions have repeatedly forced evacuations, and mega-earthquakes have killed unknown numbers.[23] The ocean too posed dangers. Tsunamis were just as fear-some as the earthquakes that caused them (they would kill several dozens of Aleuts and Russians in the eighteenth century), and harvesting the bounty of whales and seals occurred amid sudden storms, fierce currents, and perpetual fog. Still, archaeological remains attest to the fact that tidal marine invertebrates, pelagic fish, and marine mammals have long been the staples of human habita-tion. They would remain so for the Russians, despite attempts to replicate their familiar European ecologies.

Nutritious marine animals posed their own challenges, with their numbers fluctuating due to human predation and still-mysterious oceanographic factors. Sea lion, sea otter, whale, salmon, and other animal populations swing wildly based on complex convergences of oceanic temperatures, current changes, and variations in other species' abundance that contemporary ecologists still find it difficult to explain.[24] What seems clear is that cold-weather regimes have stimu-lated overall productivity of the North Pacific, and these periods have offered the greatest opportunities for high-trophic level predators such as sea lions. Humans focused on hunting one animal inevitably impacted the entire ecosystem. Some scholars conclude that human predation in fact stabilized some ecosystems, while others argue that overexploitation of large mammals in particular consid-erably reshaped local environments.[25] These are critical questions for assessing Russian impacts, as well.

The North Pacific has not only been thickly inhabited, but also thickly glossed with meaning. Aleut tales, in particular, are obsessed with the ocean and its creatures, but cultures all around the North Pacific reserved the great-est prestige and attached ritual to those who went to sea, particularly whale hunters.[26] In addition to testing a hunter's character, the ocean was an arbiter of disputes, a place of danger, and an inspiration for artwork. British writer Jonathan Raban speculates that the totemic art of the North Pacific comes from "the way in which a slight ripple will smash a reflection into an abstract of fragmentary images." He contrasts this ocean-centric world with the notion held by many European explorers and colonists that the sea was merely a "medium of access to the all-important land," of which there turned out to be precious little of use.[27] Neither the Russians, nor the French, Spanish, British and Americans who started coming to the North Pacific in the eighteenth cen-tury, ever loved the sea the way Kamchadals, Aleuts, or Tlingit did. As the Russian Orthodox monk Herman (today canonized as St. Herman of Alaska) wrote in the early nineteenth century, expressing his resistance to the North Pacific's environment: "Neither the awesome desolate places in Siberia which

I have crossed, nor the dark forests which have embedded themselves in my heart, nor the swift currents of the great rivers of Siberia could change me; not even the awesome ocean could cool my ardor."[28] Still, others found that North Pacific nature affected them deeply. The German naturalist Adelbert von Chamisso described the sublime beauty of the Aleutian Islands, glimpsed for the first time shortly after a violent storm:

> "A dark sky was overhanging the sea; the tall, jagged, snow-covered peaks of Unalaska glistened, bathed with sunlight, in a red glow.... Endless flight of waterbirds gliding low over the water surface looked from a distance like low swimming islands. Countless whales frolicked around our ship and shot jets of water high into the air in all directions within our range of view."[29]

The nineteenth-century German naturalist Friedrich Heinrich von Kittlitz captured something similar to Chamisso's lyrical description in his Kamchatkan watercolor, Figure 0.4. Today the visitor to the North Pacific gets an inkling of the contradictory feelings called up in earlier humans as a cold fog at sea lifts briefly to reveal towering volcanoes marked by snow extending to the ocean's edge, a riot of birds and whales in between (such, at any rate were my emotions as I took the photograph near Petropavlovsk in Figure 0.5). Despite such magnificence, the world Russians encountered in the eighteenth century was in many ways even more completely full of life.

The North Pacific, full of beauty and life, also possesses coherence. Many naturalists of the eighteenth and nineteenth centuries—especially those working for the Russian Empire—agreed that the seas from Kamchatka to Alaska constituted a single, coherent region. Their claims, supported by many contemporary scientists, give *Empire of Extinction* its geographical scope, roughly following the boundaries that made sense to those natural historians by concentrating on the rich, shallow seas stretching eastward from Kamchatka, between the northern extent of the sea ice in the Bering Sea and Alaskan littoral, and wrapping south to the Alexander Archipelago.[30] Though this region encompasses two continents, and is today divided politically, for most of the time period covered in this book it possessed coherence to humans (and probably to some animals too). This was the region patrolled by the Russian fur traders who hunted the sea cow to extinction, and contemporaneous descriptions of the trade necessarily touched on ports and islands from New Arkhangelsk to the Kurile Islands.

Natural historians found these and other sources of unity between Asia and America; Steller was among the first to postulate a genetic and cultural link between the indigenous peoples on both sides of the Bering Sea,[31] while Pallas, Chamisso, and the nineteenth-century governor of Russian America, Ferdinand

Figure 0.4 Starichkov Island, Kamchatka at the end of June, sometime in the 1830s. Watercolor by Freidrich Heinrich Freiherr von Kittlitz. Courtesy of the Prof Hans Engländer Collection at the Cologne University Library.

Figure 0.5 The coast of Kamchatka in early June, 2006, taken from Starichkov Island. Photograph by the author.

von Wrangel, perceived common geological features running from Kamchatka through Chukhotka and over to Alaska.[32] Wrangel put it most lyrically:

> The lofty mountains of the Kamchatka peninsula, the Aleutians, the Aliaska peninsula and the west coast of Cook's Inlet, their summits crowned with the dazzling white of eternal snows, form an enormous semi-circle which, if it could be viewed from one place at one time, when several of them are belching flame, would be conceded to be unparalleled.[33]

Due to Russian activity, the North Pacific in the eighteenth century also reacquired the cultural unity it had lost probably around the year 1100, when communication between North Pacific peoples seems to have largely ceased.[34] The Russian traders, in a sense, reestablished the long-vanished Bering Land Bridge via their island-hopping cruises. Many Kamchadals and other Eastern Siberians accompanied these voyages, reestablishing the eastward migratory pattern of the land-bridge era. Russian traders also brought Aleuts and Alutiit back to Asia, and in the nineteenth century even transported them as far south as California. The eighteenth-century North Pacific, much like the Atlantic, was woven together by patterns of migration, both free and coerced.

Natural History and the Russian Empire

European naturalists are the central actors in this book, for, after the hunters themselves, they were the most important lever upon which the living and post-humous fate of the North Pacific's animals hinged. Throughout the eighteenth and nineteenth centuries, nature and the study of nature occupied the center of imperial politics in the North Pacific. Russians founded their expansion into the region upon the harvesting and trading of marine mammals, and Russian imperial control was legitimized in part through the claim that they had mapped, described, and thoroughly understood North Pacific nature. The Russian Empire competed there with confident, aggressive Enlightenment European empires, and to win this competition it relied upon commerce and the accumulation of knowledge as much as or more than military power.

In the eighteenth century, such skills were increasingly supplied by natural historians, a group of philosopher-scientists who claimed special knowledge of the workings of the natural world. Natural historians such as Steller, Krasheninnikov, Pallas, Pennant, Sauer, Langsdorff, and Ilya Voznesenskii were astute commentators on environmental change; they advised the imperial government on environmental policies, and therefore left a particularly rich body of evidence for how Europeans understood environmental change in the region.[35] No doubt native Kamchadals and Alaskans felt these changes far more acutely than did naturalists, and I include their perspectives when possible, but this book mainly considers the views of scientists. These scientists were comprised of men hailing from a number of European nations, but most were united by employment with the Russian Empire, the main coordinator and supervisor of European activity in the North Pacific before 1800.

In part, the extensive participation of naturalists in the Russian empire was in emulation of Western European imperial practice. Empires used naturalists both in hopes of better exploiting the natural world and legitimizing conquest through a demonstration of knowledge production.[36] Natural historians, previously absent in Russian colonization, made their appearance only with the beginning of Pacific expansion. After Steller and Krasheninnikov's participation in the Second Kamchatka Expedition, the practice of integrating natural history research into imperial expansion became commonplace. The so-called "Academy Expeditions" of the 1760s, which explored Siberia and Northern European Russia, included numerous natural historians—in clear imitation of the precedent set in the North Pacific. Important in this development was the fact that most of Russia's natural historians were foreigners. As a result, natural historians not only represented a novel element of Russian empire-building, but they also provided novel viewpoints.

Once at the edges of the empire, those natural historians acted in unpredictable ways. Willard Sunderland has found that the eighteenth-century Russians rarely questioned the basic rightness of their empire's expansion.[37] However, in the Pacific, other loyalties and values sometimes overrode the duty to promote Russian imperial expansion and consolidation. Beginning with Steller, a subversive streak ran through the North Pacific's naturalists, often manifesting itself in critiques of environmental change. This is not to suggest that natural historians always heroically resisted imperial expansion—they contributed to the process as much as they undermined it—but their story refines understandings of the role science played in early-modern European imperialism and the complexity and contradictions involved in that expansion. Naturalists provide a unique perspective on Russian imperialism: that of highly literate people situated somewhere between the imperial officials who directed colonization, the soldiers, merchants, and peasants who enacted it, and the indigenous people who resisted or accommodated it.

Since the 1980s, historians have focused on the synergies between science and empire as they simultaneously have questioned earlier, triumphalist accounts of the disinterested progress of scientific ideas.[38] Scholars such as Bruno Latour, Marie Louise Pratt, John Gascoigne, David MacKay, and Richard Drayton have seen science as a powerful tool of imperial expansion, implicated in an overall European project for the domination of nature and colonial peoples.[39] As Drayton expressed it, "sciences shaped the pattern of imperial expansion ... [and] with their promise of insight into, and control over, nature, lent potent ideological help."[40] Historian of science Simon Schaffer stated this relationship in its baldest form: "the older contrast between disinterested scientific curiosity and vested commercial and colonial purposes should be abandoned. The imperial vision hinged on reliable and potent knowledge. Study of living nature was an exercise in power."[41] Some, like Latour, have seen description of the natural world as a technology that allowed Europeans to imagine, domesticate, and command faraway places.[42] Other scholars have detailed the influences of imperial modes of thinking on the development of natural history, and again concentrated on cooperation between the two.[43] Making all natures commensurable, the essence of the Linnaean project of naming and organizing, was far more than simply a way of thinking.

Not all of the new historiography portrays such a one-way correlation between science and empire: Gascoigne, for example, sees the British state's reliance on professional scientists as a sign of its own weakness. Some studies stress Europeans' entanglements with local epistemologies, and others see important shifts occurring with the onset of Romanticism around 1790. By that point, Alan Bewell has argued, colonials had begun claiming natural history as a part of local identity, and naturalists everywhere were taking stock of changing environments that could not be easily comprehended with fixed systems.[44] Indeed, there were salient examples in the Russian North Pacific of the complexity of the colonial scientific enterprise. Naturalists often relied on folk knowledge, and there is strong evidence that Aleut conceptions of animal behavior strongly influenced nineteenth-century conservation measures. Regardless of these complexities, most scholars agree on the centrality of natural history to the colonial project in the late eighteenth and early nineteenth centuries.

It seems strange, then, that the Russian Empire does not loom larger in the quest to comprehend the entangled worlds of colonialism and natural history.[45] After all, Steller's pre-Linnaean description of the sea cow stood at the very beginning of naturalists' engagement with the colonial world, and the Russians would command a colonial empire challenged in size only by Spain in the sixteenth century and Great Britain in the nineteenth. Indeed, historians have been insisting for decades now that imperial expansion has been the central factor in modern Russian history.[46] The eighteenth century saw Russians increasingly emphasizing the imperial aspects of their growing state. In the 1730s, the geographer and historian Vasilii Tatishchev redefined the border between Asia and Europe as the Urals, effectively marking off the entirety of Siberia as a colonial possession.[47] Russians and Europeans alike marveled at the breathtaking expansion of Muscovy's empire, and by the middle of the century they saw the vast size of its colonial conquests as a defining feature of the Russian state. As Michael Khodarkovsky has remarked, the eighteenth century also saw a "clear shift from previous frontier concepts...to the more modern and more European concerns of settling, colonizing, civilizing, and evangelizing the new lands."[48] Missionaries, agricultural settlers, and colonial administrators took the place of frontier garrisons.

Science, too, has come under scrutiny as a tool of Russian imperialism. Peter the Great (1672–1725) was the first to use professionally trained geodesists and cartographers in order to catalog his empire's riches, and by the nineteenth century science had proved its usefulness for the Russian state's expansion. Scholars see the relationship between science and empire in Russia as strictly one-sided.[49] The history of North Pacific naturalists, though, suggests that these men were shaped not only by St. Petersburg, but also by European intellectual traditions and, perhaps most powerfully, by the colonial environments they encountered.

The bulk of the attention of this recent return to empire in Russian historiography has focused on Central Asia, the Steppe, and Western Siberia. Few historians have treated North Pacific expansion as important in the process of Russian imperialism, except insofar as the region saw the creation of Russia's first joint-stock company (the Russian-American Company, or RAC).[50] Instead, the Russian territories in the Pacific have found their place in American historiography as a precursor to the state of Alaska,[51] or as a minor and ultimately inconsequential piece of European imperial history.[52] Meanwhile, many Russian historians have been concerned with demonstrating the kind treatment of Siberian and Alaskan native peoples or uncovering vast conspiracy theories explaining the sale of Russian America.[53] Recently, Ilya Vinkovetsky has argued that the Russian round-the-world voyages that stopped in the North Pacific colonies revolutionized how Russians conceived of their empire. These voyages exposed Russians to such Western European conceptions as race and modernity, categories which then found their way into the Russian descriptions of the North Pacific's indigenous peoples.[54] While I agree on the importance of the Pacific in Russia's imperial history, the changes to "imperial consciousness" occurred substantially earlier and as much from Kamchatka as from Alaska. It was, above all, the different concerns that arose with the control of oceanic space that caused Russians to reconceptualize their empire.[55]

Closer attention to nature and natural historians in the North Pacific can therefore substantially refine the histories of science, colonialism, and the Russian Empire. Some of the story undoubtedly looks similar to what took place in the French, Dutch, Spanish, or British colonies. North Pacific naturalists attempted to provide exactly the standard repertoire of useful knowledge, including maps, drawings, and published travel journals. They often forwarded the archetypal colonial goals of converting the natural world into commodities (notably Steller's windfall from sea otter pelts at the end of the Alaskan voyage). On the other hand, naturalists filled a complex and often uncertain role in the machinery of the Russian Empire and persistently failed to actually deliver much of value to their employer. Additionally, some naturalists harbored deep reservations about the morality of Russian colonialism and embedded these concerns in their environmental observations. These works eluded St. Petersburg's demands for useful knowledge and contained much explicit criticism of the empire. By the last quarter of the eighteenth century, a more determinedly anti-imperial natural history emerged. The nineteenth century saw a return to tamer science, but even then naturalists never delivered on their initial promise of improving Russian imperialism. Thus, what started out as an imitation of European empire building—the employment of authoritative masters of the natural world—ended with a very different outcome under Russian circumstances.

The relative failure of naturalists to materially benefit the Russian Empire had two principal causes. First, Russia was forced to employ mostly foreign naturalists, who saw the empire as relatively backwards. From Steller to Langsdorff, naturalists found much to dislike in the Russian colonies, and blame was placed as often on the Russians as on the Pacific's indigenous peoples. This happened in other empires as well—John Ledyard's criticisms of Captain Cook and British imperialism stand out as a good example.[56] However, Ledyard and dozens of others condemned Russian colonialism in the harshest terms, and these critics contributed most of the written descriptions of the region. Cook's hagiographers, by contrast, tended to drown out the critics of the British Empire.

The second explanation for naturalists' difficulties in the North Pacific comes from the environment itself. Colonial naturalists did not survey worlds of their choosing, but rather complex ecosystems never static and only partly translatable into lists of species. Kamchatka was not Tahiti, and Kamchatka in 1742 was not Kamchatka in 1800. Therefore, naturalists could not simply compile lists, draw maps, and present their work to the empire—the ground and ocean were too unstable for this. Ecosystem dynamics must be accounted for in understanding European imperialism and Europeans' understandings of imperialism.

The Russian Empire and the Changing Ocean Environment

Concluding this introduction necessitates a return to its beginning—the sea cow. Following from the insights of many environmental historians, my story takes the natural world as an important, dynamic actor in human history. While historians of the Russian empire have begun to consider the environment as a powerful historical actor, attention has remained primarily on Central Asia.[57] Russian expansion in the North Pacific offers a new environmental story, uniquely intertwined with the history of animals and taking place in an environment unlike any other in the empire. Though, as in Siberia, this was a story of a Russian-led fur trade, the maritime environment and ocean creatures exerted a powerful influence on the development of human history. The reasons why and the ways in which sea cows died made a difference for human affairs. Additionally, sea cows did not trammel an empty sea, but were enmeshed in local ecologies even as they were enmeshed in human nets. Marine mammals in the North Pacific disappeared more quickly and thoroughly than did other animals subjected to hunting in other places in the world for a number of reasons. Because they had only lived around certain islands, their disappearance showed itself dramatically in the form of totally denuded seascapes. While the interpretation of these events necessarily depended upon a host of cultural factors, the ecological aspect should not be underestimated. The changes occurring in the North Pacific environment drew Europeans to conclusions about the natural world that challenged inherited cosmologies and the power structures that produced scientific knowledge. The radical depletion of animals in the North Pacific ensured that anti-imperialism there would take on an ecological dimension.

Important environmental changes occurring in the North Pacific included a warming climate, spectacular volcanic activity and tsunamis, and the transplantation of foxes all through the Aleutian Islands. For those writing about the North Pacific in the Russian era, the decline in marine mammals stood out as most significant. Perhaps this decline was not the North Pacific's most distinctive feature—after all, animal populations throughout the world receded as Europeans expanded in the eighteenth and nineteenth centuries[58]—but the extinction of the sea cow and the near extinction of several other marine mammals in the North Pacific encouraged the still small crisis of confidence in European overseas imperialism and helped bring about an end of faith in the impervious order of nature. Empires over nature and empires over people did not end with the death of the last sea cow in 1768, but the first spears had been thrown.

Those historians who have taken into account the influence of environmental change on Europeans' modes of understanding the natural world rightly point to the unique, revolutionary effects of colonial environments on European thought. Like-minded critics found in the eighteenth century usually worked— like those studied here—in colonial locations.[59] Instead of environmentalism emerging primarily in the United States and Britain, and primarily as a means of preserving "natural" national spaces, the colonial world appears to have been an earlier source of innovative thinking about the environment.[60] Richard Grove drew attention to the theoretical advancements made by eighteenth- and early-nineteenth-century scientists on the islands of the Indian Ocean and the

Caribbean.[61] These colonial islands were ideal laboratories for observing deforestation, desertification, and climate change. The period's other great megafaunal extinction—that of the dodo—also took place on an island.[62]

Empire of Extinction offers several new examples that support the idea that
the colonial world provoked important changes in European understandings of
the natural world. The Aleutian Islands, like other colonial island locations, were
ideal places for observing environmental change—in this case, extinction. As in
France and Britain, naturalists led the debate about environmental problems in
the Russian Empire. Eighteenth-century environmental critiques were in some
ways more radical than British and American retreats into the solace of the sublime wilderness in the nineteenth century. Whereas the American transcenden-
talists spoke mainly of the individual's temporary escape from the dehumanizing
effects of industrialization,[63] some eighteenth-century natural historians hoped
to reform all of society's relationship with the natural world.

Empire of Extinction takes these insights in new directions by locating emerging
concepts of ecological justice as being as important as ideas of ecology. Whereas
naturalists such as Pierre Poivre in Mauritius developed sophisticated ideas
about the local ecosystem, the naturalists discussed here showed little appreciation for the concepts of modern ecology. In fact, Russians in the mid-nineteenth
century were still claiming that sea otters ate seaweed, and had no real notion
of the environmental links which shaped and sustained the species. What these
natural historians did understand and care about, however, were the linkages
between humans and animals, between empires and extinction. They never considered the natural world to be their only concern, and thus freely mixed analysis
of humans and non-humans, as well as natural, cultural, and political worlds. In a
word, they often did bad science. However, it was exactly these blurred boundaries that drew naturalists in the Russian Empire to their most surprising conclusions, including the idea that extinction was real and a problem. It was thanks
to these insights—generated in the complex intersection of empire and extinction—that the Russian North Pacific became an empire of extinction.

The Second Kamchatka Expedition and the Empires of Nature

> Steller went ashore. Ten hours
> Bering, with dread already imprinted
> on his brow, had granted him
> for a scientific excursion.
> Now a deep blueness
> pervaded both water and the forests
> that grew right down
> to the coast. Unperturbed
> animals came close to Steller, black
> and red foxes, magpies too, jays and
> crows went with him on his way across the beach....
> He came close to simply proceeding
> towards the mountains, into
> cool wilderness, but the constructs
> of science in his head,
> directed towards a diminution
> of disorder in our world,
> ran counter to that need.
>   —W. G. Sebald, "And if I remained by the Outermost Sea," *After Nature*

In the spring of 1742, the thirty-three-year-old German naturalist Georg Wilhelm Steller found himself shipwrecked on an uninhabited island in the North Pacific. The Russian Empire's Second Kamchatka Expedition, brainchild of Peter the Great, had ground to a scurvied halt on Bering Island. More than a dozen of Steller's Russian, German, and Siberian crewmates lay in shallow graves in the sand, picked over by the arctic foxes, which had no fear of the men. Violent earthquakes shook the island at least twice that winter. Cold, damp, and hungry, Steller and the rest of the surviving crew spent their time rebuilding their wrecked ship and hunting the marine mammals that frequented the island's shores. Melting snow rushed in torrents through the makeshift camp the men had set up on level ground near the sea. Migrating birds—loons, auks, and skylarks—began to arrive from the south, reminding Steller of the warmer climes of home.[1]

That same spring, George Frideric Handel was overseeing the inaugural performances of his oratorio *Messiah* in Dublin. Despite the drastic difference in their circumstances, the two men in fact had much in common; like Steller, Handel had studied at the University of Halle, the prestigious center of the German Enlightenment founded by the Prussian king Frederick III in 1694 (the Library at the Franckesche Stiftungen at the University of Halle, where Steller is likely to have studied, is visible in Figure 1.1). Like Handel, Steller possessed a talent for music. His father had been the cantor in the small Franconian town of Windsheim, while in his youth Steller himself had won a scholarship for his fine singing.[2] If Steller had indulged his passion for music instead of natural history, perhaps he would have at that very moment been bewigged, powdered, and serene in some Enlightenment drawing room or concert hall, instead of cold and hungry, with unkempt locks blowing in the fierce winds of the Bering Sea winter storms. One of the *Messiah*'s choruses proclaims that God would "shake the heavens and the earth, and the sea, and the dry land." Had Steller ever gotten the chance to hear Handel's masterpiece, he might have thought back to the continuous earthquakes on Bering Island and seen in them the hand of God.

Steller and Handel were united in at least one other respect: their careers had taken them out of Germany forever and placed them in the service of two of

Figure 1.1 The Library at the Franckesche Stiftungen at the University of Halle, where Steller is likely to have studied. Photograph by the author.

the eighteenth century's mightiest empires. Handel had moved with his patron to England in 1710, while Steller entered the service of the Russian empress in 1734. Both men would die in their adopted homes. While it may not be surprising that restless eighteenth-century Germans would look to the great British Empire to make a career, Steller's choice of Russia may seem an odder path. Yet he was far from the only German to look east for career opportunities. Germans were prominent in the scientific discovery of Siberia and Alaska in the eighteenth and nineteenth centuries, aware that great discoveries on par with those made in the New World in the sixteenth century were taking place. This tension between Germans, full of Enlightenment ideas, and a Russian Empire still in the process of crafting its imperial strategies, would provide some of the most creative moments in the history of the North Pacific. Steller was one of the first of these Germans to experience these tensions.

Like many ambitious Germans of the time, Steller had parlayed an excellent university education into an adventurous and consequential career. The University of Halle was famous as a center of the Pietistic movement (discussed in more detail below) initiated by Hermann Francke and for its connections with the Russian Empire of Peter the Great. Though trained to enter the ministry, Steller found a more ardent calling in natural history and medicine, and his clerical studies suffered as he botanized in the middle German forests. Dissatisfied with the limited horizons for travel in Germany, in 1734 Steller offered his medical services to the Russian army besieging the Polish city of Gdansk. Steller received free passage on a transport ship, and a month later he arrived in Russia's capital, with no employment and little to recommend him.[3]

Steller's break came when he made the acquaintance of Archbishop Feofan Prokopovich, who was instrumental in introducing him to the St. Petersburg Academy of Sciences and getting him immediately assigned to the recently launched Second Kamchatka Expedition. This remarkable expedition was, like many of the Russian Empire's ventures, breathtakingly ambitious in scope and homicidally troubled in logistics. Expedition members had been ordered to survey nearly the entirety of Russia's Arctic and Pacific coastlines, as well as to make new discoveries in the Americas. The Second Kamchatka Expedition's goals remained in flux, but it was recognized from the outset as inaugurating a new era in Russia's interaction with the Pacific, one marked by vigorous political and intellectual engagement. It would also be the first time scientists turned their attention to the region. Steller, having arrived in Russia while the expedition was already underway, was to take the place of two other German naturalists—Johann Georg Gmelin and Georg Friedrich Müller—who had decided upon reaching eastern Siberia that their health would allow them to go no further. Only the Germans' student, the Russian Stepan Krasheninnikov, found the fortitude to continue on. With such beginnings, no one in Russia or at home could have predicted the impact Steller would have on Europe's knowledge of the North Pacific.

This chapter outlines the ways that the Second Kamchatka Expedition, launched in 1739, brought exploration of the North Pacific in line with European models of imperial exploration and expansion. With the expedition's inclusion of naturalists, it anticipated later, more famous European expeditions, such as those of Captain Cook. Through Steller's and others' posthumous publications, the Second Kamchatka Expedition also brought Kamchatka and Alaska into European view. While more traditional Orthodox Christian interpretations of nature would persist, natural historians more often understood the North Pacific as part of a European colonial world, rather than as an extension of Russian Siberia. However, the road that took Steller to Alaska, Bering Island, and back to Siberia would not be straight. Along that road his relationship to both the natural world and the Russian Empire would be rerouted. Originally sent to the North Pacific to prospect for mineral wealth, Steller ended up accomplishing little of direct benefit to the empire. Instead, engagement with the North Pacific environment and with the realities of colonialism turned Steller into a sometime critic of empire and extirpation. Steller's experience contrasts with that of his Russian colleague and rival, Krasheninnikov. Despite the aggravations of shipwreck and Kamchatkan bureaucrats, Krasheninnikov retained the goal of harnessing North Pacific nature for imperial benefit and dedicated himself to cataloging the potential benefit to the empire. The national, religious, and professional differences between these two men reflected larger divisions between European and developing Russian cultures of natural history, attested to some of the difficulties the empire would encounter in applying Western cultures of colonialism to the North Pacific, and demonstrated the effects encounters with colonial natures could have on European science.

Russia and its Colonies

When Steller departed from St. Petersburg by sled for Siberia in 1738, he was joining a stream of Russian eastward colonization that had been flowing for at least 150 years. Ever since Yermak the Cossack had defeated Khan Kuchum near the town of Sibir' in 1582, Russians had been moving to Siberia, with the government providing military and bureaucratic support.[4] Russian expansion proceeded at a remarkable pace; in less than one hundred years, a handful of fur traders and *sliuzashchie liudi* (military servitors) reached the Pacific Ocean, over four thousand miles away from Moscow. While Spain, Portugal, Holland, France, and England were carving out vast overseas empires, Russians were assimilating millions of square miles of contiguous terra firma. Despite this basic difference in geography, Russians experienced imperial expansion in much the same way that Western Europeans did. As with the Western European empires, Russians had to somehow incorporate diverse cultures and landscapes into its developing imperial organization.

Expansion into Siberia, like European expansion in the New World and East Asia, inspired wonder and pride. For Russians, Yermak attained the status of Cortez or Pizarro, his valor as famed as his cruelty.[5] In the eighteenth century, Siberia was known colloquially as Russia's "Gold Mine," evoking the fabulous riches earned and robbed in the East and West Indies (though Siberia's "soft gold" came more often in the form of furs or more prosaic minerals such as iron). Siberia also resembled the New World in the opportunities it presented common people. As English peasants became freeholders in Virginia, and minor Spanish hidalgos became powerful *encomienderos* in New Spain, so did Russian serfs flee their masters and claim their own land beyond the Urals. Although the Russian colonial remained a "state peasant" and paid a *corvée* (uncompensated labor) directly to the state, the manorial serfdom that had become more oppressive during the eighteenth century never took root in Siberia. For some, Siberia took on connotations of freedom familiar from the literature of New World exploration.[6]

Many seventeenth- and eighteenth-century Russians, especially those in the literate and powerful classes, interpreted Siberia from another perspective that had close parallels in Western European literature of exploration:[7] it was an irredeemable howling wilderness. From an early date, Muscovy's tsars recognized Siberia's vast potential as a penal colony, where criminals could harass the Turkic and Mongolian tribes instead of Russians, and the voices of many politically ambitious nobles fell silent in the impenetrable *taiga* (boreal forest). While many political exiles made vast fortunes as Siberian governors, their sights were invariably set on return to Moscow, where true civilization resided. Siberia was at best a way station for the ambitious, and more usually the end of an interesting life.

Siberia was a wilderness in another sense. In comparison with the New World, it received little attention in Western Europe, and long remained relatively unknown in European Russia and beyond. At the beginning of the eighteenth century, maps of "Tartary" (as Siberia was then known) were as inaccurate as those of barely known California. Siberia had not yet gained a fixed location in the maps or minds of Europeans or most Russians. The Russian nobility's near-universal abhorrence of Siberia in part explains the lack of a substantive Siberian literature of exploration until the middle of the eighteenth century. In this way, Russian colonization to the East differed substantially from the European early modern colonial experience. Though church chroniclers retold his story decades later, Yermak had no Bernal Díaz to chronicle his conquest, and until the Second Kamchatka Expedition, no Russian Hakluyt appeared to compile and propagandize Siberian exploration.[8]

One explanation for the relative silence about Russian eastward expansion was the generally low level of literary development in early modern Russia. The first Russian printing press did not appear until the 1630s,[9] and the Russian literary tradition remained almost exclusively ecclesiastical prior to the eighteenth century. While the Russian sailor Afanasii Nikitin traveled to Persia and India in 1466 and wrote an account of his travels, he remained an exception. Few before 1740 thought Siberia worthy of study or comment and lack of an audience for travel literature in European Russia ensured that little was produced. For nearly two centuries, Siberia as much swallowed up Russians as Russia had swallowed up Siberia.

If cartography and ethnography had been neglected, next to no one concerned themselves with Siberian nature, beyond general comments about the region's extremely cold climate. Though Siberia was in many ways just as exotic as the New World, abounding in species unknown to Europe and presenting a topography and climate far different than that of European Russia, no compendia of Siberian plants or animals is found in the pre-1740 records, despite the Russians' well-chronicled taste for the exotic.[10] Part of the reason for this silence is that Russia lacked anyone trained in natural history who could conduct a professional survey of Siberian nature. With neither a university nor an Academy of Sciences, the only centers of learning in pre-Petrine Russia were the theological seminaries. Some ecclesiastics did show interest in the natural world—Peter's archbishop and Steller's sponsor Feofan Prokopovich was often found in St. Petersburg's fledgling botanical garden[11]—but their concerns were usually more otherworldly.

The seventeenth century was not completely devoid of Russian commentary on the Siberian environment. The archpriest Avvakum, renowned as the church reformer Nikon's chief adversary, was exiled to Siberia in the 1660s and wrote a narrative of the long years he spent there. In his *Life*, Avvakum invoked paradoxical images of Siberian nature as both desolate wilderness and unbelievable bounty. Mainly, Siberian nature served for Avvakum as a useful metaphor for the harshness of exile and as a vehicle for God's favor. Avvakum described the dangers of travel through the cold, harsh landscape and noted the ever-present threat of starvation due to the meager provisions. At the same time, he also described an "endless abundance" of wild fowl, pelicans, and swans on the Pacific Coast and around Lake Baikal. "Onions grow" around Baikal, he reported, "and garlic, bigger than the Romanov onion and uncommonly sweet.... There's no end to the birds, to the geese and swans—like snow they swim on the lake."[12] There are hints of an abundant heaven in a Siberia that Avvakum largely depicted as hell.[13]

Avvakum's description of Siberian nature was entrenched in a peculiarly Russian ecclesiastical tradition that saw nature as a battleground where good and evil vied for the pilgrim wanderer's loyalty. Russian hermits sought solace from temptation in the most horrid and distant wildernesses, paradoxically finding meditative peace in inhospitable landscapes. The Russian word *podvig* captured the mixture of asceticism and heroism that was the goal of this retreat into nature: a *podvig* could encompass everything from strenuous and lengthy praying to clearing the forest in preparation for agriculture.[14] In the vast forests that stretched north and east from the Muscovite heartland there were plenty of opportunities to meet the simultaneously ominous and cleansing forces of the wilderness, and Russian monks were often at the forefront of the state's colonization. One monk at the northern Russian monastery Valaam captured the Russian cleric's complex, contradictory relationship to nature, describing a love of "pure and virginal natural surroundings, threatening and savage, peaceful and majestic."[15] This Orthodox interpretation of wild nature would take root in the nineteenth-century North Pacific, enshrined in the figure of Father Herman, who arrived on Kodiak Island with the first Orthodox mission to Alaska and subsequently retired to nearby uninhabited Spruce Island to engage in a life of meditation.[16]

The theological interpretation of Siberian nature also found expression in the mapmaking and chronicles of the seventeenth and early eighteenth centuries. According to historian Valerie Kivelson, Muscovy expressed an "environmental theology" in the orientation, symbolism, and literature of Siberian cartography.[17] This theology interpreted Siberia as an epic location for the extension of God's kingdom—a dark, empty space that called for the firm hand of a conqueror to spread light and habitation. In later chronicles of Yermak's conquest, too, the natural world hastened and reflected Russian conquest. Just before the Cossacks' arrival, wolf-like beasts emerged from the confluence of the Tobol and Irtysh rivers and staged a great fight that seemed to foretell the imminent defeat of the infidel Siberians. Chronicle, cartography, and pilgrimage all produced possible bedrock for Siberian natural history. However, pilgrims rarely ventured into the howling Siberian wilderness, and mapmakers rarely managed to get further East than Irkutsk.

In at least one way, the Muscovite interpretation of the Siberian environment and its peoples would be echoed in the literature of the eighteenth-century natural historians. Muscovy, in contrast to contemporary early modern empires such as Great Britain, did not see the deracination of its conquered subjects as an integral part of its imperial project.[18] Instead, Russian expansion proceeded through a process of collection of subjects; Russian officials celebrated the empire's showcase of nations and religions. The number, diversity, and power of the tsar's conquered subjects attested to both his power and the power of God, who guided the conquests. Animals, as well as people, could accrue to the tsar's imperial grandeur, as demonstrated by an early-eighteenth-century sketch from the Tobolsk townsman Stepan Remezov. In the drawing, Remezov allegorically depicted the natives of Siberia as different animals submitting to the biblical Adam, meant to represent Russia.[19] Just as the great number of different animals signified Adam's power over creation, so the great number of different Siberian tribes signified Muscovy's power. A seventeenth-century Muscovite cosmographer listed among the riches of Siberia the magnificent monasteries and churches, the abundant grain ("in all Europe there is nothing like that land"), and "a plethora of fish of all kinds in the mighty rivers."[20] This tendency to celebrate Siberia not as a replica of Russia, but as an impressive collection of different subjects, would influence eighteenth- and nineteenth-century works of natural history, most clearly Peter Simon Pallas's *Zoographia Rosso-Asiatico*.

Overall, however, the interpretive traditions developed in seventeenth-century Siberia would exert only a weak hold over the imaginations of eighteenth-century natural historians. The dramatic changes in statecraft and culture introduced by Peter I helped break older modes of thought about Siberia, the strength of which had already been hampered by the low level of literacy in Muscovite society. While the "environmental theology" of the early maps and scattered travelogues continued to influence Siberia's government servitors, agricultural settlers, and exiles, Petrine and post-Petrine high culture imbibed little of this indigenous milk. The books Stepan Krasheninnikov brought with him to Kamchatka included works by ancient Greek and Roman authors such as Herodotus and Suetonius, but nothing in Russian, and nothing about Siberia or Kamchatka.[21] Instead of drawing on indigenous traditions, Russian conceptions of the North Pacific in the eighteenth century would draw on a new natural history based on Western European practices and preoccupations. A new mode of description was appropriate, for in Kamchatka Russians encountered an environment far removed from even Siberians' familiar experience.

Kamchatka, Environment, and Plunder

Kamchatka, a nearly insular appendage hanging off the eastern edge of Siberia, was first explored by Russian Cossacks in 1697. In that year Vladimir Atlasov, the leader of a Cossack band out of the frontier garrison of Yakutsk, initiated a bloody conquest of the peninsula, a process not yet complete by the time the Second Kamchatka Expedition arrived. Atlasov, typical of other seventeenth-century Russians, emphasized the land's wonders as well as potential for economic gain. He reported back to Moscow on the peninsula's fearsome volcanoes and abundant wildlife.[22] Atlasov tantalized his government readers in Moscow with descriptions of the "great many whales, seals and sea otters in the sea," as well as native methods of catching these animals.[23] Characteristic of the era, his accounts did not promote the economic development of the peninsula, but rather its plunder. Frontiersmen as well as state officials envisioned their empire as one of tribute collection, and Atlasov's reports induced Cossacks, government servitors, and clergymen to follow his route and institute a permanent system of exploitation of the peninsula's native Koriaks and Kamchadals. Meanwhile, Atlasov himself stole from his fellow Cossacks and in retaliation was hacked to pieces, thus falling victim to the frontier violence that was another venerable Siberian tradition.

In spite of Atlasov's traditional view of Kamchatka, the land and seas his Cossack band encountered differed greatly from any other then under Russian possession. From a geographical perspective, Kamchatka is more a part of the North Pacific than of Siberia or the Russian Far East. It forms a portion of the Pacific's Ring of Fire; in contrast to the adjacent lands, and in common with much of coastal Alaska and the Aleutian Islands, Kamchatka is a creation of volcanic forces operating at the joint between tectonic plates (see Figure 1.2). While much of Eastern Siberia is composed of rugged, but not particularly high, mountains, Kamchatka soars out of the sea (see Figure 1.3). Nowhere else along the Russian coast can fifteen-thousand-foot peaks be seen from the ocean. Kamchatka is composed of a hundred oversized Mt. Fujis, each white peak building symmetrically into the sky, and not a few spouting smoke even further into the atmosphere (see Figure 1.6). The peninsula's volcanoes find their analog (in origin if not in height) in the fiery volcanic summits of Alaska's Aleutian range still being built out of the immense depths of the Aleutian trench. Natural hot springs on both sides of the North Pacific reminded Russians of their steam baths back home.

Surrounded on two sides by the ocean, Kamchatka, with the exception of the central river valley, has a marked maritime climate. The Kuroshio Current, flowing northward from Japan, keeps Kamchatka's west coast relatively warm, though it does not protect it from frequent storms that often dump huge quantities of snow from the tips of the volcanic peaks down to the waterline. The Sea of Okhotsk to the west sends thick fogs over the boggy tundra there, confounding numerous attempts to introduce agriculture to the peninsula. Kamchatka's boreal landscape is dominated by larch, spruce, and pine forests along the coast and the southern river valleys, while further north and east tundra predominates. The habitat is ideal for moose and smaller mammals such as sable. Fed by some of the largest salmon runs in the world, Kamchatka's brown bears have evolved to attain extraordinary size, much as those on Alaska's Kodiak Island have, for similar reasons of diet and isolation. The coasts of Kamchatka are home to seabird colonies whose size and composition resemble those found in Alaska, as well as the Russian provinces around Chukotka and the Sea of Okhotsk. Puffins, auklets, gulls, and other fish-catching birds nest on the high, protected

Der Feuerspeiende Berg Kamtschatka genant.

Der untere Kamtschatka Ostrog.

Figure 1.2 "The Fire-spewing Mountain named Kamtschatka" and "Lower Kamtschatka *Ostrog* [Fort]" from Stepan Krasheninnikov, *Beschreibung von dem Lande Kamtschatka.* Courtesy of the John Carter Brown Library.

sea cliffs of Kamchatka's Pacific coast, and their prey include the herring found throughout the North Pacific. Deeper underwater live enormous halibut, flounder, and crabs. Seals, sea lions, and sea otters are the principal marine mammals, along with the larger whales. Resident and transient orcas, as well as most of the toothed and baleen whales, are seen off Kamchatkan shores. Despite the short summers and snowy winters, Kamchatka and its surrounding waters are rich in animal life, small and large.

The abundance of animals in and around Kamchatka supplied the environmental conditions necessary to support a dense human population. Huge seasonal salmon runs provided Kamchatka's humans easy access to food. In the

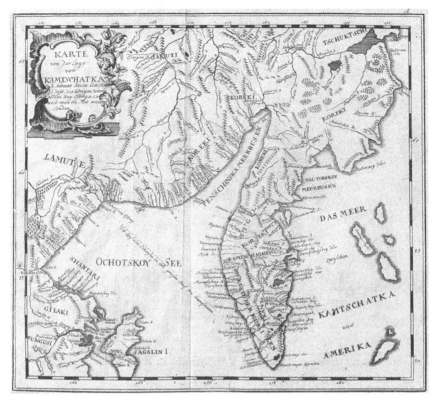

Figure 1.3 Krasheninnikov's comprehensive map of Kamchatka and Eastern Siberia, carefully delineating each river and infuriating English reviewers. From Krasheninnikov, *Beschreibung*. Courtesy of John Carter Brown Library.

south of the peninsula, the Kamchadals (also known as Itelmen) had inhabited the land for nearly thirty thousand years by the time of Russian contact. They harvested river-running salmon in the summer and fall, drying and storing them by the thousands for winter provisions to feed themselves and the dogs that pull their sleds, as illustrated in Figure 1.4. The salmon of Kamchatka, first described by Steller, provided the scientific names of five of the Pacific species (*tsawytscha, keta, gorbuscha, nerka,* and *kisutch*). Kamchadals also harvested the abundance of the sea, killing fur seals, sea lions, sea otters, and—more rarely—whales. On occasion they would also kill the peninsula's giant brown bears, impaling them to death with wooden poles (see Figure 1.5).

In these respects and others, Kamchatka represented for Russians as much an entrée into an oceanic world as a continuation of Siberia. Sables and other terrestrial fur-bearers still drew Russians to the peninsula, as they had in Tobolsk, Yakutsk, and many other places east of Moscow, but Kamchatka looked out on a very different world. True, colonists attempted to maintain Bolsheretsk

Figure 1.4 "A Kamchadal summer hut." Salmon are shown being prepared and dried, demonstrating the importance of the fish to Kamchadal life. From Krasheninnikov, *Beschreibung*. Courtesy of John Carter Brown Library.

Figure 1.5 Russians drying salmon encounter one of Kamchatka's bears. From Kittlitz, unpublished watercolors. Courtesy of Sammlung Professor Engländer Universitätsbibliothek Köln.

Tom. II. Nº XV.

VOLCAN DE KAMTCHATKOI.

Figure 1.6 This French depiction of Kamchatka emphasizes its daunting volcanic landscape. It also seems to insert a sea monster devouring a human (lower right-hand corner), perhaps an indication of the peninsula's association with exotic marine animals. From Chappe d'Auteroche, *Voyage en Siberie*. Courtesy of John Carter Brown Library.

(facing Siberia across the Sea of Okhotsk) as Kamchatka's administrative center, and Atlasov had envisioned settlements clustered along the Kamchatka River. However, throughout the eighteenth century, Russians were increasingly drawn to the Pacific shore settlements of Nizhnekamchatsk and Petropavlovsk. The latter was founded as the headquarters for Vitus Bering's first exploration of the North Pacific in the 1720s and experienced major growth during the Second Kamchatka Expedition. Meanwhile, the Kamchadals hired or forced to transport Bering's baggage across the interior of the peninsula suffered intensely, as they were taken from their homes and kept from the salmon harvest. In this way the Russian occupation of Kamchatka offered a preview of colonial relations in North America.

The Second Kamchatka Expedition and Natural History

Direct government involvement with Kamchatka began in 1719 with the dispatch of two geodists (cartographers), F. F. Luzhin and I. M. Evreinov.[24] The men were unable to determine whether America was connected to Asia, but they did discover the Kurile Islands and managed to produce reliable maps of the peninsula. Their reports back to Peter I were intended strictly for government consumption and did not reach a wider audience. Peter responded by ordering a more ambitious expedition, the so-called First Kamchatka Expedition, under the command of the Dane Vitus Bering.[25] The expedition included experienced naval officers from the Admiralty College, but no natural historian.[26] In a search terminating in 1730, Bering failed to conclusively prove the existence of a strait between Asia and America, and the results of the First Kamchatka Expedition have mostly been assessed as meager. Meanwhile, one lone botanist, the German Daniel Gottlieb Messerschmidt, traversed Siberia in the 1720s. This nearly forgotten pioneer of Siberian natural history ventured as far east as Lake Baikal, collecting many plants unknown to European science. These immense labors were too great for one man, and Messerschmidt returned to St. Petersburg lonely and broken, dying in 1735.[27] His German wife, who caused him nearly as many sorrows as Siberia had, would later marry Steller, complicate her second husband's life immensely, and see him die young as well.

In 1730, when Bering first proposed to the Empress Anna Ivanovna a second voyage to the North Pacific, Evreinov, Lukhin, and Messerschmidt were still the only scientific names associated with the region. Their written legacy at the time amounted to some pages of scattered notes. By this time, however, the St. Petersburg Academy of Science—Peter's brainchild—was established, active, and manned by literate Europeans versed in natural history.[28] Founded only a few months before the launch of Bering's first expedition in 1725, the Academy functioned as an ornament of the court, a training ground for future Russian scientists, and a disseminator of scientific knowledge to the Russian educated public. Above all a symbol of Peter's Westernization, it was about to become a part of the machinery of imperial expansion.[29]

With the Second Kamchatka Expedition, the academy would find a vast field worthy of its growing prestige. Nearly unconstrained in scope, the expedition was supposed to survey the entire Pacific and Arctic coasts of Russia and Siberia, as well as to make new discoveries in America and open trade relations with China. The expedition was a complex, overambitious mixture of Russian geopolitics, European-style exploration, and what historian Willard Sunderland has called "territoriality."[30] This last notion expressed the growing impulse in the Russian Empire to more comprehensively understand the vast territory it claimed, both to represent its claims to the international world and to better exploit the resources found within them. Better maps and better descriptions of Siberia would be crucial. Territoriality demanded considerable funds and different sorts of men. Amateur frontiersmen such as Atlasov would fade in importance, though like him, many members of the Second Kamchatka Expedition would die in the field.

The Senate and the Admiralty did the major planning for the Second Kamchatka Expedition, but they asked the Academy to become involved, initially as a consultant on cartographic matters. Joseph Nicholas De l'Isle, a French member of the Academy and a virtuoso of the popular eighteenth century art of speculative geography, produced a map indicating a large landmass just to the east of Kamchatka called "De Gama Land." Unaware of the map's gross inaccuracies, the Senate and Admiralty were pleased to procure such professional knowledge, a lack of which had slowed down Bering's first expedition. Unfortunately, De l'Isle's map would lead Bering and a second ship under the command of the Russian Aleksei Chirikov tragically off course to the south of the Aleutian Island chain, prolonging the voyage to the American coast by weeks. Perhaps encouraged by what then seemed a very useful map, the governing bodies requested greater participation from the Academy, including the inclusion of several natural historians.[31] It is not entirely clear, however, how natural historians gained entrance in the expedition. The historical literature on the subject is split between those who think that the naturalists' participation was for purely scientific reasons, and others who see the naturalists' usefulness as doctors and metallurgists as the reason for their inclusion.[32]

The question of the natural historians' inclusion is tied to a question about the ultimate goals of the Second Kamchatka Expedition. The Governing Senate stated the motive for the expedition as "the benefit of the state and the augmenting of Our [the sovereign's] interests."[33] However, different documents enumerate different aspects of the sovereign's interests, and the expedition's final instructions list various and not always compatible goals. While exploration clearly played a role, profit may have been a more powerful motive leading the organizers of the Second Kamchatka Expedition. In 1732 the Senate sent a report to the Empress Anna stating that the expedition was to

> examine the land itself with an adequate guard to see if valuable minerals and metals are there.... If there is discovered in localities subject to Russia subsurface wealth which from a large sample gives evidence of profit, notify the commandant at Okhotsk upon return or other commandants elsewhere without letting it be known afar.[34]

Besides mineral wealth, the Expedition was to look for areas rich in fur-bearing animals where the men could either convince the natives to pay tribute, or force them to hunt for the Russian state.

The profit motive, in particular the search for lands containing fur-bearing animals, was a longtime hallmark of Russian eastward expansion. The procedures outlined in the instructions for the Second Kamchatka Expedition could have come directly from any number of instructions to serving men in Siberia in the previous fifty years.[35] Precious metals, too, had played a role in the conquest and exploitation of Siberia, though gold had not been found in any quantities. Metallurgists and assayers had accompanied Siberian explorers, sometimes in the employ of government servitors. Such was the case, for example, in 1624, when the Tomsk *voevodas* (military governors) sent out a blacksmith and a Cossack to prospect for iron ore, which they found and sent back to Moscow.[36] Moscow itself sometimes dispatched *guliashchie liudi* (itinerants) to Siberia to prospect for metals. Natural historians, however, had never been employed for such tasks prior to the Second Kamchatka Expedition.

The Senate assigned prospectors to the Second Kamchatka Expedition, but none completed the trip to Kamchatka and beyond. Instead, natural historians would have to perform their work. While aspects of the expedition were indeed grounded in Siberian precedence, the inclusion of natural historians marked a departure. To a great degree, the Second Kamchatka Expedition looked past the Siberian experience and borrowed instead from Western European models of exploration. When the vice-admiral and member of the Admiralty College, Nikolai Golovin, discussed the expedition's potential, he explicitly referenced the experience of European colonization in the Americas and East Asia:

> In the exploration of America there may be the following great gains for the state: very rich mines, both gold and silver, are there which are still unknown, [and it is known] what profit the Spanish, English, and Portuguese kingdoms receive and how important the commerce and navigation to these regions are to those kingdoms now.[37]

This coupling of Russian exploration in the Pacific with Spanish, British, and Portuguese exploration in the New World was quite startling. Few in Russia had conceived of Siberia as a new world, instead thinking of its conquest as the pacification of old enemies from the steppe. It was only with the discovery of Kamchatka and the possibility of discoveries in northern North America that Russian officials began drawing parallels with the Western European experience and forming new expectations based on that history.[38] This association was, in one sense, quite natural, as the land across the water from Kamchatka was known to be part of the same continent as Mexico and Virginia—although many thought that it might be connected to Siberia north of the known extent of the Pacific Ocean. On the other hand, what little Russians knew of the lands to the east of Kamchatka suggested they would be quite unlike the prosperous colonies of Spain and Britain and more like cold, volcanic Kamchatka itself. Alaska's topography and geological history obviously resemble Eastern Asia far more than they do the Caribbean. There was little reason to expect that gold and silver might be found in Alaska, other than the fact that the Spaniards had found it in the New World. Nonetheless, the American example loomed large for the planners of the Second Kamchatka Expedition. St. Petersburg planned the Expedition with new standards of comparison and markers of success in mind, and these new standards suggested to the planners the inclusion of natural historians on the expedition.

In its conscious mimicking of Western European exploration, St. Petersburg embraced the French, Dutch, and English mixture of science and discovery. The heyday of scientific exploration had not yet arrived, but by the 1730s natural history and exploration had already been fruitfully paired. Long before Cook and Bougainville, amateur scientists had become famous through their writings on natural history, anthropology, and cartography produced on voyages of explorations. William Dampier from England and the Dutchman Abel Tasman were the earliest of these scientist-explorers, and by the late 1600s the new royal societies in London and Paris had begun to promote voyages of discovery in order to gain information on the natural world. In 1687 Hans Sloane, member of Britain's Royal Academy of Sciences, traveled to Jamaica and compiled observations in natural history that he would later publish as *A Voyage to the Islands Madera, Barbados, Nieves, S. Christophes and Jamaica, with the Natural History of the Herbs and Trees, Four-footed Beasts, Fishes, Birds, Insects, Reptiles, &c.*[39] Two decades later, the French Académie des Sciences became directly involved in exploration, assigning member Charles Marie de la Condamine to a voyage to South America to determine the shape of the earth by measuring meridians and different latitudes. The European academies of science were exerting a growing influence in the process of exploration, and it was a corresponding member of Britain's Royal Society, Gottfried Leibniz, who first counseled Peter I to send a scientific expedition to the North Pacific.

In Russia, however, natural history could claim only a short history and few practitioners. While Peter the Great had sent out two large expeditions to explore the Caspian Sea and search for gold in the region in 1714 and 1715, it was military officials, not scientists, who had surveyed the region.[40] When selecting naturalists for the voyage, the Admiralty and Senate had few choices. The St. Petersburg Academy of Sciences was a small organization in 1732 and employed not a single Russian academician. Instead, the body was packed with German scholars in every field, from mathematics to history. For the Second

Kamchatka Expedition, the Academy supplied historian Gerhard Friedrich Müller, botanist Johann Georg Gmelin, and astronomer Louis De l'Isle de la Croyère. Accompanying the German and French academicians was a host of Russian students, translators, and draughtsmen. Western personnel and Western institutions would spearhead the expedition.

From the expedition's onset, its grandiose goals inspired striking achievements and produced bitter setbacks. Gmelin botanized extensively around the Lake Baikal area and would produce a magnificent *Flora Sibirica* in the 1740s and 1750s, as well as a travel journal that drew attention in Europe.[41] Müller scoured the Siberian archives in search of old documents—labors that yielded the first comprehensive history of the Russian conquest. The two Germans also drank fine Rhine wines all the way from St. Petersburg to Yakutsk, the bottles carried by sledge over thousands of miles. Neither man ever reached Kamchatka, as they became ill in Eastern Siberia. In their stead, the young, ambitious Russian student mentioned earlier, Stepan Krasheninnikov, sailed to Kamchatka and became the first natural historian to describe the peninsula. A year later Steller—a late addition to the expedition hired as a replacement for Gmelin—arrived ready to botanize and hoping to sail to America with Bering.

The academicians who joined the Second Kamchatka Expedition found that they had to contend with an uncomprehending, obstructionist Siberian bureaucracy and populace. At the time of the Expedition, Siberia was still governed as an entity separate from Russia, like many of the American colonies subject to the state, but not to the normal organs of government. Siberian officials of the eighteenth century bitterly resented their banishment from civilization, and they expected compensation in the form of free reign over the lands and peoples they administered. The military officers and political exiles who received governorships in the towns and regions of Siberia supplemented their small or nonexistent salary with massive extortion and control of the government monopolies on furs and liquors.[42]

In this context, and given the massive distances involved and the poverty of most Siberian townships, government orders for supplying the naturalists and the expedition as a whole did not meet with immediate compliance. While the academicians became acquainted with several men who shared their interest in scientific knowledge, most Siberians viewed the scientists' requests for information as potential trouble. Müller, in particular, found strenuous resistance to his pleas to see the archival materials, which chronicled corruption and malfeasance as often as they did glorious conquest.

In Kamchatka, the poverty of the colony, the newness of the conquest, and the extreme distance from St. Petersburg exacerbated official intransigence. One of the original students at the Academy, Krasheninnikov showed early promise in botany, but in Kamchatka, he learned how difficult doing natural history in

Siberia could be. Intractable garrison commanders and their clerks continually hindered his ambitious program of measuring the peninsula's tides, surveying its rivers, and collecting natural history samples. When Krasheninnikov asked officials in Bol'sheretsk, the colonial capital, for a hunter for shooting birds, the *Prikaznaya Izba* (administration) complied by sending him a blind servitor named Nikifor Salamatov.[43] Bol'sheretsk met Krasheninnikov's demands for a more competent replacement with silence. A year later, Krasheninnikov discovered that several of his government-assigned assistants had been previously convicted of stealing government goods. Reasonably fearing that they might dip their hands into his scarce supplies, he again requested replacements and was again denied.[44]

One can hardly blame the Kamchatkan authorities for their recalcitrance. They faced demands from St. Petersburg for increased fur tributes and had to manage the Cossacks' unruly behavior, as well as the native uprisings that both provoked. It was all Bol'sheretsk could do to maintain a semblance of peace and order throughout the huge territory it nominally controlled. Colonial governors hardly had men to spare for such nonessential ends as natural history. Local government itself was composed of scoundrels and profiteers, so good men to deliver to Krasheninnikov were hard to find. Still, the young scientist was convinced that the local authorities deliberately hindered his work, and he was probably not mistaken. Kamchatkan authorities had little to gain and much to lose from the Academy's meddling in local affairs. They had scant faith that these natural historians would discover anything of material use, and detailed reports of Kamchatkan conditions could only lead to punishment for men who were often already political exiles. The new work of natural history faced serious obstacles in the North Pacific.

Strange Beasts of the Sea

While Krasheninnikov battled the local bureaucracy, Steller arrived in Kamchatka with grander plans: namely, to sail to Japan with Martin Spangenberg, or to America with Bering. But first he had to establish the hierarchy between himself and Krasheninnikov. Adjunct Steller immediately ordered the student Krasheninnikov to turn over all his notes, which no doubt strained relations between the men.[45] Steller behaved equally imperiously with his assistants and the Kamchadals. He ordered the latter to "bring to me any whales, sea animals, fish and other things thrown on shore by the sea. Under no circumstances should they cut them up, but instead should inform me of their presence as soon as is possible."[46] This short passage hints at the vigorousness with which Steller pursued his zoological research. It also gives some insight into the difficulties that natural historians such as Steller must have brought upon the indigenous peoples of the North Pacific, who depended on the products of the sea for their subsistence. In fact, everywhere naturalists went they exacted a toll on local bounty, destroying especially huge numbers of birds in their quest for the perfect specimen.[47]

After a year of such activity, Steller met up with Bering's contingent of the expedition in Kamchatka. Steller and Bering struck up a friendship, and the natural historian convinced the captain to include him as the ship's doctor and prospector. The second of Steller's positions was to cause him a multitude of headaches. The Admiralty had envisioned great finds of precious metals on the American shores, but Steller could present only the slimmest of credentials for locating substrata wealth. His theological and botanical training qualified him for prospecting only insofar as the location of precious metals was determined by divine will. Once on board the *St. Peter* with a crew of Russians, Danes, Germans, and Kamchadals, Steller seems to have compounded his awkward situation by constantly claiming advanced navigational skills and advising Bering on the proper course of sail. By the time the ship spotted Mount St. Elias, Alaska, a few days after the sister ship *St. Paul* had made landfall on the Alaskan panhandle, Steller had few friends left on board.

Complicating Steller's task, Bering's ship reached the American coastline in October 1741, very late in the navigating season. Though Bering was inclined to return immediately to Kamchatka, Steller insisted on being allowed a brief excursion onshore. Bering and the rest of the crew sent the ship's doctor onshore with a sarcastic trumpet fanfare. Natural history seemed of little import to these practical sailors. After a half a day of exploration on what came to be known as Kayak Island, Steller returned to the ship, never again to set foot on that continent's shores and having discovered nothing commercially valuable. Steller sardonically remarked to the crew, "We have come [all this way] only to take American water to Asia."[48] Bering had little choice but to return so soon, and little desire to risk his crew's safety for a few specimens of natural history. Time, distance, and the low regard in which natural historians were held choked all hopes for the Second Kamchatka Expedition's mineralogical success.

Steller's main contribution to imperial development came, ironically, at the expedition's low point. After Bering pointed the ship westward toward Kamchatka, things began to go very badly. A continuous barrage of storms coming eastward halted the ship's progress and battened its sails. At a short stop in the Aleutian Islands, the crew managed to procure only some brackish water and nothing at all to eat. Scurvy soon set in. In October, the first death occurred. November 1741 began as the worst month yet for the Expedition. Men died in scores, and by the end of the month the ship was sailing rudderless through the fierce North Pacific storms, the sailors all having died or become too weak to steer. Fear had turned to hopelessness.

Luck, though it hardly appeared as such, came in the form of shipwreck. On November 5, the ship cast up on an unknown island, and the survivors dug makeshift underground houses, in unconscious imitation of the Aleuts who inhabited the nearest islands. Many of the dugouts quickly became graves, as Bering and several others succumbed to scurvy compounded by despair.[49] Steller presided as pastor over the Lutheran commander's funeral, and the German members of the expedition grouped together. Soon, the men's acquaintance with the North Pacific natural world grew uncomfortably intimate. Arctic foxes gnawed at the faces of the dead and the dying, their fearlessness rightly suggesting to Steller that the crew had landed on an island never before visited by humans. Despite the horrors surrounding the men, the treeless island turned out to be a strange world full of surprises and, as Steller quickly realized, full of botanical and zoological potential. As soon as he had regained some strength, he began exploring the island, noting its convoluted shoreline, strange plants, and very strange beasts of the sea, including gigantic manatees grazing all about the island's lagoons.[50]

If nature had seemingly conspired against the Russian Empire, the turning point came, too, thanks to the North Pacific environment. In the spring, Steller and the other most vigorous men began hunting the island's marine mammals. They started with sea otters, animals they knew from Kamchatka. Like the foxes, sea otters initially displayed no fear of the men, and were slaughtered wholesale. Their meat, with the exception of the young otters, tasted terrible, but it helped temper the raging scurvy. In February, a totally unexpected bounty arrived: fur seals (*callorhinus ursinus*) began hauling up from the open ocean onto the island's shores in stunning numbers. The unwitting fur seals, who sought out such islands precisely because they were usually free from humans, met the same fate as the sea otters.

Now strong enough to undertake more difficult tasks, in the spring the crew decided to capture the sea cows they had seen floating in the shallows. This was no simple task. Steller's sea cows were the largest known manatees in the history of the world, roughly similar in size to an adult orca whale. The sea cows were not particularly difficult to kill, but with their limited resources, the men had no simple way of hauling the corpses to shore. One historian suggests that it was Steller who finally devised a method of harpooning, harnessing, and pulling the sea cows to shore by boat—techniques gleaned from his reading about Greenlandic whaling.[51] This new source of meat, which all agreed was delicious, gave the castaways the energy to reconstruct the ship. In April they sailed what they found to be the short distance to Kamchatka and resumed the long trek back to European Russia. Steller, fatefully, stayed on to explore Kamchatka for another two years.

The castaway months on what would be called Bering Island had revealed several possibilities for a Russian future in the oceanic North Pacific. There, the crew had lived much as the Aleuts had been living for nine thousand years in the North Pacific environment, albeit with less success. The Russians' diet consisted almost entirely of marine mammal meat and they lived in underground shelters, with timbers supplied by driftwood cast up on the treeless island. This experience provided a model that later Russian colonizers could follow, and some, especially the early *promyshlenniki* (fur traders) who hunted in the Aleutian Islands, did. Many Russians would find this lifestyle intolerable, which limited the number who could ever live in the North Pacific.

However, Russians were not mainly concerned with peopling the North Pacific, but rather with making it profitable. Steller, as a naturalist, thought that he could help in this goal. Steller's fullest expression of the imperial potential of his zoological research came in a letter to Gmelin, written upon his return to Kamchatka:

> The Channel between Kamchatka and America is not over forty to fifty miles in width and full of islands on which such an abundance of sea animals is to be met with that from them the costs of the most expensive expedition could be regained without much trouble in a few years.[52]

In his published treatise on the animals of the Commander Islands, Steller also claimed that the sea cows were so numerous "that they would suffice to support all the inhabitants of Kamchatka."[53] The peninsula faced perennial food shortages that rendered Russian control uncertain, and thus Steller's novel suggestion had strategic implications.

Though Kamchatkans would never see sea-cow steaks on their tables and scientific expeditions would rely on state support instead of fur-trade profits, the animals Steller described would play important roles in the fur trade that followed his return to Kamchatka. Some nineteenth-century writers even speculated that Steller himself counseled the *promyshlenniki* to kill sea cows as a meat supply, thereby contributing directly to the animals' extinction.[54] There is no evidence for such an advisory role, but a direct link between Steller and the *promyshlenniki* is hardly necessary to establish that Steller played a role in the beginning of the trade. He himself made a small fortune (probably three times his annual salary) from the three hundred or so sea otter pelts with which he returned to Kamchatka.[55] The *promyshlenniki* needed no further encouragement to load their boats and sail to the newly discovered islands, which all of Bering's surviving crew could describe. However, Steller's zoological work played no role in guiding the trade; natural history was not necessary to decipher the economic potential represented by the fur- and meat-bearing animals of the North Pacific.

Steller's part in the foundation of the fur trade pales in comparison with that of the expedition's naval officers. Aleksei Chirikov, who commanded the second ship in the expedition, wrote a long memorandum to the Admiralty College giving his advice on the structuring of the trade as well as the expansion of Russian naval control over the North Pacific. Chirikov recommended that St. Petersburg send a naval squadron to occupy the Kurile Islands, send settlers to occupy the Primor'ye Region (along the present-day border with China), and subordinate the already growing North Pacific fur trade to government control. He also gave explicit directions for the fur traders: they should first go to the Commander Islands, and then the following summer "or when the time is favorable for it to the south as well; and on whatever island a sufficient number of sea otters or land animals, foxes and sables, are found, they should hunt them, and whalebones should be collected in the same place."[56] Chirikov and Bering's earlier plans far exceeded in detail and ambition anything the Expedition's natural historians wrote. Chirikov submitted some Siberian ores for Gmelin's inspection, but like most of the expedition's natural historians' plans, these too were disappointing.[57]

Despite St. Petersburg's great hopes for natural history's contribution to the empire's financial well-being, the Kamchatka Expedition's natural historians accomplished little. The machinery of imperial expansion was far more capably manned by military personnel, private merchants, and the naval officers who were coming to prominence as a result of Peter I's emphasis on sea power, and the maritime nature of exploration and expansion in the North Pacific. Nonetheless, naturalists would contribute in less concrete ways to the Russian Empire's expansion into Kamchatka and Alaska, mainly through cataloging natural resources and advertising Russian possession to the rest of the world.

Cameralist and Contemplative Natural History

Though Steller had found no gold in the New World, the Russian state envisioned far greater goals for natural history. Science could be harnessed to improve all aspects of colonial development and administration. These goals can be summed up in the contemporary German term for the science of administration—cameralism (*Kameralwissenschaft*)—which gained great strength in Russia with the reign of Peter I. Cameralism envisioned a close linkage between the economy and the environment, stressing the need for the state to actively develop the productive potential of the human population and the natural world. As one German theorist put it, cameralism's ultimate aim was the "multiplication of the means of subsistence through the most advantageous use of what the earth and labor can produce."[58] Cameralism drew the state's attention to underutilized resources and dramatically increased its sphere of activity. Russia's eighteenth-century embrace of cameralist theory alerted the Empire to the underexploited potential of its colonial possessions.[59] While Siberian furs had provided a steady stream of income, the state would now attempt to develop mining, manufacturing, and any other sources of economic growth found in the East. But before it could step up the intensity of economic development, it needed better knowledge of the natural and cultural resources available in its distant dominion.

Natural historians played a key role in producing the knowledge that would lead to a more complete exploitation of nature. "All who are employed in the management and superintendency of states and nations," wrote Müller, "ought certainly to have an exact knowledge of those countries over which they preside." In his introduction to Krasheninnikov's work on Kamchatka, Müller set out the natural historian's proper research interests:

> the natural condition of any area of lands; its fertility and other quali-
> ties, its positive and negative attributes...what animals, birds, and fish
> live in what places and where what grasses, bushes, and trees can be
> found and whether any of them can be used for medicines or paints or
> some other economic purpose...[60]

For eighteenth-century practitioners of natural history, Müller must have been stating the obvious. Especially for those who had received a cameralist education in Germany, natural philosophy existed to serve the state.[61]

The North Pacific's natural historians all followed Müller's injunctions, to greater or lesser degrees. Gmelin alone described over thirty new species of plants that could have economic benefits for Russia.[62] However, not all natural historians framed their research with the same emphasis on imperial gain. A comparison of Krasheninnikov's and Steller's histories of Kamchatka demonstrates the means of resistance that natural historians could use to sidestep, and even subvert, the all-encompassing imperial project of exploiting the natural world. While natural historians served the Russian empire, the cosmopolitan and contemplative demands of natural history influenced their research and pulled at their loyalties. Not surprisingly, the expatriate Steller felt the tug of these crosscurrents more keenly than did the Russian Krasheninnikov.

In a 1750 speech he gave to the Academy of Sciences shortly before his death entitled "On the Benefits of the Sciences and the Arts," Krasheninnikov articulated his vision of natural history and its uses for the state.[63] Natural history and related "enlightened" sciences were powerful tools for a nation's betterment. The relative prosperity or poverty of nations, he claimed, "rests only on the difference in the enlightenment of their minds."[64] Enlightenment for Krasheninnikov meant mainly the practical sciences (*nauki*), including astronomy, physics, optics, and natural history. The blessings these sciences had showered upon Enlightened

Europe included better mining, better ship-building, and the discovery of the New World, a place Krasheninnikov saw as a "treasure chest" (*sokrovishcha*).[65]

These sciences would be even more powerful when fully adopted in Russia, for they would help it overcome the enormous technological difference separating Krasheninnikov's homeland from Europe. Krasheninnikov claimed that, before Peter I, "Russia was weak, and suffered all sorts of wants despite having an untold abundance in everything, but presently it is enlightening itself with the zeal of the wisest of monarchs" (the Empress Elizabeth).[66] Thanks to the sciences, Russia was now strong enough to defend itself against an aggressive Europe. For Krasheninnikov, Enlightenment was less about Voltaire's "freeing of the individual from prejudice" and far more about freeing the empire from its weaknesses. This view broadly typified Russian attitudes toward the Enlightenment, which was valued far more for its potential to more rationally organize society than as a philosophical system stressing individual liberty.

Krasheninnikov also spelled out the implications of Enlightenment for Russians' relationship with the natural world. When the sciences were combined with true Orthodox faith, "we see our superiority before all of the earth's creatures, and we have the ability to understand how to use them for benefit in our life, for tranquility, and for overcoming difficulties and dangers."[67] Krasheninnikov's pious invocation of faith, repeated several times throughout the essay, revealed that he did not part entirely with the "environmental theology" of predecessors such as Avvakum. Still, his preoccupation with the control and exploitation of nature contrasted sharply with the awe and powerlessness felt by Russian pilgrims when confronted with the Siberian wilderness. Though Krasheninnikov might express fear during one of Kamchatka's earthquakes, he read no divine portent into the event. Instead of being revealed in nature, God appeared at humanity's side in its quest to shape nature for its own benefit.

Krasheninnikov, whose career was built upon his Kamchatkan experiences, often used the North Pacific to illustrate his points in this discussion on "The Benefits of the Sciences and the Arts." The Kamchadals were presented as benighted simpletons who lacked access to the sciences that had lately blessed Russia. They required three years to build their boats, could not count higher than three without the use of their fingers, and had no notion of their own souls.[68] Boat-building was a common theme in Krasheninnikov's lecture; he marveled that the Russians now built excellent boats, and "we sail with good success not only on nearby seas for the defense of the Fatherland, but also on the very ocean."[69] For Krasheninnikov, the North Pacific—as imperial possession, proof of Russia's superiority over indigenous people, and oceanic space—was a theater par excellence for the manifestation of Russian Enlightenment.

The book that emerged from Krasheninnikov's Kamchatka research, *Description of the Land Kamchatka* (1755), put these theoretical concerns into practice, providing the environmental knowledge needed for imperial development. The book's thrust was explicitly cameralist, in ways that few other descriptions of the peninsula would be. Krasheninnikov devoted an entire chapter to naming and describing each river that he and fellow student Gorlanov had surveyed.[70] Krasheninnikov's English translator, the Scottish physician James Grieve, complained that "the Author had minutely described a great number of hills and rivers which did not serve to illustrate the subject,"[71] comments that missed the point entirely. Though Krasheninnikov offered many items of interest to the natural historian, his primary aim in *Description of the Land Kamchatka* was to supply the state with the comprehensive raw data useful for planning future settlement and future military maneuvers, and assessing the value of this distant possession. It was the beginning of a new kind of Russian imperial exploitation, one that—unlike Atlasov's fairly straightforward plans for extracting tribute—would systematically exploit all the land's resources.

The value of Kamchatka's nature lay not in its beauty, nor in the way it fed and clothed the Kamchadals, not even principally in its fitness for human habitation. An important section of Krasheninnikov's book analyzed the "advantages and disadvantages" of Kamchatka, much as Müller had advised. The disadvantages included Kamchatka's frequent natural disasters, such as earthquakes and floods, while the advantages lay mostly in the peninsula's potential for future colonization—its fertile ground ready for cultivation, the "quantity of forage" for animals, and an abundance of fish and furs for future export.[72] Here Krasheninnikov drew as neat a dichotomy between nature's unpredictability and its potential for profit as can be found in the eighteenth-century literature on the North Pacific. The value of Kamchatkan nature had to be calculated first and foremost in terms of its potential to bring gain to the Russian Empire.

Steller's approach to Kamchatkan nature had some similarities with these ideas, but differed from Krasheninnikov's in subtle but important ways. At times, Steller did lay out a plan of scientific research that resembled Krasheninnikov's insistence upon knowledge useful for the empire. While traveling through Eastern Siberia, he noted how beneficial systematic gathering of information would be for the empire:

> It occurs to me how useful and necessary it would be, not only in the whole of the Russian Empire, but especially in Siberia, that from every province and *Voevodship* [military governership] an accurate description of all places should be made. In these descriptions the benefits of a place compared to others, especially *beneficia* [blessings] and *vitia naturae* [imperfections of nature] and the richness or poverty of the inhabitants...[73]

This sort of a research program looked very similar to that proposed by Müller and carried out by Krasheninnikov, bespeaking a subordination of scientific interests to the economic and political development of Siberia. Steller also advocated using the animals he studied for imperial profits. Like Krasheninnikov, he displayed a basic faith in the desirability of imperial expansion.

However, Steller's relationship with the Russian Empire and imperial knowledge came with many more qualifications than Krasheninnikov's, and strained under the stress of contact with Kamchatka and the Kamchadals. Steller, in contrast to Krasheninnikov, often painted North Pacific nature without an imperial gloss. Steller's notes acknowledged the imperial implications of exploration, but a panoply of competing loyalties encompassing religion, sentiment, nationality, social radicalism, and natural philosophy counterbalanced the imperial element. If Steller presents a particularly conflicted case, many of these same concerns informed later North Pacific natural historians, from Pallas to Chamisso, and must be taken into account in order to understand their apprehension of North Pacific nature.

Steller's personal nexus of concerns included, most importantly, his religion and his troubled relationship with the Russian Empire. At the University of Halle, Steller had received an education strongly influenced by the seventeenth- and eighteenth-century German Protestant movement known broadly as Pietism. Pietism attempted to transcend doctrine through an emphasis on the Christian individual's direct experience with God, and the melioration of behavior that was supposed to follow such an experience.[74] While Pietism did not have much to say explicitly about the natural world, it taught that God's spirit should pervade every aspect of an individual's life. In contrast to most of the men on the Second Kamchatka Expedition, Steller adhered to a religious faith concerned deeply with worldly behavior, rather than the more outward forms of religious devotion. While Bering and his men promised to donate proceeds from the sea otter hunt to their home churches if God rescued them from their desert island, Steller focused on his and others' behavior during their exile. The apostasy, greed, and cursing of Bering's crew distressed him at every turn. Like Avvakum, Steller viewed life as a pilgrimage, in which man had to constantly guard himself from evil behavior in order to glorify God.[75] However, for him, the natural world was not there to test his faith, but rather offered opportunity for moral and immoral behavior. Steller's Pietiesm, as well as his profession, set him apart from his Siberian predecessors, and from the rest of the shipwrecked crew. Even Bering, a fellow Lutheran, practiced a faith detached from everyday life, more oriented toward miraculous intervention and the comforts of the afterlife than proper worldly behavior.[76]

Steller himself often fell short of Pietism's ideals, particularly its emphasis on controlling one's anger and avoiding "unnecessary curiosity."[77] In some ways Pietism stood at odds with the secular Enlightenment ideals which Steller and many contemporary natural historians drew upon both to establish their interests and for their methodology. Nonetheless, Steller remained a deeply pious man.[78] He saw North Pacific nature as guided by God's hand in ways that would seem foreign to later naturalists, who were more profoundly affected by the rationalist tendencies of the Enlightenment. When describing the fishes of Kamchatka, Steller claimed that they were

> even more deserving of a comprehensive description because the most wise providence and merciful love of the Almighty is clearly mirrored and revealed for all the world to see through these creatures, which He provides the Kamchadal who lack other food like bread and domesticated animals.[79]

For Steller, the act of doing natural history—describing nature—was holy work, transcribing the work of God into written form. Here Steller stood firmly in a long and continuing Protestant tradition that closely aligned natural history and theology, represented most clearly in his time by pastor-naturalists such as John Ray and Carl Linnaeus.

Though Krasheninnikov also invoked God when talking about the natural world, his and Steller's conceptions of the divine stood far apart. For Krasheninnikov, the study of nature "directs our thoughts … to our duties to God and to our Monarch."[80] For him, the relationship between the natural world and the divine was entirely conservative, reinforcing humans' duties to their superiors, and naturalizing the existing political structure. Krasheninnikov's ordering of religion mirrored the subordinate position the church had accepted vis-à-vis the state in post-Petrine Russia.

While Pietism may have played a similarly conservative role in Prussia at the time,[81] Steller's religion contained a more subversive potential, first revealed during the shipwreck on Bering Island. There, after the initial threat of starvation had receded, the men turned to killing sea otters for their pelts, as well as for sport. The pelts quickly became chips in the sailor's obsessive gambling—Steller called it an "addiction." Gambling was a particular concern of the Pietists and deeply disturbed Steller. He lamented that "Anyone who had altogether ruined himself tried to recover through the poor sea otters, which were needlessly and thoughtlessly killed merely for their pelts, the meat being thrown away."[82] Here Steller expressed both advocacy of wise use of the North Pacific's resources, as well as some sympathy for the Russians' victims. Such passages would recur later in the century, and they undercut the triumphal narrative of an enlightened Russia spreading civilization into the distance reaches of the world, instead emphasizing the cruelty and wastefulness that accompanied imperialism.

Beyond Steller's disgust with the men's sinful gambling, the exile on Bering Island had deeply affected his relationship with the natural world. With thousands of hours of enforced leisure, Steller was transformed from a collector of specimens to something resembling a modern field scientist. Though he occupied himself with measuring sea cow carcasses, on Bering Island Steller moved beyond anatomy (the obsession of contemporary zoologists) toward a study of animal ecology. He had the time and the opportunity to witness and describe some of the greatest concentrations of marine mammals anywhere in the world. The close contact with the animals awoke in him a deep affection—something one does not encounter in many accounts from the time, including those of Gmelin. As Steller noted in his journal, the sea otter "deserves the greatest respect from us all, because for more than six months it served us almost solely as our food and at the same time as medicine for the sick."[83] His treatise on the animals of Bering Island elaborated on the respect and affection he had for the sea otter, calling it "perhaps the only animal that has no comparison in the whole world."[84]

Steller was also capable of treating animals with great cruelty when science ostensibly called for it. As an experiment, he once blinded a sea lion and provoked its companions to tear it to pieces.[85] Nonetheless, he consistently condemned the wasteful killing of animals, and his interests extended well beyond the natural world's economic uses. For Steller, animals were witnesses to God's creation, and objects of beauty; consequently, they possessed the right not to be killed wantonly by humans. None of these ideas were unique to Steller, who lived at a time when European anthropocentric views of the world were coming under attack.[86] As the divinely ordained tyranny over nature that humans had enjoyed in previous centuries came under scrutiny, the right to destroy animals or treat them cruelly also began to be doubted. As the Comte de Buffon wrote in the 1760s, "is not man…the most harmful species of all? He alone slays, annihilates more living individuals than all carnivorous animals devour."[87] Even as cameralist states were harnessing nature for profit on an unprecedented scale, to many, humanity's domination of nature no longer seemed so easily justified. Among those on the Second Kamchatka Expedition, only Steller carried these attitudes—influenced by his Pietism—into the North Pacific. He also contributed to the fuller articulation of humanity's relationship with animals by drawing attention to the costs imperial expansion extracted from the animal world. If only the seeds of such a philosophy were visible in Steller's writings, these ideas would gain fuller expression from Steller's scientific successors in the North Pacific.

The relationship between Steller and Krasheninnikov appears to have mirrored their different approaches to natural history. Krasheninnikov's *Description* contains several passages that, when read through the cameralist philosophy of his "Speech on the Benefits of Sciences and Arts," appear as direct indictments of Steller's practice of natural history. As part of his introduction to the second chapter, Krasheninnikov remarked that

> The only diversions [in Kamchatka] are to gaze on towering mountains whose summits are eternally covered with snow, or, if one lives along the sea, to listen to the crashing of the waves and observe the different species of animals and consider their intelligence and constant battles with each other. If one considers only these things, it would seem more appropriate for this country to be inhabited by wild animals than by human beings.[88]

The useless "diversions" that appeared to discourage Russian colonization of Kamchatka were exactly those that Steller engaged in. In his notes that later became *De Bestiis Marinas*, Steller described sitting for days on the Kamchatkan shore, observing fur seals.[89] During his enforced exile on Bering Island, Steller spent even more time among the animals. "It happened to me on one unlucky occasion," wrote Steller, "that I could watch the habits and ways of these beasts daily for ten months from the door of my hut."[90] Such activities may have helped Steller's science, but, as Krasheninnikov obliquely noted, they did little for the Russian Empire. As Steller died before publishing anything, only a small passage at the end of his notes on Kamchatka hints at his feelings for his Russian colleague. There, he copied down a Kamchadal song poking fun at Krasheninnikov:

> If I were the student [Krasheninnikov], I would describe all the young girls.
> If I were the student, I would describe the fish *uranoscopum* (vulgar Cossack name for the female genitals).
> If I were the student, I would take down all eagle nests. etc. etc.[91]

This song captures Steller's dismissive attitude toward his Russian colleague, as well as the strange impression natural historians must have made on the North Pacific's indigenous peoples. Though studying the same nature, the two clearly perceived different environments.

Steller and the Kamchadals

In the sphere of human relations, Steller's uneasy relationship with the Russian Empire was on full display. He viewed Atlasov's conquest of Kamchatka with disgust, calling the Cossack "only the first of a long line of people who returned from there to Yakutsk and Moscow with a lot of plundered goods and ill-gotten wealth." While botanizing in Kamchatka, Steller also found time to "diligently gather a register of these thieving, unchristian overseers who, in a short time, unlawfully acquired a large capital."[92] Later natural historians would fault the Russian conquerors' savagery, but Steller was concerned to link their un-Christianity with the crimes committed in the name of conquest. The God who ensured the Kamchadals' health through an abundance of fish was also the God who punished the Russians for oppressing these people. Steller noted wryly that not one of the Russians who enriched himself in Kamchatka had been able to pass down the fortune to his descendants.

The Russian adventurers' sinfulness cast doubt upon the legitimacy of the Kamchatkan conquest. The early colonization of the peninsula had been marked by oppression and a number of uprisings and bloody reprisals. Notable revolts occurred in 1706 and 1731, the latter provoked by the First Kamchatka Expedition's demands on indigenous labor.[93] "It is safe to assume," wrote Steller, "that from the beginning to this day, Kamchatka could have been held without any rebellion and bloodshed if these affable people [the Kamchadal] had been treated in a Christian manner, sensibly and humanely."[94] The collection of *yasak* (fur tribute) was the chief cause of conflict between Russians and Kamchadals, as it was in much of Siberia. Extortionate *yasak* demands and a failure to carry out the state's benevolent policy toward the Kamchadals constituted the Russians' chief sins in Kamchatka. In Steller's opinion, the Cossacks had enjoyed too much freedom from imperial supervision in these distant provinces, though increasing imperial control had recently curtailed the worst of the offenses. By and large, the conquest of Kamchatka had been and continued to be unjust and sinful. The Kamchadals, wrote Steller, "have always been forced to rebel."[95] Steller did not advocate Russian retreat from Kamchatka, but he saw the history of Russian empire-building as deeply immoral. His views foreshadowed those of late-eighteenth-century natural historians—like Steller, foreigners—who visited the North Pacific.

Steller also anticipated later critiques with his insight into the environmental effects of Russian imperialism. In discussing the changes in Kamchatka since the conquest, Steller described how the Kamchadals had been forced to give up their traditional fur clothing, because the Russians collected all animal pelts for export.[96] The Kamchadals also faced increasing difficulties in hunting the animals necessary to replenish those lost to their Russian masters. Game was growing scarce, and with Russian demand for forced labor taking up most of the Kamchadals' time, few animals could be caught.[97] With Kamchatka's entry into the Russian Empire and the world market with which it interacted, the Kamchadals would have to adjust their relationship with the natural world. Russian imperial expansion was not only ungodly, but exploitative of the Kamchadals and their environment as well.

Krasheninnikov put an entirely different emphasis on the Kamchadal revolts that followed the Russian conquest. While admitting some lawlessness on the part of Atlasov and his band, Krasheninnikov insisted that imperial control had brought good governance, with no reason for rebellion.[98] Krasheninnikov also recognized that fur tribute lay at the heart of Russian-Kamchadal relations, but he claimed that the demands were very reasonable. He too commented upon the religious dimensions of the conquest. Instead of accusing the Russian conquerors of sinfulness, Krasheninnikov pointed out that many of the Kamchadals had converted to Christianity as a result of the Russians' missionary efforts.[99] Again, Krasheninnikov's Orthodoxy buttressed claims of Russia's sovereignty, whereas Steller's Pietism subverted these claims.

Steller, too, was interested in conversion; in fact, as an ordained Lutheran pastor, he personally baptized a Tungus (an indigenous people of Eastern Siberia) girl into Christianity on his journey to Kamchatka.[100] However, his conception of conversion ran in the opposite direction from Krasheninnikov's. When Steller asked the Kamchadals whether they approved of their children's conversion, they responded that "There is no opposing the world becoming Russian; let them like the Russian manners and company better than ours."[101] The Russians and Kamchadals both seemed to have understood conversion as mainly a symbolic exercise representing a very real submission. For Steller, however, conversion impacted the spiritual state of the person; political identity was inconsequential in comparison. Steller thought conversion actually harmed the Kamchadals:

> ...I see that more harm than good will come from baptism since, through the mingling of true religious tenets with Kamchadal superstitions, as many new sects might come into being as there are villages on Kamchatka because these people are so scattered, have such a lively imagination, and the Russians living here know so little of religion. It is utterly amazing what strange dogmas the Kamchadal learn under the name of the Christian religion by questioning the Cossack sons.[102]

For Steller, correct dogma and knowledge of biblical truth were far more important than nominal conversion. The ungodliness of the Russians guaranteed that no Kamchadal conversion would ever truly succeed.

In some ways, Steller and Krasheninnikov were not so different: both had risked their lives to study the natural world of a faraway place, and both had placed themselves at the service of one of the early modern world's greatest empires. Their paths diverged, however, at multiple points, and set the stage for personal animosity. While Krasheninnikov followed closely the dictates of cameralist natural history, the impetuous and irascible Steller was transformed in the process of engagement with the North Pacific. Lonely months on Bering Island shifted his thoughts from empire to the lives of animals, and the Pietistic faith to which he held fast in a sea of troubles awoke a pity for God's creatures. In truth, in extracting living resources and subjecting humans, the Russian Empire looked very similar to those of the British, Spanish, French, and other early modern expansionist states. But Steller was the most prominent of a very small number of interpreters of Russian expansion, and thus his opinions would take on out-sized importance, helping to define the Russians as uniquely bad imperialists.

Steller's perception of the Russian conquest of Kamchatka indicates some of the difficulties that the Russian Empire created for itself with the hire of foreign natural historians. The problem was not that Steller disapproved of Russian impe-rialism *tout court*, but that he had a fundamentally different understanding of the means and ends of imperial expansion. While Peter I had Westernized much of Russian thinking and practice, older Muscovite traditions of empire-building persisted, especially in these far corners. Krasheninnikov reflected some of these older traditions in his understanding of conversion. Even in areas where Russia had modernized, such as the application of science to imperial expansion, the practices of its imported natural historians were sometimes too idiosyncratic to mesh with the Empire's aims. In his cameralist conception of the Kamchatkan environment, Krasheninnikov partook in a newer tradition that dated from Peter's reforms, but that was not shared by his Pietistic German colleague. Even as Russia strived to emulate European practices, Europe itself continued to evolve.

Steller's metaphysical protests against Russian imperialism also had political consequences. While in Kamchatka after his return from America, Steller was entrusted with the questioning of several Kamchadals who had been accused of treason during a 1741 revolt. Kamchatkan authorities had arrested the men and marched them across the peninsula to Petropavlovsk for an audience with Steller, who, as the highest-ranking civil servant in the area, controlled their fate. Steller immediately dismissed the men (whom he claimed were true Christians) and all charges against them—an impulsive decision that would earn him the suspi-cion of local officials. He also had the temerity to accuse the Kamchatkan com-mander Chemetevskii of abusing his power over the Kamchadals. Chemetevskii returned the favor by accusing Steller of treason. These charges would hold up Steller's return journey to St. Petersburg, a delay that contributed to his illness and death in the Siberian town of Tyumen in November, 1746. Müller, who sel-dom wavered in his imperial viewpoint, complained that Steller unnecessarily got involved in matters that did not concern him.[103]

As much as the Russian Empire's excesses might enrage Steller, there was little he could do to curb them. He, Krasheninnikov, Gmelin, and Müller were caught up in a process largely outside their control. Russian expansion to the East had always relied on the exploitation of indigenous labor and natural resources, particularly fur resources. In the North Pacific this exploitation would continue, and even intensify, with the support of the same living foundations. From the moment Steller and the others yoked their destiny to that of the Russian Empire, they were swept up in a surging eastward tide of reckless resource extraction and subjection of indigenous peoples, against which they could contribute little and resist even less. Natural historians' real power lay elsewhere, in a long-term shaping of international perceptions of the North Pacific environment and its management.

The European Reception of Steller and Krasheninnikov

Apart from the search for natural resources, natural historians were engaged in the less tangible but important process of legitimizing and propagandizing Russian expansion to Western Europe. As Steller wrote in a moment of pique, he had been hired merely to "lend the undertaking greater prestige."[104] St. Petersburg saw the prestige of "enlightened" exploration as nearly as important as the discovery of natural resources, and European perception of the empire loomed large at the conclusion of the Second Kamchatka Expedition. Here, too, the results would be mixed at best.

As with every expedition St. Petersburg would coordinate in the eighteenth century, after the Second Kamchatka Expedition the government pursued simultaneous and contradictory policies of openness and secrecy. The desire to boast of Russia's feats in the Pacific collided with an anxiety that other European nations would be in better position to exploit the Russian discoveries. All journals and scientific treatises were treated as top secret during the course of the voyage. Upon the conclusion of the voyages, expedition members had to turn over materials to the Admiralty College or Imperial Senate, which carefully controlled their censorship and publication. Steller's work was singled out for immediate delivery from the Academy of Sciences to the Imperial Cabinet.[105]

This secrecy meant that news would slowly trickle out over decades. Meanwhile, there was ample motivation to smuggle journals out of Russia to London, Paris, and Germany for immediate publication. In 1746, Leonhard Euler first broke the silence surrounding the Second Kamchatka Expedition, passing on some details to the Berlin Academy of Sciences in two letters, and adding that he doubted that the Russian Empire would ever release any information on its own.[106] In 1749 Gmelin succeeded spectacularly in outwitting the censors, decamping without warning for a professorship in Tübingen, and, despite his promises to the contrary, publishing an account of his Siberian journey written from notes he had concealed. Gmelin's work pointedly praised the late and currently disfavored Empress Anna and criticized the Chancellery's role in organizing the Expedition.

Gmelin's abscondment made already troubled life more difficult for the German naturalists who stayed in St. Petersburg. The heyday of German influence at the court had ended in 1740 with the death of Anna and the ascendancy of Elizabeth I, daughter of Peter I. The Academy fell into relative disgrace and suffered extreme financial need. Professors' salaries were not paid in 1744.[107] Safely abroad, Gmelin explained to the Duke of Württemberg that he had fled "from the yearly and even daily annoyances" in Petersburg.[108] By the conclusion of the expedition, the once-favored German academicians were decidedly on the defensive.

At the same time, confusing and derogatory accounts of Steller's death, which had occurred in Siberia during his return from Kamchatka, were circulating in Germany. Steller's brother, Augustine, had corresponded with an unknown member of the Petersburg Academy of Sciences, who claimed that Steller had single-handedly saved the Bering expedition and that the Russian Empire had later persecuted him and directly caused his death. An anonymous German author, probably Müller,[109] inherited the unenviable task of pruning Steller's legacy down to size and explaining the true circumstances of Steller's death. In a letter published in Frankfurt in 1748, Müller explained why St. Petersburg had not previously allowed more exact information about Steller to leave the Empire:

> One cannot think poorly of any country—Russia included—for forbidding quick publication of materials when it spends great, almost immeasurable sums financing useful discoveries, and also richly repays its discoverers, whom it uses for these purposes.[110]

Müller also chided the German publicists for attributing to Steller the baptism of the Kamchadals, a more controversial subject than the Germans knew. In an indication that Steller's religious activism may have riled the Empire, Müller remarked that Steller had come freshly out of religion-obsessed Halle and may have been filled with a passion for conversion. However, Müller reminded his readers, "Russia has its own religion for the conversion of the heathens, and needs no foreigners' help."[111] Russia did not appreciate its hired natural historians interfering too deeply in matters of imperial administration.

Müller's letter also emphasized Steller's dependence upon the Russian Empire for his scientific exploits. The letter pointed out that Steller, though a gifted naturalist, would have had only an insignificant career had he remained in Germany. Instead, the opportunities for discovery that Russia presented had made him famous throughout the world.[112] These remarks reminded Europeans that, though Russia was participating in the Enlightenment project of cosmopolitan knowledge-gathering, the state intended to take ultimate credit for any information produced. This was an important distinction for St. Petersburg to make: it needed to be the agent gathering the information about the North Pacific if the region were to be seen as part of the Russian empire. Yes, Steller had collected botanical and zoological information in Kamchatka, Alaska, and the Aleutians, but only because Russian ships had brought him there and the Russian state had paid his salary. St. Petersburg was protecting not only the commercial advantages it might gain from natural history, but also the prestige and legitimacy it hoped patronage of natural historians would lend the Empire.

The concern with foreign natural historians received further expression in another letter that the beleaguered Müller had to write,[113] this time in response to the Frenchman Joseph Nicholas de l'Isle's outrageously inaccurate map of the North Pacific, published in Paris in 1752. De l'Isle had been employed by the Academy of Sciences, and he got much of his information from his brother Louis de l'Isle de la Croyère, who had died shortly after his return to Kamchatka. De l'Isle's widely discussed map took credit for the discoveries of others and contradicted earlier Russian maps.[114] St. Petersburg responded immediately, pointing out the absurdities in the map, smearing de l'Isle's brother's character, and claiming de la Croyère had been drunk during most of the Expedition. Müller's rhetoric in the anonymous *Lettre d'un Officier Russe* was even sharper than in his response to the Steller rumors. The few worthwhile observations in de l'Isle's account, the letter claimed, could all be attributed to de Croyère's Russian assistant Krasilnikov. While de l'Isle claimed to have personally inspired Russia to plan an expedition to the North Pacific, Müller noted that Russia had been engaged in this process since 1715, under Peter I.[115] Finally, Müller took issue with the names de l'Isle appended to the newly discovered coastlines:

> For my part I should rather have been inclined to have made use of the name of *New-Russia*, in imitation of other nations, who have called Countries of *New-England, New-Spain, New-France, New-Holland, &c.* It may be said we are not in possession of them; but as to this, it is purely at our discretion, for, at least, it is certain, that these vast countries belong to no power able to dispute the possession with us.[116]

The letter not only cleared up Russia's intentions in the North Pacific, but also stated unequivocally that the state conceived of the region as analogous to European overseas possessions. Russia, just like Western Europe, would use cartography and natural history to assert sovereignty over their conquered territories.

The strategy scored some successes in the 1750s. Müller's *Lettre* was quickly translated into English and German. Arthur Dobbs, colonial governor of North Carolina, published his English translation in London two years after the French original appeared. He conceded that it appeared "that all, or most of the merit, is due to the *Russians*, who with indefatigable labour and peril, traveled through these countries, and made these discoveries."[117] The German newspapers were similarly full of praise for the Russians' apparently successful expedition.

Yet, the European press also sounded some discordant notes. Because Steller's notes were in disarray, and because of the criticism they contained, St. Petersburg decided to let Krasheninnikov edit Steller's materials and combine them with his own. Krasheninnikov's resulting *Opisanie Zemli Kamtchatka* (Description of the Land Kamchatka) appeared in 1755; an English translation based on the type block beat the Russian version by a year.[118] The publisher, in introducing Grieve's translation, complained somewhat unfairly that, "The Russian language in which the Original of the following sheets was written, is rude and unpolished." While other countries were writing natural histories with refined languages, the publisher claimed that "in that country literature has, on the contrary, been 'till very lately rather discouraged." The Russians had a long way to go before they would be able to produce knowledge that met the demanding standards of Europe. Kamchatka and the North Pacific remained "remote, unknown, and very extraordinary."[119] As far as many Europeans were concerned, a fog of uncertainty still hung over the outlines of the North Pacific. Despite the Russians' efforts, these lands and seas were still *terrae* and *mari incognitae*.

The European scientific community waited impatiently for Steller's materials to come to light. Linnaeus in particular hungered after Steller's Siberian botanical collection, but he foolishly jeopardized his access to it by angering his St. Petersburg connection, Johann Siegesbeck. Proof of natural history's ties with eighteenth-century diplomacy, the Swedish ambassador became involved in the affair, advising Linnaeus that "It is important that Sweden be on friendly terms with him, at least until Professor Steller returns from Kamchatka and America...Siegesbeck is the only man through whom we can get a share in what Steller brings."[120] With the help of Gmelin, Linnaeus did eventually snatch up most of Steller's Siberian plants.

Otherwise, Steller's works trickled out of Russia at a maddeningly slow pace. St. Petersburg allowed the relatively quick publication of Steller's most polished and least dangerous manuscript, his *De Bestiis Marinas* (On the Beasts of the Seas), which would be translated into German in 1753, but his notes on

Kamchatka would not follow for twenty years, finally published in his native Germany in 1774. His American journal had to wait for Peter Simon Pallas' 1793 issue of *Neue Nordische Beyträge* (with some sensitive materials excised).[121] Most of Steller's work focused on a contemplative natural history ill-suited for imperial needs, and overall, Russian statesmen must have been sorely disappointed in the practical gains gleaned from Steller's mercurial employment. If other natural historians still referred to Steller as "blessed"[122] and an "uncommon genius,"[123] St. Petersburg probably shared the less flattering opinions of Krasheninnikov. It would be many decades before a Russian emperor would again employ a foreign natural historian in the North Pacific.

Thus, the legacy of Steller's and Krasheninnikov's pioneering natural history work in the North Pacific was mixed. Both failed in bringing any tangible material benefit to the empire, as gold and other precious metals eluded their tentative search. The men did, however, transform Russian engagement with the colonial natural world, providing the first systematic, published treatises describing these areas. Though naturalists would not return to the North Pacific for several decades, others such as Pallas would spend this time collating and publishing the materials of the Second Kamchatka Expedition. Science had gained a firm and lasting place in Russian imperialism. Steller and Krasheninnikov also revealed the shape of future divisions within the practice of natural history, centered on different assessments of empire, religion, and the purpose of science.

In 1771, Pallas, returning to St. Petersburg from his Siberian travels, visited Steller's grave on the banks of the Tura River. Putting to rest rumors that the grave had been defiled out of anger toward the man (when instead grave robbers had simply wanted his red cloak), Pallas described for German readers the lonely scene of his predecessor's last moments. A stone had been placed on Steller's grave, and it was likely to stay there "until the Tura River has eroded the banks on which it stands, and Steller's bones are mixed with the mammoth bones on the opposite bank."[124] For a man as sober as Pallas, this was a remarkable piece of prophecy. Not only was Steller's body washed away, but his legacy would be mixed with those of the mammoths in ways that Pallas could not fully comprehend. Steller had been intrigued by the many mammoth bones partly concealed in Siberia's permafrost, and had even concocted plans to search the Arctic coast for specimens. Pallas augmented Steller's labor by discovering mammoth remains himself and theorizing that Noah's flood had deposited Asian elephants in Siberia. Neither man thought of preserved mammoths as remains of extinct animals, but they were part of a developing global conversation on the topic that included Benjamin Franklin, Thomas Jefferson, Peter Collinson, and Buffon.[125] What neither Pallas nor Steller knew was that, in the years immediately following the Second Kamchatka Expedition, another gigantic animal had disappeared from the earth. Soon the sea cow would take its place alongside the mammoth as an emblem of extinction. As *promyshlenniki* began hunting in the Aleutian Islands after 1744, a new complication was emerging for naturalists to deal with: the rapid and largescale decline of the marine mammals Steller had just described.

2

Promyshlenniki, Siberians, Alaskans, and Catastrophic Change in an Island Ecosystem

The North Pacific Ocean remains one of the most dynamic environments on earth, and in the eighteenth century it seized Russians and naturalists in its current and cast them onto unexpected shores. Beginning soon after Steller's return to Kamchatka, a regime of even colder and stormier weather settled onto the North Pacific for the next twenty or thirty years. The great number of Russian shipwrecks during this period may be at least partly attributed to this phenomenon. At the same time, cold seas and windy weather meant greater upwelling (when nutrient-rich deep waters rise to the surface to replace depleted waters, which have been blown elsewhere), and greater overall primary productivity (meaning an increase in the numbers of organisms at the bottom of the food chain). The numbers cannot be retrieved with any certainty, but sea otters, fur seals, whales, and other large predators thrive under such conditions. And so, when the first *promyshlenniki* (fur traders) were drawn to the Commander and Aleutian Islands by news from the Bering and Chirikov survivors, they encountered waters of stunning abundance.

Russians, however, provided another source of environmental instability. Emilian Basov, the first rugged *Sibiriak* (native of Siberia) to sail from Kamchatka, gave a succinct preview of the coming onslaught in 1743. He had no sooner sighted Bering Island than his boat was caught in a storm and smashed against the shore. The twenty shipwrecked men, including Basov, set to work making a bloody mess of the shallow lagoons, killing an astounding 1,200 sea otters over the next year, or a third of the present-day numbers inhabiting the island waters. They also stabbed ineffectively at the sea cows, but when that proved unsuccessful, they settled for boiling and salting down fur-seal and sea-lion meat. After repairing the ship and sailing back to Kamchatka, Basov returned the next year and discovered an unknown island nearby. On newly named Copper Island, Basov displayed his own scientific curiosity, wondering about a species of large fish he found washed up there. He also succeeded in killing sea cows this time, and his crew of Russians and Kamchadals was well fed. Again, the take in sea otters was legendary—1,760 in less than two years.[1] In only fifteen years, there would not even be enough sea otters left to make stopping at the Commander Islands worth the Russians' time. Disaster struck the Aleutian ecosystem almost as quickly as it would strike Basov, who died an impoverished alcoholic only a few years after his rich haul.

This chapter details the ways in which the ocean ecosystem and human actions combined to produce the environmental catastrophe that, in some ways, was the defining story of Russia's eighteenth-century North Pacific empire. It tells of the total extinction of the sea cow, as well as the cascading sea otter population crashes that accompanied the increasingly complex fur trade as it proceeded eastward from the Commander Islands to the Alaskan mainland. Along the way, the Russian fur traders picked up Kamchadal, Aleut, and Alutiit subjects and allies, who each changed the fur trade in important ways. While the Russian state attempted to manage these developments, the cosmopolitan assortment of peoples and animals changed the North Pacific's environment so radically that, by the end of the century, observers were warning that unprecedented damage was taking place. Meanwhile, the ocean's power to transform Russian imperial ambitions and scientific ideas lay in its turbulent climate, its island ecosystems, and the fact that its great biological wealth was concentrated in large, fluctuating marine mammal populations.

There is some controversy over the extent of sea otter depletion caused by Russians in Alaskan waters.[2] With the benefit of detailed catch records and eyewitness reports, it is clear that local sea-otter and fur-seal depletions along the Aleutian chain were dramatic long before 1867, when Alaska passed from Russia to the United States. Sea otter declines were especially acute around the end of the eighteenth century. Complex factors induced these depletions: climate and sea temperatures shifted, with the warming trend that occurred around 1790 a potential climatic driver of fur-seal and sea-otter declines.[3] Additionally, species linkages within the ecosystem—that is, the relationships between different animal populations—meant that depletion could be partly the result of indirect factors, as seems to have been the case for the sea cow.

Russians and the imperial structures propelling and following them into the North Pacific must be accounted as the main drivers of species decline—and extinction. To serve an insatiable Chinese market for fine furs, the Russian fur trade gathered a deadly coalition of merchants, government officials, common hunters, Kamchadals, and Aleuts seemingly united only in their goal of

killing marine mammals. The relationships between these peoples and the animals they sought are key to unraveling the environmental change in the North
Pacific. Violence pervaded the long chain between sea otter and tsar, in ways
peculiar to the Russian Empire, but its full effect can be explained only at the
local level. Everywhere the Russian fur-trade empire had produced ecological
change, but in the North Pacific this change was so radical and so visible that
naturalists would later see in it a direct challenge to some of Europe's most cher-
ished beliefs about the natural world. For a while, increasing sea otter numbers
eastward along the Aleutian chain fooled *promyshlenniki* into thinking ecological catastrophe could be averted. But, due to changing climate regimes, marine
mammal ecology, and the unique visibility of declines around islands, environmental change in the North Pacific took on the appearance of catastrophe by the
1790s. While sea-otter and fur-seal numbers would stabilize (and even recover)
in the nineteenth century, the sea cow would never come back. It was in these
sixty years after Steller's voyage that Russians found themselves ruling an empire
of extinction.

The Dynamic North Pacific

Within the North Pacific, the locations most abundant in nutrients are found
at the meeting of land and sea. The Aleutian Islands—volcanic massifs rising
thousands of feet from the ocean bottom—are particularly rich places from the
perspective of marine predators, as they sit at the confluence of several major
North Pacific currents. The Alaskan Coastal Current (ACC) brings relatively
warm, fresh water from the Gulf of Alaska to the Aleutians, while the Alaska
Stream (AS) carries colder, nutrient-rich saltwater. There, water from the Bering
Sea also mixes with the North Pacific's very cold deep ocean waters, which rise
upon contact with the islands, bringing to the surface hosts of nutrients (see the
map of North Pacific currents in Figure 2.1).[4] The Aleutians are a meeting point
of extraordinary diversity and biological potential. The narrow passes between
the islands linking the Bering Sea and the North Pacific are places of special environmental opportunity for marine mammals.[5]

Looking out over these foggy straits, Aleuts and Russians saw sea lion rook-
eries, sea otter rafts, and hundreds of spouting whales, but also dangerously
swirling waters and currents that often sucked down small boats or dashed
them to pieces on the rocks. Despite the dangers, settlements tended to congregate near these straits, and the abundance of such locations in the Eastern
Aleutians contributed to a higher human population density there.[6] Within the
Aleutian Archipelago, species abundance and biomass increases from west to
east,[7] which meant that Russian colonists found progressively more bounteous

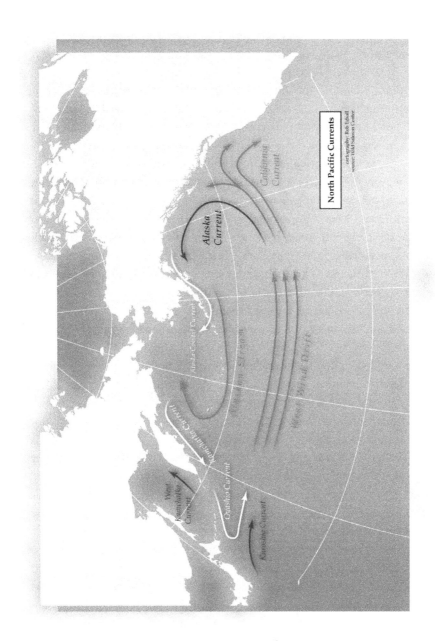

Figure 2.1 Map of North Pacific currents.

environments as they expanded the reach of their fur-trading expeditions after 1742. The Aleuts, on the other hand, when colonizing the islands from mainland Alaska,[8] found the waters progressively poorer as they went west. Those at the far western end of the archipelago had to survive on smaller, less nutritious food such as shellfish and migratory birds, whereas those to the east ate larger fishes and marine mammals.[9] Thus, the first islands the Russians encountered, the Near Aleutian Islands, had the smallest Aleut populations.

The Aleuts colonized the islands during a time of relative cold—a climate regime still in effect, though waning, when the Russians arrived in the North Pacific.[10] Cold air and sea temperatures had variable effects on local fauna. Fish populations, especially Pacific cod, seemed to have flourished under those conditions, and numbers of sea birds that fed on the fish were particularly high during cold periods.[11] Sea lions, an extremely important food source for the Aleuts and a source of boat-building material for both Aleuts and Russians, also thrive under cold conditions.[12] The generally cooler ocean temperatures and greater precipitation in the past would have been beneficial to most marine mammals, because of associated increases in upwelling.[13] Steller's sea cow, on the other hand, is one of the few North Pacific mammals whose population decreases during cold periods, probably because it is the only one that feeds on kelp.[14] Ironically, with the incipient warming trend that began after 1760, the sea cow was poised for a recovery in numbers, after having dipped perilously close to extinction.

Several periodic phenomena are known to occur in the North Pacific, affecting the relative abundance of several species of fish and mammals.[15] Most important of these is the Aleutian low-pressure system (Aleutian Low), which prevails from September through April. The Aleutian Low pulls a constant flow of cyclonic storms from Japan eastward to the Gulf of Alaska, bringing along with it plankton and, after 1742, an intermittent stream of Russian ships. Bering fought against a strong Aleutian Low against which on the return voyage, and which helped kill him. Periods of strong Aleutian Lows are known as the Pacific Decadal Oscillation (PDO), a phenomenon that favors most predatory fish and the sea mammals that feed on them, but depresses other fish, and thus seabird, populations.[16] The PDO appears to shift every twenty to thirty years, with a particularly strong swing toward a cooler and wetter regime around 1750.[17]

The 1750 PDO was associated with strong growth in glaciation in Southeast Alaska, and can perhaps be seen as the beginning of accelerated environmental change throughout the North Pacific.[18] After a period of intense cold lasting until 1760, temperatures increased until around 1800, when another fifteen years of cold followed. Powerful earthquakes hit the North Pacific in 1788, 1792, 1844, and 1854, often with sudden and dramatic effects on coastal topography. The Commander Island shoreline, for example, has been significantly lower over the last 750 years than previously—a factor that limited foraging area for both sea cows and sea otters. Volcanic activity has been almost continuous.[19] Taken together, recent centuries in the North Pacific have seen, according to some scientists, "environmental change on a scale almost unsurpassed anywhere else on the planet."[20]

It is no simple task to correlate historical marine mammal populations with climatic and oceanographic trends. Even biologists assessing the impacts of the 1989 Exxon Valdez oil spill have had a difficult time isolating the oil as the most significant factor explaining a variety of ecosystem changes.[21] Nonetheless, some broad trends can be discerned. The colder oceanic and climatic conditions were favorable to marine mammals. Most ecological modeling also assumes a far higher fish biomass in 1750 than in the twentieth century,[22] a factor that would have had greater effects on fur seals and sea lions than on sea otters, which eat relatively few fish. It is possible that sea otters have been subject to a long-term decline throughout the North Pacific due to falling sea levels leading to a reduction in productive shallows,[23] but human predation seems to have been a more powerful factor in determining sea otter—and all marine mammal—numbers. According to evidence recovered from ancient garbage heaps (known as middens), North Pacific sea otter populations were comparatively high from about 1700 BCE to 1 CE, then decreased substantially from 1 to 800 CE. Their numbers then rebounded, but never regained their initial abundance. Similarly, sea lions have decreased in abundance over the last 3700 years—again, probably due to Aleut exploitation. Fur seals, on the other hand, do not seem to have been declining at the time of initial Russian contact.[24] As would be the case in the eighteenth century, anthropological factors already seem to have been decisive in determining sea mammal populations for at least several thousand years in the North Pacific. Whether Aleuts stabilized marine mammal populations or drove them continuously downward is debated.[25] Whatever the case, with the beginning of warming, the onset of a strong PDO around 1740, and no known changes in Aleut hunting, the North Pacific's marine mammals seemed to be in no particular danger. This changed suddenly with the arrival of the Russians, and an entirely new relationship between humans and beasts.

Promyshlenniki and Sea Otters in the Commander Islands

When the members of the Second Kamchatka Expedition returned from Alaska with reports of amazingly abundant animals, Russian fur traders already in Siberia almost immediately began organizing maritime voyages to the newly discovered

Commander Islands (Bering and nearby Copper). The first men who gathered together the necessary complement of hunters and navigators were often what Russians referred to as *raznochintsy*, that is, people who had no firm place in Russia's rigidly structured caste system. Neither landowners nor serfs, the *promyshlenniki* were sometimes runaways from European Russia who had gained experience in the Siberian fur trade, but more often government officials who were part of the loose bureaucracy of the Far Eastern provinces of Kamchatka and Okhotsk. Later, an increasing number of well-capitalized merchants from Moscow or the Siberian metropole of Irkutsk captured the bulk of the maritime fur trade, but the trade's first years were truly democratic.

Basov, the first *promyshlennik* to hunt in the North Pacific, was a government servitor then living in Okhotsk, in Eastern Siberia. Before embarking to the North Pacific, he had to take the laborious step of traveling to Moscow to obtain official government permission to hunt in these waters.[26] Though it had not explicitly claimed the lands and seas discovered by Bering, the Russian state controlled its subjects' access to the region. In fact, any Russian who wanted to travel from his or her hometown had to obtain a passport from the appropriate government official.[27] Additionally, the state claimed *de facto* ownership of all the natural products under its dominion.[28] In 1739, Krasheninnikov had felt obliged to inform the Bolsheretsk Chancellery in Kamchatka that the Empress had given him permission to shoot local birds for scientific purposes.[29] His actions indicate that not only were animals considered government property, but in the centralized Russian state, from the very onset of the trade, ultimate control of the Russian North Pacific lay with St. Petersburg.

In a strict sense, then, there would be no "tragedy of the commons" in the North Pacific. A tragedy of the commons occurs when, because of lack of clear ownership, people harvest natural resources at an unsustainable rate for fear that others will harvest them first.[30] The Russian state had both the legal structure with which to claim the North Pacific's resources and the means to enforce its edicts. Because *promyshlenniki* had to assemble a crew, build a boat, and disembark from and return to one of very few ports in the Russian Far East, the government could track their movements relatively easily. St. Petersburg succeeded in taxing the *promyshlenniki* regularly from the trade's inception, keeping thorough (and presumably fairly accurate) records of catches brought in to Russia. Additionally, the Aleut people who had been harvesting sea otters for generations claimed their own ownership over the animals around their islands.[31] They thus had a continued incentive to spare at least the sea otters found closest to their home islands. Later fur traders would claim that the companies' ruthless competition for furs had depleted the sea otters. This was true, but was only one of many factors leading to the long-term decline of marine mammals in the North Pacific.

Basov's pioneering voyage of 1743 seemed to demonstrate that the animals of the North Pacific were as abundant as advertised. Steller's recent harvest notwithstanding, the Commander Islands were perhaps the only unexploited population in the North Pacific at that time. In the twenty-first century, once again free of hunting pressures, there are as many as thirty-one individual sea otters per kilometer of shoreline, which is an extremely high figure (see Figure 2.2).[32]

Figure 2.2 A raft of sea otters in numbers suggesting the abundance the first *promyshlenniki* encountered. Photograph taken at Cordova, Alaska, by author.

The presence of a vigorous sea otter community is also seen in Steller's reports of abundant kelp forests, a result of sea-otter predation on kelp-eating sea urchins.[33] In 1743 Basov's men were able to kill up to fifty sea otters and one hundred arctic foxes per day (see Figures 2.3 and 2.4 for eighteenth-century renderings of sea otters).[34] Although sea cows were more difficult to kill, Basov's report indicated that these animals were especially abundant, enough "to feed many people."[35] In one winter of hunting, Basov and his crew killed 1,200 sea otters and 4,000 arctic foxes.

Upon his return to Kamchatka, Basov quickly got together another crew which sailed the following summer, this time expanding the hunt to the newly discovered Copper Island, located just to the southeast of Bering Island. On this voyage, the men hunted fur seals in addition to sea otters and foxes. The crew also finally had success in catching sea cows, using a hook procured from the Chancellery. Despite blundering around the North Pacific for several months in search of undiscovered islands, on their second voyage Basov and crew killed an astounding 1,760 sea otters in the Commander Islands. Upon their return the fur traders felt flush enough to donate one-thirty-second of the catch to the small church in Nizhnekamchatsk—the Church of St. Nicholas, patron saint of sailors.[36] It was a very successful start to the trade.

Figure 2.3 See Otter. These two grossly inaccurate depictions of a sea otter were published by the St. Petersburg Academy of Sciences to accompany Steller's article "De Bestiis Marinis." *Novi Commentarii,* T. II (St. Petersburg, 1751).

Figure 2.4 One of the only drawings of a sea otter in the eighteenth century was produced by the English artist John Webber. Courtesy of Alaska State Library. Alaska Purchase Centennial Commission PCA 20–137.

Basov's profits drew other *promyshlennik* to the sea-otter-fur trade, and to head off the competition Basov succeeded in obtaining an edict from the Bolsheretsk Chancellery prohibiting any other traders from hunting on Bering or Copper Island, ostensibly for fear that they might not hesitate to steal parts of Bering's ship still lying on the sands of Bering Island, which was legally still the property of the state.[37] One of the motives behind Basov's pleas was surely the dwindling number of sea otters found on the islands after the last three years' ravages (including Steller's hunting parties). Although the Commander Islands were some of the richest sea otter grounds in the entire North Pacific, the population was very likely already in serious decline by 1747.

In fact, by 1747 it was probably becoming clear to Basov and his men that the marine mammals of the North Pacific were very different from the sables that had formed the backbone of the Siberian fur trade. Sables are prolific breeders that, moreover, are highly mobile. Their populations are prone to quick booms and busts depending on climatic factors and availability of prey, and they range far and wide in search of prey or to flee from enemies. Sea otters, on the other hand, typically give birth to only one pup every other year, producing a stable population that has little reserve against catastrophe. Exacerbating this problem, at least on the Commander and Aleutian Islands, was the animals' relative isolation and inability to migrate. The Commander sea otters were part of a larger community stretching from the Kurile Islands to California, but open ocean hindered migration between the Commander Island animals and neighboring groups. Even the Bering and Copper Island groups had little or no contact with each other. Though the two islands lie only twenty-nine miles apart, this distance is farther than sea otters normally travel over open water. Relatively small creatures unable to dive deeply in search of food, they find the long passages with swift currents between islands inhospitable and dangerous. Sea otters are capable of traveling between island groups, but migration normally takes place accidentally, as when a group is blown by a storm across open ocean. Outside these rare occurrences, the animals do not venture into water deeper than ninety-one meters (fifty fathoms), shallower than the 130-meter-deep sea between the two Commander Islands.[38] After the disappearance of the Copper Island sea otters in 1762, they did not reappear for over one hundred years.[39] In the short run at least, the Bering and Copper sea otter populations were distinct. Nor would sea otters arrive from the Aleutian Islands, several hundred miles farther to the east of the Commanders. In the lifespan of a *promyshlennik*, and certainly within the span of two or three voyages, the Commander Island sea otters would be unable to recover from hunting pressure through in-migration; nor would they be able to flee persecution through out-migration.

At this early point St. Petersburg did, in fact, contemplate the regulation of the North Pacific fur trade. In a 1748 decree granting a one-year monopoly over the Commander Island trade to one of Basov's successors—the *promyshlennik* Emilian Yugov—Empress Elizabeth referenced earlier laws on the Siberian fur trade that regulated when and where private fur traders could catch animals. Laws from 1727 and 1731 had prohibited hunting in the spring, summer, and fall of "young animals, mothers, and nursing or pregnant animals (*podsosov*)," and Elizabeth seems to have wanted such measures extended to the North Pacific.[40] This and other similar laws had aimed partly at preserving high-quality animals for the government's own tribute collection, but they demonstrated the state's willingness to legislate the trade and contained some sensible conservationist measures learned in Siberia (and research shows that limiting sea-otter hunting to males would have drastically curtailed population decline).[41] Yugov's monopoly (in exchange for which the state took 33% instead of the usual 10% of the catch) also had the effect of limiting the hunting burden on marine mammals, as one trader could hardly catch as many animals as the whole fleet.

However, after disappointing results, Yugov's monopoly was revoked and the short history of eighteenth-century conservation in the North Pacific ended. The following year the state prohibited fur hunting in the Commanders in order to protect government property, but this attempt at regulation was half-hearted;

most if not all traders violated it with impunity. Later decrees became adamantly anti-conservationist. In 1758 the pro-*promyshlennik* Siberian governor Fedor Soimonov commanded the government servitors accompanying the fur trader Bechevin not to

> attempt to issue any orders other than those which lie within their competence, without the consent and permission of the *prikashchiks* [foremen] and supervisory personnel. While they are hunting animals, Bechevin's agents and laborers are not to be hindered, nor is anyone to interfere with their private lives.[42]

Soimonov, who trumpeted the North Pacific's abundance, emerged as a strong proponent of unregulated hunting. In 1761 he convinced the Imperial Senate to open up sea otter hunting in the Kurile Islands, which had previously been closed due to concerns over alienating the Japanese. This decree allowed anyone who wished to sail to the Kuriles and catch "as many animals as they can," as long as they did not conceal the catch numbers from the government.[43] In his lobbying for this change, Soimonov had not acted alone. Müller's reports of the richness of the sea otter grounds south of Kamchatka in an earlier edition of the *Monthly Compositions* had been crucial in getting the law enacted.[44] Though Müller would at other times advocate conservation, in this instance the work of a natural historian had led directly to the destruction of the sea otter.

Withdrawing from regulation of the trade, St. Petersburg had essentially given the state's property away to private interests. The reason for this was clear: the empire, chronically short of money, found it more economical to collect tax revenues than to finance expensive trade regulation. As long as they vigorously collected taxes on the catch, local officials were encouraged to provide licenses and even material support to any fur traders desiring to sail the North Pacific. As Empress Anna had expressed in a 1733 decree, local governors should assist fur traders "because it is more advantageous and without loss to the treasury if the merchants and *promyshlenniki* themselves search for distant places."[45] What applied to Siberia was even truer for the very distant North Pacific. Weak government in the North Pacific was the sea otter's worst enemy.

Hunting in the Commander Islands proceeded unhindered for the next several years, until traders suddenly ceased taking sea otters there in 1757. By using present-day sea otter population figures, it is possible to reconstruct a rough chart of what happened to the Commander Islands sea otters in the 1740s and 1750s (see Figure 2.5). In the first decade of the twenty-first century, Russian zoographers reported a stable population of up to 5,300 sea otters around the islands: 3,300 to 3,600 on Bering Island and 1,500 to 1,700 on Copper Island. They believe these numbers to be near the pre-exploitation population.[46]

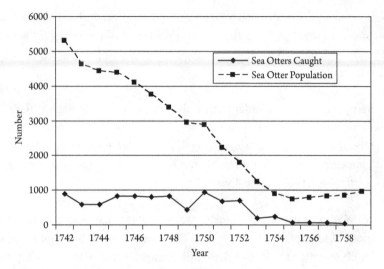

Figure 2.5 Estimated Sea Otter Population in the Commander Islands 1741–1758, with Number of Sea Otters Killed Each Year. Catch figures are compiled from two early-nineteenth-century sources, which show some discrepancies and thus cannot be accepted as completely accurate. The original population estimate comes from twenty-first-century surveys, which may not reflect populations around 1742. The equation used for calculating historical population is: $N_2 = N_1 - K1 + (N_1 - K_1)(b - d)$. (T.D. Smith and T. Polacheck, "Analysis of a Simple Model for Estimating Historical Population Sizes," *Fishery Bulletin* 78, no. 4 (1979): 771–779.)

While the sea otter population had been in steady decline since 1741, it probably began a steep drop in 1749 and 1750, when at least four crews were hunting in the Commanders. Basov was then leading another hunt on Copper Island and finding sea otters very rare, while three other companies were hunting on Bering Island. Another *promyshlennik*, Rybinskii, caught more sea otters than Basov had, but only by staying on Copper for three years and killing 120 *medvedki*, or juvenile sea otters. The *medvedki* furs were nearly worthless, and killing them was even then recognized as a death blow to the herd.[47] Rybinskii's was the first recorded catch of *medvedki*, and it is an indication of the awful toll that the 1749–1750 hunt had taken on the Commander Island sea otter population. In what must have been a vast and ceaseless slaughter, in these two years at least 1,380 (the true figure is certainly higher since some of the data has been lost) sea otters had been killed.[48]

After 1750, hunters would have to chase (an estimated) less two thousand sea otters out of an original population of at least five thousand in the Commanders. Signs that the animals had become scarce were seen everywhere. Rybinskii also killed over 7,000 fur seals and 1,900 foxes during his three-year stay on Bering Island, which is indicative of an attempt to make up for the

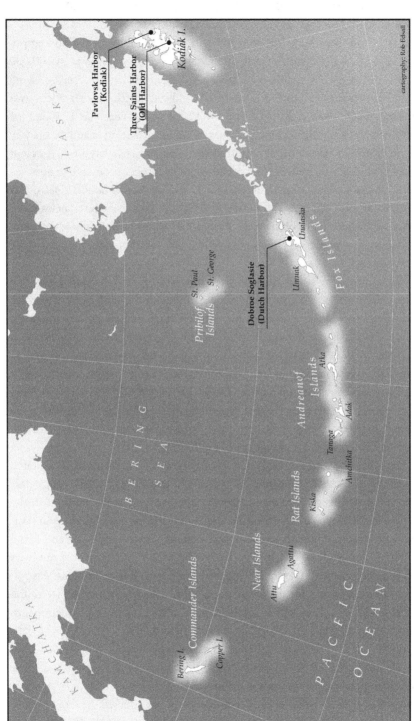

Figure 2.6 Island groups in the North Pacific, with places mentioned in this chapter

reduced sea otter catches. This was by far the largest fur-seal catch of the 1750s, but it brought the company little income. Despite staying for two seasons on Bering Island, the catch was sold for only 61,000 rubles, while contemporary voyages to the Near Aleutian Islands were bringing upwards of 100,000 rubles. When the *promyshlennik* Trapeznikov tried his luck on Bering Island in the years from 1752 to 1757, his crew could only catch 218 sea otters over the course of 6 years, a dismal average of about 36 per year.[49] In 1756, a boat captained by the *promyshlennik* Bashmakov landed at Bering Island on the way to the Near Aleutians, and he reported that, "no animals were hunted except [sea cows]."[50] By the mid-1750s it seems it was no longer profitable to hunt sea otters on the Commanders. There were likely only several hundred sea otters scattered around the coasts of Bering and Copper Islands, where once several thousand had lived. Sea otters were elusive animals even when abundant; now, Russians crews would very likely see no sea otters at all when they landed at the Commanders.

The impact also seems to have been long-lasting. In subsequent decades, *Promyshlennik* crews still stopped at the Commander Islands to provision for their long years in the Aleutians, but very few reported taking any sea otters there. In 1792, as the Billings Expedition sailed by the islands once described by Steller as abounding in sea otters, Christian Bering reported that "On these islands *promyshlenniki* go to hunt sea lions, fur seals, and foxes. Sometimes a few sea otters are found on Copper Island, but very few."[51] In 1811, a hunting party spent seven years on Copper Island and managed to catch only fifteen sea otters.[52] More than sixty years later, the Commander Island sea otters still had not recovered from the onslaught of 1749–1750.

The speed and visibility of the Commander Island sea otter decline separated it from depletions of fur-bearers elsewhere. On two lonely islands, completely isolated from the rest of the world, the sea otters seemed to melt away before the *promyshlenniki*'s eyes. Unlike the sable depletions that plagued Siberian fur traders, the sea otter reduction was stark and seemingly irreversible. The end of the cold PDO around the 1770s may have contributed to keeping sea otter numbers permanently small. However, the data demonstrates that hunting alone was sufficient to nearly wipe out the entire population. Though the percentage of the global sea-otter stock killed was small, the separation of animals' population into discrete island groups made local hunting catastrophic.[53]

While some of the hunters thought that the sea otters had migrated to other islands, most recognized that overhunting had caused their disappearance.[54] The Commander Islands crash warned the fur traders of the potential for crisis. Early hunts by individual companies in different years had stressed the Commander Island sea-otter population, but had not exhausted it. In 1749 and 1750, the rush of companies quickly decimated the herd. This short, intensive burst of hunting was dangerous for the long-term health of the trade. At the same time, discovery of new hunting grounds also gave hope that a new bonanza would replace the loss of the Commander Islands sea otters.

Kamchadals, Yakuts, and *Promyshlenniki*

Though success in the Commander Islands could merit serious attention, it rarely lasted long for the *promyshlenniki* involved. Basov drank away his fortune, then counterfeited coins in an attempt to make it back; he ended up in prison, and died young. After hunting for three years in the Commanders, Yugov died of unknown causes on Bering Island in 1751, never to enjoy the fruits of his company's lucrative haul. By the time hunting shifted to the Near Aleutian Islands, these pioneers had given way to better-capitalized merchants from Irkutsk and Moscow. The ethnic composition of the hunters, too, was changing. Indeed, to speak of the *Russian* colonization of the North Pacific is misleading, since Russians on the frontiers of empire relied on indigenous labor to accomplish their commercial and political goals.

On his first voyage to Bering Island, Basov brought a hunting crew composed entirely of Russians and had a fairly successful voyage, catching four hundred sea otters per year. On his second voyage, however, Basov brought with him seven Kamchadal hunters and caught an astounding 835 sea otters per year, again on Bering Island. Encouraged by this success, on his third voyage Basov employed twenty-five Kamchadals, almost double the number of Russians on the voyage.[55] After Basov's second voyage, few ships sailed without a substantial number of Kamchadals—usually about half the crew—though their presence did not always guarantee hunting success. Kamchadals slip into the historical records fitfully, usually appearing in order to mark their participation in warfare against the Aleuts or to mention their deaths by starvation, drowning, or exposure (a rare, lifelike drawing of a Kamchadal man, shown in Figure 2.7, was made by the British artist John Webber later in the century). In 1747, Basov reported, one Kamchadal was killed by a landslide on Copper Island, and in 1750 another was killed by an avalanche near the same location.[56] That same year the first Kamchadals paid for Russian expansion in the Near Aleutian Islands with their lives, as Aleuts killed several of them while they were hunting on Attu in 1750.[57]

These lonely, violent deaths serve as a reminder that for the Kamchadals too, the Aleutians presented a challenging new ecosystem. Though they lived surrounded by seas, Kamchadals did not depend primarily on the ocean for their subsistence and did not inhabit the ocean the same way the Aleuts did. Their

Figure 2.7 John Webber, *Native of Kamtschatka*. Courtesy of Captain Cook Memorial Museum.

traditional economy was instead based on salmon, which were mostly caught as they swam upriver during the spring and summer.[58] Still, compared to the Russian *promyshlenniki*, Kamchadals had a great deal of experience with marine mammals.[59] The Russians valued the Kamchadals' hunting prowess and ability to maintain "good health despite the poor provisions"[60] on the voyages, an endurance that speaks to the men's familiarity with a sea-based diet. Steller claimed that Russians were far better hunters and trappers of land animals, but everyone acknowledged the native Siberians' advantage in killing sea mammals.[61] While most Kamchadal men probably had prior experience hunting sea otters, sea lions, and whales, they would have shared the Russians' inexperience in killing sea cows. The animals did not inhabit the Kamchatkan coasts, though their corpses sometimes floated across the two-hundred-mile strait separating the peninsula from Bering Island. Such scattered incidences may have led

Kamchadals to wonder where these floating bounties came from, but there is no record that they traced the currents to find the sea cows' home.

Kamchadals would serve as important participants in the fur trade at least through the end of the eighteenth century, even as the trade moved farther and farther from their homeland. Archaeological evidence on Kodiak Island (south of present-day Anchorage) reveals that Kamchadals and Yakuts made up a large proportion—perhaps a majority—of the "Russian" settlers at the colony's principal settlement at Three Saints Bay.[62] Records of the private companies involved in the fur trade show that at least some of the Siberians signed on willingly to hunt.[63] By the end of the century, Russians were even recruiting heavily from parts of Siberia relatively distant from the North Pacific. Yakuts, in particular, made up a heavy portion of the crews and often occupied the more prestigious position of carpenter. Other Europeans joined in the hunt too, such as the Baltic German Johann Maltsan. After sailing with Bering and Steller on the Second Kamchatka Expedition, Maltsan decided to join several of the early expeditions back to Bering Island in pursuit of furs. Either out of a desire to better immerse himself in local culture or out of sincere religious conviction, he was baptized into the Russian Orthodox Church, taking the new name of Ivan Iosafovich Khotuntsevskii.[64] In 1752, after surviving two shipwrecks, Khotuntsevskii/ Maltsan died in a third, on Adak Island.

The Kamchadals and Yakuts hunting in these unfamiliar waters brought their own environmental ethos to the North Pacific—one which is, however, very difficult to recover. In Siberia, Yakuts sometimes justified their killing of animals by blaming the Russians and their weapons. When, with great reluctance, the Yakuts killed a threatening bear, they would ceremonially cook the meat and apologize, saying, "We are not eating you but the Tungus [another Siberian people] or the Russians; they make the powder, they sell the guns; but you know that we do not know how to do these things."[65] Kamchadals seemed to have had no such reluctance. As stories handed down by oral tradition attest, killing animals was a fundamental part of life on Kamchatka. "They began to live" and "They killed animals" occur in tandem in Kamchadal folklore.[66] On the other hand, some stories tell of kindness for wild animals, and reports from both early-modern and contemporary observers show the Kamchadals to have been very familiar with the behavior and ecology of large mammals.[67] Steller reported that Kamchadals sometimes even teamed up with killer whales in pursuing baleen whales, together cornering the large cetaceans and driving them into nets.[68] Whaling did not play a central role in Kamchadal economic life, but whales were important in spiritual life. The peninsula's active volcanoes were thought to be the result of local gods cooking whale blubber.

Some Kamchadal beliefs could have encouraged overhunting. In 1823, Otto von Kotzebue wrote that, "On their own immortality, as well as those of all animals, the Kamchadals firmly believe."[69] No animal killed was truly dead, so the possibility of hunting something to extinction would have been difficult to accept or meaningless, because the animals would have gone on living—albeit in a different form—forever. Kamchadal stories tell repeatedly of dead animals being cut open and releasing a hidden person or demigod living inside—an indication of the magic that adhered to the hunt as well as the close identification of animals with humans. When Kamchadals killed sea cows, it must have been an intense religious experience, as it meant encountering an unfamiliar animal that may have harbored exotic new beings inside of it as well.

At times differing religious approaches to hunting made relations tense between Russians and other North Pacific peoples. The Russian hunters, who were great believers in the efficacy of Orthodox ritual, usually prefaced their hunting contracts with a plea to God to grant them success in killing sea otters.[70] At the conclusion of the voyage, the men often donated part of their catch to the church in Kamchatka or Okhotsk. Similarly, Kamchadals traditionally donated part of any catch to their god, Kutq, and their preparations for hunting included ritually abstaining from washing. However, in an ironic inversion of Russian practice, at least some Kamchadals were careful not to make the Orthodox sign of the cross before embarking on a hunting trip, lest they anger their own god and hinder their own success.[71] In 1795, a long list of complaints submitted by Russian hunters to their company leader related tensions with the Yakuts and Tungus, describing them pointedly as *inovertsy* (literally "different believers").[72]

On the other hand, Russian fur traders' ideas about animals sometimes dovetailed with those of the Siberians, no doubt in part from years of cross-cultural exchange. Logbooks kept by *promyshlenniki* reported that fur seals around the ship, "acting very much like people, lay forward and put their fins on their heads and necks and prayed,"[73] an indication that Russians commonly saw marine mammals as sentient beings. Russians also sensed magic in animals, which sometimes became clear when Enlightenment Europeans came in contact with the *promyshlenniki*. In 1790, as the English captain Joseph Billings led a crew of scientists and fur traders across the Sea of Okhotsk, a fierce storm blew up. The *promyshlenniki* pinpointed the storm's origin in an eagle that Billings had captured in Siberia and brought with him on board. They pleaded with him to free the bird, but Billings would not relent to their superstitions. The men survived and the eagle arrived in America still in slavery.[74] As this and other stories demonstrate, no strict Cartesian separation between rational humans and unfeeling animal automatons seems to have operated on hunters' minds in the North Pacific. Kamchadals, Yakuts, and *promyshlenniki* broadly agreed that animals were intelligent and sometimes magical creatures. Such sentiments, however, seem to have done little to discourage killing them.

The Sea Otter Hunt in the Near Aleutian Islands

Since the Second Kamchatka Expedition, fur traders had been aware that sea otters were present in the islands east of the Commander Islands. However, the location of these otter-rich islands was uncertain. Many of the early *promyshlenniki*, including Basov, sailed to the East without finding new islands. It is possible they were misled by fur seals migrating from the south to assume that land lay in that direction, making the same mistake as Bering and Chirikov in their search for North America. Finally, in 1745 the ship *Evdokim*, led by the merchant A. F. Chebaevskii, stumbled upon Attu and Agattu Islands, the so-called Near Aleutian Islands.[75] With Chebaevskii's rediscovery and the simultaneous decline of the Commander Island sea otters, the North Pacific fur trade moved eastward, and in the process took on very different characteristics. Most notably, in the Aleutian Islands, Russians first encountered dense populations of humans already very experienced in the hunting of marine mammals.

At the time of initial contact with the Russians, the Aleut way of life had diverged substantially from their distant genetic relatives on the other side of the Bering Strait. Aleuts, even more so than other North Pacific peoples, lived from the sea. To a large degree this was the result of superb adaptation to the challenging local conditions. Their foggy, treeless islands bore little of nutritional value, while the seas around them were rich with nourishing life, fed by the productive zone of nutrient mixing between the North Pacific and the Bering Sea and rich upwellings of cold water along the continental margin.[76] The Aleuts procured most of their foods from the intertidal zone, the exposed rocks that yielded sea urchins, chitons, small fish, and octopi, and usually situated their villages near shallow lagoons.[77] The offshore environment played an important role in Aleut life too. Among the most important animals for Aleut sustenance were the large marine mammals, seals, sea lions, and sea otters. Seals and sea lions provided food, while sea otter furs were used for clothing.[78] To capture these large animals, which often were found in deep water or on difficult-to-reach rocks, Aleuts had developed sturdy but maneuverable canoes, called locally *igax* (one-hatched) or *ulyuxtax* (two-hatched), known to the Russians as *baidarki*, and to Americans as kayaks (after the Inupiat word for the craft). Even after a century of contact with Native Americans down the Northwest Coast, most Russians remained convinced that the Aleut version of the kayak was far superior to any others, and the Aleuts the best handlers of the craft. There was good reason for this proficiency, for not only were the Aleuts' home waters full of treacherous riptides, waves, and sometimes ice, but an Aleut could rightly said to be more often on the water than any other people north of the equator.

Aleuts of the late nineteenth century reported that they had still been hunting sea cows at the time of the Russians' arrival, and later archaeological evidence would seem to confirm that there was a small sea cow population remaining. Apparently,

Near Island Aleuts hunted the sea cows opportunistically, rather than counting on what must have been a limited resource for reliable food. An especially propitious time for capturing the huge animals was shortly after a storm, when the sea cows would seek shelter in shallow coves. Just as Steller had reported, the animals apparently had so little fear of humans that they would scarcely react to being stabbed with a spear. For this reason Aleuts considered hunting sea cows to be a "woman's game."[79]

If Russians too hunted sea cows on the Near Islands, they left no records of it. Instead, they were mainly interested in sea otters. Most of the sea otter grounds lay on the southern, Pacific side of the islands, areas rich in nutrients because of the cold upwelling. Typical of sea otter colonies, the animals stayed relatively near to shore, and were rarely found more than six miles away from land. Aleuts located their permanent dwellings away from the grounds so as to give the animals peace, and in the summer months would paddle across the dangerous passes that connected the Pacific with the Bering Sea.[80] Aleut hunting of marine mammals throughout the archipelago took place on a large enough scale to register long-term changes in the animals' populations. Even before Russian contact, the islands' sea otter populations were likely smaller than they had been before Aleut arrival, around 1,000 BCE. In 1745, the Near Islands marine mammals would have been rare near populated areas. Aleut hunters likely had to travel long distances to catch sea otters.

At the onset of Russian invasion, the sea otter population was large by contemporary standards. The *promyshlennik* Novodchikov, part of the crew of the *Evdokim* in 1745, reported that marine mammals "abounded around Attu, Agattu and Samych Islands," and that the Aleuts killed them with spears and arrows made of bones.[81] Initial sea otter catches in the Near Islands show relatively abundant animals, even greater than the population in the Commander Islands. Initially, the Russians hunted the animals themselves. Taking advantage of the numerous sea otters visible around the island, the Russian and Kamchadal crew divided up into small *artels*, or hunting groups, and began shooting at the sea otters in the ocean. This hunting did not go unchecked by the Aleuts. The Near Island Aleuts initially met Nevodchikov with hospitality, offering him gifts including a club carved with the head of the seal.[82] From there accounts diverge. One version indicates that the Aleuts attempted to seize the Russian firearms, but instead found themselves fired upon. Another report has it that the Attuans were incensed by the Russian crew's robbery and hostage-taking.[83] Despite the conflict, hunting proceeded successfully, but when fall came the invaders began to suffer. The same seasonal storms that had bedeviled Bering kept the *promyshlenniki*'s tiny *shitik* (small boats sewn together with cordage) in the harbor, where the men began to starve. Finally risking a voyage into the turbulent seas, their boat wrecked on the Kamchatkan shore. Fourteen Russians and Kamchadals perished, and many of the sea otter skins were lost to the waves. Several of the survivors were called in front of local officials to answer for their "murders and thefts," but they were acquitted. The crew's cargo of sea otters and attendant tax paid to the Kamchadal authorities probably helped their defense.[84]

Catches in the Near Islands continued to be large for the next decade and a half. The skipper Durnev, hunting on Attu and Agattu in the 1750s, made the extremely rich catch of 3,117 sea otters, or 779 per year,[85] figures that exceeded even the best years of the Commander Island hunt. In the late 1750s the famous skipper Andrean Tolstykh managed to surpass even these numbers, catching 5,360 sea otters in the Near Aleutians, including some *medvedki*. Part of Tolstykh's success came from his gift of nets to the Aleuts on Attu, which he used to recruit them into the hunting force.[86] Tolstykh spent two years hunting on Attu and Agattu, and at the end of this time added the Aleuts' catch to his own. The methods used by the *promyshlenniki* to encourage the Aleuts to hunt included hostage-taking as well as offering attractive trade goods, especially metal. Tolstykh, at least, was able to establish cordial relations with the Agatuans.[87] Co-opting indigenous labor, which had been impossible in the uninhabited Commander Islands, increased hunting efficiency, though in the Near Aleutians the relatively small size of the human population limited the gains. Large-scale exploitation of Aleut labor would begin with the discovery and slow conquest of the Fox and Andreanof Islands.

Some fifteen years after the first Russian crews began hunting sea otters there, the Near Island sea otter population began showing the same signs of decline. The reason was the same as in the Commanders: an intense rush of several vessels over the short span of several years that decimated the population before it had time to recover through natural growth rates. Added to this was the addition of Aleut hunters to the trade, which increased the speed of the depletion and allowed Russian hunters to move on to other island groups while the local Aleuts continued hunting locally. In the Near Islands, the barrage came during the years 1756 to 1762, when at least eight hunting voyages sailed specifically to these islands in search of sea otters. A peak occurred in 1759, when Tolstykh and four other hunting parties were dispatching the animals. Over three thousand animals were caught that year, approximately three times the highest yearly numbers the Commander Islands ever yielded. The years 1759 and 1760 saw a massive, chaotic slaughter in the Near Islands. Scores of Aleuts died from Russian firearms, dozens of Russians died of hunger and shipwreck, and over five thousand sea otters were killed by Russian guns and Aleut harpoons—some of the bloodiest years in the eighteenth-century North Pacific (see Figure 2.8). What followed immediately was a near cessation of the hunt.

Sea otter numbers have never recovered entirely in the Near Aleutian Islands, so it is impossible to estimate the original eighteenth-century population in order to gauge the effect of contemporary hunting. The animals were completely

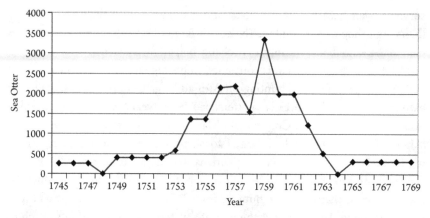

Figure 2.8 Sea Otters Caught per Year in the Near Aleutian Islands.

eliminated there in the nineteenth century, and only in the middle of the twentieth century did they recolonize portions of their original habitat. There is little doubt that the population must have been far higher in the late 1750s, when the equivalent of the modern colony was killed each year. Whatever the population had been, the slaughter of the late 1750s and early 1760s was enough to radically deplete it. Catches began to drop steeply in 1763, and the Near Islands were offering unprofitable hunting by 1765. The ship *Nikolai*, cruising by Attu in 1768, reported that there were "not enough animals" there, and sailed on to the Andreanof Islands.[88]

As with the Commander Islands, the eighteenth-century *promyshlenniki* did not exterminate every animal from the Near Islands. They hunted in the islands until the killing became so difficult that it was cheaper to sail farther, in search of untapped waters. However, until the sea-otter population had fallen to a very low level, it was cheaper to hunt at an established location. The costs involved in eastward expansion were significant, including additional voyaging years and the process of establishing friendly or dominant relations with the peoples newly encountered. *Promsyhlenniki* hunted on known and pacified island groups for as long as possible. Thus, the sea-otter population in the Near Islands likely fell to something under one thousand animals, as it had in the Commanders, before hunters moved eastward. While Aleuts had been hunting sea otters in the Near Islands for hundreds of years, there is no evidence that they had ever killed such a large percentage of the population.

Andreanof and Fox Islands

Just as had happened in the Commanders, as the Near Islands sea otter population crashed, an even-richer source of furs was found. In 1760, the celebrated navigator Andrean Tolstykh sailed to Attu, found it too crowded with *pro-myshlenniki*, and ventured farther east to discover the Andreanof Islands (named after Tolstykh himself).[89] Using his practiced tact, Tolstykh established good relations with the Andreanof Islanders. Dividing its hunters into several *artels* (hunting groups), the Company killed and brought back to Siberia over three thousand sea otters, almost one-third of which were *medvedki*.[90] Whereas the presence of *medvedki* in earlier catches had indicated the decline of the local sea otter population, this clearly was not the case on Tolstykh's maiden voyage to the Andreanofs. Tolstykh seems to have realized that—based on prior experiences in the Near Islands—the Andreanof sea otters would soon be gone, so it made sense to kill every animal possible, no matter the harm done to the population. While the discovery of the Andreanofs provided immediate relief from the crisis threatening the trade in the 1760s, traders were already anticipating the next crash.

The central islands in the Aleutian chain—of which the Andreanofs constitute the largest portion—today contain the most abundant sea otter populations, and catch figures from the eighteenth century suggest that this was the case then as well. Over six thousand sea otters were found around the Andreanof Islands in the 1960s, at their peak population, though this number had declined below 4,000 by the 1990s.[91] This lower figure was still around three times that of the Rat Islands population, the second largest population in the Aleutians. The *promyshlenniki* were finding that, despite increasing human population, sea otter populations also increased in an eastward direction along the Aleutian chain as the productivity of the ecosystem grew.[92] Each discovery not only resolved impending crises, but also expanded sea otter yields from previous highs. The Andreanof decline came around 1770, when three ships were on the islands. The process is familiar by now: several ships wintered over in the Andreanofs at the same time or in short sequence resulting in massive catches, with a sharp downward turn in the following years. With the Andreanofs' large sea otter population, the fall-off does not seem to have been as steep as in the Commanders and the Near Islands, but the falloff in activity in the 1770s was similar to previous declines. Never again would catches anywhere in the Aleutians exceed 350 animals per year—a figure that would have been low for the first voyages.

Aleuts and Extinction

The role of the Aleuts in the destruction of the sea otter and other marine mammals in the North Pacific is composed of a complex blend of cultural, economic, and environmental factors. At a basic level, the Aleuts themselves probably killed a large majority of the sea otters brought to market in the North Pacific after the

1750s. While Russians and Kamchadals did the hunting on the Commander Islands themselves and initially tried hunting in the Near Islands, elsewhere Russians quickly became dependent on Aleut expertise to bring in sea otters. When the naval officers Krenitsyn and Levashov visited Unalaska and Umnak in 1771, they reported that the Russians did almost no hunting on their own. In part this was because they feared being killed at sea by the increasingly hostile Aleuts. The Russians also handed out fox traps to the local populace, since Aleuts did not hunt the animals for their own subsistence.[93]

The terms on which Aleuts assisted the Russian fur traders are much disputed. Many scholars depict Aleuts as having been near slaves of the Russians, cowed by superior firearms and the ruthlessness with which the bearded invaders took hostages and constantly wielded the threat of deadly violence.[94] Certainly, hostility attended relations between the invaders and the Aleuts from the first contact. In 1753, for example, a number of Kamchadals and Koryaks who had chosen to remain permanently in the Aleutians grabbed some Aleut women and were killed in retaliation.[95] Hostage-taking constituted the central Russian strategy when encountering new people—a tradition borrowed from the Siberian experience. Often these hostages had to travel long distances on behalf of the Russians. Some went to Siberia, while others sailed with pioneering *promyshlenniki* looking for new sea-otter grounds.[96] Additionally, European diseases hit the Aleuts hard, and some scholars estimate that the Aleut population had declined by 50%, or even 80%, by the end of the eighteenth century.[97]

While initial contact in the Near Aleutian Islands in the 1740s seems to have been relatively peaceful (though the *promyshlenniki* did take hostages), outright warfare broke out in the thickly populated Fox Islands in the 1760s. The Aleuts scored some initial successes, including the massacre of almost an entire *promyshlennik* crew, which temporarily slowed the incoming tide of Russians and outgoing tide of sea otters. However, when reinforcements arrived several years later, the Russians gained the upper hand. A brutal hunter named Solovev led the counterattack, slaughtering those who had led the resistance. An eyewitness reported that Solovev killed about two hundred Aleuts and destroyed their houses and boats.[98] After these bloody reprisals, Aleut-Russian relations reached a certain equilibrium, with the Russians holding women and children hostage in return for a guarantee that the men would both trade and deliver a yearly tribute.

Soviet scholars tended to portray this relationship as comparatively enlightened, and some modern historians have broadly accepted this view, noting what they claim were Russians' positive contributions to Aleut culture, such as literacy and a reduction in internecine warfare.[99] In the final analysis, however, the Russian North Pacific empire depended on the constant threat of violence. In exchange for a written language, a new religion, and an introduction to the world economy, the Aleuts paid the price of population loss, a wrenching dislocation of their culture, and severe environmental degradation. Perhaps, had the Russians found the North Pacific empty of people, they could have forged an empire based on their own commercial prowess and native Siberians' hunting skills. Instead, Aleut proficiency in sea-otter hunting held the golden promise of immense profits for tsar and *promyshlennik*, and hastened the end of Aleutian independence.

Because of the Russian reliance on their labor, Aleut environmental beliefs and practices were a significant factor in explaining ecological changes in the North Pacific after 1742. While the sea otter was not an important source of meat in the Aleut diet, the animal served both clothing and ceremonial purposes in pre-contact Aleut culture. As with the Kamchadals, animals in the Aleut world often took on a human persona; sea otters were said to have originated as a pair of incestuous human lovers who were punished by the gods and made to inhabit the ocean. Aleut stories suggest that they endowed the sea otter hunt with special significance, and killing them (and fur seals) was thought of as defeating a rival warrior. Accordingly, a host of rituals and beliefs surrounded the hunt. Hunters had to be careful that their wives were not menstruating and were not unfaithful during the hunt, or the expedition would be unsuccessful. Sea otters were believed to behave like humans, taunting hunters by coming close to their boats, then swimming away. Talismans, such as special pebbles, were taken on hunting voyages to attract sea otters. In fact, Aleuts usually thought of sea otters as finding a worthy hunter, rather than the hunter finding the animals. Sea otters often played the role of moral arbiter of human affairs, judging the worth of the hunter either by avoiding capture or submitting to it.[100] One Aleut song tells of a "sluggish man" whose spears bounce harmlessly off the hide of a "sea lion surfacing joyously."[101]

According to some observers, after Russian occupation, Aleuts (really a combination of Kodiak Island Alutiiq and Aleutian Islands Aleuts—the Russian sources mix the two) continued to hunt sea otters with ardor. The English explorer George Vancouver, who had numerous interactions with Alaskan natives, claimed that they joined the "quest of sea otters . . . with the greatest cheerfulness."[102] Even elderly Aleuts who had earned the right to stay home continued to hunt sea otters "if their vanity was flattered."[103] According to Veniaminov, who probably knew the Aleuts better than anyone else in the nineteenth century, they considered it "glorious" to "kill as many wild animals as possible."[104] Others reported that the Aleuts considered sea otter hunting their "natural and hereditary art."[105] Ferdinand von Wrangell, governor of the colonies in the 1830s, spoke of the convenient but destructive merging of Russians' pecuniary interests with Aleuts' "inborn passion" for killing animals.[106] Certainly, Aleut culture had changed significantly between the 1740s and the 1830s, and other sources speak of Aleuts disinclined to hunt sea otters, especially if they were not given the right inducements. Their "inborn laziness" meant that Russians had to import all sorts of luxuries in order to increase the hunting yield.[107] After decades of contact with Russians, and under conditions of semi-forced labor, it is very difficult to determine the evolution of Aleut attitudes toward the sea otters they had once thought of as transformed humans.

One factor seems not to have changed substantially after Russian contact: Although Russians provided the Aleut hunters with new technologies, including nets and guns, for catching sea otters, these new tools seem to have accounted for very little increase in the sea otter take. Timofei Shmalev, a government employee in Kamchatka in the 1770s, reported that initially Aleuts were able to kill many more animals by taking advantage of the increased range that Russian firearms added. However, these methods frightened off the sea otters, so Aleuts soon returned to the traditional method of using a throwing board, a flexible wooden implement attached to the hand that provided lethal force to a projectile.[108] Even in the late nineteenth century, very few sea-otter hunters used firearms. An American observer concluded

> neither does it appear that any particular style of hunting is more destructive than the rest.... In the western districts, Attu and Atka, where only the spear was used, the decrease has been quite as marked as in the eastern districts, where the gun has been used almost exclusively.[109]

The extirpation of the sea otter in the Aleutian Islands cannot be explained by technological change. Instead the Aleuts, very seldom of their own accord, but apparently with great success, hunted the animals to near extinction using time-honored methods (see Figure 2.9).

In fur trades in other parts of the New World, anthropologists have often maintained that the European commercial ethos eroded Native Americans' more spiritual attitudes toward animals and caused them to relax their pre-contact restrictions on the hunt.[110] This does not seem to have been the case with the Aleuts. Because of the correspondences between Aleut and Russian religious beliefs, conversion seems not to have affected Aleut hunting practices. In other words, no desacralization of nature followed Christian conversion, and thus cannot be blamed for Aleut willingness to overhunt the sea otters upon which they had long depended.[111] Russians in Alaska perceived strong similarities between their and Aleut beliefs and practices. In the 1750s the Russian *promyshlennik* Stepan Cherepanov wrote:

> As we Russians call and invoke the name of God, our Lord, whenever we commence any activity, and call [upon him] to come to our aid and bless [our enterprises] or when we set out to hunt on the sea to hunt in

Figure 2.9 An Aleut paddling past sea lions on the Pribylof Islands, the richest hunting ground for fur seals. The male sea lions fight in the foreground, much as Steller had described them, while a Russian ship is seen behind the island. From Choris. Courtesy of the Huntington Library.

> our baidaras and observe a silence and then say "God aid us," so these foreign people also, commencing the hunt say a prayer like "Lord bless." The same when they travel in baidaras just like us, they call out "God will aid us." They are very understanding of the Orthodox Christian faith and do not doubt that we possess the truth.[112]

With Russians calling on a multitude of saints, Kamchadals supplicating Kutq, and Aleuts imploring their shamans, there was no shortage of supernatural beings taking perverse aim at the animals they had created for the North Pacific.

Even the Orthodox clergy was not impervious to Aleut cosmology. Bishop Ivan Veniaminov, in a letter to his superior in Irkutsk from 1829, reported strange doings on Akun Island. In 1825 the islanders had experienced great hunger. The inhabitants secretly asked an old *toion* (clan leader), Ivan Smirennikov, "thought by many to be a shaman," to summon a whale. After a few days, the shaman told the islanders where a whale could be found, and an entire, freshly beached whale was discovered at the location he had named. "There were many such examples, proving

[Smirennikov's] unusual conduct and strength, but I will keep silent about them," Veniaminov added cryptically. The priest was intrigued enough to ask the shaman how he was able to perform such feats, and Smirennikov explained that, shortly before his baptism, two glowing figures (Veniaminov recognized them as saints) had come to him, instructed him in the Christian belief, and appeared to him ever since, always helping in times of need, including informing him about the doings of animals.[113] While the incident may have had a satisfyingly Orthodox conclusion for the Russian priest, the interpenetration of the spiritual and animal realms needed no explanation for Aleuts, or Russians. For both peoples, animals embodied spiritual meaning, acting out the consequences of humans' behavior.

The Aleuts of course had methods in place for regulating human relations with the environment. They considered it a sin to "pollute and defile a stream at home or in another locality, so that the fish will not come into it, or to pollute the sea in the vicinity of a village and thereby drive away the fish or game forever."[114] Additionally, Aleuts attached strong property rights to productive streams and intertidal regions, prohibiting non-owners from procuring resources there. These measures protected the most important ecosystems for the Aleut economy: the riverine and near-shore environments where salmon and shellfish could be found. The emphasis on animals being "driven away," rather than depleted, suggests that Aleuts conceived of habitat disturbance—rather than overhunting— as the principal environmental threat. Certainly, by the early nineteenth century, at least, Aleuts were conceiving of massive ecological change. In 1817, Russian artist Louis Choris reported an Aleut tale telling how the explosion of the human population meant the diminution of various kinds of animals, "because they had all been eaten by the people." As a result, the humans migrated en masse to another island.[115] Other means and expressions of environmental restraint were likely lost due to Russian conquest.

What does seem certain is that Aleuts had few institutionalized means of limiting their sea-mammal hunting. For example, archaeological evidence suggests that Aleuts preferentially took juvenile fur seals, since they were easier to catch, a practice that had the potential to deplete the population if done without selection by sex.[116] Based on centuries of interaction with fluctuating marine mammal populations, Aleuts were accustomed to sea otters disappearing from hunting grounds, then reappearing elsewhere.[117] This experience may have led them to misinterpret the decline in sea otters around their islands after Russian incursion as another natural and temporary disappearance. Certainly Russians took that approach, insisting for decades that sea otters migrated away from hunting pressures.

Russian hunters, at least, felt that god would restore nature's balance when they overhunted fur-bearing animals. As the fur trader Alexander Baranov wrote to his employee Stepan Larionov in 1801, "We must consider it the sacred will of the Creator to recompense us for the diminished catch of land animals by increasing our principal catch [sea otters]."[118] At other times, this faith seemed to wane in the face of continued depletion. Larionov replied to Baranov that, "We cannot continue to make profits on the islands without the help of other places and with God's help, and there is no hope for that. In my locality this summer, working hard we obtained barely 170 sea otters, not counting young ones."[119] Larionov's attitude came, not coincidentally, at the end of 55 years of hunting sea otters in the Aleutians. If some Russians still maintained the hope that God would refresh their sources of wealth, others had read in the animals' dramatic disappearance in one island group after another the sign of a more radical, permanent environment change, out of the hands even of the Almighty. Larionov's thoughts were to be extended, debated, and sometimes denied by the natural historians who became increasingly preoccupied with the same problem the Russian *promyshlennik* had identified.

If Larionov's despair was shared by the Aleuts who were hunting for the increasingly scarce sea otters, their concerns have not survived the amnesia of time and empire. The eighteenth century has left a gaping lacuna in knowledge about Aleut practices and beliefs, so the historian is left either to extrapolate forward from pre-contact oral histories or backward from the better-documented nineteenth century. However, the Aleuts' most effective pre-contact conservation mechanisms—including defense of proprietary hunting grounds and careful, ritualistic hunting practices that took care not to frighten animals away—were precisely those taken from them by the Russian conquest. Russian *promyshlenniki* forced Aleuts to hunt in all seasons, disease erased many of the former owners of hunting grounds, and Aleuts often found themselves transported to distant islands where they took over others' guarded hunting grounds by force. This last phenomenon, especially, encouraged depletion of marine mammals. Since the Aleuts associated killing marine mammals with defeating human enemies, they likely did not resist stripping a conquered neighbor's animals. That attitude certainly predominated among nineteenth-century Aleuts who sailed up and down the Northwest Coast and California, taking sea otters from the Tlingits and others. Without such proficient hunters, Russians never could have eliminated the sea otter with such effectiveness. Of course, by right of conquest, the Russian empire held the ultimate responsibility for conserving the North Pacific's fur-bearing animals, and in this it failed spectacularly in the eighteenth century.

The North Pacific Commons and the *Yasak*

In fact, the Russian state's desire for additional profits from the fur trade directly encouraged the total extirpation of local sea otter herds. As they had with conquered Siberian peoples, the state imposed an annual tribute (*yasak*) on the

North Pacific islanders, payable in furs. The *yasak* was both an important fiscal instrument of the state, used to buttress tax collection, and one of the most
important signs of its lordship over conquered subjects. The collection of the
yasak was the responsibility of the government servitor present on most pri-
vately organized voyages. In the absence of a servitor (a frequent occurrence),
collection was left in the hands of the company foreman and was open to tremendous abuse. Collection lists could be falsified, extra furs could be extorted,
and the Aleuts complained that company men would collect prime pelts from
the Islanders and present tattered ones to government officials in Kamchatka
or Okhotsk.[120] Although they were not large compared with the commercial
catches, Aleuts bitterly resented *yasak* demands. Russian hunters would often
leave an Aleut group with hunting implements, which would be thrown away as
soon as the boats sailed out of sight.[121] Catherine II suspended *yasak* payments
in 1788 due to widespread abuses. Nonetheless, collection continued, and the
state does not seem to have turned away any fur marked for the treasury.

Yasak collection may have been small compared to tax receipts or private
catches, but it bit into sea otter populations already reeling from the *promyshlenniki's* attacks. As Russian control of the islands was usually consolidated only
after major hunting operations had been established, *yasak* collection tended to
increase as sea otter, fur seal, and fox populations decreased. Once Russian hunters had moved on to farther islands, they would still call at nearer islands to collect tribute. Even when sea otter populations had declined to the extent that they
were no longer profitable for Russians to hunt, continued forced local catches
kept the animals' numbers down. In this way the Russian fur trade differed from
the early stages of the Canadian and American beaver trades. There, indigenous
hunters responded to market forces in determining how much to hunt, and
depleted herds often gained reprieves.[122] Only when European fur traders were
willing to increase prices would the Amerindians find it worthwhile to hunt a
severely depleted beaver stock.[123] In the North Pacific, political control over the
fur-catchers meant that they could not decrease their hunting as herds declined.

Records gathered by members of the Billings Expedition during their stay
on Unalaska Island in 1791–1792 show how *yasak* increased fur collection.
Members of the expedition surveyed *yasak* lists dating from the first payment
to *promyshlenniki* in 1764 until the expedition's own tribute collection during
that winter. The *yasak* totals, pictured in Figure 2.10, show an intensification of
collection in the Fox Islands after 1772, at a time when sea otter catches were
already in decline. Even as Russian hunters increasingly abandoned the region
in the last quarter of the century, native hunting increased until it too leveled
off and began to decline by 1783. The increase was not accomplished by raising
yasak demands on each Aleut, but by subjugating additional villages throughout the Fox Islands. By the 1790s most villages were paying tribute, though

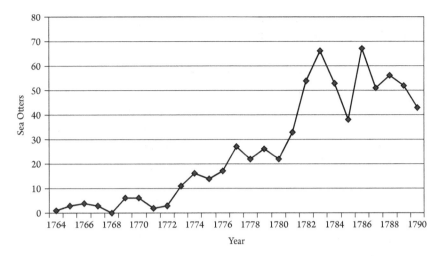

Figure 2.10 Total Collection of Sea Otters for *Yasak* in Fox Islands, 1764–1790.

the population of each village was declining. *Yasak* collection was not the main engine of species decline in the North Pacific, but it did ensure that depleted fur-bearing populations would not recover quickly, and if a population was already in serious jeopardy, it could deal the final blow.

With this two-pronged attack on sea otter populations—initially from hunting companies co-opting indigenous labor, and subsequently from government collectors keeping their populations low—the Aleutian sea otter hunt never significantly recovered under the Russian Empire. When a new bonanza began, this time around Kodiak Island, the costs of organizing such a long voyage prohibited many of the smaller companies from joining the rush. The death of the Aleutian sea otters spelled the death of the small trader as well.

Kodiak, Monopoly, and the Chain of Exploitation

The exploitation of the Kodiak Island sea-otter colonies restored the trade's profitability in the 1780s. The sea otter population around Kodiak and the Northwest Coast was the most numerous of those anywhere the Russians hunted in the eighteenth century,[124] and those few companies with the means to outfit ships to these distant shores and wait years for a return on their capital outlay made very successful catches.[125] However, Kodiak's inhabitants, the Alutiiq (known to the Aleuts as Koniags, which is also what the Russians called them), did not yield their animals easily. The first *promsyhlennik* expeditions to the island, in the early 1760s, were repulsed and returned without any furs.[126] In 1785, the Irkutsk merchant Grigorii Shelikhov attacked Kodiak Island's Alutiit (plural of Alutiiq) near present-day Old Harbor, defeating them after several days of battle that exacted a heavy toll in Alutiiq life. While Shleikhov soon returned to Siberia, the Russians who remained formed the nucleus of the first Russian permanent settlement in the New World. The competition among companies in Alaska was even fiercer than it had been in the Aleutian Islands, often erupting into armed warfare, especially between Shleikhov's men and the rival Lebedev-Lastochkin Company. By the last decade of the century, these two were the only two companies remaining, all others having been sidelined by the high costs.[127]

As the companies consolidated and planned more distant, longer-term, and increasingly expensive operations in Alaska and the near-shore islands, the relationship between company and hunter began to change. Since the beginning of the trade, individual hunters had joined voyages on short-term contracts and worked for a predetermined share of the catch. With the ascendance of Shelikhov and Lebedev-Lastochkin, the hunters lost much of their earlier freedom. Late-eighteenth-century company charters show a compulsion to control all aspects of employees' lives. They spell out in great detail all behaviors that would be punished, threatening legal action for any disorders whatsoever, and especially for any attempt to hide furs from the company.[128] Debt enhanced the men's powerlessness. Christian Bering reported in 1790 that

> When the *promyshlenniki* return [to Siberia], having been in the islands seven, eight or ten years, they are mired in deep debt to the company master, and not having anything with which to repay the debt they have to return to the sea. And because of deceits the *promyshlenniki* have never-ending debts, and have to serve like serfs.[129]

The company would commonly indebt hunters by advancing payment and allowing them to purchase alcohol and tobacco at the company store in Okhotsk. Once afloat, the skipper controlled company wares and sold them at a hugely inflated price, also often on credit. The debts at the end of the trip would be enormous, and the individual trader would have no choice but to ship out for another voyage.

The consolidating companies reaped several benefits from these tactics, including payment of lower real wages and the assurance of an available labor force for multiple voyages. Both were essential for the success of a trade so far removed from its markets. One effect of these practices was the increasing desperation of the hired men. According to Bering, the men responded by forcing the Aleuts, with violence if necessary, to increase their hunting of fur-bearing and edible animals.[130] By this means the *promyshlenniki* hoped to increase their take enough to repay their debts, as well as to avoid purchasing more food from company stocks. There was, of course, an environmental toll to be paid from what might be called a chain of exploitation. The *promyshlenniki* and the Aleuts both stepped up the intensity of their marine mammal hunting in the 1780s, and the North Pacific sea otters and fur seals ultimately bore the burden for the large companies' profits. Count Nikolai Rezanov recognized the essence of this problem on his survey of the American colony in 1805. In his opinion, resolutions restricting hunting would be fruitless as long as the *promyshlenniki* were desperate to pay off their debts. In order to avoid "the complete extinction of fur-bearing animals," wages would have to be raised.[131]

The catch-per-year totals of some of Shelikhov's ships had not been seen since the heyday of the Andreanof hunt.[132] As had been the case elsewhere, initial catches harkened a new boom in the fur trade. Shortly after the Kodiak conquest, hunting on that island alone yielded over five thousand sea-otter pelts. The decline, however, came just as quickly as it had elsewhere. Ten years later, in 1793, Baranov, Shelikhov's agent in Kodiak, was reporting that the once-rich grounds on the nearby Alaskan coast were "almost hunted out."[133] That year only 480 animals were taken—hardly complete extirpation, but enough to induce Baranov to explore further down the Alaskan panhandle to Yakutat Bay.

As Shelikhov's Company grew in strength, it began eyeing the possibility of gaining a monopoly concession for sea-otter hunting in the North Pacific—the goal first articulated by Basov in 1746. Empress Catherine rebuffed Shelikhov's first monopoly request in 1787, but various factors gave his pretensions momentum as the century came to a close.[134] One of the arguments for consolidation advanced by Shelikhov was the "visible decrease in furs," which presumably threatened the profitability of smaller companies. There are hints, even, that Shelikhov advocated a more sustainable rate of capture of fur-bearers that could be better regulated through one powerful company, rather than through many desperate companies. A law of August 5, 1797 mentioned Shelikhov's report of the "harm done by many companies, and the usefulness of their consolidation into one company."[135] The nature of the "harm" was not spelled out, but it may have referred to environmental damage as well as to the armed conflict that had erupted between the companies.

In 1810, Johan Adam von Krusenstern, captain of Russia's first round-the-world voyage, wrote that the decline in sea otters had been the driving force behind consolidation in the fur trade. He gave credit for reversing this devastation to Shelikhov:

> The hunters…without taking account of the future only hurried to collect as many pelts as possible and return to Okhotsk. The valuable sea otters, as well as other wild animals whose pelts brought the rapacious hunters great profits, were quickly going extinct (*ausgerottet*). The trade would have ended on its own accord or at least stagnated over a

long period. Convinced of the great necessity of halting these methods Shelikhov attempted to unite the various participants in the trade into one company, and through it to manage the trade with intelligence and care.[136]

Unfortunately, Krusenstern made no mention of the source for this tantalizing information. Some of his men had spent time at the RAC Kodiak Island headquarters in 1805, and had perhaps heard this version of events from Baranov. Krusenstern's expedition occurred at a time when concerns over extirpation had increased significantly, and it is probable that the RAC was indulging in a bit of historical refashioning, as there is little evidence from the 1790s that Shelikhov was concerned with conservation. At any rate, Shelikhov's company managed the trade little better than had the competing companies. By 1789 Shelikhov was already looking for the next hunting ground, and advising his factors to investigate the newly discovered Pribylof Islands. "Do not lose this golden opportunity," he implored them, "Soon the animals will be frightened away and the price will be as before."[137]

Fur Seals

As sea otter populations diminished in the Fox Islands and around Kodiak Island in the 1780s, fur traders looked not just to Alaska, but also renewed the long search for the fur-seal breeding grounds they knew must exist somewhere near the Aleutians.[138] In 1786 the "old voyager" Gavriil Pribylov, in the employ of the Lebedev-Lastochkin Company, discovered the islands of St. George and St. Paul, now known as the Pribylof Islands. The two islands were covered with fur seals and sea lions, and were home to many sea otters as well. Pribylof and company hunted in the islands for two years, killing over thirty thousand fur seals.[139] These huge numbers, more than six times the largest sea otter hunts, were typical of the fur seal trade, which Shelikhov's company had practiced intermittently since the early 1770s in the Commander Islands. Fur seals congregate in extremely large herds during mating season and are so preoccupied with mating activities that they are easily killed in large numbers. In 1768, total herd size on the Pribylofs may have numbered between two and three million animals.[140] Nowhere else in the North Pacific could such a concentrated abundance of animal life be found.

The *promyshlenniki* had apparently found a market in China for the formerly worthless fur seal hides,[141] and they expanded the hunt rapidly. Following Pribylof's pioneering voyage, the fur trader Protasov caught over seventy thousand fur seals the following year. Shelikhov's company, too, joined the Pribylof hunt, his men catching over one hundred thousand fur seals near the end of the century. In 1809 Shelikhov's company transplanted an entire village of Aleuts to the Pribylofs in order to prosecute the hunt on a permanent basis. The Aleuts who lived there reported horrific living conditions. The stench of rotting fur-seal carcasses overwhelmed the senses. Veniaminov described how the "uninterrupted stench in summer from the decaying carcasses of sea lions and the stench from the local so-called firewood—rotted blubber and bones—so pollute the air of the village that it becomes intolerable.[142] Streams fouled with seal innards and blood nonetheless provided the only drinkable water.[143] Food, in the form of marine mammals, sea birds, and sea bird eggs, was plentiful, but often dangerous to procure. Many Aleuts met their death scaling down the islands' steep cliffs in search of eggs when the rope supporting them snapped, or (in a small act of retribution from the animal kingdom) when a fox gnawed it off.[144] Still, the profits that could be made from the rich hunting made many Aleuts reluctant to leave, even after their contracts expired. Some Russians even wondered whether the Aleuts brought were "surfeited with debauchery," causing a very high incidence of illness.[145]

As Veniaminov remarked years later, "hunting on both islands had been carried on with absolutely no foresight and husbandry because then there were many companies—and consequently many owners, each of whom tried to take as much as possible."[146] As with the sea otters, the intense competition to kill the animals before another company did resulted in huge catches. The Pribylof hunt was prolific and profligate, and with such huge numbers of animals being killed, waste was an inevitable by-product. Though the *promyshlenniki* could not kill the entire Pribylof herd before the century's end, the dramatic decline that did result was shocking in its own way. The fur seals' concentration, and the ferocity with which the *promyshlenniki* attacked them, made the herd's decimation clearly visible within the span of two or three voyages. In spite of their initial almost unfathomable abundance, it had taken only twenty years for the Pribylof fur seals to decrease to the point that their future survival seemed in doubt. In speed it resembled the sea-otter decimations; in scope it surpassed anything the Russians had seen.

Veniaminov reported in 1840 that, "Almost all the old voyagers believe and assert that a fur seal closed season, that is, not to kill them several years, is wholly useless for their increase and means that they are lost forever."[147] Perhaps some of these old voyagers had hunted before the 1799 monopoly. Even if they had not, their attitude could be taken as representative of the free-wheeling *promyshlenniki* of the eighteenth century, who saw any animal they failed to catch as "lost forever." With stiff competition, little or no regulation, and a need to turn quick profits, the fur traders exhibited a mixture of greed and insecurity. The hieromonk (celibate clergyman) Makarii, part of the first Russian Orthodox mission sent to Kodiak Island in 1792, reported that, "On the islands they simply say,

'The sky is high, the sovereign is far away, so do whatever you wish.' They also say, 'As long as there are sea otters there will be no problems.'"[148] Makarii had captured the essence of the *promyshlenniki* worldview, one common to many resource extractors operating on the far edges of imperial control: having ventured this far, through so many dangers and hardships, they had earned the right to make a fortune—no matter what the cost or method. Their greed was tinged with a fatalism derived from the knowledge that the sea otter and fur seal might not survive the slaughter, and that nobody in St. Petersburg seemed to care about the animal's destruction as long as it was profitable.

The North Pacific without Sea Otters

The large-scale subtraction of sea otters and fur seals from the North Pacific did not constitute Russians' only contribution to the region's environmental history in the eighteenth century. Russians also introduced rats, some pigs and cattle (which, however, did not thrive), wheat, and other Eurasian species into the Aleutian Islands.[149] In return, some Alaskan species found their way to European Russia. Steller's dream of domesticated sea otters never came true, but plants, in particular, were attractive to Russian botanists, who requested that seeds of large pines be transported to Russia in order to grow forests of timber-bearing trees for the navy.[150] In a practice that reaped more immediate environmental impacts, Russian *promyshlenniki* tried to increase the pelt harvest by spreading arctic foxes to all islands that had been without them. The foxes often flourished, feasting on unprepared seabirds, whose numbers in turn declined radically. It is possible that the double-crested cormorant disappeared entirely from some islands due to predation by transplanted foxes.[151] Environmental change in the wake of Russian incursion was wide-ranging.

However, the maritime, subarctic environment of the Aleutian Islands kept most Eurasian plants and animals out, and the process of "ecological imperialism" associated with many European overseas ventures never eased Russian colonization. Instead, direct Russian intervention in the ecosystem—in the form of the massive decline in sea otter numbers—had the widest range of environmental consequences, and it drew the most attention from observers at the time. The sea otter has become something of a symbol of the notion of "keystone species" in the scientific literature. These animals, it has been shown, exert an extraordinary amount of control over species assemblages in their habitat. Sea otters are voracious consumers of shellfish, especially sea urchins, so when the mammals are removed these invertebrates flourish, consuming and reducing kelp in the nearshore habitat. Because kelp provides a protective environment for large numbers of fish, in its absence their populations quickly fall. Mussels and barnacles, which depend on chemical properties that the kelp provides, also decrease when sea otters are gone. The effects of sea-otter removal even extend to wave and current patterns as well as populations of glaucous-winged gulls and bald eagles.[152] The complex events that occur after the extermination of a keystone species, referred to as "trophic cascade," leave an ecosystem relatively impoverished in terms of variety of species and overall biomass. As biologists have observed, the return of the sea otter in the 1940s was accompanied by an increase in almost all other smaller organisms in the North Pacific.

The principal victims (after the sea otters themselves) of this trophic cascade were the Aleuts. While the loss of sea otters did not directly rob them of much nutrition or clothing, the resulting reduction in shellfish and fish populations did. Aleuts depended on the nearshore environment for the majority of their food, and had few alternative options. Male hunters were too busy chasing sea otters and fur seals to redirect their hunting toward the whales that periodically supplied villages with bonanzas of protein. Meanwhile, introduced foxes bit into the seabird populations that also provided important sources of Aleut food. The women and children left behind increasingly had to depend on sea urchins, salmon runs, and whatever access to Russian food sexual alliances could provide.[153] This radical decline in nutrition undoubtedly played a central role in increasing Aleut susceptibility to the introduced diseases that cut into their population, and thus provided a concrete link between sea-otter and human decline that later European observers would find so striking.[154]

A number of longer-term processes impacted marine mammal populations in conjunction with human predation. First, the changing climate had different long- and short-term effects on sea otters. The cool climate of the first half of the eighteenth century encouraged sea-otter population growth, but the rise in volcanic activity likely had the opposite effect. The major eruptions of Shishaldin Volcano on Unimak Island in 1775 and 1790 had particularly strong effects in its immediate vicinity.[155] In addition to instigating short-term climate changes, large volcanic eruptions can directly kill large numbers of marine mammals.[156] The North Pacific environment often produced promethean changes that made Russian actions seem a mere scrape on the surface of the sea.

Situated within a context of constant change, however, the Russian impact still stands out as decisive for the sea otter. Whatever other longer-term dynamics may have been operating in the sea otter populations, humans only observed them to be in decline after several years of *promyshlennik* hunting. Nowhere was extirpation reported independent of Russian incursion. Furthermore, the outcome for every distinct sea otter population was identical—near extinction— an outcome unlikely to have been produced by local volcanic eruptions. Only widespread, dramatic climate change or disease could have produced such a rapid disappearance of the animals, and neither factor appears strongly in the

historic or paleographic record. Instead, the deadly combination of Aleut hunting proficiency attached to the global market dominated by Chinese demand
killed sea otters most effectively. Certainly the North Pacific's distance from St.
Petersburg, which contributed to a lack of government control over the trade,
hastened the sea otter's and other species' decline. Russians' lack of familiarity
with the local ecosystem, another common characteristic of colonialism, meant
that even the conservation measures available to the state did not appear immediately necessary to those on the ground. In these ways, the destruction of the
sea otter was a story mirrored throughout the colonial world of the eighteenth
century. In other ways, however, this was a distinctly Russian story. Sea otter
exploitation followed the models, developed in Siberia, of the appropriation
of indigenous labor and the combined public and private collection of *yasak*.
The former was the only means by which the Russians could have removed so
many sea otters from the North Pacific, and the latter ensured the animals did
not quickly recover.

Understanding the effect of sea otter declines on the Russian Empire and
European natural historians, however, requires a return to the North Pacific
environment. In its broadest outlines, sea otter decline repeated a worldwide,
early-modern story of animal decline in the colonial world.[157] The Russians
were well aware of this from their colonial experience with sables in Siberia,
and everywhere Europeans hunted marine mammals, swift decline followed.[158]
Two factors distinguished the Russian experience in the Aleutian Islands from
those other early-modern experiences. First, uniquely, the Russians based their
fledgling empire on the exploitation of marine mammals, and thus sea-otter
and fur-seal decline posed a deeper threat than did, for example, the decline of
elephant seals pursued opportunistically by itinerant British sailors in the South
Pacific. Second, the island ecosystem the Russians encountered in the North
Pacific both hastened the extirpation of sea otters (because they could not
migrate from one island group to the next in the short run), and rendered it visible in a way that sable decline was not. Islands served as more readily compre-
hensible synechdoches for nature as a whole, and provided a way of challenging
orthodox thinking about extinction. The sea cow gives the best example of this.

The Extinction of the Sea Cow

The extinction of the sea cow—the only known megafaunal extinction to take
place in the eighteenth-century North Pacific, and one of the first in the modern world—was also tied to the region's island geography and may have been
a consequence of the extirpation of sea otters. The sea cows Steller had found
in 1741 grazing in the bays of the Commander Islands were the remnants of

once-abundant herds that had swum in Pacific waters as far south as California.[159] The Russians arrived in the Commanders at a difficult time for the animals. Archaeological evidence demonstrates that sea cow populations waned during colder periods. In the Medieval Warm Period (ca. 1000–1300), sea cow numbers may have been two or three times greater than they were at the time of Russian discovery,[160] but as global temperatures cooled, especially after 1600, the sea cow population diminished. By 1741, the animal's population had dwindled to several thousand.[161] Human predation contributed to this decline, as Aleuts hunted sea cows (though not in the Commanders), at least sporadically.[162] Though it was formerly thought that Aleuts had exterminated the sea cow from the Aleutian Islands at a distant time, recent evidence suggests that some animals lingered on there until the beginning of the eighteenth century. If so, they were part of an increasingly lonely group. The sea cow in 1742 had reached what journalist David Quammen has called a "rarity unto death," or, a population so small that any disturbance could tip it into the black hole of extinction.[163]

Those sea cows that remained were already eking out a precarious living. Steller described the animals he saw as emaciated in the winter, and some were so weakened that the ice would trap them underwater and drown them.[164] Some archaeologists even speculate that Aleutian sea cows might have taken to eating marine invertebrates and small fishes because kelp had disappeared in the cold temperatures of the early eighteenth century.[165] Despite the animals' weakened state, however, their meat still tasted delicious. Steller described the sea cow's flesh as "extremely pleasant," comparing it to "may butter" and "almond oil,"[166] and the *promyshlenniki* used the animals as their main food source during their hunting voyages. Typical itineraries included wintering on Bering Island and catching as many sea cows and sea lions as possible for the years of hunting that lay ahead. The flesh and fat were cured in the open air, providing meat, oil, and leather for the construction of *baidarki* (Aleut-style kayaks). The sea cows were so large that one carcass could feed thirty-three men for a month.[167]

With the *promyshlenniki's* crude instruments, killing the sea cows was extremely wasteful, and as many as five times more were killed than were consumed.[168] Many of the harpooned animals swam out to sea, died, and never floated to shore. In 1754, thirteen years after Steller's reports of huge numbers of sea cows on Bering Island, the population was already in crisis. That year the government sent the mining expert Peter Yakovlev to survey the Commander Islands. Yakovlev reported to Catherine's *Bergkollegium* (Advisory Body) that sea cows had vanished from Copper Island, and that they were increasingly rare on Bering Island as well. He noted that the sea cows could not take refuge from the hunters, as the animals' seaweed diet limited them to inshore waters. Yakovlev also emphasized the dramatic change from abundance to poverty through the observations of the hunting crew he was with: "on their previous hunting trips they saw hundreds of sea otters and just as many sea cows, but now the cows have been so extirpated (*iskoreny*) that the hunters never even see one."[169] Yakovlev recommended that the Bolsheretsk Chancellery immediately forbid further hunting of sea cows, so that "they will not be exterminated from Commander [Bering] Island."[170] In the admittedly fragmentary source base, this is the first record of the possibility of the sea cow's extinction.

Neither Bolsheretsk nor St. Petersburg responded to Yakovlev's warning, and the sea cows continued to decrease. A hunting party from 1762 still reported animals around Bering Island, and in 1766 a cursory description of the islands mentioned the continued existence of *korovy morskie*, though it gave no indication of their remaining numbers.[171] Fur traders were increasingly avoiding the depauperate Commander Islands, so reports of the fauna dwindled. Then, in 1783, Shelikhov stopped on Bering Island and listed all the animals found on the island, without mentioning the sea cow.[172] Silence surrounds the fate of the animal until 1802, when Martin Sauer, a member of the Billings Expedition, reported that the sea cow had gone extinct in 1768, just two years after its last reported existence.[173] Sauer could not have witnessed the extinction himself, so he must have been relying on the word of *promyshlenniki* who had either killed the last of the animals themselves, or had stopped at the Commander Islands and found no sea cows. By the early nineteenth century, *promyshlenniki* were reporting finding mysterious bones on Bering Island: these were the last remains of Steller's sea cow, now completely forgotten by the successors of the men who had hunted it to extinction.[174]

Promyshlennik hunting had dealt the rare sea cow its death blow. The early-twentieth-century biologist Leonhard Stejneger estimated the pre-contact sea cow population in the Commander Islands at around 1,500. He also estimated that Russian hunters killed over 2,000 of the animals between 1741 and 1763, more than enough to exterminate it.[175] However, the mechanism by which the sea cow met its end might not have been so straightforward. One recent theory suggests that the massive decline of sea-otter populations in the Commander Islands indirectly caused its death.[176] Once sea otters disappeared from the ecosystem, sea urchins proliferated and competed with sea cows for food. In many places where sea otters went missing, "urchin barrens" resulted, the name giving a sense of the oceanic wasteland that resulted. Ironically, the tiny sea urchin helped starve the giant sea cow, one more effect of the removal of sea otters from the North Pacific ecosystem. Other research has shown that, whatever the effects of sea otter depletion and sea urchin population explosion, *promyshlennik* hunting was more than sufficient to exterminate the entire sea cow population in the Commander Islands before 1768.[177] Whatever the proximate cause, the ultimate causes of sea cow extinction were Russian hunting in the North Pacific and the island ecosystem, in which the remnant sea cow population was confined. Even if Sauer's date of 1768 cannot be confirmed, the sea cow's extinction is certain.

The extinction of Steller's sea cow had immediate consequences for Russians in the North Pacific. Gone was the cheap source of protein that had fueled the fur trade and had lowered the cost of entry for aspiring companies. Without sea cows, capital needs increased, as companies had to procure food in Okhotsk or Kamchatka. With the failure of agriculture on the peninsula, much of this food had to be imported at inflated costs. Larger, better-capitalized companies were able to dominate the trade, and conditions for the hunters deteriorated.[178] Environmental degradation was both consequence and cause of human misery in the North Pacific. Aleuts, Alutiit, Kamchadal, and Russian *promyshlenniki* grew hungrier, colder, and less free during the course of the eighteenth century. Unlike the Aleuts and Alutiiq, the common *promyshlennik* had only himself to blame for his increasing servitude to the Company masters, however, for he had exterminated the source of his wealth.

The sea cow's and sea otter's extirpations rippled throughout the North Pacific ecosystems. The waters were set in motion by the Russian empire, represented by a coalition of marine-mammal killers barely attached to St. Petersburg, but still operating under its strictures of property and tribute relations. The diversity of these killers was dazzling, encompassing Siberians, government officials, Kamchadals, and Aleuts—in their variety altogether representative of the Russian empire's ecumenical structures. However, these men's prey was remarkably circumscribed, as they focused only on large marine mammals with luxuriant furs or delicious meat. North Pacific humans had long extracted energy from the ocean, but after the 1740s their diverse predation was channeled toward a few similar species. In this way, the Russians fused eclectic diversity with ruthless single-mindedness, producing a creative new empire and a newly monotonous ocean.

3

Naturalists Plan a North Pacific Empire

In 1776, the St. Petersburg Academician Peter Simon Pallas announced a European-wide competition, asking for ideas about how to conserve timber resources used to build ships in Germany and Great Britain; the insights gleaned would be used to preserve similar trees in Eastern Siberia.[1] Indeed, Pallas fashioned himself as an expert on German *Forstwissenschaft*, the nascent science of forestry. He wrote long treatises proposing forestry legislation for the Russian Empire that apparently went unpublished. In them, he even suggested measures for protecting forest animals, pointing out that in places where the forests were poor, the animals faced greater dangers.[2] In the 1780s, when helping to plan the abortive Mulovskii Expedition to the North Pacific, Pallas advised the imperial government that valuable sources of timber might be found in the Kuril Islands, Sakhalin, and Japan.[3] On several occasions he met with Catherine II personally, who enquired about his opinion of the French naturalist Buffon and ordered the naturalist to continue his work on forestry.[4] When traveling through Southern Russia in 1793, he encountered many deforested regions—a blight he thought could be easily remedied through the application of simple German forest science. "There would be no reason," Pallas wrote,

> to apprehend a scarcity of [oaks] or any other species of wood, if the indolent proprietors and their vassals could be induced to bestow some attention on the increase and preservation of that useful article on the rural and domestic economy of man. This object might in some degree be obtained, if a proper forest-police, as the allotment into annual falls, and the consequent re-planting and sowing could be introduced...[5]

Pallas's concern was justified, and in 1798 the Emperor Paul I took Russian forest protection under state control, inaugurating a pattern of progressive forestry that persisted even through the Soviet era.[6]

This chapter investigates the personal experience of conducting natural history research for the Russian Empire in the second half of the eighteenth century, and describes the contributions naturalists made to ongoing debates about Russian nature. In several ways forestry work was representative of naturalists' engagement with North Pacific nature during the era of unrestrained fur-trading that decimated sea-otters. Academicians like Pallas carefully juggled their European intellectual backgrounds and loyalties with their employment by the Russian Empire, parlaying their supposedly superior knowledge into a greater degree of influence over government policy in the North Pacific than Steller or Krasheninnikov had enjoyed. Though no naturalists visited the region between 1745 and 1790, the Academy of Sciences remained engaged in Kamchatka and Alaska. Through a network of correspondents, natural historians gathered information about distant events, and used this knowledge to advise the state on imperial policy. This knowledge was surprisingly important, for ideas about the natural world loomed large in Russia's self-perception and foreigners' critiques of the empire. Claims about the relative abundance or decline of the natural world under Russian suzerainty redounded throughout imperial courts. Thus, naturalists occupied a strong position in the informal machinery of imperial governance in the last half of the eighteenth century.

As demonstrated by Pallas's concern with timber supplies, natural historians in Russia were developing an interest in conserving the empire's natural resources. In the North Pacific, however, initial reports of the region's superabundance seemed to make such concerns unnecessary. Additionally, naturalists often showed a much greater interest in developing the area's trade and agriculture, which reflected their close relationship with the structures of power in the Russian Empire. However, signs of a growing emotional attachment to wild nature also begin to appear. Unlike with forestry, though, naturalists did not yet contribute to the conservation of marine mammals before 1790. Their very claims to possess special knowledge made them discount the reports of unlettered *promyshlenniki* about the decline of sea otters and fur seals. They did, however, define the scope of the debates about Russians' and empire's effect on the natural world that would set the stage for a far fiercer engagement with environmental decline in subsequent decades. An examination of naturalists' engagement with North Pacific nature in this period illuminates just how radically their successors in the 1790s would transform Russian and European understandings of the environment.

The Abundant North Pacific

Amid the haze of information about the North Pacific, the relatively copious publications resulting from the Second Kamchatka Expedition long shaped both

Russian and European conceptions of the region. Herein lay the true power of St. Petersburg's natural historians to shape the environment—both in the imagination of their readers and the practical ways in which their successors would shape Russia's environmental policies.

Abundance (*Izobilie*) emerged as a defining feature in mid-century Russian descriptions of the North Pacific. Steller, Krasheninnikov, and others on the Second Kamchatka Expedition described an Arctic nature almost unbelievably rich in species and overall numbers of plants and animals. The trope of abundance began early; the seventeenth- and early-eighteenth-century writings of Avvakum and Atlasov express similar wonder at the number of animals in Siberia. In the eighteenth century—an era in which statesmen were obsessed with population growth—the picture of abundance possessed enormous economic and metaphorical attractiveness.

Fish and large mammals, especially, impressed North Pacific observers. Krasheninnikov reported that, "All the fish in Kamchatka swim upriver in such huge throngs in summer that the rivers swell and overflow...If one thrusts a harpoon into the water, it is rare that one does not hit a fish."[7] Steller added that foxes, sables, and wolves roamed the peninsula in far greater numbers than in Siberia.[8] Krasheninnikov told the fabulous tale that, "Before the conquest of Kamchatka, there were so many wild animals...that when the natives wanted to feed their dogs, they had to chase the other animals away from the feeding troughs."[9] Kamchatka was a veritable promised land for the Russian traders who had always counted their wealth in the "soft gold" of furs.

Steller's brief glimpse of Alaska suggested that it might be home to an even greater abundance of animals—certainly the trees and plants were better than in Siberia. Untouched by Europeans until the eighteenth century and not yet hunted commercially, many of the North Pacific's animals had flourished when limited only by the hunting of a relatively small indigenous population and competition with other animals.[10] Steller wrote about fur seals that "If I were required to state how many I saw on Bering Island I should truthfully say that I could not guess—they were countless."[11] His descriptions were not exaggerated; the North Pacific is one of the most productive seas in the world. Additionally, the animal populations in places like Bering Island had never experienced human predation. Europeans must have read the scientists' published journals with a mixture of wonder and dread at nature's unconstrained multiplication in this far corner of the world.

Steller's and Krasheninnikov's readers would have recognized the trope of abundance from earlier European writings about exotic locales. While some newly discovered lands were condemned as barren and unfruitful, Europeans had also consistently found locations of remarkable abundance. In 1650 Massachusetts, for example, "The abundance of Sea Fish (was) almost beyond believing," while in the early eighteenth century, flocks of pigeons in the Carolinas were said to "obstruct the Light of the day."[12] Further north, John Cabot termed Newfoundland the "Baccallaos, because in the adjacent sea he found so great a quantity of a certain kind of great fish like tunnies, called baccallaos by the inhabitants, that at times they even stayed the passage of his ships.[13] As Richard Grove has pointed out, Europeans were inclined to see the faint image of Arcadia or the Garden of Eden in the exotic landscapes they encountered on tropical islands.[14]

However, for many Europeans, the North Pacific resisted associations with abundance, not to mention hints of Arcadia. Eighteenth-century visitors from Western Europe were more likely to see paucity and hostility in North Pacific nature. The paintings of John Webber, full of luxurious plant growth when depicting the South Pacific, typically showed barren mountains of ice in the North, such as in Figure 3.1.

The Frenchman Jean Baptiste Barthelemy-de Lesseps, whom the explorer Jean-François de Galaup, Comte de la Pérouse left at Kamchatka in 1787, thought the peninsula "dreary," a "barren dessert (sic)" with "frosts, mountains, and seas of ice as barriers."[15] Georg Forster, a naturalist on Cook's second voyage, gave a theoretical explanation of the North Pacific's barrenness. During the course of his voyage he had noticed a more or less uniform decrease in the richness and diversity of flora from the equator to the poles. Forster extended this correlation to include animals and men. There was, he believed, a general loss in "splendour," "nobility," and variety in countries far from the tropics.[16]

A View of SNUG CORNER COVE, in PRINCE WILLIAMS SOUND.

Figure 3.1 John Webber. A View of Prince William Sound. Courtesy of Alaska State Library.

Forster never visited the North Pacific himself and knew little of the actual numbers of the local species, or relative "nobility" of Arctic regions. Steller, for one, was impressed by both:

> All the fish migrating far up the rivers [of Kamchatka] are types of salmon, in which Mother Nature has made so many changes that on Kamchatka alone one encounters as many unknown and different species as all the naturalists have so far described in the entire world.[17]

Russia's natural historians, in contrast to those from Western Europe, did not have a Tahitian paradise with which to compare the North Pacific, and their evaluations were correspondingly sunnier. Steller and Krasheninnikov also gained far greater familiarity with the region than would any other natural historians before the end of the century. Viewed from their more intimate perspective, Kamchatka and Alaska entered the Russian literature of exploration as sites of abundance, as indicated by the nineteenth-century artist Louis Choris's depiction of Kamchatka (Figure 3.2).

Figure 3.2 Plate from Louis Choris showing a verdant Avacha Bay (present-day Petropavlovsk). Courtesy of John Carter Brown Library.

The theme of abundance would influence policy long after the deaths of Steller and Krasheninnikov. Twenty years after the Second Kamchatka Expedition wrapped up, the governor of Siberia, Fedor Soimonov, articulated the equation of the North Pacific with abundance in an article for Gerhard Friedrich Müller's magazine *Monthly Compositions* (*Ezhemesyachnye Sochinenie*) entitled "Concerning the Ancient Saying 'Siberia is a Gold Mine'" (*Drevnyaya Poslovitsa Sibir' Zolotoe Dno*). In 1761, Soimonov contributed the first of what would be a two-part essay, in which he described to St. Petersburg readers the riches found in Siberia and the North Pacific. Although he admitted that he could not be sure where this apparently well-known saying came from, the former Siberian governor speculated that the term "Gold Mine" came from the amazing abundance of fur-bearing animals found in Siberia during the initial phases of the Russian conquest in the early seventeenth century.[18] Probably with Steller's reports in mind, Soimonov confirmed that nature's abundance had impressed the first settlers in Kamchatka as well, who found that the fish surpassed all others in quantity, taste, and satisfaction, "so that it would be impossible to wish anything better."[19]

Soimonov was also interested in the present situation in Siberia and the North Pacific. A model cameralist statesman, he had extensive surveys done of the vast territory under his jurisdiction, in an attempt to better manage known resources and discover new sources of imperial income.[20] A large part of his *Monthly Compositions* essay concerned the wealth of the far eastern regions of the Russian Empire, including the developing fur trade in the North Pacific. The *promyshlenniki*, Soimonov marveled, did not even have to bring bread on their journey, for the meat of the sea creatures they caught was sufficient for voyages of several years' duration.[21] The hunt for sea otters was so rich, he reported, that it had had even tempted a Greek merchant (Evrstat Delarov) out to the North Pacific. All this abundance led the governor to conclude that, "although the [Gold Mine] saying is meant allegorically... it has entered into use for good reason."[22]

Though the abundant North Pacific continued as the dominant trope until the 1790s, a less confident counter-narrative tagged on its heels. Among all the scarcely credible numbers of animals, natural historians perceived a threat of depletion—which was not a new phenomenon. The increasing scarcity of sables, foxes, squirrels, and wolverines by the middle of the seventeenth century throughout Siberia was well known locally. Those responsible for Siberian policy had responded by commuting fur tributes to cash payments, or lowering tribute demands. In addition, imperial officials prohibited the Cossacks from hunting in some parts of Siberia, leaving them to native hunters who were known to better conserve fur-bearing animals.[23] By the 1740s the shortage of furs in Siberia seemed to have approached crisis proportions. Traveling overland from St. Petersburg through Siberia, the members of the Second Kamchatka Expedition heard from trappers, natives, and government officials throughout the woodland regions of the precipitous decline in Siberia's fur-bearing animals.[24] While on the Lena River in Eastern Siberia, Krasheninnikov reported that, "It used to be that one could trap many sables in the woods near that river, but in order to find any today, one must go all the way up to the headwaters of the rivers tributary to the Lena."[25] Gmelin and Müller reported similar problems throughout Siberia.[26]

Steller discovered that, even on Kamchatka, sables were no longer found in their former abundance. Whereas once

> A man could bring in sixty, eighty, or more sable pelts in a winter without exerting himself...after [the First Kamchatka Expedition] the number of these animals declined to such an extent that nowadays less than one-tenth [the previous quantity] is taken out of Kamchatka.[27]

Here, Steller expressed for the first time that loss of abundance seemed to go hand-in-hand with imperial expansion. Krasheninnikov also noted the decline in the sable harvest, but, characteristically, he blamed it on the Kamchadals: they were so lazy that they would "trap only as many as they need to pay their *yasak* and their debts."[28] Even on the question of historical sable populations, Steller and Krasheninnikov's descriptions of the natural world reflected their divergent imperial viewpoints. Despite the anxiety over the decline, abundance would remain the dominant image through the 1780s. The natural historians of the Second Kamchatka Expedition had done much to establish a confident, imperial perception of the North Pacific.

D'Auteroche, Catherine II, and the Russian Environment

One notable incident illustrates the stakes involved in perceptions of the Russian environment. In 1761, the French Abbé Jean-Baptiste Chappe d'Auteroche arrived in Western Siberia to observe the transit of Venus (part of the cosmopolitan attempt to determine the size of the globe, of which Cook's first voyage was also a part). D'Auteroche made his observations and then published a scathing book defaming the people, roads, and nature of Siberia, extending his distaste to Russia as a whole.[29] The abbé thought that the Siberian climate rendered its inhabitants lethargic, and that the despotism of the Russian state robbed them of any energy that might have remained. D'Auteroche's criticisms mirrored those of the Russophobe faction of the French Enlightenment, represented by Gabriel Bonnot de Mably, Étienne Bonnot de

Condillac, Guillaume Thomas Raynal, and Honoré Gabriel Riqueti Mirabeau.[30] Particularly noteworthy were d'Auteroche's depictions of Russian nature as dreary, uniform, and "torpid," characteristics he applied to the Russians themselves as well (see Figure 3. 3).[31]

D'Auteroche's attacks on the Russian Empire hit their mark. *Journey into Siberia* was published in 1768, six years after Catherine II (the Great) had ascended to the throne. Catherine took such offense at the denigration of Russian nature and

les Kamtchadals préparent les poißons pour les faire secher, et font fondre la graiße dans des vases de bois, par le moien des pierres rouges au feu

Figure 3.3 "The Kamchadals preparing fish to dry…" Typical of the plates in D'Auteroche's description of Siberia, this depiction of Kamchadals was wildly stylized and inaccurate. His Europeanized Kamchadals and unrecognizable salmon did at least demonstrate the importance of fish in the local economy. Contrast this image with the drawing by Webber in Figure 2.7. Such flights of fancy did not help the credibility of D'Auteroche's book, but information about the Russian North Pacific was hard to find in Europe in the 1760s. Courtesy of John Carter Brown Library.

culture that she composed a lengthy page-by-page rebuttal of the Frenchman's book. She was particularly touchy about Siberia, writing that:

> I do not suppose there is a country, to which nature has been more boun-
> tiful than to Siberia: it quite resembles the fairy lands: the Russians give
> it the nick-name of *Sibir Solotoie dno*, i.e. Goldensoiled Siberia... and all
> this in the country, where, according to the *Abbé*, 'nature seems torpid.'[32]

Catherine went on to describe Siberia's abundant harvests of corn and its numerous rich mines. She also emphasized d'Auteroche's poor cartography (the Frenchman had said the same thing of the Russians) and expressed shock that he had omitted mention of Gmelin's journal, which provided clear travel directions in Siberia.[33] Finally, the Empress rebutted d'Auteroche's claims that Russians were timid by listing Russia's recent imperial conquests: "Go, *Mons. Chappe*, ask the Swedes, the Prussians, the Poles, and Moustapha the Victorious [all recent victims of Russian imperial expansion]... whether the Russians are timid!"[34]

D'Auteroche's attack and Catherine's defense highlight how nature was a prominent field upon which battles over national prestige and imperial politics were fought. According to a prominent strain of thought, exemplified by Montesquieu's *The Spirit of the Laws* (1748), a society's characteristics were seen to mirror those of its environment.[35] Also, the quality of the information produced about that environment (e.g. Russian maps and description of nature) indicated the level of a society's "enlightenment." These equations were about much more than image. As historian Larry Wolff has written, "one may observe [how] the intellectual formulas of the Enlightenment... [were] deployed in the military maneuvers of the next generation."[36] In fact, Enlightenment formulas would impact military matters in the North Pacific even sooner, by the end of the eighteenth century. Though none of d'Auteroche's criticisms touched upon the North Pacific specifically, the abbé's critique would form the framework within which natural historians produced information about Russian nature.

The second point d'Auteroche's book made was a remedial lesson for Catherine: foreign commentators on Russia's colonies presented a danger. Thus, natural historians would have to be as carefully monitored as in years following the Second Kamchatka Expedition. In fact, national competition within the scientific community in Russia had already intensified. In the Academy of Sciences, native Russians gained favor over German and French professors. Krasheninnikov had advanced to full professor before his premature death in 1747. Meanwhile, the Russian Mikhail Lomonosov had risen from the peasant ranks to become an adjunct in 1742 and then full professor in 1745.[37] Lomonosov consistently resisted the advancement of Germans in the Academy and advocated for a more nationalistic science. Müller, the lone holdover from

Figure 3.4 Levashov's Sketch of a Sea Lion and Fur Seal, from RGAVMF. Very little information was gathered about the North Pacific's natural world between the 1740s and 1790s.

the Second Kamchatka Expedition, found himself embroiled in controversies with Lomonosov over questions of Russian history.[38]

Whether by design or coincidence is not recorded, but no natural historians would accompany Russian voyages of exploration in the North Pacific for four decades. Several small voyages of exploration launched in the interim were manned by government servitors. Though tasked with extracting information from native Alaskans, expeditions led by P. K. Krenitsyn and M. D. Levashov mostly avoided contact for fear of Aleut attack. Without naturalists on board, the voyages contributed to cartographical knowledge of the region, but produced almost nothing of scientific value. The situation would not change until international politics dictated a renewed engagement with the North Pacific, and Catherine launched the Billings Expedition in 1785. Russia did learn something of the North Pacific between Bering and Billings, but the state had little direct contact with the region's natural world, especially its animal life, during this period (see Figure 3.4).

German Naturalists, Russian Nature

The failure of these expeditions to contribute to natural history can be blamed in large part on the sidelining of the Academy of Sciences. After the difficulties encountered with Steller, Gmelin, and d'Auteroche, the Russian state treated its foreign natural historians with understandable circumspection. Natural historians, though shut out of the North Pacific, nevertheless actively engaged in defining Russian nature, especially as the Academy gained renewed favor under Catherine. A network of like-minded colonial administrators kept the Petersburg Academicians informed about events in the North Pacific, and natural historians found themselves deeply involved in the economic and ecological changes in the region.

The Academy scored a significant success in 1767 when it hired the brilliant young Peter Simon Pallas from the University of Leiden. The Berlin-born Pallas was already well-known in scientific circles for his publications on invertebrates, and he infused the Academy with innovation and new European contacts. Over the course of his long career, Pallas would be at the forefront of developments in pre-evolutionary zoology, geology, and paleontology (meriting a mention in Darwin's *Origin of the Species*). He would also strike up a deep friendship with the older Müller. Pallas's immediate task was to lead a new government-sponsored expedition throughout the Empire—the first of its kind since the close of the Second Kamchatka Expedition. The so-called Academy Expedition left St. Petersburg in 1768, and traveled as far east as Lake Baikal. In a departure from earlier scientific expeditions, Academicians studied the flora and fauna of the Russian heartland. Practices developed in the North Pacific were now applied to the rest of the Empire. And, just as the Second Kamchatka Expedition had taken several lives, the Academic Expeditions had deadly moments. One German scientist was captured and killed by the Tartars, and the Swedish Academician Johann Falck (a student of Linnaeus) killed himself in a melancholic fit. Empire and natural history remained a dangerous combination.

Pallas himself stayed safe. He got no further east than Transbaikalia, but in Siberia he met administrators who talked of the developing fur trade and the new discoveries being made. A particularly poignant moment for Pallas was his visit to Steller's riverbank gravesite in Tyumen in 1771.[39] Pallas remarked that no natural historian had been in the North Pacific since Steller, and the combination of events seems to have awoken his interest in the region. He had to admit that, though he had the courage for such a journey, he lacked the strength.[40] Upon his return to St. Petersburg, Pallas dedicated himself to organizing and publishing Steller's papers, and he struck up correspondence with North Pacific administrators.[41] Pallas even expressed hope that a new voyage of natural history might soon visit the newly discovered islands (though in fact this would take another twenty years).[42] Along with Müller's continued interest in the region, the Academy of Sciences reestablished a strong engagement with North Pacific events by the 1770s.

In the Far Eastern colonies, colonial administrators themselves brought the practice of Enlightenment natural history to the North Pacific. Chief among these were the Shmalev brothers, Timofei and Vasilii, whose father had been stationed in Anadyrsk (north of Kamchatka) in 1753. After their father's death, the brothers remained in the Far East: Timofei became commander of Kamchatka and Vasilii served in a variety of lower offices. Timofei Shmalev took an active interest in the discoveries of the *promyshlenniki* in the Aleutian Islands, and he transmitted their reports faithfully to Müller. Shmalev, "full of the desire to serve the Fatherland,"[43] compiled essays on the Russian North Pacific Empire on everything from navigation to agriculture to Russian relations with the region's indigenous peoples.[44] Müller published some of Shmalev's essays in his *Monthly Compositions*.[45]

Friedrich Plenisner, who also served as governor of Anadyrsk, represented the more cosmopolitan type of colonial administrator-naturalist. Plenisner had taken part in the Second Kamchatka Expedition, during which he had befriended Steller and acted as his draftsman. It is to him that the few existing sketches of Steller's sea cow can likely be attributed. In 1763, as governor, Plenisner led a major military action against the Chukchi in the North, but he never achieved the successes Siberian officials had hoped for. Before leaving for Siberia, he had consulted with Müller in Moscow and promised to send him information from the North Pacific.[46] Plenisner fulfilled his promise faithfully, sending parallel reports to the Admiralty Senate and the Academy.[47] Like so many Germans in the North Pacific, Plenisner met a sad end. He was accused of embezzlement and failure to prevent the smallpox epidemic that hit Kamchatka in 1768, and then had to endure the Empire's slow judicial machinery. His plea that other governors had embezzled just as many sea otter pelts as he had was perhaps not the most advisable defense.[48] Though exonerated, Plenisner had a difficult time recovering his good name. In the late 1770s, he could be seen shuffling pitifully through St. Petersburg society, trying to convince anyone in government to give him a pension in exchange for his knowledge of North Pacific geography. Pallas wrote unmercifully that, "Plenisner is soliciting here in vain. People find little new in his reports, and I do not find everything he says to be reliable."[49] Plenisner died in penury the following year. [50]

Plenisner's military and scientific exploits depended on support from indigenous peoples. A Christianized Chukchi, Nikolai Daurkin, aided the Russians in locating his clansmen during the invasion of Chukhotka, and provided Plenisner with the first accurate information about the American lands lying just to the east of Anadyrsk. Daurkin would later render invaluable assistance to the government's Billings expedition during its overland trek through the same region in the 1790s. Timofei Shmalev also provided a direct link between native and natural historian. He escorted the Aleutian *toion* (chief), baptized as Osip Ivanovich Kuznetsov, all the way from Kamchatka to St. Petersburg in 1770, where the Aleut met with Müller and provided him with a map of the Aleutian Islands.[51] Despite their valuable assistance, neither Daurkin nor Kuznetsov's names would appear in the official eighteenth-century histories of the Russian North Pacific.

If the conquered peoples of the North Pacific had to make complicated decisions about whether or not to abet Russian expansion, German scientists faced a similar dilemma, though with less personal risk at stake. Pallas, Müller, Plenisner, and other Germans employed by the Russian Empire in the North Pacific, like Steller, played a careful game in defining their loyalties. They experienced a fundamental tension between their commitment to cosmopolitan science and their employment by the Russian state. Underdeveloped but expanding, Russia promised rapid career advancement and unique research opportunities, but these came with attendant frustrations and moral pitfalls.

Lack of opportunities in Germany drove scientists eastward to St. Petersburg. Though Germany boasted perhaps eighteenth-century Europe's best university system, patronage for naturalists in the German imperial courts lagged behind the efforts of the French, English, and even Russians. The Prussian Academy of Sciences (later the Imperial Academy of Sciences), founded in 1700, was an exception. However, for those Germans interested in the natural world, St. Petersburg proved an exceptionally strong draw. German princes simply had no way to compete with the temptations of exotic travel that St. Petersburg offered on its eastern and southern frontiers. Lacking colonial territories, eighteenth-century German princes witnessed a steady trickle of their universities' best naturalists to countries that could offer the exotic. The famous Forsters, father and son, left Halle for Russia and England and found new worlds of plants and animals in the Russian steppe and the South Pacific of Cook's Second Voyage.[52] Fame and the professional satisfaction of adding new species to Enlightenment Europe's growing catalogue of the natural world were some of the substantial rewards awaiting Germans who defected.

As Steller could attest, being a German naturalist on a Russian expedition could be especially frustrating and lonely. Wilhelm Gottlieb von Tilesius von Tilenau, who sailed as the naturalist on Krusenstern's round-the-world voyage from 1803 to 1806, wrote onboard that his private journal "gives my oppressed heart some air, and this book is my only, silent confidant on this voyage."[53] To lessen the hardship, many naturalists brought with them an improbably large amount of luggage, with contents ranging from the books necessary for their profession, to the casks of fine Rhenish wine that Gmelin insisted on. The books they read reflected a society still transitioning from reliance on classical accounts of history and geography to the modern genre of travel literature. Steller brought a number of books all the way to Kamchatka (and perhaps America and back), including Greek and Roman classics, such as works by Herodotus and Sallust, and a new, German version of Pliny's *Geography*. More modern works included those by the eclectic (and quasi-Pietiest) philosopher Johann Franz Buddeus, and the great German Enlightenment thinker Christian Wolff. These serious works were balanced out by a collection of *Nuges Venales*, a collection of comic and bawdy works popular among Pietists and Puritans.[54] Taken as a whole, Steller's reading list suggests that he discerned few boundaries separating the natural from the philosophical and religious worlds.

Naturalists visiting the North Pacific a half century later and into the nineteenth century concentrated their reading on the travelogue genre, reading Cook and LaPerouse (and even Pallas) instead of contemporary philosophers or classical historians. They also had the by-then-classic works of Steller and Krasheninnikov to guide them. Doing natural history apparently got even easier in the nineteenth century: for example, the Russian naturalist Ilya Voznesenskii received two assistants, paid for by the Russian American Company.[55] By that time a wider variety of colonial officials had become involved in interpreting the natural world. Russian-American Company governors, for example, collected plants and animals for the Imperial Botanical Garden.[56]

Back in St. Petersburg, naturalists like Pallas could count on a steady diet of frustration in working with an empire they did not completely comprehend. In the 1770s the Academy's director insisted that all scientific work be first published in Russia, before distribution abroad.[57] While Pallas was still new to Russia, in 1768, he had to apologize to the Academy of Sciences for not submitting his reports from Siberia in Russian. "Only after my last report," he wrote,

> did it become known to me that, in accordance with the Academy of Science's demand, I should write the names of places in Russian, and that because of negligence on my part there was no Russian written in the last report. I ask your forgiveness for this oversight.[58]

Pallas improved his Russian and complied with the Academy's demands in the future. Sometimes the German's relations with European scientists appeared too cozy to the Russians. During his Siberian journey Pallas sent several boxes of specimens to Dutch colleagues instead of to St. Petersburg. Furthermore, these boxes were unmarked, suggesting that Pallas was attempting to defraud the Academy of Sciences. After the Academy opened one of the boxes, fellow Academician Leonhard Euler reprimanded him: "You send the best and the rarest things to foreign lands...without asking the Academy, and we can assume that you've done this previously as well, as the [European] learned newspapers are reporting your finds."[59] In the end, though, the lure of knowledge in Russia was great enough to counter the intermittent annoyances. "If I were to return to Germany," Pallas once wrote, "I would die of boredom."[60] The money did not hurt either. Pallas wrote to Joseph Banks in 1782 that,

> There was indeed some possibility of my quitting this Country last year. But since the Empress has almost doubled my Salary, & bestowed emoluments & honours on me more than I expected, I believe I shall remain ever fixed in Russia.[61]

The flatteries and briberies of empresses were a powerful factor in the natural historian's career choices, especially in the status-obsessed eighteenth century.[62]

While the state and the Academy often disagreed over immediate politics, their ideas of the meanings of civilization and progress closely correlated, ensuring broad agreement over imperial policies. Academicians often moved to the forefront of the development of imperial policies, especially when they touched on the questions of resource extraction and development. That foreign natural historians should have participated so eagerly in the Russian Empire's expansion may seem surprising. While natural historians often chafed at the difficulties of working in an underdeveloped, semi-European nation, they were encouraged by a Russian society looking to them for cues on what civilization meant. With the accession of the enlightened Catherine to the throne, Academicians such as Müller and Pallas could reasonably consider themselves at the forefront of the Empire's identity-formation.

National politics also made German naturalists sympathetic to Russian imperial expansion. Support of Russia's interests often aligned with a more general anti-British sentiment that pervaded the courts of continental Europe in the late eighteenth century. Though Pallas respected British contributions to exploration and natural history, he was always on the lookout for opportunities to discredit their imperial claims. In 1777, Pallas begged Müller to publish his writings on the Russian discoveries in the North Pacific, in order to expose Britain's false claims on the existence of a Northwest Passage. Müller's planned publication would "finally prove to the public that the English geographers (the angels of the public) and not the Russians, are liars."[63] Here Pallas's jealousy of British exploits, his concerns that British expansion threatened to upset the European balance of power, and his professional interest in deciding the question of the Northwest Passage combined to push him into an unusually strong support for Russian claims in the North Pacific. Distrust of the Chinese played a similar role. German naturalists in Russia led exciting lives full of professional opportunity compared with the dreary prospects at home. If the empire they served had its unsavory aspects, these could often be dismissed as customs destined to be wiped away by the enlightening spirit of Catherine and, of course, the natural historians themselves.

Arcadia and Wilderness

While natural historians often had to explicitly define their political loyalties, they said much less about their feelings regarding the natural world. Taken up with the tasks of collecting, organizing, and corresponding, these men rarely felt the need to explain their reasons for doing natural history. Steller, as we have seen, interpreted studying the natural world as a religious act. He was, in general, far more voluble and far more exuberant about nature than were his contemporaries. His passion shines through in a passage he wrote to Gmelin: "I would not exchange the experience of nature that I acquired on this miserable voyage [with Bering] for a large capital."[64] Yet, Steller's overtly emotional relationship with North Pacific nature was not the norm.

A rare glimpse into the sentiments of Steller's successors comes in the shape of a poem written by Pallas and preserved for posterity by his daughter. Entitled "*Immergrün*" (Evergreen), it gives a sense of the bucolic sentiments current in European scientific circles.

> Here is a little tree, everywhere in growth,
>   May none so marvelously bloom!
> No stormwind bends it, no summer beam
>   bleaches its green leaves.
> The beggar knows as much as the king,
>   How to plant and care for it,
> Young and old, Husband and child,
>   gather in its shadows.
> Its whispers heal the sick,
>   and kindle new warmth;
> When the evergreen so kind and good
>   blooms on pain's hearth.
> When in the dark dungeon of night
>   tears of unhappiness fall,
> then comes in bright display of light
>   my brave Evergreen.
> There, where a friend is called to rest,
>   then blooms another branch,
> and he sinks, with the scent of flowers blessed,
>   to doze in his grave.
> Goodwill to all on this pilgrimage,
>   who praise the little tree!
> My Evergreen, what do you say to me?
>   What is this wonder tree called?
> It is called hope! It grows everywhere,
>   May none so marvelously bloom!
> No stormwind bends it, no summer ray
>   bleaches its green leaves.[65]

While not a direct commentary on North Pacific nature, Pallas's stanzas indicate the general mindset with which natural historians approached the region. For Pallas, the soft, tame nature of the planted and tended tree signified health and hope. With such an attitude, Pallas took part in a long tradition of European longing for benevolent, ordered nature, often symbolized as a botanical garden, or the Garden of Eden.[66] Such landscapes required, and benefited from, man's intervention through both the axe and the seed. Across eighteenth-century Europe, men rhapsodized about the beauty of well-tilled fields and orderly forests.[67]

The flip side of this pastoral ideal was abhorrence for the wildness of untamed nature. As Buffon expressed it, "Wild nature is hideous and dying; it is I, I alone, who can make it agreeable and living."[68] Pallas himself took comfort in the image of the Siberian wilderness falling before the march of civilization. In his *Neue Nordische Beyträge* of 1793, he published accounts of the growth of towns and mining in the Eastern colonies. Besides satisfying his readers' curiosity, Pallas "had another reason for making known" these developments:

> I want to root out the harmful prejudices that many, especially those abroad, have of Siberia. Siberia is as splendid (*vortrefflich*) a country as any other in the world at a similar latitude. Here, in an almost unbeliev-able manner, huge, impenetrable woods and wildernesses have been turned into inhabited boulevards, while desert steppe has been turned into fruitful fields, all through the tireless care and the matchlessly wise governance of our most glorious monarch Catherine II.[69]

These sentiments were meant largely for foreign consumption. The reference to boulevards, in particular, was directed toward d'Auteroche's criticism of Siberian roads.

The hostility toward wilderness, however, was moderated in St. Petersburg. Unlike Buffon, Pallas and others in the Academy found wild nature deeply interesting. Pallas's opus, the *Zoographia Rosso Asiatica*, described domestic ani-mals, but, unlike Buffon's *Natural History*, the bulk of the work was taken up with exotic wild animals. In part, this was because the vast Russian Empire was a far wilder place than the Paris in which Buffon spun his epic. To some extent, the aesthetics of European Academicians had changed through their close expe-rience with the untamed steppe and forest that made up most of Asia. Pallas, Steller, Müller, and others had won their botanical, zoographical, and historical knowledge by traveling through some of the most remote parts of the globe, and one sees traces of an altered ethos in their writings. As Pallas was about to depart from Siberia in 1773, he wrote to Müller that he was loath to leave Daurien (the mountainous region south of Lake Baikal toward the Mongolian border), for there were "still many things left undone in those romantic (*romanenhaften*) mountains."[70] The destruction of trees, in particular, aroused Pallas's ire. In Southern Russia he could "not help feeling great indignation, when I observed here, in every direction, the remains of large oak forests in a desolate state ... cut down by the Russian boor, without the least hesitation."[71] The wilderness had become for Pallas a place of unexpected beauty and culture. As Pallas wrote to Müller, he had enjoyed much hospitality in Siberia, "as wild as that Land and even its name is."[72]

Pallas and the others never relinquished their preference for mild, controllable nature. In an age when wilderness inevitably brought danger, discomfort, and often death, such an imaginative leap would have been daring, if not foolish. But the Siberian experience tempered the revulsion for wilderness and encouraged some to find beauty even in the tangled vines and awesome precipices. The evergreen of Pallas's poem seems the perfect symbol for naturalists' conceptions of the vast eastern environment—a tree found throughout Siberia and the North Pacific growing wild, but that nevertheless could be domesticated. The evergreen indicated a conceptual shift that would, by the end of the century, ripen into the romanticism of Joseph Billings and a host of naval officers in the North Pacific.[73]

North Pacific Agriculture

The desire to temper the wilderness played out in several projects for the improvement of North Pacific nature. First among these was the establishment of agriculture, a project that had strategic as well as cultural value. Despite repeated and bitter failures throughout the century, natural historians would not give up on the idea of turning Kamchatka into a land habitable by Europeans. In no other location of Russian imperial expansion were the natural historians of mid-century more active.

To guage the region's potential for food-bearing crops, natural historians first had to evaluate the climate. Reports about Kamchatka's climate were contradictory and confusing. After his two-year visit to the peninsula, Vladimir Atlasov reported in 1709 that, "Winter in Kamchatka is warmer than in Moscow. There is not much snow there."[74] Later observers were less sanguine. Krasheninnikov, who spent three years traversing the peninsula, reported cruel winters and found it "difficult ... to believe that the winters preceding were any milder, because during the four years I spent in Kamchatka, the temperature remained constantly cold."[75] German Magnus Behm (who served for seven years as the governor of Kamchatka and was Pallas's frequent correspondent) reported that the climate was "extremely moderate."[76] At the same time, Pallas sounded a cautionary note, passing on reports of cold fogs and early frosts that plagued Russian settlers.[77]

The harsh but changeable climate surrounding the North Pacific islands elicited even wilder swings of opinions. After his 1762 trip to the Aleutian Islands, the Cossack Peter Kulkov reported clear, healthy air and a mild climate. Kulkov admitted that the snow sometimes got very deep, but after wintering on the islands, he felt it necessary to contradict other *promyshlenniks*, who reported long, hard winters. On his visit the snow did not stay on the ground for long, and his crew encountered no severe frosts. Most remarkably, Kulkov claimed that "summer is quite warm and lasts almost nine months," contradicting everything observers have said before or since.[78] Perhaps more accurate was Sven Waxell's observation in 1739 that around the Aleutians "there is continual fog and mist, and the weather never clear."[79] Accounts of continual cold and a short navigation season recur in the journals of eighteenth-century North Pacific exploration, though Kulkov was not the only dissenter.

On balance, it seems that those with more pessimistic views of the North Pacific have been justified by climate history. Tree ring and glacial records indicate that eighteenth-century Kamchatka was both colder and wetter than it is today, as were Alaska and the Aleutian Islands. The very end of the seventeenth and the beginning of the eighteenth centuries were times of particularly dramatic glacial buildup and slow tree growth.[80] Thus, the Kamchatka Atlasov encountered in this period had truly ferocious winters. There is considerable variation within the peninsula though, with especially marked differences between the coast and inland regions. Influenced by the cold Oyashio current, winters on the southwest coast of Kamchatka (where Petropavlovsk is located) are roughly equal to those of Moscow. The interior portions of Kamchatka—those explored by Atlasov and settled first—are sheltered from coastal weather patterns by high mountains, and are thus subject to a continental climate regime. With an average January temperature of -22 °C, central Kamchatka winters are far colder than those in European Russia and comparable to Eastern Siberian winters. While the Kamchatka River valley offered temptingly warm summers, winter's long and firm grip did not bode well for European grains.

Nonetheless, more often than not, state servitors and natural historians chose to listen to the sunnier reports of Kamchatka and the North Pacific's climate. The government confidently planned agricultural settlements from top to bottom on Kamchatka, and from the Second Kamchatka Expedition onwards, the St. Petersburg Academy of Sciences added its voice to the development of agriculture in the peninsula. Krasheninnikov was given instructions to investigate the progress made in establishing agriculture at the various settlements and to conduct experiments of his own. He was happy to report that, in 1738, the Kliuchovka monastery on Kamchatka was growing barley and vegetables and producing very large turnips.[81] (Krasheninnikov's own attempts at agriculture, however, were less successful. On the foggy shores of the Sea of Okhotsk his turnips and radishes failed to attain an edible size.[82]) Attempts to supply Kamchatka with Siberian grain were frustrated. Mountainous passages and hostile, unpacified Siberians blocked the land routes, while the sea route from Okhotsk claimed many ships in the eighteenth century.[83]

Of course there was another alternative to developing agriculture in Kamchatka: a colony based on the subsistence practices of the local Kamchadals (who lived near the bottom of the peninsula) or Koryaks (who lived in the interior and near the Northern end of Kamchatka). As Atlasov had remarked, the Kamchadals practiced no agriculture whatsoever, [84] but they managed to subsist and even flourish in their environment. According to Steller, Krasheninnikov, and other early visitors, the Kamchadals survived mainly on the great abundance of fish found in the rivers, eating them fresh in summer and fermenting them for winter consumption. For clothing the Kamchadals dressed in the furs of sea mammals and dogs. Steller, for one, claimed that the peninsula was thickly populated before the Russian occupation.[85] Many of the Russian settlers inclined toward a Kamchadal lifestyle; in 1761 Governor Nedozrelov reported that the peasants were neglecting agriculture because it interfered with catching fish, a far easier means of sustenance in Kamchatka.[86]

But, for the Academicians and other practitioners of natural history who visited or lived in Kamchatka in the eighteenth century, agriculture presented the only acceptable means by which to build a colony. Krasheninnikov best expressed this viewpoint. In evaluating the peninsula's potential for colonization, he set off the disadvantages of wilderness against the advantages of a cultivated landscape blessed by agriculture and domesticated animals. Such a Kamchatka could be just as fit for human habitation as the settled lands of Europe.[87] In fact, this equation of agriculture with empire had long been enshrined in the basic assumptions of the Russian colonial state. "Breadless" (*bezkhlebnaya*) was a common term for newly conquered territories, and Russian commentators referred to Kamchatka in 1742 as that "breadless and distant land,"[88] its two chief problems from St. Petersburg's point of view. Krasheninnikov can claim precedence among Academicians for his agricultural promotion, but he was merely stating a truism that would echo throughout the writings of eighteenth-century natural historians: the realization of Russia's imperial project in the North Pacific demanded the transformation of the wild landscape into something recognizably European.

Steller explicitly linked the development of agriculture with an enlightened approach to empire-building in the region. He explained that St. Petersburg had ignored agriculture in the region until recently, when it "recognized that many important projects depended on the cultivation of this land—without it, these projects could either not be carried out at all or resulted in a hundred times greater harm than benefit to not only the Kamchatkans but also their adjacent provinces." Though Steller did not specify which projects he had in mind, he most likely was referring to the First Kamchatka Expedition, whose leaders had press-ganged many of the Kamchadals and confiscated their foodstuffs. Steller blamed the failure of the agricultural reforms on the Cossacks, who "cared little about grain but rather about tobacco, brandy, and furs with which to return to Yakutsk," and the "drunken, greedy and thieving commanders of Kamchatka, who are only concerned with their own interests and never with the interests of the country and its progress (*Aufnehmen*)."[89] Steller contrasted the responsible, imperially minded naval officers and scientists who actively promoted agriculture with the lower-level civil servants who gave no thought to the state's long-term interests. Here the supposed disinterest and technical expertise of enlightened empire-builders found expression in the devotion to agricultural advancement. In the argument over the agricultural prospects of Kamchatka, natural historians invariably came down in its favor. Agriculture seemed to align naturally with enlightenment.

Of course Academicians had not suddenly discovered the enlightened properties of agriculture when contemplating North Pacific colonization. Europeans colonists throughout the world had self-consciously attempted to create "Neo-Europes" with economies based on the production of European grains.[90] Agriculture served both as a means of survival and as a symbol of continuity with the civilization colonizers had left behind. Nor had Russians been unaware of the power of ecological transformation in the colonization process. The center stage of Russia's eighteenth-century imperial expansion— the Steppe—produced an entire corpus celebrating the transformation from desert to cultivated garden.[91] Prince Potemkin extolled Catherine's greatness with reference to her ecological power: "This country [The Crimea], with your care, has been turned from a place of uninhabited steppes into a garden of abundance, from a lair of beasts to a pleasing refuge for peoples from all countries."[92] Krasheninnikov and Potemkin fully agreed that beets were better than beasts in the new colonies.

Besides expressing an ideal ecological state, rhetoric such as Potemkin's served to naturalize colonization.[93] A process that was in fact bloody and extremely disruptive of long-established ecological relationships could be re-imagined with the metaphor of a peacefully blooming garden. Images of fruitfulness and abundance replaced those of rapine and destruction. Just as the domesticated plants of European Russia grew to support human life, so too would Russia breathe life into inhospitable distant regions. Agricultural transformation in Kamchatka, as elsewhere, functioned both as an ideal state and a trope that justified the process of colonization.

Promoters of North Pacific colonization faced some difficult obstacles in establishing agricultural development. This is where natural historians sensed their opportunity to serve the imperial project, for agriculture was a realm in which they could provide special technical knowledge. Pallas and Steller possessed botanical expertise that few administrators could match, and furthermore had direct experience with exotic Siberian plants that might be profitably transplanted to Kamchatka or the Aleutian Islands. Just as they had been sanguine about the climate, as a group the natural historians of Kamchatka and the North Pacific were far more optimistic about the possibilities for agriculture—especially grains—than were the government officials assigned to the peninsula in the 1740s, 1750s, and 1760s.

Steller, trained in botany, was an early enthusiast of grain production on the peninsula. Though he had misgivings about Kamchatkan weather, Steller believed that in the area around the Upper Kamchatka, fortification farmers could grow "not only the amount of grain necessary for the local population, but in the course of time, as much as would be needed for supplying Okhotsk *Krai* (Region) and other enterprises."[94] Despite his dismal results with agriculture around Bolsheretsk, Krasheninnikov agreed with Steller that Upper Kamchatka offered a suitable location for spring and winter grain. He also pinpointed the Lower Kamchatkan *ostrog* (at the mouth of the river, in northern Kamchatka) as a promising location and noted the success the monks of the Monastery of Our Savoir of Irkutsk had had with barley. While he was pessimistic about the prospects for oats, Krasheninnikov concurred that, in time, Kamchatka might even export grain. When it came to cattle, the Russian student threw caution to the wind, claiming enthusiastically that, "There are few countries where forage is better or more suited to pasturing herds."[95]

Sailors and administrators, less confident in the efficacy of scientific knowledge, found agriculture's prospects dismal. Two naval officers who headed different parts of the Second Kamchatka Expedition came back with bad news. Sven Waxell noted the success of the monks of Uspenskaya Hermitage with growing barley, but he added that it was "not possible every year, but only in a dry summer, and when there are not too many mists off the sea, and such favourable weather will scarcely come once in ten years."[96] Aleksei Chirikov, another no-nonsense sailor, reported that snow persisted in Kamchatka until June, never leaving the higher mountains; that fog was prevalent; and that frosts began in September. He noted reasonably that grain could not ripen in such a short growing season.[97]

Despite the failure of the grain-growing projects initiated in the 1730s, St. Petersburg chose to believe the reports emanating from the Academy of Sciences and continued to finance the development of agriculture and animal husbandry in Kamchatka. In 1760, the Senate, apparently influenced in particular by Steller's optimism, hoped that new peasants they were sending to Kamchatka would be able to "supply with grain not only the Kamchatka military command but also the commands found at Okhotsk Port and at Anadyrsk Ostrog."[98] Grain yields continued to be miserable, and new projects initiated by Governor Soimonov proved just as futile. These failures induced Timofei Shmalev in 1774 to despair that there was no hope whatsoever for grain cultivation in Kamchatka.[99]

As efforts to establish grain production in Kamchatka flagged, a new organization was established in St. Petersburg that would maintain and even intensify the struggle. In 1765, enlightened members of the gentry along with many of the Academicians formed the "Free Economic Society for the Encouragement in Russia of Agriculture and Animal Husbandry," which enjoyed the patronage of Catherine II.[100] The establishment of Russia's first voluntary association was not without controversy: Lomonosov opposed it on the grounds that its members were mostly foreign, and thus had no roots in local agriculture.[101] Catherine's cosmopolitanism prevailed, however, and, inspired by the French physiocrats, the Society began applying the best of European agricultural techniques and theories onto the Russian landscape.

The Free Economic Society buttressed the already strong links between Academicians and the imperial bureaucracy. While a high-ranking member of the nobility often headed the Academy, in the Society Academicians, nobility, and provincial servitors worked side-by-side. This is not to say that the Society's output inevitably reflected the concerns of the state. For example, the Society's first essay competition was on the subject of the benefits and disadvantages of serfdom for the national economy, with the winning essay coming down against it. Still, the Society's charter included a statement of its mission to bring an "increase in the national prosperity" and "to strive to bring the economy by a process of natural development to the best possible condition."[102] Thus, the goals were explicitly national and closely tied to Catherine's overall project of state management of the economy. The Society gathered rich rewards for such imperial service, including state-subsidized publishing and freedom from censorship.

The Free Economic Society did not confine its interest to encouraging agriculture in the European heartland. Its members took a special interest in improving farming techniques in the southern territories recently conquered under the campaigns of Potemkin. Siberian agriculture, too, came in for analysis. Pallas became a member of the Society in 1770,[103] and turned his attention to the state of Kamchatka's farming and husbandry in a 1783 article entitled, "News of the Livestock and Agriculture Introduced to Kamchatka and around Okhotsk." Pallas reported that he had new information from several Siberian governors about developments on the peninsula over the past ten years, which would be "of great importance to Russian Patriots."[104] As a measure of the importance of the empire in Pallas's economic thought, all seven of the articles he submitted for the Society's *Trudy* (Works) at least indirectly concerned newly acquired imperial provinces.[105]

In his Kamchatka article, Pallas admitted that agriculture had suffered many setbacks, especially around the Port of Okhotsk. While on his trip to Irkutsk he had spoken with many who thought Kamchatka's agricultural prospects were dim. Strong hoar-frosts had killed all the barley planted in the state's latest attempt in 1770, and 1771 "was not much better." However, Major Magnus Behm, an enlightened governor and corresponding member of the Free Economic Society, had taken over command of Kamchatka from Shmalev, and Pallas expected great things of him. This year's harvest, he claimed, "promises to produce almost as much grain as in the northernmost fields of Europe." If this seemed like an overly humble goal in comparison with other assessments of the perpetually promising Kamchatkan fields, Pallas suggested trying to improve yields with several other sorts of crops. He proposed introducing *kraipivo* (Siberian stinging nettles) and hemp into Kamchatka for the purpose of rope production,[106] along with flax for consumption. Drawing from the Society's recent success with planting potatoes in European Russia, Pallas recommended the introduction of this useful American tuber into Kamchatka. Thus the potato completed its near-circumnavigation of the globe, from its home in Peru to its furthest eastward outpost in Kamchatka.[107]

By the time of Pallas's report, the Academy's views had gained broader support from Kamchatkan officials, despite agriculture's poor historical performance on the peninsula. This was due in part to the growing collaboration between the Academy and the provincial elite, encouraged by the formation of the Free Economic Society. As Pallas had hoped, Governor Behm proved an active administrator, promoting Kamchatka's development in a myriad of ways, including salt production, iron smelting, the establishment of the peninsula's first hospital, and tax reform.[108] Behm had supplied much of Pallas's information about the agricultural situation in Kamchatka, since Pallas himself had never been to the region. In addition, Behm submitted an article for the *Trudy*, in which he reported on his attempts to restart grain production, though "never before has it succeeded."[109] Behm imported large quantities of grain seed into Kamchatka, as well as herds of horses and cattle. The governor personally oversaw the planting of the seeds, after selecting the fields. "To date," he proudly reported, "all has gone as successfully as we have wished."[110] Kamchatkan grain and cattle production experienced a renaissance under the enlightened governor, buttressed by the support and advice of the Academy of Sciences and the Free Economic Society. During Behm's tenure, which lasted until 1779, the Kamchatka garrison managed to produce a surplus of over 36,000 pounds of grain, and only one crop failure occurred during the six years of his administration.[111]

The 1780s saw agricultural optimism extended to the islands of the North Pacific. Previously, few positive reports had come back from the Aleutians, whose treeless islands were so beset with fogs and storms that they resisted even the most optimistic imperialist's Arcadian vision. Nor had the Alaskan mainland elicited much interest from the Empire's planners. This changed, not coincidentally, with Shelikhov's attempt to establish the first permanent Russian settlement in the New World, at Three Saints Bay on Kodiak Island. Shelikhov was a crafty promoter of his own interests, and he knew that agricultural promise would encourage the state to support his venture. In a report submitted after his conquest of the island, Shelikhov noted the fertility of the lands, and claimed that "there are also good lands suitable for agriculture," borne out by his own experiments with barley and several different vegetables."[112] Meanwhile, the results told a different story. Shelikhov's men died en masse of scurvy, eating only "worm-eaten bitter yukola (dried fish), covered with mold."[113]

The Irkutsk governor Ivan Iakobi, for one, was impressed with Shelikhov's reports. He advised Catherine II that Shelikhov's "most important responsibility, and the very first point to be made, is to see to it that all reasonable means are used to ameliorate the savagery of the natives, and to work on behalf of their needs, using all available means to improve their life." The best course for the natives' illumination, he thought, was to establish agriculture. "Shelikhov has made observations," Iakobii continued, "concerning the superb climate in the places he has visited in America."[114] In Shelikhov's promotions the connection between agriculture and civilization emerged quite distinctly—just as apparent for Russians as it was for the British, Spanish, and the vast majority of European early modern colonizers.

After Russia's experience in Kamchatka, it should have come as no surprise that Shelikhov's Kodiak agricultural aspirations would be largely frustrated. In 1805, a ship under the command of Adam Johann von Krusenstern arrived at Pavlovsk Harbor, a new, more favorably situated Kodiak settlement. The company's naturalist, Georg Heinrich von Langsdorff, agreed with Shelikhov about Kodiak's excellent climate, but remarked that the island's inhabitants subsisted largely on fish and other sea products. "The few attempts that have been made to grow grains," he reported, "have not succeeded."[115] Yuri Lisianskii stopped at Kodiak the following year and noted the same thing, though he still held out hope for agriculture's future development.[116] European staple crops never succeeded to a degree that would allow Kodiak to feed itself. Its continuing dismal agricultural performance later necessitated the establishment of Russian outposts in California, where the climate was far better suited to grain production.

The stock-raising (*Skotovodstvo*) that Behm had so vigorously supported represented another attempt to replicate a European Russian diet in the far reaches of Asia and was another of the Academy's active concerns. Steller noted that, in 1739, cows and horses were new arrivals on Kamchatka, from Okhotsk. He predicted great success for the animals and expressed confidence that "both the Cossacks and Kamchadals will declare great pleasure in raising livestock."[117] Livestock stood a better chance of survival in Kamchatka than did wheat, but cows, pigs, and goats faced their own challenges in the hostile landscape. Cold killed many of the animals, and Pallas later reported that the giant bears and the semi-feral dogs inhabiting the peninsula had also acquired a taste for beef and pork, killing substantial portions of the herds each year.[118]

Nonetheless, when Captain Cook's *Resolution*, under the command of Charles Clerke, landed on Kamchatka in 1779, Governor Behm was able to supply the Englishmen with twenty head of cattle. The men devoured them gratefully, though the cows were "skeletons compared with those of England." Lieutenant John Gore reported that Kamchatka contained no other livestock but poultry, and that no cow was seen in the country except one that was delivered on board as a present to Captain Clerke.[119] British voraciousness contributed to the decline of Kamchatka's livestock herds; the number of cattle on the peninsula fell from 587 in 1773 to 272 in 1781.[120] It is no coincidence that 1781 saw Behm importing new cattle from Siberia in an attempt to reestablish the herd after the Britons' departure.[121] Though Gore and others aboard the *Resolution* praised Behm's hospitality, the unfortunate governor suffered greatly due to the British beef banquet. St. Petersburg never reimbursed him for the cattle he had supplied out of his own budget, and later repeatedly denied his requests for a pension. Behm became so desperate for a means of support after his Kamchatkan tour of duty that he ended up at Sir Joseph Banks' house in London asking for assistance in obtaining a pension from the British state. Though justice demanded that Behm finally receive some compensation from the British, this request was also refused.[122]

Despite the continuing hopes of scientists and administrators, Russia's North Pacific colonies remained almost entirely dependent on local, non-Russian sources of food, most of which were procured by Kamchadal and Aleut subjects. For example, in the 1830s Kodiak residents still subsisted mainly on fish, and it was mainly parties of Alutiit, accompanied by one or two Russians, who did most of the fishing.[123] These "colonial foods," as they were called, represented the environmental compromise most Russians in the Pacific ended up making. Those watching the North Pacific from St. Petersburg may have found these compromises unsatisfying, but they fueled any imperial consolidation Russia was able to make.

Commerce and Empire

In Academicians' plans for the North Pacific, agriculture played but one part in an ambitious scheme to develop the region as a productive, Russian colony.

Another, equally important part of developing the region was the encouragement of commerce. Though Gavriil Sarychev considered Petropavlovsk a miserable little town in 1789, "In a short time it might become an important station,
if our merchants paid due attention to the advantages they could derive from
their trade with China, Japan, and the East Indies."[124] The North Pacific occupied a unique location in the Russian Empire and in the imperial imagination
of the empire's planners and promoters. As the only portion of the empire truly
maritime in character, Kamchatka, Alaska, and the intervening islands offered
a wealth of temptations to the natural historian interested in the region's development. Its proximity to the lucrative and strategic markets of East Asia also
tempted naturalists to develop a host of commercial schemes novel in Russian
history. Few of these plans succeeded, but they indicate natural historians' search
for development strategies in the North Pacific and illuminate the ways in which
these men believed they could use their knowledge of the natural world in the
service of the Russian Empire.

The Empire's other important ports—Archangelsk and St. Petersburg—both
suffered from the disadvantages of ice-bound harbors and distance from the most
lucrative export markets. Both the Americas and East Asia were separated from
these ports by foreign nations and great distances. While the state had planned
voyages to Asia and the Americas, the lack of provisioning stations en route frustrated these efforts. Therefore, from the beginning of Kamchatkan exploration,
the promise of finally establishing American and (even more promising) Asian
trade beckoned. Kamchatka lies less than 1500 miles from Tokyo, and it was
not uncommon for Japanese sailors to shipwreck on Kamchatkan and Aleutian
shores. The seventeenth-century Russian settlements in the Amur River Valley
had offered even easier maritime access to China and Japan, but these had been
lost to the Chinese in 1689. Since the loss of the Amur, Russia's trade with China
had been confined to several isolated Mongolian border outposts, and Japanese
commerce remained merely a dream. Kamchatka, if properly developed, promised new products and new access for East Asian trade.

Bering was the first to elaborate the idea of a trading system between
Kamchatka and East Asia. In his proposal for a second expedition of discovery to the North Pacific, he wrote that "It would not be without advantage to
explore the water passage from Okhotsk or Kamchatka to the mouth of the
Amur river and farther to the Japanese Islands...Also if the possibility of carrying on trade with Japan permits, no small profit may develop for the Russian
empire in the future."[125] St. Petersburg responded by devoting much of the expedition's resources to an exploratory voyage to the Kurile Islands and Japan under
the command of the Dane Martin Spangsberg. Spangsberg successfully located
Japan on his first voyage, but his enemies in the administration considered his
accounts untrustworthy, and ordered him to repeat the voyage the following

year. Spangsberg once again sailed to Japan and met some Japanese sailors along the coast who treated the Europeans with suspicion. Unable to gain access to Japanese authorities, Spangsberg returned to Okhotsk having failed to establish relations with the Tokugawa Empire.[126] The Japanese seemed fond of Russian spirits, but otherwise showed no willingness to engage in trade.

Once the Russians had located Japan, they faced two problems in establishing commerce with the Tokugawa Shogunate: Japan was closed to all foreigners but the Dutch, and the Russians had nothing to offer the Japanese. Natural historians stepped in, claiming that by virtue of their technical knowledge, they might be able to find marketable products. Steller, who had wanted to sail with Spangsberg and shared Bering's enthusiasm for Asian trade, offered his ichthyologic expertise in service of his adopted empire. "On the Sea of Okhotsk," he wrote in his journal, "an equally great stockfish and cod fishery could be established as in Iceland or New England in America if it were ever needed, or if one found out that the neighboring peoples wanted to include it in trade, which I do not reliably know of either the Chinese or the Japanese."[127] As Steller's stockfish suggestion indicated, natural historians also claimed an understanding of commerce beyond plants and animals, gained through extensive traveling and reading.

Steller was right to express doubt about the Japanese and Chinese willingness to buy fish, given that both nations had productive fisheries. But other products found in the eastern regions of the Russian Empire might find ready buyers. Steller noted that walrus tusks lay "unused" in several known places on Kamchatka and further north.[128] Russia had long conducted a limited commerce in walrus ivory, exporting it to Western Europe from the Arctic Sea coast near Archangelsk. In the North Pacific the first known harvesting of walrus ivory occurred in 1762, when *promyshlenniki* under the command of Stepan Glotov submitted for taxation thirty-two puds (or just over 1000 pounds) of walrus tusks gathered in unknown places.[129] Initially fur traders visited the walrus hauling-out grounds to collect those tusks that had fallen out or were left behind when the walrus died. With the 1786 discovery of the Pribylof Islands, summer home to one of the world's largest walrus herds, the *promyshlenniki* began a short-term, but large-scale slaughter of the beasts. On Pribylof's initial voyage of discovery, over 464 puds of walrus tusks were taken. Later voyagers took over two thousand puds from slaughtered animals.[130] Walrus ivory never found a market in Asia, however, but went instead to Moscow and on to Western Europe, where it was used for decoration. Overall, the trade was of limited value to the *promyshlenniki*, as much liability as opportunity. It did little to help either the Treasury or the development of the North Pacific.

The Academicians' passion for finding products suitable for trade with East Asia resulted from their zeal to develop the North Pacific colonies, but it also had geopolitical ramifications and emotional undertones. Chinese tea, silks, and porcelain fetched high prices in European Russia, and the state made a fine profit off customs duties extracted from the merchants. In exchange, China purchased vast amounts of Siberian furs, sometimes with silver bullion which buoyed the repeatedly devalued Russian ruble. However profitable, trade relations with China had been a source of frustration and shame to the Russians since the 1650s, when conflict over the Amur River Valley provoked the Chinese to cut off trade relations. By 1689, the Russians had ceded most of the Amur, but regained some limited trading privileges in China. By the Treaty of Kiakhta in 1727, China was allowing one Russian caravan to travel to Beijing every three years, a practice the Russians ended in 1753 due to its unprofitability. Trade was also allowed at two border locations, Selenginsk and Kiakhta (shown in Figure 3.5), both near present-day Mongolia south of Lake Baikal.[131]

While the Chinese willingly purchased Russian goods, their justified suspicion that Russia desired to retake the Amur made the Qing administrators (China's ruling dynasty in the eighteenth century) extremely sensitive to any border disturbances. Conflict along the border erupted throughout the turbulent eighteenth century, as the two expanding empires squeezed the nomadic Dzughurs and Mongols who had lived in Transbaikalia for centuries. With Russia sometimes providing (nominally covert) aid to rebels within Chinese borders, and with continual problems involving cattle rustling, the Chinese found many excuses to shut down the border trade. During Catherine's thirty-four-year reign,

Figure 3.5 "View of Maimayschin" (Kiakhta). Most of the North Pacific's sea otters found their way to this desolate, inland border post in present-day Mongolia. There Chinese merchants got the better of their Russian counterparts, at least according to the empire's natural historians. Courtesy of John Carter Brown Library.

seventeen years saw trade limited or shut down entirely, with the longest stoppage occurring for seven years between 1785 and 1792.[132]

Natural historians were tempted to see the politics of this trade as a moral battle. The Chinese were "crafty" traders, employing every means to keep their bullion out of Russian hands. Müller had gotten involved with the China issue when, in 1757, he was commissioned to write a history of the Amur for his *Monthly Compositions*. In the article, Müller claimed that the "cunning" Chinese had tricked the Russians at Nerchinsk and Kiakhta and that Russia still retained a right to the area.[133] In 1764, Müller went further, presenting a memorandum to Catherine II explaining what must be done to force the Chinese to resume commercial relations with Russia, which had been broken off earlier that year. As customs revenue plummeted, Catherine threatened war with China. Müller recommended peasant settlement around the Amur and the courting of rebellious Mongols in order to force the Chinese back to the negotiating table. He even went so far as to recommend to Catherine a preventative war, while other senior advisors advocated for more peaceful tactics. Finally China agreed to negotiate, and border trade was reopened in 1768.[134] Müller, however, always retained a somewhat extreme Sinophobia.

In later years, Pallas joined Müller in his distrust of the Chinese, with frequent letters bemoaning the "tricks" that kept commerce on unequal footing.[135] When he visited Kiakhta and the Chinese sister city of Mai-Mai-Chen in 1772, Pallas noted that the Chinese merchants always gained the upper hand in trade negotiations, though he also pointed out that this imbalance was due to the Russian merchants' inability to organize into a single company. As a result of Russian disorder and the Chinese cunning, the Chinese were the "master of the price."[136] He lamented in a later letter to Pennant that the border trade with China was bringing little monetary wealth to the Russian state, as Russian demand for Chinese rhubarb, tea, and "trifles" was so heated.[137]

The mercantilist impulses that invigorated Pallas and Müller's Sinophobia differed from those of eighteenth-century naturalists, such as Linnaeus in Sweden. Linnaeus vigorously pursued programs of transplantation and domestication of exotic plants in an attempt to negate his country's import needs and enable an autarkic domestic economy.[138] The St. Petersburg Germans shared Linnaeus's belief in natural history's usefulness for imperial commerce, but the empire they served had needs different from those of the retracting, conservative Swedish monarchy of Linnaeus. Russia under Catherine II was energetically expanding both its borders and its commerce. For Russia, imperial natural history's task was not principally one of finding plants that could substitute for imports, but rather locating products from the natural world that could flourish in export markets. Also, Russia's natural historians never articulated the kind of sophisticated relationship between natural history and national interest that Linnaeus had. They reacted to state policy much more than they shaped it, understanding their role as privileged servitors endowed with special technical knowledge. Pallas, Steller, Müller, and others working in the Academy were subject to the same realities as the Empress's other subjects; they served at the state's pleasure and participated in political life only to the extent that they were allowed.

Sea Otters

With Russian merchants chronically unable to unite, natural historians suggested finding new, more attractive items that the Chinese would be unable to resist. As the Russians began to discover from the 1720s, sea otter pelts might even the balance. The 1727 state caravan to Peking carried the usual squirrel, fox, and ermine pelts, but also 582 sea-otter pelts from recently conquered Kamchatka. The pelts fetched a lower price than did squirrels and foxes, but a greater proportion of sea-otter pelts were sold than of any of the staples, indicating a promising market.[139] Caravans in the following years, however, left no record of having sold any more of the furs. Nonetheless, some must have been sold, as the Kamchatkan sea-otter population quickly dwindled by the time the Second Kamchatka Expedition arrived on the peninsula.

Steller, who traveled to Kiakhta on his way to Kamchatka, judged the sea otter to be a powerful weapon in the battle for the China trade, and advocated for the colonization of the Kurile Islands for the hunting of sea otters. Fancifully inverting the actual balance of power, Steller opined that once the Kurile Island colonies were flourishing, "If discord came about between China and Russia, one could also stop the trade between the two and large profits could be won." Apparently, if Russia suddenly withheld a theoretical supply of Kurile furs to China, the latter would be forced to increase their payments, as their inability to sail to the fur islands left them no other option. Steller made the strategic implications of the trade clear, stating that in such a situation, "Without much trouble, the Japanese and Chinese could be forced to do anything."[140] In this way, trade could be a weapon of imperial expansion.

A veritable explosion in the sea-otter trade at Kiakhta followed the return of the Second Kamchatka Expedition. The Chinese valued sea-otter pelts not for their limited warmth, but for their lustrous quality as lining for mandarins' jackets. By the 1750s, North Pacific sea otters commanded almost unheard-of prices at the Chinese border. Müller, writing in 1755, marveled at the high prices the Chinese paid for the animals at Kiakhta—sixty to seventy rubles—while foxes were selling for just above twenty rubles. Pallas reported that, by the 1770s, prices had increased to between one hundred and one hundred forty rubles.[141]

Since the Moscow Treasury paid only fourteen to fifteen rubles for sea-otter pelts, nearly the entire catch was sold to the Chinese.[142] Some of Müller's readers could be forgiven for not even knowing what a sea otter was: "From these high prices it is clear why the Kamchatkan beavers are rarely seen and even entirely unknown in Russia."[143] The Russian supply of furs was insufficient to meet Chinese demand, and beaver pelts imported from America and transshipped across Eurasia to Kiakhta were needed to make up the deficit, though these could not compete with the sea otter in price.[144] The sea otter seemed to be the only animal with a fur luxurious and rare enough to consistently bring the Chinese to the negotiating table.

Another potential market existed in Japan. The Japanese had been importing sea otter pelts and transshipping some to China since at least the fifteenth century.[145] In the eighteenth century, sea-otter pelts had become one of the most valuable commodities in Japan's trade with the Ainu of the Kurile Islands. Otter skins commanded prices up to five hundred times higher than those for seals.[146] The Japanese ascribed mystical therapeutic powers to the skins, believing that they relieved abdominal pain and could halt the spread of smallpox. If one did not suffer from health problems, then the skins could be sold to the Chinese, who, according to the Japanese, believed that the pelts were the "cushion of the emperor."[147] Though Russians knew little of these trade relations, they picked up bits of information from Japanese sailors shipwrecked on North Pacific shores. For example, in 1787, the French traveler De Lesseps met a group of Japanese in Kamchatka who had been on a trading voyage to the Kuriles and were shipwrecked on Amchitka Island.[148] Luckily for the Russians, the ship's captain was the scholarly Kodayu, who quickly learned the Russian language. After many years of exile in Irkutsk, the unfortunate castaway was granted an audience with Catherine II in St. Petersburg, in which he told the empress much about his homeland.[149]

Her interest piqued by what Kodayu told her about the Japanese trade, Catherine ordered the organization of an expedition to Japan that would return the castaways and open trade negotiations with the Shogun. Irkutsk governor Adam Laxman undertook the expedition and reached Edo (Tokyo) in 1792. Pallas wrote excitedly about this mission, informing readers of his *Neue Nordische Beyträge* that it was sure to open up new and important "*Handelsvortheile*" (advantages or benefits of trade) to the Russian Empire, with sea-otter pelts at the top of the list.[150] The Japanese, however, received Laxman and Kodayu with caution and were willing only to issue the Russians a permit to return to Edo to conduct further negotiations. Kodayu seems to have impressed his compatriots greatly with his descriptions of Russia, and the Japanese were disappointed when the Russians did not follow up on Laxman's visit for nearly fifteen years.[151]

Despite the failure to develop a Japanese market, the sea otter trade was flourishing by mid-century. With a Chinese market dependable as long as the border remained open (and smuggling continued during the Kiakhta closures), sea otter catches rose. While Russian *promyshlenniki* were never able to bring more than eighteen hundred sea otters to market in the 1740s, by the 1750s this mark was regularly exceeded. In 1752, over five thousand pelts entered the Chinese market, and though the figures varied from year to year, the sea otter trade was firmly established.[152] The state had found a pleasant new source of riches. Kamchatka and Okhotsk's populations swelled as traders arrived to join the hunt. Pallas remarked during his stop at Kiakhta that to the Chinese Kamchatka sea otters, "both large (dams) and medium (juveniles), are the most important and pleasing commodity."[153]

Some naturalists tried to get rich off the developing sea-otter trade too. Steller was the first—and most successful—example, earning a small fortune from the nine hundred sea otter pelts he sold in Kamchatka after his stay on Bering Island. Despite the fact that state servitors were forbidden from trading furs, the Japanese reported that Steller's contemporaries on the Spangsberg voyage had stuffed their ship so full of Kurile Island sea otters that there was hardly room for anything else on board.[154] Sometimes the fur mania reached such a pitch that it hindered the work of naturalists. Pallas reported that nearly everyone on the Academy Expeditions was trading pelts on the side, and his student, Zuev, had joined them, leaving Pallas with no one to help him collect specimens.[155] Pallas implied that he had kept his hands clean of the fur business, and given his dour personality and fanatical work ethic, it might just be possible that he was one of the few to resist the temptation. Even Orthodox priests were sometimes caught with illegal furs.[156]

By the last quarter of the eighteenth century, the sea-otter trade and the developing fox and fur-seal pelt trade gave the far eastern Russian colonies their identity. The fur trade so dominated life in the colonies that other potentially profitable industries such as whaling never had a chance to develop, despite persistent attempts by state and naturalist to encourage them. Large-scale agriculture, too, was mostly abandoned; its prospects had always been based on wishful thinking anyway. With a Chinese market rendered more pliable by the demand for sea otters, this reliance on a single export item seemed feasible. However, two problems with this development soon emerged. First, European traders in the wake of Cook began poaching sea otters from waters Russia considered its own and sold the pelts at Canton, undermining the monopoly the Russians had enjoyed. Second, as the sea otter population began showing signs of fragility, evidence of a coming ecological crisis became increasingly difficult to ignore. The Russian Empire's natural historians would soon have to grapple with both of these problems.

Promyshlenniki and Natural Historians

Russian naturalists had access to a great deal of reliable information regarding the decline of marine mammals. Unlike other European colonists, who showed little curiosity about the plants and animals of the New World,[157] the Siberian fur traders who sailed the ocean thoroughly explored the North Pacific's natural world and reported their discoveries back to officials and scientists. The *promyshlenniki*'s reports included long lists of indigenous plants and animals, often transcribed directly from Aleut and Alutiiq names. They also sent to St. Petersburg objects collected from people they met, curiosities that eventually landed in the Academy of Science's Kunstkammer.[158] Having lived among the Kamchadals, Aleuts, and Alutiiq on intimate terms, the *promyshlenniki* had acquired an extensive knowledge of herbaria, marine mammal migration and breeding, and hunting techniques. The fur traders mixed cultural chauvinism with a practical admission that the North Pacific's indigenous peoples knew the North Pacific environment far better than they. Even if many of the *promyshlenniki* disdained sea lion meat and few adapted to living in Aleut dugout houses, they adopted indigenous names for plants and animals and quickly became skilled handlers of the Aleut kayak. After the Alaskans, the *promyshlenniki* had the most complete view of the progressing extirpation of the sea otter.

Nonetheless, natural historians approached the *promyshlenniki*'s harvest of information with caution, and even disdain—a pattern established as early as the Second Kamchatka Expedition. Krasheninnikov was continually frustrated by the local Russians' inability to provide them with detailed information about Kamchatka. Gathering information for his exhaustive description of Kamchatka's physical geography, Krasheninnikov found that the "Cossacks" he interviewed could tell him nothing about land that lay beyond their immediate concern, for "they do not have much curiosity about things they have not seen."[159] Steller thought that the Cossacks possessed valuable knowledge, but rarely put it to good use. "On my arrival in Kamchatka in 1740," Steller reported,

> I immediately made a diligent effort to obtain such information [about Kamchatka's geography and natural history], questioning all arrivals, traders, and Cossacks in the most friendly way; where it would not come out by fair means, I made them confess with brandy, the pleasant torture.

The naval officers on the expedition, however, discounted the Cossacks' knowledge, saying, "People talk much. Who believes Cossacks?"[160] Steller thought that the Russian sailors showed even less curiosity.[161]

Pallas and Müller, who had relied on "enlightened" informers in the North Pacific, showed much more skepticism toward the *promyshlenniki*'s knowledge. Pallas wrote in his *Neue Nordische Beyträge* that much of the information about the North Pacific came from the "inexperienced" (*unkundig*) traders and voyagers who "composed their maps arbitrarily, without making observations and calculations."[162] Natural historians distrusted *promyshlennik* cartography with good reason, but the German scientists' ignorance of indigenous and Russian knowledge of the natural world underestimated the depth of local knowledge.

Natural historians drew a self-serving contrast between the Cossacks' and *promyshlennikis'* hazy disinterest and their own keen-eyed awareness as they absorbed the environment they traveled through. In the introduction to his published account of the Billings Expedition, Martin Sauer—an aspiring natural historian—remarked that, "My object has been to travel with my eyes open."[163] He could provide the reader with information that common sailors and hunters could not. Pallas also referenced a dedicated use of his senses as a foundation of his identity as natural historian: "The observer of natural history cannot determine the importance and usefulness of his discoveries. The natural historian can do no more than to exercise tireless attention and diligently use his senses and insight."[164] The natural historian may have traveled to the same places the *promyshlenniki* did, but he saw these places differently.

The natural historian's impartial eye functioned as a metaphor for the increasing distancing of professional natural history from the layman's haphazard accumulation of knowledge of the world.[165] The ultimate marker of professionalism belonged to the imperial academies of sciences. Steller's and Krasheninnikov's positions in the St. Petersburg Academy of Sciences gave their observations of Kamchatka privileged status among the various reports and remarks issuing from the fur traders in the region, which is why Krasheninnikov could claim to "discover" Kamchatka some twenty-five years after the first Russian penetration of the peninsula.[166] Later, other Russian naturalists and explorers would make similar claims about the Aleutians.

Knowledge produced by natural historians and other trained professionals attracted the favor of the court in St. Petersburg. When the *promyshlennik* Solovev returned from his discovery of the Fox Islands and the mainland of Alaska, the state responded by sending the Krenitsyn-Levashov Expedition in search of "more exact" information.[167] The state and navy were interested in maps that accurately depicted safe harbors and charted ocean depths, but the *promyshlenniki* often navigated by the rudimentary means of a compass and the memory of old voyagers. What maps they did produce were helpful, but never satisfied the needs of the state to know the territory thoroughly. Even the disastrous Krenitsyn voyage had "shed more light" on Aleutian geography than had the uneducated fur traders.[168]

The state and the Academy's suspicion of the *promyshlenniki*'s knowledge of the natural world effectively limited the transfer of information about the scope of the decline in marine mammal populations in the North Pacific. Without access to the details of the geography of the hunt, those in St. Petersburg had little idea of what was transpiring. Their reactions to *promyshlennik* reports reflect their deep mistrust of nonprofessional knowledge. When discussing a *promyshlennik*'s report concerning the lack of sea otters around Kodiak Island, Pallas noted that, "we must not give complete confidence to the reports of the Russian sailors in matters affecting their interest, particularly when they say that they have seen no sea otters in so many islands."[169] Distrust and scorn hamstrung the experts' attempts at understanding North Pacific nature.

Still, the Academy did have some idea of the decline in marine mammal populations in the North Pacific. In Pallas's 1781 *Beyträge*, he reported that, "Sea otters come only in small numbers to [the Near Aleutians] and almost never to Bering Island, though the shipwrecked discoverers of that island, and the first hunters who tried their luck there were able to kill as many as they wanted."[170] Though sea otters had been mostly eradicated around the Near Aleutians for about twenty years, this was the first mention of the event in the scientific literature. Later in the article, Pallas noted that the animals were already becoming scarce in the Fox Islands, which he claimed had previously been the *promyshlennikis*' richest hunting grounds.

Therefore, by the 1780s, knowledge of the periodic declines in sea otter numbers was beginning to spread through academic circles, and knowledge of the fur seal disaster would come in the following decade. However, no one in St. Petersburg knew the full extent of the decline of either species, despite existing *promyshlennik* reports. On the eve of a new era of governmental activity in the North Pacific, populations of sea otters in the Aleutian Islands were nearly eradicated, and the Kodiak Island populations too were beginning their decline. When St. Petersburg responded to Cook's third voyage and the influx of foreign fur traders with the first large-scale expedition since Bering and Chirikov, it would discover a seascape in decline, the fur wealth uncovered in the 1740s mostly exhausted. By the end of the century, the state, the Academy, and the world would learn far more about the extent of the sea otter decline as well as the extinction of the sea cow. When they did, many of the naturalists' certainties about empire, commerce, and the environment would falter.

Extinction and Empire on the Billings Expedition*

Thus terminated an expedition in which neither time nor expense had
been spared—a *nine-years* expedition—wherein not one of the points
for which it was undertaken was ascertained.... It was the error of
Catharine, and it has ever been the error of all despots, to think that
every thing is to be accomplished by their almighty fiat.... To set up
a Captain Cook was like her own imitation of Shakespeare.... The
luxuries of London and the vices of Paris might be transplanted to
Petersburg, and would thrive there, but science is not to be so procured.
The Annual Review, and History of Literature, 1802.

In the spring of 1794, the English stockbroker Martin Sauer lay in his bed in St.
Petersburg, sick, like Steller, from a fever caught in Siberia.[1] Sauer had recently
returned from Siberia and Alaska as part of the Russian government-sponsored
Billings Expedition and was hoping to soon leave Russia. Somewhere in his
apartment he had hidden a diary, notes, and possibly other secret materials from
the voyage. The expedition's commander, Joseph Billings, alerted members of the
Admiralty that Sauer might "plan to reveal these to the world through publishing them before Her Imperial Majesty would like." Billings received permission
to search Sauer's room, but found only a few draft notes. The sick man claimed
he had burned the materials, but a few years later, in 1804, they resurfaced as
part of the first printed description of the expedition, Sauer's own *Account of a
Geographical and Astronomical Expedition to the Northern Parts of Russia.*[2] The
Russians suspected that the illness had been feigned, a ruse to obtain a release
from Russian service and to keep government officials from searching his apartment too thoroughly.[3]

* Parts of Chapter 4 previously appeared in Ryan Tucker Jones, "'A Havock Made among Them':
Animals, Empire, and Extinction in the Russian North Pacific, 1741–1810," *Environmental History*
16, no. 4 (October, 2011): 585–609.

Europeans had known of the semi-secret Billings voyage since 1790, but had been unable to gain any information about it. The German press even spoke of a "secretive darkness" surrounding the expedition,[4] and George Vancouver's naturalist, Archibald Menzies, wrote of the "odium of secrecy" observed by both Russians and Spaniards.[5] Thus, readers received Sauer's book with great anticipation. Reaction, however, was mixed. Even though (or perhaps because) Sauer had enlisted the help of the Romantic poet William Beloe to help with the style,[6] one reviewer found the book full of "bloated phraseology,"[7] while another thought it contained "as dull, tedious, and uninteresting a narrative as was ever committed to the press."[8] Others thought Sauer had produced a "simple and perspicuous narrative" and wished that the author had produced more words about these poorly known areas of the Russian Empire.[9]

What united all Sauer's British reviewers was their reading of his travelogue as an indictment of the Russian Empire. London's *Annual Review* thought that the expedition had proved the savagery of common Russians and the rotten heart of Russian despotism. Russian priests were termed "savage bigots" and the late Empress Catherine II a misguided autocrat, all of her grandiose schemes poisoned by her subjects' lack of freedom.[10] Three pieces of evidence gleaned from Sauer's account demonstrated the Russian Empire's corruption. First, Russians were barbarously mistreating their conquered subjects in the North Pacific, murdering the men and stealing their women; the massive decline in population there spoke for itself. Second, the Russians were destroying their colonial fur resources as a result of the empire's poorly conceived commercial policies and the overzealous hunting practices of the *promyshlenniki*. Things had gotten so bad that "some of the species of animals producing furs have been entirely extirpated, and the whole thinned to such a degree as to be nearly annihilated."[11] Finally, the Russian Empire, despite this massive investment in hiring sailors and naturalists and outfitting the expedition, had failed once again to produce accurate knowledge of its domains. As far as the learned magazines were concerned, Catherine had done nothing to overcome, as one reviewer wrote, "the icy ignorance of Russia." Despotic, ignorant Russia had a poor claim to its colonial possessions, these reviews suggested, and it is not surprising that Sauer's book made some British mouths salivate about the expansion of their own empire into places that Russia claimed. "In a commercial view," wrote one paper, "it might probably be advantageous to our government, to have that part of America explored, which Mr. Sauer was desirous of visiting."[12] Russian officials must have wished Sauer had died from the Siberian fever that only temporarily laid him low in St. Petersburg.

The foreign reviews of Sauer's book, and the machinations he used to smuggle his notes to Britain, illustrate the dilemmas faced by the Russian Empire in the late eighteenth century and the growing attention paid to environmental problems in the North Pacific. In the 1790s, Russia's perception of the region changed from one of unbounded optimism over the new commercial and imperial opportunities offered by this rich source of furs, to a growing sense of trouble due to St. Petersburg's inability to successfully manage its fledging overseas empire. Foreign factors played a role in this transformation, as the English Captain James Cook's 1778 voyage through the Aleutian Islands, and the fur traders who followed, presented a real challenge to Russian sovereignty. Catherine responded by launching the Billings Expedition, which had mixed results for Russian knowledge of the North Pacific and furthered unflattering comparisons with the Spanish Empire. The natural world, too, presented difficulties for the Russian Empire. Massive ecological destruction seemed to show that Russia's Pacific Empire was badly run and on the verge of disintegration. In the journals and reports of the Billings Expedition, destruction of animals emerged for one of the first times in European history as a basis on which to criticize imperial expansion. At the center of that critique was an entirely new problem: that of species extinction.

Cook and the New Cosmopolitanism

The period after the conclusion of the Second Kamchatka Expedition was marked by a nationalization of discovery in the North Pacific. Russia allowed few foreigners into the region, and natural historians lost direct contact with events there. Everything changed for the Russians with the arrival of the celebrated English navigator Captain James Cook into the North Pacific. Instructed to determine whether the Northwest Passage existed, Cook sailed from Hawaii to the southwest coast of Alaska in the summer of 1778. Surveying the coast, he reached the Aleutian Islands late in the summer and met one of the fur-trading factors, Gerasim Izmailov. This was the first direct contact Western Europeans had ever had with the Russian fur traders in the North Pacific. Izmailov gave Cook a suitably exaggerated idea of the scope and power of Russia's colonization of the Aleutians, leaving the captain with the impression that Russia controlled much of mainland Alaska as well.

Revealing Western Europe's ignorance concerning the North Pacific, Cook thought that he observed sea cows swimming around his ship while sailing through the Aleutians: "We sometimes saw an animal, with a head like a seal's, that blew after the manner of whales. It was larger than a seal, and its colour was white, with some dark spots. Probably this was the sea-cow or manati," Cook concluded.[13] In the years since the publication of Steller's description of the sea cow (likely Cook's source for his assumption), no one else had publicly commented on the sea cow or produced a better drawing of it than the one found in the Academy's 1753 *Commentarii*. That Cook should have confused the animals he observed—probably beluga whales—with the sea cow is understandable, given the description he possessed.[14] Of course, Cook could not have seen sea cows anyway, since they had likely been extinct for at least a decade.

After Cook's death in Kealakekua Bay, Hawaii, in 1779, his ships returned to the North Pacific, docking at Petropavlovsk for supplies and more news about Russian Alaska. While Petropavlovsk's Governor Behm treated Captain King and the dying Captain Clerke to a beef feast, Timofei Shmalev suspected hidden imperial intentions. He sent detailed reports of the English activities back to St. Petersburg, along with a plea for reinforcement of the port's defenses.[15] When Captain King returned again the next summer, Petropavlovsk, formerly vulnerable only to Kamchadal attack, began looking more and more like part of a new invasion route to Siberia.

The Academy of Sciences received the news of Cook's voyages with great interest. On October 28, 1779, before Western Europe had even heard details of the voyage, Pallas wrote excitedly to Müller of Siberian officials' reports concerning two English ships that had sailed through the Aleutian Islands the previous year. "This can be no one else," Pallas concluded, "than the famous Captain Cook." Pallas received further information about Cook's activities in December, when he reported that Cook had finally found the passage between Asia and America. Pallas was soon pushing Müller to publish a long-planned book on the Russian discoveries in the North Pacific, which would have the effect of showing the English "whom the honor [of discovery] belongs to." Cook's voyages, so exciting from a scientific point of view, had strategic potential as well, and Pallas recognized early that they could threaten Russian dominion in the North Pacific. The sensitivity Russia felt about Cook's voyages was made clear later that year when Pallas was denied access to most of Cook's materials sent overland from Kamchatka.[16]

The threat to Russia lay in Cook's claims to first discovery of much of the North Pacific lands, and his improvement over Russia's geographic knowledge. Because the extent of Russia's Pacific exploration was unknown to most of Europe, Cook did effectively "discover" much of the North Pacific for Europe, which constituted a powerful claim for dominion in eighteenth-century Europe. Further increasing St. Petersburg's insecurity, two other European voyages of discovery got underway before 1790. A French expedition led by la Pérouse, sailed through the Western Pacific, mapped Sakhalin Island, and landed at Petropavlovsk before being wrecked and lost in the South Pacific in 1789. The following year Alejandro Malaspina set sail for the Spanish Empire on a voyage of discovery that took him to Alaska, where he obtained rich information about the Northwest Coast's natural history. Europe was beginning to break the "icy ignorance" surrounding the North Pacific.

Just as threatening as these government-organized voyages were the English attempts to establish a fur trade in the North Pacific in the early 1780s.[17] Upon return to Canton, Cook's crew was surprised to find that the sea-otter furs they had haphazardly collected in the North Pacific commanded tremendous prices with the Chinese merchants. Although all English commerce in the Pacific was reserved for the East India Company, English merchants made several licit and illicit trading voyages in search of North Pacific furs. It took some time to finance and organize these ventures, but in 1785 James Hannah, in command of the *Sea Otter*, reached the Northwest Coast. Others followed in droves, and they encountered little interference from the Russian companies already hunting in the area. James Strange, another trader who reached the coast in 1785, wrote that:

> It is a singular Proof of the Inactivity and want of Enterprise in the Russians, belonging to Kamchatka, that they have not yet availed themselves of this new source of Wealth, laid open to them, by the Discoveries of Captain Cook. [18]

This was alarming criticism for those concerned with Russia's interests in the North Pacific. Russia, though the first European discoverer of most of mainland Alaska, had not exploited its natural resources, and this inactivity, as Strange implied, was an invitation to the rest of Europe.

Responses to Cook

Russia thus faced a triple challenge to its North Pacific empire: Europeans were unaware of the extent of Russian discoveries; they were skeptical of Russia's ability to produce information on the North Pacific's natural world; and they doubted that Russia was capable of exploiting the North Pacific's natural resources. A bolder proclamation of Russian sovereignty over all the Aleutian Islands would have helped Russia's claims, but St. Petersburg hesitated, doubtful that it possessed the naval power necessary to protect such faraway lands. While the state was not ready to forcibly extract other Europeans from the North Pacific, as some Russians urged it to do, it was clear that something had to be done.

First and foremost, Russia needed to inform Europe of the empire's activity in the Aleutians and mainland Alaska before 1778. In 1781, while the English were still preparing a public account of Cook's voyage, the Russian Navy produced a chart showing the tracks and landfalls of earlier Russian navigators and merchants, along with their own map of Cook's travels.[19] Reversing decades of policy, the

Russian state also gave Pallas permission to share detailed accounts of Russian voyages to the North Pacific with influential foreigners.[20] Pallas was the ideal man for the job, for he sat at the hub of a wide network of foreign academicians and travelers interested in Russia and the North Pacific. One of his most influential correspondents, the Comte de Buffon, received Pallas's extracts from Russian journals of exploration first, and he incorporated information on North Pacific mammals into the twelfth volume of *History of Quadrupeds*. While this openness was a clear shift in Russian policy about its North Pacific activity, old fears persisted. "Be so kind," Pallas requested of his friend Pennant, "to leave also out…the wanton cruelties committed by the first Russians that visited the Islands."[21] Pallas recognized that it was still dangerous to share information too liberally.

From the Russian Empire's perspective, the most important recipient of the North Pacific information was another Englishman. The Reverend William Coxe, traveling through Russia in 1778 as tutor to Lord Herbert, son of the Earl of Pembroke, became interested in the North Pacific through his acquaintance with Pallas. After some persuasion, Pallas agreed to give Coxe access to several documents concerning Russia's Pacific voyages. Coxe had some of these manuscripts translated, then edited and published them in London in 1780 as *Russian Discoveries between Asia and Russia*. The documents Coxe received concerned the Krenitsyn-Levashov voyage as well as seventeen private fur-trading voyages, a combination that could indicate both the early date of Russian discoveries and the seriousness with which they had surveyed and mapped these territories.

St. Petersburg's hopes that Coxe's book would give the world notice of Russia's claims in the North Pacific largely succeeded. In particular, the reverend's book stressed Russia's credentials as equal to those of European enlightened voyages of discovery. Coxe praised Catherine for planning the Krenitsyn-Levashov Expedition, expressing "the warmest admiration of that enlarged and liberal spirit, which so strikingly marks the character of the present Empress of Russia." The best proof of Catherine's enlightened approach was her commitment to sharing information on Russia's exploration:

> The authentic records of the Russian history have, by her express orders, been properly arranged; and permission is readily granted of inspecting them. The most distant parts of her vast dominions have, at her expense, been explored and described by persons of great abilities and extensive learning; by which means new and important lights have been thrown upon the geography and natural history of those remote regions.[22]

Perhaps this sycophancy was the price Coxe paid for access to the Russian materials; at any rate it was effective propaganda for Russia's North Pacific claims.

Couched in terms of the disinterested pursuit of knowledge, these lines in fact made much more worldly claims. Russia, not England, had paid for the first explorations of the North Pacific, and Russian support was responsible for most of the knowledge about the region. When Coxe noted that his book allowed the reader to compare the Russian discoveries with Captain Cook's,[23] he was referring to more than just the possibility of putting various maps side by side. With Coxe's book, one could compare the extent of Russian activity in the North Pacific with the relatively recent arrival of the English.

While Coxe gave notice that Russia had been active after Bering, his editorializing sometimes veered onto dangerous grounds. Coxe readily praised Russia's enlightened sovereign, but was less kind toward her servitors. Borrowing from some of Müller's earlier papers, he began his account of the Russian discoveries by discussing the Cossack Yermak's sixteenth-century conquest of the Khanate of Sibir. According to Coxe, Yermak invaded Siberia because of a "passion for riches," the same passion that had driven the Spaniards to conquer the Americas. Yermak led, in Coxe's words, a "band of adventurers less civilized, but at the same time not so inhuman as the conquerors of America [Spaniards]."[24] Such comments detracted from Russia's claims to have led an enlightened conquest of Siberia and the North Pacific, suggesting instead that greed and banditry had led the charge.

Coxe's low opinion of Yermak and his men's civility was borrowed from Müller, who in the 1750s had engaged in a long debate with Lomonosov over the morality and civility of Yermak and his men. While Lomonosov praised Yermak as a Russian hero, Müller pointed out that he had in reality been little more than a bandit.[25] The Spanish comparison was Coxe's own, and it enriched the old Yermak debate with some international context. Contemporary European readers would have associated this debate with the Black Legend of Spanish cruelty in the Americas, and the Spanish conquest's devastation of native populations. Coxe's criticisms of Russian colonization centered on this second part—population loss. "The present population of Kamchatka is very small," Coxe noted. "Formerly the inhabitants were more numerous; but in 1768, that country was greatly depopulated by the ravages of the small-pox." The reverend also reported that the population of Unalaska had fallen greatly, for its inhabitants "have suffered greatly by their disputes with the Russians, and by a famine [in reality the Solovev massacre] in the year 1762."[26] Coxe did not condemn Russian colonization outright, but he offered a powerful line of argument for those already inclined toward such a condemnation. The new policy of openness about Russia's North Pacific discoveries was already revealing some drawbacks.

Cook and the private fur traders who followed him also spurred Russia to more concrete countermeasures to European encroachment. In 1785, at the suggestion of several prominent members of Catherine's War Cabinet, the Russian state began planning two ambitious North Pacific expeditions, both to be led by naval officers. One expedition, under the command of Grigorii Mulovskii, was to sail from St. Petersburg, through the Baltic, around the Cape of Good Hope, through the Indian and Pacific Oceans, and finally land at Kamchatka, where one warship would stay behind for permanent protection of the garrison there. Another naval contingent, under the command of Joseph Billings, would travel overland to Okhotsk. From there, the expedition would explore the Kolyma River up to the Arctic Ocean and attempt to find a sea route around Cape Dezhnev. The next year the men were to explore the Aleutian Islands and mainland Alaska before returning to Chukchi land (the Billings route is illustrated in Figure 4.1). Far more explicitly than Bering's voyages had, these expeditions aimed to ensure Russian sovereignty in the region.[27]

Both expeditions were linked in man and spirit to Captain Cook.[28] Georg Reinhold Forster, who had accompanied Cook on his second voyage, was chosen as the Mulovskii voyage's natural historian. Forster excitedly made grand plans for his part in the Expedition. However, due to renewed war with Sweden and Turkey, Catherine had to cancel Mulovskii's voyage and redeploy the captain to the field of battle, where he was killed.[29] If the voyage had materialized, Forster would have been the first scientist to sail on a Russian voyage of exploration since Steller, an early indication of the change of emphasis in this new round of activity.

With the cancellation of the grander Mulovskii voyage, all plans for the North Pacific had to rely on the voyage of the English Captain Joseph Billings. Billings had sailed on Cook's last voyage, and this seems to have been his main recommendation for command of the complex and difficult expedition. Joseph Banks did not think this much of a qualification for such a great responsibility, as he wrote to Pallas:

> Not deriving much hope from the station Mr. Billings held on board the Discovery ships that he could gain insight into the manner of conducting an expedition and consequently not forming any sanguine expectations of his success I postponed answering your last letter. I may, however easily be wrong in my judgment of that gentleman not having any personal acquaintance with him although I believe he has been sometimes in my Library, which I hope is open to all who have any pretense to science.[30]

As Banks's letter hinted, Billings had dubious ability, but fashioned himself a man of science. He would collect assiduously for Pallas during the North Pacific voyage,[31] and he contributed much to Pallas's *Zoographia Rosso-Asiatica* (ZRA).

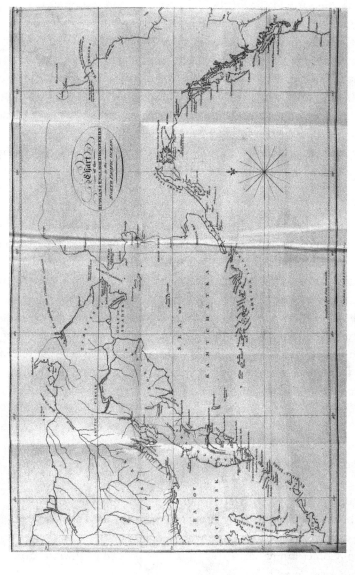

Figure 4.1 Map of the Billings Expedition (detail). Expedition members spent significant time in Kamchatka, Unalaska, and among the Chukchi in Siberia. This map also indicates the extent of Russian knowledge of the North Pacific around 1800. Martin Sauer, *An Account of a Geographical and Astronomical Expedition to the Northern Parts of Russia*. London: For T. Cadell, Jun. and W. Davies, in the Strand, 1802. Courtesy of John Carter Brown Library.

This good work did not pay personal dividends, however; he has been savaged by Russian historians for his tentativeness at the command,[32] and his marriage proposal to Pallas's daughter would later be rebuffed, possibly because of his humble social status.[33]

Pallas was deeply involved in the planning of the Billings Expedition, in contrast to the lack of Academy participation in the Krenitsyn-Levashov voyages. The Expedition even went so far as to christen one of the ships built in Eastern Siberia the *Pallas*, "as a mark of respect to the very learned Doctor of that name, who was the chief cause of the expedition taking place."[34] Pallas suggested Billings's appointment to the Empress Catherine, [35] and he found the chief draftsman, Luka Voronin, who would produce marvelous drawings of the expedition.[36] In the eyes of many in the outside world, this was Pallas's expedition.[37] However, in appointing a natural historian for the voyage, he ran into difficulties. Forster did not wish to participate in this smaller expedition, and it was difficult to find a replacement of his stature. Pallas asked Banks in June 1785 whether the Englishman knew any "collector" who could accompany Billings.[38] After hearing nothing back from Banks, Pallas nominated a Frenchman named Patrin,then living in the Western Siberian town of Barnaul, for the position. Patrin seems to have been a last-ditch option, as Pallas did not think much of the man's work.[39] Adding to the complications, Patrin became ill before he could join the Expedition, and another replacement had to be found.

The natural historian who finally accompanied the Billings Expedition was a German, Carl Heinrich Merck. Merck, already living in Siberia, was the nephew of the paleontologist Johann Heinrich Merck, who was acquainted with Banks and Pallas. This connection undoubtedly brought the younger Merck to the expedition, for he was completely unprepared for the work of natural history.[40] Two years after the completion of the voyage he died, leaving behind only the fragments of a journal and a Siberian vocabulary. To Billings, Merck seemed at least to be a "steady young man." [41] The highest-ranking Russian on board, naval officer Gavriil Sarychev, described him as a "man combining an almost puerile timidity with extraordinary intelligence."[42]

Not only the naturalist, but Billings's entire crew was cosmopolitan. In addition to the stockbroker Sauer, Robert Hall, an Englishman, captained a second ship, an Italian physician named Alegretti served as surgeon, and Christian Bering—Vitus's nephew—worked as navigator. Sarychev, second-in-command, was the highest-ranking Russian. In Kamchatka the Expedition picked up several of the "old voyager" *promyshlenniki*, including the renowned Pribylof, who would die of scurvy on the journey. These men represented the only link to the recent Russian voyages to the region; otherwise, the Billings Expedition resembled far more Bering's second expedition and, more recently, Cook's expeditions.

Russians and Spaniards

Billings's long eastward journey got underway in 1787. Expedition members were initially enthusiastic about Russia's colonization of Siberia. "The Siberians through-out are more industrious and independent than any Russian peasants, live more comfortably, and drink home-brewed beer," proclaimed an impressed Sauer.[43] Sarychev marveled at the exiles he encountered in Yakutsk, who "not only have their liberty, but use it with the greatest moderation."[44] Sauer and Sarychev were among the first to debate whether Siberia brought freedom or slavery to Russia.[45] Early in the expedition both agreed that Siberians enjoyed great freedom of movement and conscience, which they attributed to Catherine's enlightened, liberal governance of the region. Back at home, Pallas echoed the travelers' praise of Siberia. Although inns and hotels were rare, the hospitality of the inhabitants made for pleasant trav-eling. "With one word," he wrote to the readers of his *Neue Nordische Beyträge*, "Siberia, with great strides, is approaching the most enlightened nations (*Ländern*) of Europe."[46] At the same time, Siberia provided hints that progress had come at a price. Inspecting the site of a new factory in Ekaterinburg, Sauer was shocked by the sudden absence of trees in the clearing hewn out for the factory (a sensitivity devel-oped no doubt, by Sauer's experience with a rapidly industrializing Britain). Still, with events in the North Pacific shrouded in relative silence, the members of the Billings Expedition could not have been prepared for the depletion they encoun-tered when they reached the ocean in 1790. Their most recent accounts came from Steller and Krasheninnikov, who had wondered at the North Pacific natural world's seemingly limitless abundance, and from Krenitsyn and Levashov, who had little to say about the environment. A shock awaited them in Alaskan waters.

As the expedition reached the Eastern Siberian capital of Yakutsk in 1786, it ran into complications. As Sauer reported, no provisions had arrived, no hous-ing had been arranged for the expedition members, the town was in a state of extreme poverty, and the weather had become bitterly cold. A generous gift of meat from the local Yakut elders probably saved the Europeans from starva-tion.[47] While expedition members formed mixed opinions of the Siberians, they criticized the Russian occupiers mercilessly. According to Sauer,

> The lordly Cossac... These last of mankind, unworthy of the name, these hardly animated lumps of clay, exert the most savage barbarity over their wives, children, animals, and the poor neighbouring tribes whose miserable lot it is to pay tribute to them...[48]

Echoing d'Auteroche's famous indictment of Siberia, Sauer's criticism of the Cossacks' treatment of animals foreshadowed the equally bitter accusations that would follow in the North Pacific.

In 1787, after a summer survey of the Arctic Ocean coast, the Expedition returned to Yakutsk to find a surprise visitor. John Ledyard, an American who had sailed with Cook and was acquainted with Billings, had turned up in the town. He hoped to ship with the expedition in order to reach the northwest coast of America, as part of a plan to investigate its fur resources. Only by remarkable good fortune had Ledyard been able to get this far. He had received uncommon hospitality throughout his journey through Siberia, for which he had Pallas to thank. The two had become acquainted in St. Petersburg, and Pallas had written letters of introduction for the American.[49] Not everyone supported Ledyard's plans, however. Catherine, who had been away when Ledyard had obtained travel permission, had deep reservations about his plans. As she wrote to the Baron Grimm in Germany, "Regarding Ledyard, discovery for others is not always discovery for us."[50] Ledyard's gossipy familiarity with Thomas Jefferson, Joseph Banks, and others hardly held happy portents for the Russian Empire.

This was certainly the impression of Russian colonial officials. Governor-General Iakobi in Irkutsk, who would become closely involved with the Billings Expedition, reported to St. Petersburg that

> [Ledyard's] confused travel pattern and his way of putting thoughts into words were sufficiently strong grounds for me to doubt him, especially since he does not have a proper passport even to this place.... It is entirely possible however that he was sent here by the English to obtain information on these places.[51]

Ledyard had a penchant for meeting notable people. Grigorii Shelikhov, future founder of the RAC, happened to be in Irkutsk at the same time and suspiciously took notes of their conversation. Shelikhov reported that Ledyard asked "with ardent curiosity" about Russia's possessions in the North Pacific, to which the Russian trader responded with lies and disinformation. When Ledyard informed Shelikhov about new European settlements on the Northwest Coast, the Russian told him that, "people from other states had no right to exercise power over these areas without permission from the Russian Monarch."[52] Imperial rivalry in the North Pacific was heating up considerably.

Perhaps Ledyard should not have been surprised by his sudden arrest shortly after reuniting with Billings in Yakutsk. While historians debate the exact reasons for Ledyard's arrest, one of his letters to Pallas may help explain the mistrust.[53] In December 1787, Ledyard wrote at length to his friend in Petersburg with his collected impressions of Siberia. Russian colonists, he claimed, reflected none of St. Petersburg's enlightened spirit. The conquered natives knew nothing of the "wise & polished Catherine... nor of the spirit of humanity... Billings is the first officer who ever gave them an honest account of this." If the Billings Expedition succeeded in bringing the North Pacific islands under greater control, Ledyard predicted that the same tyranny would extend there. Never one to check his language, Ledyard informed Pallas

> in positive terms that there is not a Captain Isprawnik [Commander] in the country where I am...who is not as vile a scoundrel (tho w/o his abilities) as the Man whose Conquest of Mexico has damned to fame—nor is there even a scoundrel of a Consul who does not like him...deeply prostitute the dignity of the sovereign & the laws of this Empire for a foxes skin, and is worse than the vilest miscreant in the armies of Cortez or Pizarro—and to crown this narration this troop of infernals are followed by the holy priesthood to sanctify this enormous mass of black Iniquities.[54]

Ledyard pressed the comparison with the other European empires, claiming that the Russians were even greater scoundrels than the Spaniards, the Portuguese in Brazil, or the English in the East Indies.[55] Though he spared Catherine his rancor, after his arrest she too felt the sting of Ledyard's pen. The incident would set off a string of anti-Catherine publications in America and Britain.[56]

Before Ledyard's arrest, Billings had agreed to let him sail to America with the expedition. During his months in Yakutsk, Ledyard spent many hours with Sauer and the other foreigners, even traveling with them to nearby attractions.[57] While it is uncertain whether Ledyard shared his criticisms of the Russian colonial bureaucracy with the others, the Billings Expedition's members would strikingly echo his sentiments in their journals. The emphasis on Russian despotism, and the unflattering comparison with historical colonial regimes, are particularly noteworthy. Ledyard's themes would reappear—with an ecological angle—once the Billings Expedition sailed on to the North Pacific.

Leaving Ledyard to his fate, the Billings Expedition continued on to the seaport of Okhotsk (shown in Figure 4.2) that summer. There, they made another acquaintance who would be instrumental in shaping their views of the fur-trading companies' relationship with the Aleuts and Alutiit. While preparing for the journey to the Arctic Ocean, they met a fur trader and surgeon named Britukov, who had recently returned from a stint with the Shelikhov-Golikov Company. Distrusting Shelikhov's glowing reports of the Kodiak conquest, Catherine had instructed Billings and his crew to investigate the company's behavior.[58] Now, meeting with Britukov, the expedition had its first chance to look into this matter. Britukov, glad to have the ear of someone in contact with St. Petersburg, told Billings that the company's Kodiak conquest had been far bloodier than reported. He explained that Shelikhov had ordered one of his men to "put (two

Figure 4.2 "A snow sledge drawn by dogs, as used in the vicinity of Ochotz," Gavril Sarychev, *Puteshestvie*. Expedition members traversed much of Eastern Siberia and Kamchatka on dog sleds. Courtesy of John Carter Brown Library.

natives) together so that he could shoot them both with one shot from a gun," and "tortured them with whalebone and gunsticks."[59]

A story nearly identical to Britukov's appeared in Billings's later report, which contained complaints made by some Aleuts encountered on the voyage. The Unalaska natives related how the *promyshlennik* foreman Solovev "lined up men one behind the other to see how many could be killed by one shot from his firearm."[60] These stories of sport killings had appeared almost verbatim in Bartolomé las Casas's 1542 *Destruction of the Indies*, which recounted numerous Spanish "massacres and strange cruelties" against the Hispaniola Islanders. The *promyshlenniki*'s behavior mimicked that of the cruel Spanish conquistador—or perhaps the reports of *promyshlenniki* behavior were molded to suggest this correspondence. Either way, Coxe's and Ledyard's comparison of the Russian and Spanish New World conquests gained credibility among the members of the Billings Expedition.

Ironically, Shelikhov himself promoted the connection between his company and Spanish colonization. The published version of his 1786 journey to Kodiak had opened proudly with an engraving depicting Shelikhov trading for furs in the North Pacific, as seen in Figure 4.3. In it, a Russian fur trader accepts what

Колумбы Росские презрѣвъ угрюмый рокъ,
Межъ льдами новый путь отворятъ на Востокъ,
И наша досягнетъ въ Америку Держава,
И во всѣ концы досягнетъ Россово слава.

Figure 4.3 The frontispiece to Shelikhov's account of his conquest of Kodiak Island shows a Europeanized Alaskan peacefully trading what may be a sea-otter pelt to a Russian *promyshlennik* (and his Siberian allies?). A walrus, squirrel, and another unidentified marine mammal wait their turns. The accompanying poem by Russian scientist Mikhail Lomonosov compares the fur-traders to "Russian Columbuses," an unfortunate association in European eyes. Courtesy of Alaska State Library.

seems to be a sea otter fur from a strangely European islander, flanked by a fierce, shrunken walrus. An angel of concord blesses the entirely fabricated scene. Finally, the caption below the picture quoted Lomonosov's poem honoring the "Russian Columbuses" making new discoveries for the glory of Russia. In retrospect, the Spanish comparison was one Shelikhov may have been wise to avoid.

Shelikhov and Billings

The Billings Expedition entered the North Pacific at a time when administrators were first beginning to worry about the decline in fur-bearing animals, and as aggressive entrepreneurs such as Shelikhov were reshaping the trade. The sea otter, whose fur commanded the highest profits, had become the primary animal of concern by the late 1780s. Governor-general Ivan Iakobi, who had generously supported the Billings Expedition during its stay in Yakutsk,[61] was recalled to St. Petersburg late in 1787. In an important report sent to Catherine at that time, he warned that sea otter depletion was about to become a serious problem:

> Merciful Sovereign, we know from many examples that the hunting has decreased substantially each year. There is absolutely no doubt, when one realizes that millions (sic) of animals have been taken [in the North Pacific]....One can therefore suppose that in a few years the animals will be completely depleted, or at least, that the great expenses associated with hunting will not continue to be rewarded at the same level.

One of the problems resulting from the sea otter's depletion was the worsening trade balance with China. The goods the fur traders obtained from the Chinese had "become necessities, almost indispensable to Your Empire."[62] With the supply of furs drying up, Russia in the future might have to pay in hard currency for Chinese imports, which was anathema to mercantilists who devised Catherine's economic policy.[63]

Iakobi had little hope that the decline in the fur trade could be stemmed and suggested instead that government expeditions look for new sources of profits—perhaps the old chimeras of precious metals or the Japanese trade could be revived. He noted hopefully that "neither the islands nor the American coast inhabited by savages have yet been explored by naturalists"—maybe the Billings Expedition could remedy this.[64] Furthermore, sea otter decline threatened more than imperial profits and the balance of trade. With Cook and La Pérouse's recent incursions, successful management of the North Pacific Empire required new thinking and decisive action. Shelikhov had recently argued to Iakobi that European fur traders were "damaging the interests of Russia" by snatching up some of the diminishing supply of animals.[65] Iakobi strongly suggested that Catherine give limited monopoly control over Aleutian and Alaskan commerce to Shelikhov's fur trading company (then known as the Shelikhov-Golikov Company, later called the Russian American Company) in order to encourage further colonization and ensure that the indigenous people caused no more problems. If fur profits were in irreversible decline, then permanent settlement might have to substitute for a vigorous trade. According to Iakobi's reports, Shelikhov had done a marvelous job of subduing the Alutiit on Kodiak Island, and other natives feared and respected his company. If various trading groups were allowed to hunt sea mammals near Kodiak Island, "one simply cannot suppose that all, in the multitude who will visit the islands, will behave in the same manner." Remembering Solovev and other reckless *promyshlenniki* of the past, Iakobi warned that small bands of hunters simply stirred the natives to violence without having the means to sufficiently subdue them. It was particularly important to keep the Aleuts and Alutiit in submission as "these American natives must be protected from all foreign interference."[66] Both strategic and conservationist reasons seem to have been instrumental in securing Iakobi's support for Shelikhov's venture.

In the meantime, Billings was fortunate merely to be able to continue the expedition. He had forwarded Britukov's report detailing Shelikhov's abuses to St. Petersburg along with another similar report through Iakobi's replacement, Governor Ivan Pil, who most likely had substantial monetary interests in Shelikhov's Company.[67] Pil passed Britukov's statement on to St. Petersburg, but included complaints that Billings was overstepping his duties, and suggested that the expedition be discontinued. The new governor claimed that "the enlightenment (*prosveschenie*) which presently pervades Europe" would instantly alert Europeans to the Russians' actions and might provoke retaliation.[68] Thus, the Enlightenment could also hold negative connotations for some in eighteenth-century Russia.

Making matters worse, Billings had compromised himself by engaging in lucrative, semi-legal dealings with the Yakuts, actions that had also solicited negative reports.[69] The empress, under budgetary pressures due to war in Europe, was already considering canceling the expedition. News was also reaching Siberia that a Swedish warship was cruising in the North Pacific and looking to sack Russian possessions. On June 20, 1790, the empress sent the order to cancel the expedition if it had not yet left port.[70] Luckily for Billings, he had already set sail from Kamchatka and could not be recalled. If not for Billings's timely departure, the environmental crisis in the North Pacific would have gone long unnoticed in European scientific circles.

On the peninsula, the expedition enjoyed its last happy moments, with "views...more beautiful than anything [Sauer] could remember to have seen." Much time was devoted to pilgrimages to sites associated with Cook,

Figure 4.4 View of Captain Clerke's Tomb at St. Peter & St. Paul. Charles Clerke, Captain's Cook's second in command, died of tuberculosis while the ships were in Petropavlovsk harbor. The picture also depicts one of the last heads of Kamchatkan cattle being driven away for slaughter to feed the British. From Martin Sauer, *An Account of a Geographical and Astronomical Expedition*, 1802. Courtesy of John Carter Brown Library.

including Clerke's grave (shown in Figure 4.4). Sauer reported meeting several Kamchatkans who had known those on Cook's expedition; they had even composed a "song to their memory, with a chorus to the tune of God save the King; which is frequently sung in perfect harmony."[71] The men also enjoyed the blend of Kamchadal-Russian culture, attending dances in the Russian, Polish, and Kamchadal styles, the latter of which would make "every modest woman...blush to be a spectator, much more a partner in it." The Kamchadals had meanwhile moved out of their subterranean houses and built in the Russian style.[72] From this unexpected idyll, this strange Russian expedition—successors of Cook under a different sovereign—sailed on, into the stormy Pacific, and into a world utterly transformed from the days of Steller.

Sea Otters and Savages

In one sense, Russians who came to the North Pacific were prepared for the problem of the decline of fur-bearing animals. In contrast to the Europeans who traveled to the North Pacific, Russians first passed through Siberia, where the demands of the fur trade had long since caused local extinctions of sables, foxes,

Figure 4.5 "Man & Woman of Oonalashka" Gavril Sarychev. This drawing by expedition artist Luka Voronin depicts some of the Aleuts' maritime technologies, including their marine-mammal intestine parkas (*kamleikas*) used to keep them remarkably dry at sea. The man also wears a hunting visor designed to shade the eyes during the hunt. The woman wears the facial tattoos then typical. Courtesy of John Carter Brown Library.

wolverines, and wolves. Even in Steller's time Siberian hunters reported increasing scarcity of animals, though no one yet contemplated the possibility of the entire eradication of a species. The Siberian frontier moved continually eastward, partly because of the continual hunting out of fur-bearing animals. Coxe, among others, noted this phenomenon in his *Russian Discoveries*.[73] The members of the Billings Expedition also encountered Siberian hunters who complained of the drying up of formerly rich hunting grounds. Fur depletion was a long-standing problem for both the *promyshlenniki* and the Russian state that counted on revenue derived from the fur trade.

Nonetheless, the scene awaiting the Billings Expedition in the North Pacific was astonishing. After negotiating foggy seas which forced them to bypass the Commander Islands, the two ships landed at *Bobrovaya* (Sea Otter) Bay on Unalaska. A fleet of Aleuts (two of whom may be depicted in Figure 4.5) came to meet the ships, astonishing crew members with their agility in the sea. They "paddled in among the breakers, which reached to their breasts, and carried the baidars (large skin boat) quite underwater, sporting about more like amphibious animals than human beings."[74] There were only two Russians and one Kamchadal then at *Dobroe Soglasie* ("Good Concord," the darkly ironic name Russians had given their settlement after suppressing the 1762 Aleut uprising), but the Aleuts readily told of severe repressions. No wonder Billings's journals never found a publisher, for in them he claimed the Russians take "the fruit of their Labour to themselves, not even allowing the Natives company Clothing. They select the youngest and handsomest women without Ceremony of asking their consent they Live entirely on the Natives who frequently hunger to satisfy their Lordly virtues." Furthermore, Russian hunting parties often engaged in slave raids of other Aleuts, and the few imperial officials in the North Pacific were mere "idle spectators of insults and say that they think themselves happy, if they are not forced by the Companies to bear an active part."[75] Sauer reported similar abuses, and Sarychev summarized briskly that the Aleutians had been "the theatre of many oppressions."[76]

Worse, all these oppressions were bringing precious little wealth. The expedition found that the sea otter trade had nearly ceased altogether, as it had in Kamchatka and the Commander Islanders. Nothing in the literature on North Pacific exploration could have prepared the expedition for the barren fur deserts in the Aleutian Islands. Steller, their primary guide, had described an incredible abundance of marine mammals everywhere he went. Now, as the expedition passed from one island group to another, it met with few, if any, sea otters, declining numbers of fur seals, and no sea cows. Though many had tried to explain the disappearance of the sea otters as mere migration, those on the Billings Expedition, having seen over two thousand miles of otter barrens, would reach very different conclusions. The island context made the decline uniquely visible, with each island offering a microcosm of a larger process taking place throughout the Russian possessions in the North Pacific. There was no refuge left for the marine mammals that had once swarmed these islands, no forests into which they might have disappeared, and no hidden cove where they might have congregated.

By the time they reached Kodiak Island in the late summer of 1789, the expedition members had seen enough destruction on the islands to come to some conclusions about the state of marine mammals in the North Pacific. Sauer reported that sea otters were gone from nearly every spot they had formerly inhabited in the North Pacific: "They are no more on the coast of Kamtschatka; they are very seldom seen on the Aleutian islands; of late, they have forsaken the Shumagins." Sauer predicted that, because sea otters were found only in this part of the world and because they had been hunted so savagely, "fifteen years hence there will hardly exist any more of this species."[77] Island foxes, seals, and sea lions too were now becoming increasingly scarce. Sauer, the stockbroker, turned out to be the best naturalist on board, and he mentioned repeatedly locations where sea otters and other animals were "almost forgotten."[78] Others also found the decline striking and disturbing. The naturalist Merck noted that, "concerning the sea otter: the annual catch has diminished by half, until they are now quite rare."[79] He, in contrast to Sauer, believed that the sea otters might have moved to "quieter regions." Sarychev found the decline in sea otters most noteworthy on Unalaska, where a portion of the crew overwintered. "Since the stay of the Russians here," he remarked, "the number of these animals has been greatly diminished, and they are now very scarce."[80] Christian Bering matched Sauer's pessimism in predicting that the entire trade would soon be exhausted.[81] Among the officers, only Billings failed to mention the shocking decline in sea otters, though he too later predicted that ecological ruin would threaten Russian imperial interests. He had turned out to be less of a naturalist than he had presented himself. Even Pallas, his great supporter, in the end found Billings's efforts on the voyage disappointing.[82]

Sauer became the first to publish news of the extinction of the sea cow, as part of his contraband journal. In Kodiak, he claimed that "the last of this species was killed in 1768 on Bering's island, and none have ever been seen since."[83] Sauer probably received information about the end of the sea cows from one of the hunters in the Three Saints Bay settlement on Kodiak, perhaps, as the historian Stejneger suggests, from the old hunter Evrstat Delarov,[84] with whom Sauer certainly had long conversations. Unfortunately, Sauer did not elaborate further on the sea cow's extinction, so momentous in the history of humanity's interaction with the natural world. Curiously, none of Sauer's shipmates confirmed the extinction. Merck mentioned only that the sea cow was gone from Bering Island, but added that it "was not to be found in the Pribyloffs either"—a place sea cows had never lived.[85] Some confusion clearly still surrounded the animal. With its extinction already nearly thirty years in the past, the *promyshlenniki* themselves may have been uncertain to what exact animal *morskaya korova* (sea cow) referred. By the early nineteenth century, many of the hunters would claim that Steller's animal had never existed.[86]

It is clear that the still-loose definition of "naturalist" enriched the Billings expedition's environmental awareness. Sauer, who lamented not being trained in natural history, in fact read important works in the field. He and Sarychev turned out to be far more insightful commentators than Merck, who ostensibly trained in the subject. Merck's journal is full of pious exclamations, a few observations on Aleut culture, and almost nothing on the natural world. Langsdorff, a well-trained naturalist, would later build and improve on Sauer's observations, but his companion, naval officer Lisiansky, also wrote with much insight. In short, nearly every educated European on the Russian voyages enthusiastically plunged into the North Pacific's natural history.

This Billings Expedition's nearly unanimous declaration of environmental catastrophe in the North Pacific was remarkable by eighteenth-century standards. Though contemporary naturalists were worrying about deforestation and climate change in some colonial locations, they had little to say about the decline in animals, and almost nothing at all about the possibility of extinction.[87] When people did worry about hunting animals to extinction—Bermudan officials in 1620 for example passed ordinances protecting sea turtles because of the "danger of an utter destroying and loss of them"—the concern was purely local.[88] In contrast, the members of the Billings Expedition inaugurated a new era of sustained concern over extinction in the North Pacific, and by publishing their accounts widely, they brought these concerns to a larger European audience. The reasons for their interest in the perilous fate of marine mammals lay first of all in the animals' visible decline, but also in a mixture of economic, political, and cultural concerns unique to the Russian North Pacific.

Some of the Billings Expedition's concerns about North Pacific fur-bearing animals were familiar from Siberian colonization. *Yasak* and taxation of the North Pacific fur trade were very lucrative for the perennially cash-strapped Russian state, and the Billings Expedition served the warning that overhunting threatened this commerce. Sarychev noted the problems developing in Eastern Siberia, including figures that would catch St. Petersburg's attention: "The quantity of skins…taken near the river Kolyma was so considerable as to furnish a yearly revenue of 4,000 [rubles] to the state…. The sables having now all disappeared from this quarter, the fair [where furs had been sold] has, of course, been totally abandoned."[89] The decline in the sea-otter trade similarly threatened imperial revenues. Indeed, since the American colonies were entirely based on the sea-otter hunt, that threat was especially pressing here.

However, the Billings Expedition's environmental critique encompassed much more than economics. The members of the expedition drew conclusions from environmental decline that revealed the power in the unique confluence of North Pacific environment, natural history, and the cosmopolitan construction of Russian voyages of exploration. Sauer, Sarychev, and others combined Enlightenment arguments about noble savages and Russian barbarians into an environmentalist critique of the sea-otter trade that challenged the moral legitimacy of the Russian Empire.

First of all, expedition members noted that the decline in the Aleut and Alutiit populations and the decline in sea mammal populations were related. Sarychev remarked that the sea "remains, at all times, [the Aleuts'] grand resource; one while supplying them with an abundance of fish or animals for their pursuit, and another time casting on its shore many delicacies."[90] Sea mammals provided the North Pacific peoples with food, clothing, and weapons. But now, noted Merck, as the sea otters, fur seals, and foxes disappeared, the islanders, clad only in grasses, were freezing to death.[91] The Russians forced the native men on longer and longer hunting voyages to find the dwindling supply of animals. Unable to provide for their families while on these long trips, the men would return to find their community starving and unprepared for winter.

Here the second main thrust of Coxe's critique of Russian imperialism in *Russian Discoveries*—that colonization was depopulating the North Pacific—appeared in the Billings Expedition's reports. In Okhotsk, Britukov had informed Billings that the Shelikhov-Golikov Company had exterminated so many Alutiit that "one village was completely eradicated."[92] Upon reaching the main Russian settlement on Unalaska, and then the Shelikhov-Golikov Company's headquarters on Kodiak, they discovered more evidence of population decline. Taking a census of the native population of the North Pacific, the Billings Expedition members found the numbers far lower than had been reported. "The number of males," Sauer estimated, "does not exceed eleven hundred.... Formerly, one village on this island [Unalaska] contained more than the above number."[93] Billings noted that many islands in the Aleutian chain had been completely depopulated since the Russian arrival.[94] The Billings Expedition's unique contribution to early modern environmental literature was to tie the widely recognized ill effects of European colonization on native peoples with the corresponding decline in animals.

The men on the expedition gave several reasons why native population was in decline. Russian hunters subjected the Aleuts to various depredations, reducing them to servitude and sending them on long hunts that killed many men and kept them from providing for their own families.[95] In contrast to the Siberian administrators' hopeful reports, Billings and his crew found the *promyshlenniki* and the Shelikhov-Golikov Company to have poisoned Russian-native relations. Christian Bering managed to see a silver lining in the sea otter's decline: "in a few years the sea otters will be completely gone from these islands, and perhaps, this poor nation will rebound a little as a result [of the hunters leaving]." In the meantime, Bering described a sorrowful scene of women and children so hungry that they were reduced to eating the *promyshlenniki*'s discarded fish bones.[96]

The decline in animal populations and the related decline of native numbers mattered for more than just humanitarian reasons. In the late eighteenth century, population growth was considered one of the main responsibilities of government. That population equaled prosperity was a truism that few philosophers (before Malthus) or statesmen questioned. Taking on increasing responsibility for the health of the national economy, self-proclaimed "enlightened" governments focused on increasing the productive resources of their country. In Europe and in Russia, the human population was considered the primary productive resource, and by simple arithmetic, increasing population would increase production.[97] Population increase, in fact, was one of the main criteria upon which foreign travelers judged the success of the Russian Empire.[98] A particularly nasty review of Sauer's book allowed that "This unhappy woman (Catherine) could desolate, but she could not people."[99] The St. Petersburg Academy of Sciences made the study of the Russian population one of its principal goals, and the pages of its journals are filled with estimates of St. Petersburg's population, along with year-by-year birth and mortality records. These early practitioners of statistics always emphasized increasing population and the ways in which government policy could achieve this goal.

Not only the population of European Russia, but also of Russia's eastern empire, figured in the balance sheet of autocratic rule. From the Steppe to the North Pacific, enlightened Russian statesmen saw increasing population as a mark of governmental success.[100] Imperial concern for the indigenous peoples on the margins of empire had not always been the standard. Government officials often claimed to desire benevolent treatment of distant imperial subjects, but just as telling was the Empress Elizabeth's 1742 order for the "total liquidation" of the Chukchis and Koryaks (fortunately never carried out).[101] However, the international position had changed so dramatically with the incursions of Cook and LaPérouse that, by the 1780s, native well-being had become a priority. Officials in Eastern Siberia, responding to Aleut complaints (sometimes presented in person), attempted to guarantee the *promyshlenniki*'s good behavior, something that was difficult to achieve at such a distance and difficult to reconcile with the greed for furs in government circles. Nonetheless, there were at least some points of overlap in Aleut and government interests. A note to the Aleuts from the commandant of Nizhnekamchatsk in 1787 noted the particular problem of the Russian hunters substituting poor-grade skins for the quality furs rendered as *yasak* by the Aleuts. The commandant advised the Aleuts to "place certain signs or marks on the skins, sewing bits of wood or something else on them so that they cannot be substituted."[102] Though the Aleuts would show such orders to visiting hunters, demanding that they sign them, the guarantees seemed to have little effect on *promyshlennik* behavior.

By the 1790s, with the North Pacific's lucre and vulnerability exposed, officials in St. Petersburg and Siberia sensed they would have to rely on the native population for political, in addition to economic, purposes. Good treatment might prevent the possible formation of a native fifth column.[103] As Catherine put it in her orders to the Billings Expedition, "humane and friendly behaviour keeps them quiet."[104] Indeed, Billings grilled the Aleuts about their relationship with foreign ships passing by and found that they differentiated little between Russians, Spaniards, and Englishmen.[105] Furthermore, with Cook's example squarely in mind, Russians and foreigners in Russian service hoped for more civil relations between conquerors and conquered—something that went beyond the casual violence of the Siberian conquest. Cook was the gold standard for enlightened voyages of exploration, and despite his death at the hands of enraged Hawaiians, his relations with non-Europeans were thought to have been exemplary in their civility. Sauer reflected something of the prevailing conception when he praised "the liberality with which the Expedition under Captain Cook treated the natives of every place they touched at."[106] As explorers who styled themselves after the mold of Cook,[107] the Billings Expedition's officers saw native welfare during the voyage as their responsibility, and thought they could provide a useful example for the Russian conquerors after they returned to Europe.

The members of the Billings Expedition perceived a second, deeper link between sea mammal and native welfare in the North Pacific. The ocean's natural abundance—an idea borrowed from earlier explorers in the region—had seemed to guarantee its inhabitants a carefree existence. Spared the harsh struggle for scarce resources, the natives of the North Pacific represented what some called "noble savagery," a state of moral purity and true happiness untainted by the decadent concerns of modern civilization.[108] Sauer termed Siberians "great Nature's happy commoners,"[109] and Sarychev remarked about Eastern Siberia's Tungus,

> No matter how poor the state of these people might seem, they are much happier in it than enlightened rich people who have their pleasures all the time. They do not know any troubles or worries; their needs are limited; and their whole welfare consists in the abundance of fish.[110]

Sauer was surprised to find liberality and order among the Aleuts, as "the capacity natives of these islands infinitely surpasses every idea that I had formed of the abilities of savages.... Their behaviour...is not rude and barbarous, but mild, polite, and hospitable."[111] Local social relations seemed to short-term visitors like Sarychev to be pure and uncomplicated, but the destruction of the environment threatened the North Pacific natives' innocence. Merck remarked that the Aleuts "have few needs, particularly because their clothing came to them together with their food [in the form of sea mammals]." But, with the arrival of the Russians, the "stingy greed of the civilized world robbed them of their leisure.... Therefore now the Aleuts have to live in constant anxiety."[112] The *promyshlenniki*, in particular, were complicit in the natives' loss of innocence, for by hunting sea mammals they destroyed the natural resources upon which noble savagery depended, and their use of forced native labor robbed the Aleuts and Alutiit of the fruits of whatever environmental bounty still remained.

Defending the natives' purity was fraught with contradictions that mirrored the problematic use of the concept of noble savagery.[113] Many aspects of the supposedly pristine Aleut and Kodiak Island culture disgusted the Billings Expedition, such as their lascivious dancing, the smell of their houses, and their deceitfulness—though Sauer was pleased to find that the natives did not practice nudity (perhaps unsurprising in such northern climes). On the other hand, the natives were showing signs of becoming more civilized, receiving the Billings Expedition with courtesy and adopting some aspects of European culture.

Sarychev felt that they should take up agriculture in order to become more like Europeans, lamenting that the *promyshlenniki* had not "turned their thoughts to the introduction of agriculture and every rural occupation."[114] According to theories of noble savagery, however, development of agriculture would end the state of happiness by introducing the vices of civilization.[115]

The Billings Expedition's tentative and contradictory enthusiasm for noble savagery signifies one of the first adoptions in Russia of the contemporary European enthusiasm for primitivism. The idea had been current in European intellectual circles since at least the early seventeenth century, and had recently gained renewed prominence through Jean-Jacques Rousseau's celebration of uncivilized virtue. However, the idea had previously found little purchase among Russians. As historian Yuri Slezkine puts it, "Most Russian travelers seemed well aware that the absence of civilization and enlightenment (ignorance) could also be interpreted as the absence of pride and affectation (innocence), but it was the ignorance that struck them the most." As a result, "there were no noble Tungus or perspicacious Buriats, and the "obscurantist and retrograde ravings" in Rousseau's first *Discours* met with stern rebuke from all quarters."[116] In the last quarter of the century these attitudes began to change. The re-internationalization of Russian North Pacific exploration, embodied best in the Billings Expedition, was partly responsible for the embrace of primitivism. Sarychev, the lone Russian officer, was also the most insistent on the need to "Russify" the natives. His education in the St. Petersburg naval school would hardly have prepared him to see ignorance as innocence, yet he too warmed to the narrative of the noble savage in the North Pacific. Cook's example and his foreign shipmates' enthusiasm for primitive culture influenced the Russian's mindset.

Another effect of Cook's influence was an increasingly romantic view of wilderness (see Figure 4.6). Pallas and others in St. Petersburg preferred ordered nature, though those who had traveled to Siberia had gained some appreciation for dark forests and endless steppes. European voyagers to the North Pacific such as Georg Forster had found little to love in the region's icy wastes. But by the last decade of the century, British voyagers—including some on Cook's last voyage—were beginning to find the region's towering peaks, immense trees, and overall desolation to be "sublime."[117] These preferences were carried onto the Billings Expedition. Billings wrote that in Chuckchi land, "you sometimes meet mountains of an Amazing height, you are often presented with prospects that are really romantic."[118] Sauer spoke of "romantic desolation," and even Sarychev was bewitched by the pines and firs, which he found made the landscape "agreeably diversified."[119] Diversification of flora was an essential component of the new romantic landscape aesthetic, and Sarychev seems to have assimilated it completely.

Despite the expedition's confidence in their own enlightenment, its members despaired that the Russians could ever emulate Cook. The problem lay

Figure 4.6 This illustration from the Russian traveler Litke's *Atlas* depicts both the majesty and abundance of Alaskan nature (here near the Russian capital of New Arkhangelsk, present-day Sitka). The toga-wearing Tlingits hearken back to earlier, primitivist fantasies that had begun to grip Romantic Russians' imaginations. Fedor Petrovich Litke, *Atlas Lithographié d'après les dessins originaux d'A. Postels…et du Baron Kittlitz.* Paris, 1834. Courtesy of the Rasmussen Library, University of Alaska Fairbanks.

in their tyrannical nature. As naturalist Georg Heinrich von Langsdorff wrote a decade later, the fur trader in the North Pacific "enjoys no protection of his property, lives in no security, and if oppressed, has no one to whom he can apply for justice." Langsdorff also had seen "fur hunters dispose of the lives of the natives solely according to their own arbitrary will, and put these defence- less creatures to death in the most horrible manner."[120] In a passage much resented in the empire, Sauer wrote that, "Nothing in the world can astonish a Russian more than disinterested liberality, or any kindness without some prospect of future benefit."[121] Such statements reflected the tumultuous state of the North Pacific in the last decade of unrestrained hunting, but they also used the longstanding European equation of Russia with tyranny. Russian subjects were thought to be irredeemably corrupted by their slavery under the Russian autocracy, and reduced to a state of barbarity that caused them to act like brutes. By contrast, Western Europeans, secure in their personal liberty, were free to behave rationally. As Sauer put it, while wintering on Unalaska he and the crew formed a "little republic, in perfect congeniality of sentiment...uncontrolled by severity,"[122] a model of English liberty, he hardly needed to say, which that island had never seen before.

Such notions were attributes of what some have termed "Russian Orientalism," the idea developed by Enlightenment thinkers that Russians possessed essential differences from Western Europeans. As Russians themselves often accepted such ideas and brought them home, this response has also been termed "internal colonization," after the persistent, almost desperate attempt to erase their back-wardness. These differences might stem from the tyranny thought to be endemic to Russia's political culture, or, as d'Auteroche had claimed, they might be rooted in Russia's natural world. Often, the two came together. The Billings Expedition added an intriguing outline of an environmentalist twist, whereby Russian tyr-anny degraded its own nature and undermined its own imperial interests.[123] Proof lay all around the North Pacific: in the tyrannized and tyrannical Cossack, in the cowed and declining Aleuts, and, fundamentally, in the empty coves where sea otters had once grown their luxurious pelts.

While population decline of both people and animals threatened Russia's colonial success in the North Pacific, hope lay in an enlightened new policy of naval control. Thus, in the conversation about securing Russia's North Pacific empire that followed in the wake of Cook, the members of the Billings Expedition cautioned against ceding control to private trade, in the form of either individual *promyshlenniki* or a monopoly for the Shelikhov-Golikov Company. Sarychev and Billings pointed toward a permanent naval presence as the best means of securing the North Pacific. They foresaw a North Pacific enlightened by direct government involvement and better relations with the natives.

Sauer, with his close attention to the environment, was far more pessimistic. After noting the savagery of the *promyshlenniki,* he opined that "the authority of government can never reach these distant regions," agreeing with Christian Bering that the only prospect of relief for the Aleuts was the total extermination of the sea otter, upon which the Russian hunters would leave the North Pacific.[124] Sauer even encouraged the British government to send its own fur-trading ves-sels to islands claimed by the Russians—a position of course deeply at odds with his concern for sea otter numbers.[125] Sauer's journal could only cast doubt on the legitimacy and feasibility of Russian sovereignty in the North Pacific. Such were the dangers of launching a cosmopolitan expedition to a contested region of the world.

Foreign reactions to the expedition tended to cement in European readers' minds negative characterizations of the Russian Empire. Sauer's account, which was translated into German, French, and Italian,[126] elicited the most comments. Some reviews honed in on the environmental message found in his account. London's *Monthly Review* remarked that "on account of the remoteness of these

Aleutian islands from the seat of government, this inhumanity is not likely to be checked, and will terminate only with the extirpation of the chace (sic); an event which Mr. S. considers as by no means improbable."[127] In fact, Sauer's explanation for the threat of extinction was more complex, including the vulnerability of the animal populations to the tyrannical nature of Russians, no matter how close or distant from St. Petersburg.

Colonialisms Compared

The Billings Expedition's claims that human and animal populations in the North Pacific were declining sowed seeds of doubt about the morality and effectiveness of Russian imperial expansion. The numerous reviews of Sauer's journal demonstrate that Europeans understood exactly this to be the message. Observers elsewhere had, like Billings and his crew, lamented the economic problems associated with the overexploitation of the natural world, but the Billings Expedition's assessment that environmental destruction hurt Russia's conquered subjects was subtler and more novel. The expedition members' observations of the link between animal and human population suggested that successful colonization of the North Pacific would require conservation of animal populations, and a cessation of the profitable, but heedless slaughter that had defined the *promyshlenniki*'s empire-building. As St. Petersburg and Siberian officials increasingly recognized the need to sustain native population and encourage their loyalty, a better understanding of the indigenous economy and culture was necessary.

The cosmopolitan composition of Billings's expedition explains in some part the willingness to criticize Russian empire-building in the North Pacific. The Russian Sarychev offers an interesting counterpoint. On the whole, he agreed with his foreign shipmates, while insisting on some significant qualifications. He pointed out that Sauer, when criticizing Russia, could not have been referring to the "whole Russian nation," but rather only to the hunters he encountered while on the expedition. These men, he admitted, lacked generosity and benevolence, but then again, so did the English East India Company's employees.[128] Imperial comparisons could work both ways. The *promyshlennikis'* lack of civility, their cruelty toward the natives, and their reckless killing of North Pacific animals resulted not from their Russianness, but from their social status. Sauer may not have agreed with this, but the other Englishman (Billings), probably shared Sarychev's distinction between civilized Russians and the *promyshlenniki*. His journal praises that "Liberal hospitality which forms the Characteristic of Russian Nobility."[129] Nonetheless, in private, Billings would share with his friends that, "the conduct of the Russians toward the defenseless people is so shocking that it appears almost incredible."[130] From a distance, the fine distinctions between different sorts of Russians tended to dissolve into a general condemnation of the entire nation.

Comparing the environmental critiques developed on these Russian voyages with other European concerns over depletion of fur-bearing animals, the crucial importance of Russian Orientalism becomes apparent. Since at least the 1650s, Europeans had held Native Americans responsible for declines in animal populations—an attitude still prevalent in the mid eighteenth-century. As one Jesuit remarked about the Iroquois, conservation "would be asking The Impossible from the savages."[131] Contemporaneous with the Billings Expedition, in Western Canada, where the beaver had grown scarce by the beginning of the nineteenth century, the trapper David Thompson warned that, "the avidity with which the furr-bearing animals is sought, almost threatens their extinction." Thompson laid the blame, at alternate times, on the introduction of firearms by "White People," the lack of central control among the "Natives," the stationary nature of the beaver, and the desire of the Cree to make war on the animal. Though Thompson hinted at a linkage between European imperialism and environmental change, he too tended to see the conquered subjects as authors of their own environmental downfall. In the North Pacific, the Aleuts, Alutiit, and Kamchadals in fact probably did kill the vast majority of the sea otters and fur seals. However, in the eyes of foreign observers and some enlightened Russians, Russia itself was blamed for environmental destruction, playing the role that "Natives" did in other European accounts of environmental change. Thus, Russian Orientalism inflected the environmental criticism of the Billings Expedition, lending it an anti-imperial edge that similar critiques elsewhere did not possess. [132]

Even those observers, such as the Swede Peter Kalm, who perceived a direct link between European colonization and species diminution usually presented this change as inevitable, even beneficial, and in no way an indictment of the practice. "Beavers were formerly abundant in New Sweden..." Kalm reported in 1770, "but after the Europeans came over in great number, and cultivated the country better, the beavers have been partly killed, and partly extirpated." Here, extirpation was the natural result of progress, and elsewhere Kalm blamed American environmental degradation on the "spirit of freedom which prevails in this country," hardly an indictment of American colonization (and the exact opposite of the tyranny that was thought to cause Russian environmental destruction). There was no similar sense in the North Pacific that Russians had "cultivated the country better" as recompense for species loss. In fact, Russians were consistently condemned for their inability to bring agriculture to the North Pacific, yet another sign of the inadequacy of their colonization. Russians may have been fellow colonizers, but not all colonizers were equal.[133]

This powerful reversal of roles, with Aleuts behaving nobly and Russians perpetuating savagery and tyranny, was not in itself too original, though in the charged political context of the time it was consequential. The Billings Expedition was unique in its focus on human relationships with the natural world, in particular with wild animals. Sauer, especially, judged the relative merits of each culture on its actions toward the sea otter. On one side, Aleuts used these resources wisely to produce happiness and leisure; on the other, Russians stripped the seas bare for distant commerce and immediate tyranny. That focus can be explained only by the colonial Pacific environment, in its unique array of charismatic animals, those animals' vulnerability to the hunt, and the stark visibility of their absence.

Russia, Enlightenment, and the Natural World

The problems faced by the Russian state in the wake of the English challenge to its North Pacific empire reveal some of the ways that the natural world and its study in an age of Enlightenment affected Russia's imperial ambitions. Russia acquired its North Pacific empire in an era when its most powerful competitors—France, England, and, to a lesser extent, Spain—subscribed to a set of Enlightenment notions with which Russia also aspired to identify. A junior partner in the effort to embody Enlightenment ideals, Russia was particularly vulnerable to criticism from the centers of the international intellectual culture. Philosophers and statesmen in London and Paris defined the Enlightenment, Russia attempted to meet these definitions, and often it failed. When criticism was directed at Russia's unenlightened imperial expansion, Russian statesmen felt the danger that came with being culturally dependent and militarily inferior. In the North Pacific, Russia's most exposed colonial possession, this provincial position led to real geopolitical vulnerability.

More important for the environmental history of the North Pacific, the foreigners hired to buttress Russian imperial claims brought with them the Western European values and critical stance toward Russia necessary to focus attention on the overhunting taking place in an obscure corner of the globe, thus raising international awareness of the danger of species extinction. The decline of marine mammals had been ongoing for several decades, and Europeans had possessed knowledge of it, but it took the men on the Billings Expedition to first interpret this decline as a true environmental crisis and to make some attempt to explain its causes. Historians of early modern European empires have described a close affinity between European attempts to dominate nature and to dominate foreign cultures.[134] The members of the Billings Expedition, on the other hand, used protests of environmental degradation as a criticism of Russian domination of the indigenous peoples of the North Pacific. This conjuncture points to the possibilities in the eighteenth century of using criticism of empire-building as a bridge to environmental critique.

Such new attention to the state of colonial environments in some ways paralleled contemporary developments in Britain and Europe, where the health of colonial tropical forests was of primary concern. Europeans had seen the benefits of conserving environmental resources long before the 1790s, but historians have located an important shift in thinking about the environment in Western Europe during the late eighteenth and early nineteenth centuries. Increasingly sophisticated scientific methods, exposure to a diversity of exotic flora and fauna, and the obvious destruction of forests and fisheries that accompanied European expansion throughout the world prompted scientists to formulate more ambitious conservationist measures. European writers on the natural world also began considering the aesthetic value of natural environments, and colonial administrators in the Caribbean and South Asia took concrete steps to maintain virgin forests and replant those that had been degraded.[135] In the North Pacific, extinction was added to the list of colonial environmental concerns for the first time.

The history of the Billings Expedition suggests that late-eighteenth-century changes in thinking about the natural environment had a wider geographical and intellectual pedigree. The Russian Empire also participated in the process of colonial expansion, assimilation of knowledge about distant parts of the world, and the involvement of science in empire-building, all of which seem to have been essential ingredients for paying close attention to environmental degradation. The environmental history of Russian expansion in the North Pacific was not only one of senseless slaughter and ruthless commercial exploitation by the *promyshlenniki*.[136] Rather, the Russian Empire employed disparate personnel and methods in expanding its power into the North Pacific, and not all of them unquestioningly exploited the region's environmental resources. Important actors in Russia's North Pacific expansion included sailors and scientists as well as *promyshlenniki*, and these groups had diverse goals and ideas about the North Pacific's land, animals, and people.

Though its personnel were British, German, and Italian, as well as Russian, the Billings Expedition was truly a Russian imperial phenomenon. Its cosmopolitan composition was typical of Russian imperialism in the eighteenth century—Bering was Danish, after all, and Pallas German. Finally, its critical attitude toward Russia itself was part of Russia's Enlightenment culture, and Sarychev shared many of his shipmates' concerns. The Billings Expedition possessed precisely the explosive combination of Western ideas and personnel thrust into the North Pacific's changing environment that made the Russian Empire the best place to discover extinction. Back in St. Petersburg, however, the evidence would not seem so straightforward.

Ordering Arctic Nature: Peter Simon Pallas, Thomas Pennant, and Imperial Natural History

Welshman Thomas Pennant was one of the eighteenth century's greatest natural historians, but sometimes even he succumbed to professional despair. In the 1760s, Pennant had decided to write a comprehensive zoology of North America. He assiduously cultivated contacts in the British colonies and amassed an unprecedented amount of information about animals large and small. Alas, in 1776 thirteen of those colonies declared their independence from Great Britain, and in 1783 "that fatal and humiliating hour arrived, which must strike every feeling individual at losing his little share in the boast of ruling over half of the New World."[1] Pennant decided that after the American Revolution he no longer had the right to write the zoology of North America. Instead, he had to recast the work as an Arctic zoology that would span the northern portion of the entire globe—a massive reworking of his labors which required the cultivation of many new acquaintances, including Peter Simon Pallas in Russia. Improbably, Pennant's reconceptualization would provide the crucial intellectual tools to help convince Martin Sauer that the sea cow was entirely extinct. The same intellectual trends that lay behind Pennant's reconceptualization guided Pallas's own opus, his *Zoographia Rosso-Asiatica*, and ironically caused him to miss the significance of the growing environmental crisis in the North Pacific.

The crucial conceptual category, again, was empire. Empire's dissolution caused Pennant to recast his North American zoology, and empire's glory guided Pallas's *Zoographia* in directions that did not allow for the extinction of any species under the auspices of the glorious Russian scepter. This chapter describes the divergent outcomes of Pennant's and Pallas's similar works of zoology by considering the changes that natural history was undergoing in the late eighteenth century, and the real-world consequences of the intellectual boundaries drawn through the natural world. In doing so, it reveals the roots of

Russian conceptions of extinction, many of which were tied to the supposed uniqueness of the empire. It also shows why naturalists around Europe were so slow to integrate the Russian experience into their ideas of the natural world. Taken together, the intellectual labors of Pallas and Pennant reveal the centrality of the North Pacific in changing conceptions of species extinction. As one of the European world's most contested imperial arenas at the turn of the nineteenth century, the region attracted imperial hubris and imperial despair, both of which were interwoven with its declining animal populations.

Imperial Natural History

In the second half of the eighteenth century, the study of natural history underwent a marked change, as attention shifted from geographically defined regions to units of analysis aligned with political boundaries. Since the sixteenth-century rebirth of natural history, studies had predominantly focused on exotic lands. Such works collected all the known creatures of some distant geographical region and briefly described their characteristics and economic uses. The monumental and lavishly illustrated *Histoire Naturelle des Indes* of the late sixteenth century was an outstanding example of this type. Its authorship is disputed, but it is thought that the *Histoire Naturelle* was written in French by an Englishman. It described lands mostly claimed by the Spanish state—an indication of the cosmopolitan tastes and practices of the era. Characteristically, the book ignored the question of the political character of the West Indies.[2] In the East Indies, Dutch natural historians produced works such as the *Hortus Indicus Malabaricus* (1678–1693) and the *Herbarium Amboinense* (1741–1750).[3] The purpose of such works was to satisfy Europeans' curiosity for exotica, as well as to point the way to commercial profit in distant lands. Steller's and Krasheninnikov's histories of Kamchatka also fit these parameters—describing an exotic region defined by geography—even if Krasheninnikov's *Opisanie* looked forward to a time when Kamchatka would become more Russian.

As interest in natural history grew, Europeans turned their attention to the world immediately around them, producing in many cases the first systematic studies of the flora and fauna of their home regions.[4] In 1660, John Ray, the great English systematizer of the seventeenth century, produced the *Catalogus Plantarum circa Cantabrigiam nascentium*, which described the plants of his parish of Cambridge.[5] Carl Linnaeus's first work, the *Flora Lapponica* (1737), described a colonial region within Sweden. Like the studies of large, exotic regions, these homegrown natural histories took as their subjects regions defined by geographical rather than political borders.

By the second half of the eighteenth century, European botanists and zoologists began to shift the focus of their works from description to synthesis. Building on the studies of exotic and regional plants and animals, two new directions of research opened up. The first was the possibility for grand synthesis based on information collected from around the world on one group of plants or animals. The most notable of works in this genre were several sections of Buffon's *Natural History* (1749–1788), such as "History of Animals," "Natural History of Quadrupeds," and "The Carnivores."[6] Buffon, using information mostly gathered by others, used local natural historical knowledge to speculate broadly on the relationship between humans and animals, the difference between Old World and New World environments, and the possibilities of the transmutation of species. In a similar vein, Pennant published a grand *Synopsis of Quadrupeds* in 1771, which attempted a comparison of all the world's known four-legged creatures.[7] Linnaeus, who had published a first edition of his famous *Systemae Natura* in 1735, sent his students around the world to compile the local natural histories needed to perfect his system.

Linnaeus was also at the vanguard of the second trend in European natural history in the eighteenth century: an increasing preoccupation with political space and the naturalist's obligation to serve his country. In a 1741 lecture at Uppsala University, Linnaeus expounded on this theme:

> Good God! how many, ignorant of their own country, run eagerly into foreign regions, to search out and admire whatever curiosities are to be found; many of which offer themselves to our eyes at home. I have yet beheld no foreign land, that abounds more with natural curiosities of all kinds, than our own.[8]

Natural history's cosmopolitanism had gone too far, Linnaeus declared; it was time to focus on plants and animals in one's own country. This approach would yield political and strategic benefits, he thought. The Uppsala professor engaged in several schemes to cure Sweden of its dependence on imports of exotic spices and other culinary items by trying to locate indigenous substitutes and encouraging the indigenization of South Seas plants.[9] For Linnaeus, natural history was ripe with potential to serve the state in matters of both economics and prestige.

Others followed Linnaeus's lead. In his 1768 *British Zoology*, Pennant remarked that,

> we are unwilling that our own island should remain insensible to its particular advantages; we are desirous of diverting the astonishment of our countrymen at the gifts of nature bestowed on other kingdoms, to a contemplation of those with which (at least with equal bounty) she has enriched our own.[10]

Nature's productions functioned not only as sources of commercial advantage for the country they happened to be found in, but also, as Pennant pointed out, as sources of national pride. Pennant went on to praise the richness of Britain's vegetable resources, the usefulness of its minerals, and the various natural monuments, such as the Giant's Causeway in Ireland. Such homegrown wonders should inspire British men to devote their hours to the contemplation of the empire's nature.

The link between the study of natural history and imperial rivalry was quite explicit for Pennant, who lamented the great advances Buffon and the French were making in the field. Zoology, in particularly, had helped the French discover new, useful ways of manufacturing clothing. "If we reflect but little on the unwearied diligence of our rivals the *French*," Pennant commented, "we should attend to every sister science [of Zoology] that may any ways preserve our superiority in manufactures and commerce."[11] Others around Europe in the eighteenth century perceived these same advantages to both national pride and commerce, and the century saw an increasing production of national or imperial natural histories. Pennant's *British Zoology* was accompanied by, among others, Niels Horrebow's *Natural History of Iceland* (1752), Erich Pontoppidan's *A First Natural History of Norway* (1752), Georg Christian Oeder's *Flora Danica* (1761), Nicholas von Jacquin's *Flora Austriaca* (1773–1778), and Pennant's *Indian Zoology* (1790), which described the animal resources of Britain's new colony. Each of these works took political boundaries as the outline for their field of study, with the stated aim of improving the state's knowledge of its natural resources and glorifying these resources. Some of the works were even directly funded by the state. Similar trends can be detected in the North American colonies.[12]

In Russia, the reforming state of Catherine II took up the task of national natural history with gusto. Since the reign of Peter I, Russia had devoted resources to thoroughly cataloguing the state's territorial possessions, a process that included producing accurate population figures, clarifying Russia's borders, and identifying potentially productive locations for mines, factories, and fur extraction. Under Catherine, the Academy of Sciences and the Free Economic Society launched the "Academy Expeditions," which sent professors throughout the Russian Empire, from the White Sea in the north to the far side of Lake Baikal in the east. The main goals of these expeditions were to increase the state's knowledge of its resources, and to intensify the exploitation of those resources.[13]

One part of the Academy Expeditions was led by Pallas, then a newly hired professor of natural history. As he wrote,

> The Empire wished natural science to be increased and sent out observers alone through the most desolate places.... I and others were

ordered in the year 1768 by the Divine Catherine the Great, Empress of the Russias, to produce a complete and renowned natural history...[14]

The Russian state, never content to plan on a small scale, had decided to produce not just a "national" natural history of Russia, but a natural history of the entire empire. Pallas, Samuel Gottlieb Gmelin, and Johann Peter Falck spread out through the eastern portions of the empire to fully study its flora and fauna. Fellow academicians Johann Anton Güldenstadt, Ivan Lepekhin, Johann Gottlieb Georgi, and a team of adjuncts and students handled everything from topography to political economy. The results were spectacular. As English cleric William Coxe observed, "In consequence of these expeditions, perhaps no country can boast, within the space of a few years, such a number of excellent publications on its internal state, natural productions, topography, geography, and history."[15]

Pallas had a complicated relationship with the new school of national or imperial natural history. In his 1778 *Betrachtungen über die Beschaffenheit der Gebürge* (Observations on the Nature of Mountains), Pallas took Buffon and others to task for using too small a sample when coming to large conclusions. Those philosophers had, according to Pallas, "judged the entire world based on national prejudices (*Naturalvorurtheilen*) and their own knowledge limited to the mountains of their fatherlands." Pallas, instead, preferred projects of Humboldtian scope (two decades before Alexander von Humboldt would patent the approach) that encompassed truly behemoth portions of the earth. Traveling "under the protection of our great and sublime Monarch," he wrote, "I have traversed almost the entire breadth of Asia," an opportunity for which he had to thank the "wide circumference of the Russian Empire."[16] It was a nice trick, celebrating the size of the empire while claiming a space supposedly free of the limitations of a national viewpoint. Pallas's conception of Siberia mirrored that of most imperial officials: it was both a part of Russia and yet different at the same time, its definition varying to suit the observer's needs. Such ambiguity afforded conceptual benefits for the naturalist as well.

Returning to St. Petersburg in 1774, Pallas set to work on the first major publication resulting from his and others' observations during the expeditions. He published his *Flora Rossica* between 1784 and 1788, and in the meantime began to compile the *Zoographia Rosso-Asiatica* (hereafter ZRA).[17] The ZRA was intended to describe "the natural history of the large animals, above all their habits and uses (*utilité*), the description of those which are particular to this country...in short a complete list of all of the species observed to be living in the extent of this vast Empire."[18] Work on this massive catalogue occupied Pallas throughout the last quarter of the eighteenth century and into the nineteenth. He thought the work was nearing completion as early as 1777, when he promised Thomas Pennant a copy of a "compleat Fauna of the Russian Empire," which was to be printed "within the year."[19] This proved to be a very overly optimistic estimate. Pallas still had too little information on the North Pacific's animal life to complete the sections on the empire's furthest borders. For decades, Steller's observations had remained the only scientific source on North Pacific zoology, ichthyology, and ornithology, and Pallas felt the lack of information keenly.[20]

Only when Billings and naturalist Merck returned from the North Pacific in 1793 did Pallas get new specimens and reports to incorporate into his growing list. Though by then Pallas had moved into semi-retirement in the Crimea, he fairly quickly assimilated this new information into the *ZRA*. However, further setbacks delayed its publication. In 1803, the Academy demanded that Pallas submit the first volume. Pallas asked for more time, explaining that the engravings, ordered from Leipzig, were not yet finished. He was unwilling to see the book, "which he had been working on for 36 years," go to the printer in an imperfect form.[21] The first volume was published in 1811, only after the Academy finished most of the engravings itself. Finally, Russia had its own imperial natural history. Pallas had died two years earlier.

The Zoographia Rosso-Asiatica and the "Vast Russian Empire"

Pallas's *ZRA*, an imposing, if ultimately incomplete, masterpiece, ended up being more than a compendium of animals. The book also expressed a peculiarly Russian notion of the nature of empire, and this imperial inflection guided Pallas subtly, but consequentially, toward some omissions. Much like similar works of the period, the *ZRA* aimed not just for a description of the empire's nature, but sought, through these animals, to make statements about the nature of the empire itself. In the interplay between nature and empire in the *ZRA*, the North Pacific played a large role, especially concerning the questions of the empire's diversity and emerging oceanic orientation. As such, it is a key document revealing the ways in which the North Pacific was imagined as part of the Russian Empire in the late eighteenth century.

Producing an "imperial" natural history was in some ways extremely awkward. In contrast to studies of smaller geographical regions, Pallas's *ZRA* brought together many animals that would never meet in the natural world. For instance, the common domestic dog and pestiferous rat found everywhere in European Russia, and familiar to all readers from daily experience, shared pages with the exotic Steller's Sea Eagle, a gigantic bird found only in Kamchatka and the islands of the North Pacific. Such animals had nothing in common other than being mammals, and unlike Buffon or Pennant, Pallas had little interest here in comparing mammal morphology or behavior.

Pallas's readers could gain little by considering such animals together, other than an appreciation of the amazing diversity of animal life in the Russian Empire. That, of course, was part of Pallas's goal. While d'Auteroche had criticized Russian nature for being uniform, the animals Pallas marked as "Russian" varied from the tame to the wild, the mundane to the exotic, and the boreal to the equatorial. The *ZRA* presented perhaps the greatest number—and certainly the greatest variety—of species of any of the national or imperial natural histories produced in the eighteenth century. The size of the *ZRA* reflected the size of the empire, and this correspondence was more than just coincidence. Through its heterogeneous mix of animals, Pallas's *Zoographia* portrayed for readers an empire vast in extent and diverse in economic resources, one that could take its place among the preeminent empires both past and present, and even overtake them in some important aspects.

Pallas began his *ZRA* with a description of the extent of the Russian Empire, from the cultivated heartland in the west, to the "vast Steppes" of the south, to the mountains of the east (where "almost all of Tartaria lies under Russian power"), to the icy seas of the north and the far eastern corner. Outside of the well-known European parts, the "Russian empire everywhere presents regions vast and little populated."[22] Pallas was not the only one in Russia to note the staggering extent of the empire. Russia's great size was one of Lomonosov's favorite themes,[23] and other members of the St. Petersburg Academy of Sciences wrote enthusiastically about the "vastness" of the Russian Empire.[24] According to Sauer, Russia's territorial gains were the most popular topic of conversation in St. Petersburg salons in the last decades of the eighteenth century,[25] and a host of court poets praised the motherland's vastness.[26]

The focus on the empire's size pressed home at least two points. The first was the rather desultory observation that the state's huge expanse of territory made for difficult governing. For Catherine II, size was a key argument in defense of Russian autocracy. Borrowing from the legal and climatic theories of Montesquieu, as interpreted by the Russian historian Tatishchev, she explained that, "the Extent of the Dominion requires an absolute Power to be vested in the Person who rules over it."[27] More liberal and dispersed forms of government were fine for England or Holland, but the vast Russian territory demanded a concentration of authority. A second, and more optimistic, interpretation of the empire's growing bulk was that it placed Russia on par with other European empires, both past and present. The Moscow jurist S. E. Desnitski, writing in the 1760s, proclaimed Russia's conquests greater even than those of Greece and Rome, the two classical imperial archetypes.[28] If, as many admitted, the Russian Empire lacked the mercantile success of the British Empire and the intellectual clout of the French Empire's philosophes, then it did at least impress based on its sheer size. And, as Russia advanced in the arts and sciences, these vast spaces meant that the empire could embark on a civilizing mission as grand as that of any of its predecessors or competitors. "Our great empress has still more to hope for," wrote Pallas's friend Müller. "She can give an entire quarter of the globe a new appearance."[29]

Contained in its immense terrestrial extent was an equally impressive variety of life. Academician Johann Gottlieb Georgi, who produced the anthropological counterpart to Pallas's *Zoographia,* wrote that, "There is hardly any other Empire in the world that possesses such a great variety of different nations, tribes, and colonies, as the Russian Empire."[30] The abundance and variety of the empire's human life paralleled its animal creation. In Siberia alone, wrote Pallas, "the empire is extremely vast, with great rivers flowing from the mountains of Asia toward the north … with salmon from the ocean coming up them, in great variety and great abundance."[31] The Russian Empire could boast of more of almost everything—more territory, more subject peoples, and more animals as well.

Evidence of the Russian Empire's diversity came at the beginning of each animal's description. Many of the ZRA's animals were introduced with long lists of names, both native and European. For the sea otter alone seven different names were listed, from the Russian *morskoi bobr* to the Kamchadal *kalan.* This long list compared with only four names in Pennant's *Arctic Zoology* (two borrowed from Pallas). The key name contributors were the native tribes of Eastern Siberia and even the semi-dependent Kurile Islanders were allowed to contribute their *kaiku.* As an example of the politicization of natural history, an early Latin version of Pallas's *Flora Rossica* included the Polish name *Mozdrew* for the larch, whereas a later Russian version, published when Catherine was suffering international scorn over the partition of Poland, omitted the name taken from the offending imperial possession.[32] In the hundreds of pages of the ZRA, the reader experienced the Russian Empire marching before his eyes, with distant subjects and exotic animals stretched in a seemingly never-ending parade.

Variety and abundance engendered not only imperial pride, but also a vast potential for scientific knowledge and economic growth. Lomonosov crowed, "the wealth of [Russia's] internal resources equaled that of the first European states and even exceeds many of them."[33] The Russian Empire contained peoples, plants, and animals unknown elsewhere that, with the proper scientific treatment, would add greatly to Europe's collective body of knowledge and commercial development. As Pallas had mentioned when drawing up plans for his *Flora Rossica,* by describing all of the "useful and curious plants which nature has brought forth in the vast Russian Empire," he would bring to light the "usefulness of species heretofore known too imperfectly."[34] If the Enlightenment had hitherto been only a casual visitor to Russia, nonetheless the nation's vastness promised much to the worlds of science and commerce.

Russia's men of science were especially eager to emphasize the diversity of the empire's climates and the resulting diversity of its natural products. From the deserts in the south to the temperate forests of European Russia to the frozen tundra of the north, Russia was characterized by climatic variety. Pallas and his fellow academicians stressed this diversity in various projects. In its 1777 plan for the study of the Russian Empire's geography and topography, the Academy noted that Russia "occupies a great part of two continents," a geographical uniqueness that gave it great diversity. While European Russia offered interesting material for political geography, Asiatic Russia was characterized by abundant natural riches that were still imperfectly known.[35] So, Russia could match European empires with a heartland boasting a long history of civilization, and, because of its vastness, it could also offer all the benefits associated with uncivilized lands, e.g. new herbs and medications, new animals for hunting or domesticating, and possibly precious metals.

The North Pacific in the Zoographia Rosso-Asiatica

In the ZRA, North Pacific lands and oceans played a particularly important role in establishing the Russian Empire's character. The Russian Empire's most productive maritime environment—the rocky cliffs, icy bays, and wind-tossed seas of Kamchatka and the Aleutians—provided an ideal habitat for a variety of animals which were well-protected from the cold and adapted to fish-based diets. Most of the seals and whales (and the only manatee) in the Russian Empire were found in the seas between Kamchatka and Alaska. In the *Zoographia* mammals found exclusively in the North Pacific regions made up about 10% (or, at least 12 of 151) of Pallas's total for the entire Russian Empire, a remarkably large number considering the comparative smallness of the region. An even greater percentage of Russia's birds called the North Pacific home.

The North Pacific, full of animals found nowhere else in Russia, was also the part of the empire least known to European men of science. This exotic quality—the fact that the North Pacific was one of the last major regions of the world discovered by Europeans—helps explain its prominence in Pallas's work. Transbaikalia and the Crimea, both better known to Pallas personally, were also important, but their lesser degree of ecological diversity (especially their lack of marine mammals) and their rather greater familiarity to European science, meant that they would play only supporting roles in the *ZRA*. Though he had collected most of the information for the *ZRA* during his own Siberian expedition in the 1760s and 1770s some twenty-five years previously, Pallas held up completion until he could get a fuller accounting of the North Pacific's wildlife—a mark of the region's importance to the work. Pallas gave Merck and Billings detailed instructions on specimen collection, and the two brought back many valuable specimens that are still prominent in the Academy of Science's zoography collection.[36] Though Pallas often envied Banks his superior access to rarities, on one occasion Pallas offered some North Pacific specimens to the Englishman, describing them as "some peculiarities unknown in other parts of the world & more difficult to procure, as the great distance by land and the scarcity of Collectors make them rather rare."[37] The North Pacific provided the main chance to give Pallas's *Zoographia* real luster and add to its stated goal of demonstrating the Russian Empire's great natural diversity.[38]

North Pacific fauna brought other benefits to Russia. One was the establishment of the empire's maritime credentials. Since the founding of the Russian navy by Peter the Great in the late seventeenth century, the empire had looked for access to ice-free seas. Never had the possibility of real naval power seemed as close as it did in the late eighteenth century. Russian imaginations had been fired by the first appearance of the Russian navy in the Mediterranean (1769), and the victory over the Turks in the Battle of Chesme in the Black Sea (1770).[39] Control of the Dardenelles as well as overseas colonies seemed within Russia's reach; both would enhance its status as a great European empire, and overseas maritime possessions would cast it in the mold of England or France. All these possibilities seemed to be the fulfillment of Lomonosov's 1761 prophecy of Russia's maritime destiny, which Shelikhov had adopted as his own slogan, despite its unfortunate reference to Spanish colonizers:

> The far-flung Russian state, like a whole world, is surrounded by great seas on almost every side. On all of them, we see Russian flags flying... Here new Columbuses hasten to unknown shores to add to the might and glory of Russia [etc].[40]

Lomonosov expressed poetically what others expressed more prosaically: namely, that there was a meaningful link between maritime activity, including discovery and conquest, and Russia's identity as an Enlightened European power.[41]

The recently colonized Crimea best symbolized Russia's maritime imperial optimism of the 1770s through the end of the century, and Pallas drew much of his material from the south. But, as Lomonosov reminded Russians, their nation was surrounded by great seas on all sides. The North Pacific played a crucial encircling role at the empire's eastern end. No other European nation, in fact, could claim contiguity with both the Atlantic and Pacific (though Spain did have colonies touching on the Pacific). Furthermore, while possession of the Crimea might give a nod toward the classical Greek and Roman empires, the North Pacific offered a more thoroughly maritime, and exotic, environment in which to express Russia's aspirations. Kamchatka, in particular, answered to the description of a hub for maritime activity, especially with the ice-free harbors further to the south (including the present site of the port city of Vladivostok), then still under Chinese control.

In the last years of the eighteenth century, the naval officer Johan Adam Kruzenstern—soon to become Russia's first round-the-world voyager—composed a court memorandum that reflected the desire to redefine Russia as a maritime empire. "The possession of Kamchatka and the Aleutian Islands," Kruzenstern informed the state, "perhaps has the potential to awake Russian commerce from its slumber, and to insert Russia into the politics of the trading nations of Europe."[42] He went on to recap the history of Western Europe's ascension, pointing to maritime commerce as its key component. First the Portuguese, then the Dutch and the English, had grown rich from trading across the oceans.[43] Wealth was to be found on the waves, and, with access to the Pacific, Russia could now catch up with the winners. The memorandum worked to great effect with the state, and many of his suggestions were soon acted upon. Krusenstern's vision of imperial progress—like those of many of his contemporaries—was thoroughly maritime, characteristic of this time of growing hopes and growing naval influence.

Imperial Natural History and Extinction

Pallas's orientation of the ZRA toward the definition and glorification of the Russian Empire had distinct consequences for the ways in which he and others thought about the growing scarcity of North Pacific animals, especially the sea cow and the sea otter. The effects of the imperial approach can best be seen through a comparison of the ZRA with Thomas Pennant's Arctic Zoology. Both Pennant and Pallas were writing about a part of the world that had recently seen an extinction—Steller's sea cow—and was currently experiencing a massive decline in other animal species, including sea otters. The natural histories that these men wrote shed light on the way that eighteenth-century natural historians understood or failed to understand these North Pacific extinctions, and how they addressed the question of extinction in general. In naming, categorizing, and describing these animals, Pallas and Pennant had the opportunity to inform Europeans about which North Pacific species were unique, which were threatened, and which were still prolific.

Pallas, Pennant, and other eighteenth-century natural historians faced conceptual obstacles when confronted with the possibility of extinction. Most leading writers on the natural world believed strongly in what was sometimes called "nature's economy." The term was coined in 1749 with the publication of Carl Linnaeus's "The Oeconomy of Nature." Historian Donald Worster locates the essence of Linnaeus's "Oeconomy" as a "thoroughly static portrait of the geo-biological interactions in nature." [44] Linnaeus took the hydrological cycle—the continual evaporation and precipitation of water from the oceans to the land and back—as representative of all change in nature and posited a long-term steady state, where no species grows or shrinks in number. Though animals are being killed and being born, and their numbers might fluctuate in the short term, in the long run the cycle operates at equilibrium. God had ensured this equilibrium through a fine balancing of predator and prey, and also by setting each animal in a fixed geographical location where it could flourish, but whose boundaries it could not transgress. The wonders of this "oeconomy" were seen everywhere; even rates of reproduction had been regulated so that herbivores produce excess offspring in order to feed the carnivores and sustain their own numbers at the same time. Through this conception of nature, Linnaeus was able to reconcile the visible changes taking place in the natural world with the insistence that God had created the universe in a perfect, unchanging form.

Nature's economy held clear implications for the question of extinction: namely, that it was impossible. Though numbers might wax and wane, no part of God's creation would ever vanish from the earth. This held true even in this era when, as many natural historians admitted, humans had become an exceptionally successful predators against the animal kingdom. Luckily, God had designed the world so that even humanity's ravages contributed to nature's balance. The order of nature could not be otherwise, as the entire creation was meant for humans' use. As Linnaeus put it,

> All these treasures of nature, so artfully contrived, so wonderfully propagated, so providentially supported throughout her three kingdoms, seem intended by the Creator for the sake of man. Every thing may be made subservient to his use...By the help of reason man tames the fiercest animals, pursues and catches the swiftest, nay he is able to reach even those, which lye hidden in the bottom of the sea.[45]

For Linnaeus, at least, humans were the whole reason nature's economy existed, so it would be absurd to think that they could disturb its ultimate balance.

Other natural historians were less enthusiastic about humanity's capacity for destruction. Still, most agreed that nature's reserves were deeper than humans' grasping hands could reach. Buffon, for example, lamented humans' greed and cruelty toward animals, but in the end concluded that, "we would exhaust Nature if she were not inexhaustible." He even counted human dominance—with all its brutality—as a key indicator of civilization.[46] John Bruckner, whose 1768 *Philosophical Survey of the Animal Creation* enjoyed wide popularity, worried that the progress of the human species sometimes harmed other species. He noted that the Americans, for example, in clearing forests to cultivate the land threatened ten animal species for each species of grain whose propagation they aided. Bruckner could not accept Linnaeus's easy positioning of humans at the center of creation, and he maintained that each part of nature had equal value. Fortunate, then, that humanity was incapable of destroying its fellow creation:

> It is, I say, five thousand years at least that one part of the living substance has waged continual war with the other, yet we do not find that this Law of Nature has to this day occasioned the extinction of any one species.[47]

Buffon and Bruckner were more pessimistic than most about their species' environmental behavior, but their faith in nature's self-regulation and endless bounty was typical.

Bruckner's claim that not one species in nature had gone extinct was of course false, but it points to another limitation eighteenth century natural historians faced: few, if any, had direct experience with extinction. Those extinctions that had taken place either involved species too small to take notice of, were too far in the past, or had occurred in parts of the globe too remote to impact the European consciousness. When the dodo went extinct on the island of Mauritius sometime shortly before 1700, its loss went unnoticed through the eighteenth century. In 1778, the French naturalist M. Morel reported that inhabitants of Mauritius had not seen any sign of the dodo for sixty years, though he stopped short of making a definitive statement about the bird's total extinction.[48] Other turn-of-the century French travelers to Mauritius echoed Morel's claims, some holding out hope that the dodo might yet be seen somewhere.[49] Others began to doubt it had ever existed. But the dodo, long gone, still lingered in most popular natural history books, such as Buffon's *L'Histoire des Oiseaux* and George Edward's *Gleanings of Natural History*. Edwards' book, for example, included colored plates of the dodo with no mention that the bird no longer existed.[50] Most other famous extinctions—the great auk, the Tasmanian wolf, the passenger pigeon—lay in the future. Evidence of more ancient extinctions was for the most part discounted; fossils of wooly mammoths found in Siberia were dismissed as the sad fate of elephants that strayed too far from the tropics,[51] and those of strange sea creatures found in mountain soils were considered artificially produced "wonders of nature."[52]

Still, Enlightenment natural historians sometimes found the evidence difficult to reconcile with an entirely harmonious nature. New evidence of unknown animals unearthed in Pennsylvania vexed Thomas Jefferson. When presented with news of a strange fossilized rhinoceros in Ireland, Joseph Banks admitted that it "appeared to confirm the puzzling observation that at some distant period of remote antiquity many animals were to be met with on its surface whose species are now extinct." But Banks would not be persuaded of the possibility of the accidental disappearance of species, and instead postulated that, "the Whole of existing beings had been once if not oftener swept from the Face of the Earth & a new set of beings created in their stead."[53] Even this cautious statement represented a daring intellectual risk in a science that held stability at the heart of its philosophy. More typical was Pennant's statement, when considering mammoth bones, that, "Providence maintains and continues every created species, and we have as much assurance, that no race of animals will any more cease while the Earth remaineth, than seed time and harvest, cold and heat, summer and winter, day and night."[54]

One of the few exceptions to the general belief in stability was the French naturalist Georges Cuvier. In 1796, he published an article declaring that European and Siberian fossil elephants (drawing on Pallas' publications) represented extinct species, and postulated that similar fossils found in Ohio had shared that fate.[55] Cuvier, despite the undoubted importance of his proclamation, stopped short of declaring any species contemporaneous with humans extinct. In other words, like Banks, he postulated "revolutions of nature" in prehistoric times, eras when entire assemblages of now unknown species had disappeared entirely. Cuvier made no mention of the dodo or sea cow. Additionally, he theorized that one or several global catastrophes had been responsible for the loss of former organisms. While daring, the antiquity and mode of Cuvier's extinctions did not leave humans wielding the executioner's ax, and thus did not challenge the practical import of nature's economy—that humans' activities could not so harm the natural world that they might eradicate species.[56]

The idea of nature's economy enjoyed great influence in Russia, as did Linnaeus himself (Pallas once half-jokingly referred to him as the "dictator of natural history").[57] As Pallas's antagonist in the Academy, Ivan Lepekhin, wrote in 1783,

In one word; each production of our globe, each phenomenon, if we examine it well, clearly announces the powerful hand of the Creator, who has given existence to everything and who has established an inalterable harmony in nature, for the reciprocal utility of all creatures. The celebrated naturalist Linnaeus has shown us the traces of this harmony in his different public works... above all in his work... "On the Oeconomy of Nature."[58]

While Pallas had his disagreements with Linnaeus, especially over the Swede's classification system, he was still faithful to the spirit of nature's economy. When discussing the arctic foxes found in the Aleutians, Pallas noted that, though the *promyshlenniki* slaughtered thousands every year, the animals compensated with rapid reproduction and every year recovered their numbers. In Mangazeia, in Western Siberia, up to forty thousand pelts were annually exported, and Pallas noted that the fox population had declined in the region. Pallas reasoned that their disappearance was not due to their extirpation, but must be explained by the fact that they had only been migratory visitors to Mangazeia.[59] Nature's economy, it seemed, sometimes needed help from humans' creative accounting.

One way out of the conceptual dead end of nature's economy was the emerging discipline of biogeography. It was here that the different parameters of Pennant's and Pallas's zoographies revealed their importance. While Pallas was working on the *ZRA*, he shared much of his information about North Pacific animals with Pennant. The two had met in The Hague not long before Pallas's departure for Russia, and they frequently exchanged information and books on natural history.[60] As part of Russia's policy of increased openness after Cook's voyage to the North Pacific, Pallas sent a great deal of his collected information on the region's animal life to Pennant. With Pallas's help, Pennant was able to embark on a project as monumental as his *Arctic Zoology*, which described animals found in northern latitudes, from his native Britain to Greenland and boreal North America (see Figure 5.1).

In many ways the *Arctic Zoology* resembled the *ZRA*. The two men described many of the same animals, and mostly gave them the same scientific names. But, despite the similarities in subject matter, Pennant and Pallas diverged greatly in the ways they presented North Pacific nature. While Pallas was concerned with the animal life of a political empire, Pennant described the region as defined by science. As indicated by its title, the *Arctic Zoology* took not an imperial or national space to define its purview, but rather a space determined by geographical location. Ironically Pennant, like Pallas, had initially conceptualized his study as another imperial zoology. In the third volume of the *Arctic Zoology*, Pennant explained that he had begun his work as a "sketch of the Zoology of North America."[61] He continued, "I thought I had a right to the attempt, at a time I had the honor of calling myself a fellow-subject with that respectable part of our former great empire." After the American Revolution, Pennant lamented that he "could no longer support my clame (sic) of entitling myself its humble Zoologist; yet, unwilling to fling away all my labours, do now deliver them to the Public under the title of the ARCTIC ZOOLOGY."[62] Just as he had with his earlier *British Zoology*, Pennant had felt entitled to write the zoology of North America as long as the region had an imperial identity which he also shared. Now, the "humble Zoologist," committed to the benefits of a nation reading about its

Figure 5.1 Frontispiece to Pennant's *Arctic Zoology*. A fox and a two birds of prey prepare to do battle under a dramatic sky.

own natural world, could find no meaning in a book about North American animals. This remarkable conception—that animals should be described only by a scientist who shared with them a political identity—made little sense outside the parameters of late-eighteenth-century natural history.

In order to publish the result of his many labors without transgressing such principles, Pennant had to invent a space unassociated with any political power. To do this, he drew a line at a latitude of 60 degrees north and extended his study around the entire globe to encompass other northern lands. By cutting across multiple empires, Pennant could imagine a coherent space that possessed no national or imperial character. For the most part, the Arctic's human inhabitants were nomadic peoples who had long roamed the icy tundra. These peoples had the great advantage for Pennant of possessing nothing that Europeans would recognize as state formations. The land they inhabited, therefore, seemed open to anyone—either to possess later or to study now. If there were imperial claims to some Arctic regions, nonetheless enough flexibility remained that European natural historians could still characterize the territory as open and natural. Pennant could claim to possess the authority to write a natural history of this region.

Pennant called the region above 60 degrees the "Arctic." The latitudinal divide served more as a guideline than a rigorous parameter for deciding which animals to include in the *Arctic Zoology*. If any examples of an animal species had been found above 60 degrees, then its entire range and history were included in the study. Essentially, any northern cold-weather animal merited inclusion in Pennant's zoology, so in practice the area of study extended well to the south of 60 degrees, a practical consequence of the earlier scope of the project. Still, there was a great deal of climatic homogeneity in Pennant's work, especially in comparison with Pallas's ZRA.

Though he had stumbled upon his geographical focus, Pennant gained much from his non-imperial approach. The *Arctic Zoology* became one of the first representatives of an emerging biogeographical orientation in natural history that focused on distinct environments.[63] Biogeography—the study of the geographical distribution of living organisms—was still in its infancy in the late eighteenth century, but several new works had begun to draw Europe's attention to its importance. The outstanding example of eighteenth-century biogeography was Eberhard Zimmermann's *Geographische Geschichte des Menschen und der vierfüssigen Thiere* (Geographical History of Man and the Quadrupeds), which appeared between 1778 and 1783. Zimmermann drew natural historians' attention to the usefulness of a rigorous accounting of the present distribution of species.[64] Of particular interest was Zimmermann's attempt to construct a worldwide map of species distribution, which gained wide praise among natural historians. Pennant called it "a most curious map . . . in which is given the name of every animal in its proper climate; so that a view of the whole Quadruped creation is placed before one's eyes, in a manner perfectly new and instructive."[65]

Biogeography was destined to be the crucial conceptual step needed to formulate a coherent theory of evolution. Both Charles Darwin and Alfred Russel Wallace later turned to species mutation to explain seemingly incomprehensible species distributions in the tropics.[66] More immediately, in the eighteenth century, biogeography enabled natural historians to recognize the profound relationship between species and environment. Earlier attempts to explain distribution based on lines of migration from a common source, or global, imprecise associations of latitude and species were replaced with more sophisticated explanations of the ways that climate and terrain determined which species were found where. Natural historians had gained the sense that discrete regions of the world contained discrete fauna, and that the naturalist would have to look at the ecological relationships of a species in order to determine where it could survive.

Pennant's regional—as opposed to imperial—focus allowed him to make statements about species distribution far more easily than Pallas. The *ZRA*'s animals did not possess any inherent relationship with the Russian Empire, while many of Pennant's animals flourished in the Arctic and nowhere else. Pennant could analyze his animals, consider their relationship to cold climes, and speculate about their possible range and former distribution. As an example, he remarked that the reindeer was found only in the coldest parts of the Arctic and mused that its range might once have extended to Iceland and Newfoundland, where very cold temperatures were also to be found.[67] Even if his speculations were sometimes off the mark, Pennant's methodology encouraged theorizing and prompted him to carefully delineate the limits of each of his animal's ranges.

Pennant's engagement with biogeography yielded important insights for the history of the North Pacific. In his description of the sea otter, Pennant first cleared up a misconception common in the eighteenth century: namely, that the North Pacific sea otter was the same species as the river otter in Brazil. Pennant admitted that he had made the same mistake in his earlier *Synopsis of Quadrupeds*. Now, with new confidence in the uniqueness of the sea otter Steller first described, Pennant outlined the animal's range:

> These are the most local animals of any we are acquainted with, being entirely confined between lat. 49 and 60, and west longitude 126 to 150 east from *London*, on the coast and seas on the north-east parts of *America*; and again only between the *Kamtschatkan* shores and the isles which intervene between them and *America*. They land also on the *Kuril* islands, but never are seen in the channel between the north-east part of *Sibiria* and *America*.[68]

While Pennant's geography of the sea otter functioned as a hunting manual for would-be British fur-traders, it also constituted the most complete and accurate accounting of the animal's distribution published in the eighteenth century. In addition, it prompted the reader to consider the relative scarcity of this very "local" animal.

One of Pennant's readers was Martin Sauer. The *Arctic Zoology*'s first volume was printed in 1782, a few years before Sauer left England for Russia, and passages from Sauer's journal indicate he knew the book's contents.[69] In one of his strongest statements about the danger the sea otter was in, he seems to have quoted, nearly word for word, parts of Pennant's entry for the animal:

> There are no more [sea otters] on the coast of Kamtshatka; they are very seldom seen on the Aleutian islands; of late, they have forsaken the Shumagins; and I am inclined to think, from the value of the skin having caused such devastation among them, and the pursuit after them having been so keen, added to their local situation between the latitudes of 45 and 60, that fifteen years hence there will hardly exist any more of this species.[70]

Sauer amended Pennant's estimation that the sea otter ranged down to 49 degrees north latitude, around Vancouver Island. Working with information likely gleaned from later fur traders working the Northwest Coast, and possibly reflecting firsthand conversations with *promyshlenniki* in Kamchatka and the Aleutians, Sauer expanded the sea otter's southern limit to 45 degrees, around the present-day latitude of Portland, Oregon. In fact, Sauer's latitude was also too far north. In the eighteenth century the sea otter inhabited land as far south as 22 degrees latitude, near the southern tip of the Baja peninsula, but British and Russian fur traders had as yet had no experience with the California sea otter populations. Pennant himself had been a little uncertain of where to mark the sea otter's southern extent. In the *Arctic Zoology*'s first edition, he placed the animal at 44 degrees north latitude, based on a conversation he had had with an unspecified member of Cook's third voyage crew. As the official account of Cook's voyage later stated that sea otters were first seen in Nootka Sound, at 49 degrees, Pennant wrote in his introduction that this should now be considered the southern boundary.[71] Cook's official account likely deliberately misled readers about the sea otter's distribution in order to keep potential hunting grounds secret. Sauer left Pennant's northern boundary intact, as the sea otter did not inhabit the seas further north than about 60 degrees, just south of present-day Anchorage, Alaska.

Whatever the exact extent of the sea otter's range, Sauer's reference to the sea otter's local situation clearly marked Pennant as his source. Pennant's claim that the sea otter was the "most local" of any animals dealt with in the *Arctic Zoology* impressed Sauer with the fact that the animal suffered an especially great risk of extirpation, and was the crucial conceptual link that allowed him to expand his concern with the sea otter from commercial distress to outright extinction. Others on the Billings Expedition lamented the sea otter's decline, but none save Sauer saw in its overexploitation the possibility of total disappearance. The importance of biogeographical conceptions stands out clearly in comparison to Steller's musings fifty years earlier. When encountering fur seals, sea otters, and sea cows, Steller operated on the assumption that these species were mere northern analogs of animals found around the world. Steller assumed his sea cow must have been the same as the one that William Dampier had seen in the Caribbean, and that the sea otter was probably of a species with a Brazilian river otter.[72] Biogeography for Steller (as for Linnaeus and many others at the time) meant that like species would be found at similar latitudes north and south. Pennant's and Zimmermann's conceptions, on the other hand, pointed out the bounded nature of species' ranges and was one of the keys to conceptualizing extinction.

Pennant's *Arctic Zoology* also helped Sauer conceive of the sea cow's total extinction. Sauer's mention of the death of the last sea cow occurred immediately after his prediction for sea otter extinction. Using the same biogeographical logic, and the fur traders' reports that they no longer saw sea cows, Sauer deduced that the animal was entirely gone. There were no analogs in the Caribbean. In this way, one could say that the American Revolution—by forcing Pennant to reconfigure his *Arctic Zoology*—led indirectly to the discovery of extinction.

While observers had long commented on the decline of certain animals, they had lacked a global view of species distribution. If an animal disappeared in one place, it seemed likely that it had merely migrated somewhere else, or that it still existed in a more distant corner of the globe. Now, the Linnaean scheme for dividing the natural world into discrete species had led natural historians to develop comprehensive and usable lists of species proper to different regions of the world, even if Linnaeus himself had remained wedded to older biogeographical notions. The growing sophistication of biogeography led men of science in the late eighteenth century to begin to gauge the relative abundance of these species and to connect the idea of local extirpation with the eradication of an entire unit of nature. Above all, those who understood biogeography realized the finitude of animal distribution. Animals could not flee indefinitely, for climatic and topographical barriers barred their escape. Given that biogeographers recognized that each region in the world contained animals found nowhere else, local extinction often meant total extinction.

In Sauer's journey through the North Pacific, with Pennant's *Arctic Zoology* in hand or mind, the intellectual development of European natural history met for the first time a species truly in danger of extinction. Sauer was the first to announce the sea cow's extinction to Europe, and he was the first to recognize that the sea otter faced the same danger. Although the trend of sea otter depletion had been clear for at least a decade, and the extinction of the sea cow should have served as a warning, it was only in the conjunction of Sauer's avid reading and Pennant's cosmopolitan biogeography that Europe learned the full scope of the destruction the North Pacific fur trade was causing.

The importance of Pennant's cosmopolitan approach to natural history becomes apparent when Pallas's contributions to biogeography are considered. Pallas, too, participated in the late- eighteenth-century study in the global distribution of animal and plant species. His *Zoographia Rosso-Asiatica* began the description of nearly every animal with an enumeration of its range within the Russian Empire. About the walrus (see Figure 5.2), for example, he wrote that,

> These beasts are frequently found in the Arctic Ocean, along the northern shores of all of Asia, and in Europe in places where ice flows, and in the islands and promontories most toward the East, where they swim gregariously. They are copious on the Island Novaja Zemlya, and on the shores of the far corner of Eastern Siberia, and especially in bad weather they haul out onto the land in great herds...and in autumn they celebrate their union...[73]

Not only did Pallas list all the known areas of the Russian Empire where the walrus is found, but he also described its preferred habitats and seasonal migrations. If Pallas himself did not comment on the relationship between the walrus and its habitat, his description included all the information necessary for a biogeographer to map out the animal's Russian distribution.

Pallas was one of the early theorizers in the field of plant biogeography. During his journey through Siberia, Pallas noted several profound and sudden changes in plant species east of the Yenisei River. Though the climate of the region was fairly uniform, Pallas noted that the topography was extremely variable, and the character of the land seemed to determine its flora.[74] Though Pallas's work was less then systematic, it represented an early, serious attempt to map species distribution onto something more sophisticated than climate or latitude. Along with the work of the Forsters in the South Pacific and Ramond de Carbonnière's studies of the vegetation of the Pyrenees, Pallas's work was some of the first to extend analysis to the "physical principles underlying the differing distribution of plant groups."[75]

Recognizing Pallas's commitment to biogeography serves to highlight his failure to note the limited distribution of the sea otter. Such recognition would have led him and others interested in Russia's North Pacific Empire to doubt the sea otter hunt's continued profitability, and possibly fear for the animal's ultimate survival. But Pallas's biogeography remained constricted to the confines of

Pall. Zoogr. 1. p. 268.

Rosmarus arcticus. Pall.

Figure 5.2 The ZRA's depiction of the walrus, a species found in both the Russian Arctic and the North Pacific. *Zoographia Rosso-Asiatica*, v. III, p 628.

the Russian Empire, and his choice of geographical parameters shrank his field of vision. While he achieved brilliant insight in his study of plants distributed through the Russian Empire, other life forms escaped Pallas's analysis. Because the sea otter (and many other animals) inhabited lands and seas that traversed imperial claims, they could not be comprehended by an imperial natural history.

Truly comprehensive biogeography, in fact, constituted a blind spot for imperial natural history. Imperial natural history focused its lens both too widely and too narrowly to catch some of the salient features of the plants and animals it pretended to contain. By including so many animal species, in its celebration of size and diversity Pallas's ZRA lost the focus on a cohesive region that Pennant had (inadvertently) captured, thereby ignoring some of the links between species and environment. Because the Russian empire was so big, it could not be only "arctic" or "desert." There was no sense of an animal population unique to Russia. On the other hand, by drawing its borders in the middle of some species' ranges, the ZRA's focus was too narrow to fully describe the empire's animals. When animals strayed outside the Empire, that part of their lives did not come under the ZRA's consideration.

The imperial blind spot was more than just an intellectual shortcoming that might reduce the scientific value of natural histories written in this style. Because the eighteenth-century natural historian functioned as synthesizer and disseminator of knowledge useful for national commerce, misunderstandings of the importance of geographical distribution had economic and political consequences. The decline in sea otter numbers would have a profound impact on Russia's imperial aspirations in the North Pacific; the animal's disappearance drew Russian hunters further eastwards, but once the animals were commercially extinct in the Aleutians and Southeastern Alaska, there were no further unoccupied hunting grounds to tap, nor were there other populations that could be used to restock. A note of caution from the great encylopedist of Russia's fauna, or at least a recognition of the sea otter's precarious existence, might have alerted imperial administrators and Far Eastern fur barons that the object of the hunt was not inexhaustible. This is, in fact, what the less influential Sauer and Merck had done.

Instead, Pallas remained one of the staunchest doubters of the sea otter's decline, and his geographical focus likely played a role in his shortsightedness. Pallas initially dismissed hunters' reports of growing scarcity as a product of their ignorance and disinformation. Later, he admitted that "it is said that [sea otters] are becoming somewhat scarce [in the Aleutians]," but he explained the scarcity by mentioning that the animals "are beginning to frequent Kadiak, seldom visited by the Russians, in correspondingly greater numbers."[76] Both arguments—that hunters could not be trusted concerning the abundance of commercial species, and that decline in animal numbers was a sign merely that they had migrated away from humans—had long found favor with natural historians, and it is understandable that Pallas should have fallen back on them when confronted with the unexpected news of the sea otter's decline. However, armed with a fuller understanding of the sea otter's biogeography—as Pennant was— Pallas could have seen his way through to the realization of the animal's precarious position.

Pallas's ZRA, conceived as a glorification of the Russian Empire's size, diversity, and commercial and scientific potential, left serious lacunae in its descriptions of the empire's animals. The whole concept of imperial and national natural histories, by drawing political lines through animal populations that recognized only geophysical and climactic borders, was destined to miss important aspects of these animals' biogeography. Yet imperial and national boundaries were such dominant ways of organizing knowledge of the natural world in the late eighteenth century that it took the dissolution of the British Empire in North America for a zoology to appear that could capture the perilous state of the North Pacific's animal life. Grand syntheses of zoographical knowledge, like Zimmermann's exemplary works, did exist, but their wide, theoretical focus did not capture the dynamic reality in the North Pacific. Even Pennant, at home lamenting the loss of North America while writing an innovative natural history, missed the reality of extinction. It was only when Pennant was read by Sauer, who saw firsthand the animal's decline, that eighteenth-century natural history managed to describe and predict the threat of the sea otter's extirpation.

Perhaps the most poignant example of the shortcomings of imperial natural history, however, was Pallas's failure to mention the extinction of Steller's sea cow. Inclusion of this event in the ZRA might have guaranteed Pallas a legacy of rare farsightedness among early modern natural historians. Pallas, in fact, had made one of the key contributions to understanding the animal's extinction by classifying Steller's sea cow as a unique species. Extinction, after all, would not have been an issue if the animal roamed the coastal seas worldwide. Steller himself had confounded the sea cow with other manatees found around the world.[77] Pennant had made this same mistake. In the *Arctic Zoology*, Steller's *vaca marina* appears as the "White-Tailed Manati." Although he noted that the genus was not found anywhere else in the Northern Hemisphere, Pennant was convinced that the manatee found in the Arctic was the same species as that about which Joseph Banks had collected accounts from the South Indian Ocean island of Diego Rodriguez.

Pallas took a more reasonable stance on the issue. In his introduction to the *Manatus Borealis* or northern sea cow (see Figure 5.3), he emphasized that this was an entirely different species from any other previously described:

> This sea beast frequents the Eastern Ocean from the Islands between Asia and Eastern America to the American Coast (but not the Asian), but the Manatee on the Eastern coast of America is a very different species, and our species is only known from the labors of the immortal Steller, who produced a picture of it and described its nature, structure, and habits.[78]

Pallas acknowledged that other natural historians (in particular Buffon) had recently produced descriptions of manatees and often lumped Steller's sea cow in with them, but he declared that they were not all the same species. In short, Pallas was well aware that the *Manatus Borealis* was a unique species, and that local extirpation in the North Pacific would be tantamount to its permanent extinction.

By the time Pallas had finished with the ZRA, ample evidence of the extinction was available. The nineteenth-century naturalist Leonhard Stejneger speculated, credibly, that Pallas actually gave Sauer, with whom he was acquainted, special instructions to determine whether the sea cow was still extant.[79] Other early-nineteenth-century scientific travelers to the North Pacific read Sauer's

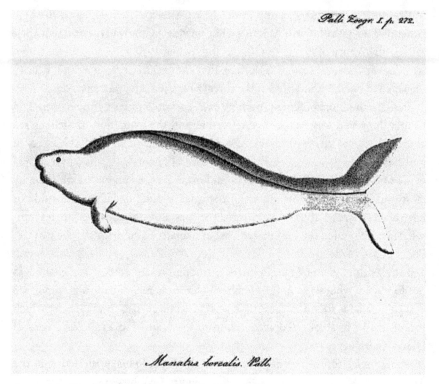

Pall. Zoogr. I. p. 272.

Manatus borealis. Pall.

Figure 5.3 Sketch of a sea cow published in *Zoographia Rosso-Asiatica*, Volume III, p 630.

journal and understood its importance. On Russia's first round-the-world voyage (1803–1807), the German naturalist Georg Heinrich von Langsdorff wrote:

> My greatest curiosity was particularly directed to the *trichecus mana-tus Stelleri*, or Steller's sea cow. This noteworthy animal, of which we first received an account from this worthy man of science [*verdienst-volle Gelehrte*], and which in former times abounded upon the coast of Kamchatka and upon Bering's Island and other islands of this sea, was at one time the preferred food of the Russian fur hunters. (Sauer says on page 185 of the German translation of his journal that in 1768 the last of these animals was killed and had not been seen in this region again.)[80]

Langsdorff agreed with Sauer that "though known to be in existence not more than forty years ago, [the sea cow] must now be ranked among the list of beings lost from the animal kingdom, like the dudu, the mammoth, the carnivorous elephant of the Ohio and others." Langsdorff's remarkable statement was the most complete account of anthropogenic extinction in European literature up to this point. His views were far more radical than Cuvier's. Pallas organized the results of Langsdorff's voyage[81] and thus would have had at least two definitive accounts of the sea cow's extinction, as well as Cuvier's writings.

Yet Pallas remained silent on the sea cow's extinction. Perhaps in his old age he had become too tired to touch on controversial scholarly issues. Perhaps, in the face of the evidence, he still could not believe that nature's economy would permit the loss of any link in the chain of being. Or perhaps in publishing a book on the abundance and variety of Russian nature, a book that was meant to augment the Russian Empire's glory, there was no place for an empty space where Steller's sea cow was supposed to be. In the half-century environmental history of the North Pacific, it would certainly not have been the first time that questions of empire had imposed upon the empire of nature. Only later in the nineteenth century, when Russians themselves substantially changed their ideas of empire, would extinction become part of the scientific culture.

Empire of Order

Yuri Lisiansky may have been the first European since Steller to be emotionally affected by the plight of the sea otter. Lisiansky, who sailed with Krusenstern on his round-the-world voyage, observed the sea-otter hunt in Russian America in 1804. By this time the hunt had moved away from the Aleutians and Kodiak Island to Southeast Alaska, but native laborers still did most of the hunting, traveling long distances to the less-exploited hunting grounds. "When these hunters attack a female otter, swimming with her young one" Lisiansky wrote,

> a picture of maternal affection presents itself, that would induce a feeling mind to desist from its cruel purpose; but a Cadiack man, hardened to his trade, has no frailties of this kind, and can pass nothing without darting his arrows in it. When she finds herself pursued, the poor mother takes her cub in her arms, if I may so speak, and plunges with it, to save it.[1]

Lisiansky was a man of sentiment; his rapturous descriptions of the views from atop Alaskan mountains made him one of the first to describe the North Pacific in a Romantic manner.[2] He approached marine mammals in the same way, focusing on his emotional responses to their suffering. Characteristically, Lisiansky also blamed the "Cadiack" men instead of Russian hunters for the animals' destruction.

Both of Lisiansky's reactions—pity and accusation—signified the new directions Russian environmental policies and perceptions in the North Pacific would take in the nineteenth century. Beginning with the Krusenstern Expedition (1803–1806), rising concern for the emotional plight of sea otters and fur seals paired with fears over the empire's future prosperity and international reputation to forge new ideas about managing the North Pacific. In 1805, the newly formed Russian-American Company (RAC) instituted conservation measures for fur seals, and a decade later began protecting sea otters as well. While the measures began in a piecemeal fashion and enjoyed mixed success, by the 1840s they were some of the most progressive anywhere in the colonial world. Increasingly confident about their Pacific empire, Russians reversed their eighteenth-century focus on environmental mismanagement and looked to lay blame elsewhere for the declines that had taken place, and in some places continued to plague the North Pacific. First, they targeted the Aleuts, then American and British fur traders. Yet other, unforeseen problems cropped up. In the 1860s, the question of environmental justice threatened the continuation of the Company's monopoly, and the troublesome question of the sea cow's extinction was reopened.

Naturalists, despite a growing presence in the North Pacific, played a minimal direct role in the implementation of colonial conservation. In the nineteenth century, numerous Russian voyages of exploration criss-crossed the Pacific, carrying with them a host of naturalists, ship-captains, and philosophers interested in the natural world, who brought with them Romantic ideas that elsewhere in Europe strengthened criticisms of empire. However, few of these men provided the trenchant commentary that Steller and Sauer had. Instead, the Russian Orthodox priest Ivan Veniaminov may have had the largest role in influencing the Russian-American Company on methods of conserving animals. Colonial officials and Aleut hunters, too, contributed both important ideas and necessary manpower to conservation efforts. All these members of the Russian Empire, however, took from naturalists the essential conceptual pairing of empire and extinction—the idea that care for the natural world marked enlightened colonial governance. The timing of North Pacific conservation was no accident. It directly folllowed the bitter criticism delivered by the Billings Expedition, criticism that was sharpened by Lisiansky and other members of the Krusenstern Expedition at the turn of the century. Colonial administrators co-opted the language and concerns of critical naturalists, and their subsequent attention to environmental problems neutralized the latters' concerns. Indeed, naturalists almost unanimously approved of the nineteenth-century RAC's conservation measures, taking it as evidence of progressive Russian imperialism. However, as Lisiansky's concerns showed, this "empire of order" could also be used to justify continued exploitation of the North Pacific's indigenous peoples. As Russians prepared to sell Alaska to the United States in 1867, the relationship between empire and extinction remained fraught with contradictions, as well as marked by productive intellectual tensions.

Circumnavigation, Empire, and Animals

The Krusenstern Expedition, Russia's first round-the-world voyage, inaugurated new maritime links between St. Petersburg and Alaska and signaled a shift in perceptions and presentations of the North Pacific colonies. In 1799, despite the protests of members of the Billings Expedition, St. Petersburg granted merchant Grigorii Shelikhov a monopoly over the North Pacific fur trade. His Russian-American Company, under several different imperial charters, would retain its privileges until the sale of Alaska. Johann Adam Krusenstern, a Baltic German, was chosen along with Lisiansky to lead a voyage intended to provide supplies to the new government-chartered company and to attempt to open trade relations with Japan (the longstanding desire of those interested in the North Pacific). The influential courtier Count Nikolai Rezanov sailed as supernumerary, with authority whose vagueness would bedevil the expedition. Krusenstern actually ended up with two natural historians, both Germans who made enormous personal efforts to secure passage. Johann Tilesius von Tillenau was studying in Leipzig when he read in the newspapers about the proposed voyage and immediately dashed off a letter to Krusenstern, begging to be admitted to the expedition.[3] After Tilesius was accepted on the voyage, University of Göttingen (then a major center of European natural history) graduate Georg Heinrich von Langsdorff was turned down, but he traveled at his own cost to Copenhagen to intercept the ships and was finally allowed on board.[4] Additionally, Swiss astronomer Johann Kaspar Horner, another Göttingen student, sailed as astronomer.[5] German enthusiasm for Russian voyages had not cooled since Steller's days, and naturalists on Russian expeditions had become even better connected with the main currents of European intellectual life.

Great pomp and ceremony accompanied the two ships of the expedition, whose members were repeatedly reminded that they were officially the first Russians to cross the equator, pass the Cape of Good Hope and Cape Horn, and circumnavigate the globe. As the ships passed the equator, the imperial flag was raised, guns were discharged, and everyone joined in a rendition of "Success to the Russian Flag."[6] Krusenstern, keenly aware of the damaging reports like Sauer's then appearing in the foreign presses, wrote at the beginning of the voyage that he felt an enormous pressure to see the circumnavigation succeed, for "Those who delight in censuring and vilifying Russia would have triumphed over an unfortunate event." [7] In fact, the voyage did suffer a great deal of bungling, strife, and absurdist comedy, some of which Krusenstern experienced directly. While in Kamchatka, Rezanov attempted (unsuccessfully) to have Krusenstern removed from command and had another member of the expedition, Fedor Tolstoi, sent home. Lisiansky's ship did provide crucial firepower in helping the RAC retake the new Russian fortress of New Archangelsk (today Sitka) from the native Tlingits, but the attempt to open up trade with the Japanese was spectacularly unsuccessful. To crown the tragedy, one expedition member committed suicide on the return voyage.[8]

The natural-historical results of the expedition also brought some disappointment. Tilesius, in particular, found it extremely difficult to work his observations

into publishable form, in part because of the immense labors involved in helping to edit Pallas's *Zoographia*. His marriage and divorce from a St. Petersburg
girl (he should have kept Steller's experience in mind) also delayed matters.
Krusenstern had hoped that Tilesius would illustrate the commander's account
of his voyage, but after several years of footdragging, the wait became intolerable.
The German critic and prominent naturalist Lorenz Oken publicly questioned
both Tilesius's industry and his competence, claiming that, "this well-traveled
man has the strange habit of describing everything only halfway and piecemeal (*stückweise*)."[9] Tilesius would never complete the captions, much to
Krusenstern's and many others' disappointment. Negligence like this tarnished
the Academy of Science's reputation, but overall the Krusenstern expedition still
counted as an international sensation.

Nonetheless, problems ran deeper than onboard strife and occasional
incompetence. Given the history of past expeditions, criticism came, predict-
ably, from inside. A Russian officer, Gavriil Davydov, reported the enslaved
Alutiit's "hatred of the Russians," while also describing the detailed environmental knowledge of the natives and the appalling lack of curiosity among the
promyshlenniki. He bemoaned the declining profit gained from the Aleutian
posts and painted a startling picture of rippling sea-otter extirpation following Russian advances from Kamchatka to Sitka. Some of this criticism sprang
from Davydov's full-blown Romanticism, present only sporadically on earlier
Russian voyages. In Kodiak, Davydov wandered through the mountains on
Kodiak Island, staring out at the open ocean and musing on human loneliness
and the sublime effects which wilderness produced on the soul. The Romantic
stress on freedom also strengthened his identification with the subjugated
Alaskan natives.[10]

Langsdorff, who wrote the most complete reckoning of the sea cow's extinction, also included an attack on the barbarity of Russian traders that strongly
echoed those of Sauer, Billings, and other predecessors. According to Langsdorff,
the tyrannous *promyshlenniki* were too short-sighted to see that their overhar-
vesting of sea otters would soon bring an end to the trade that was making them
rich.[11] As he wrote to Krusenstern in an apocalyptic vein, "now there are no sea
otters, and almost no one left to kill them. Sitka is certainly the most miserable
place in the world."[12] In the self-confident style of the German natural historian,
Langsdorff felt, with the application of a little science (lacking in the Russians),
he could make everything better. Kamchatka, which had grown "close to [his]
heart," would flourish with more intensive potato cultivation and the introduction of reindeer breeding.[13] Conscious of a long tradition of improvement literature on Kamchatka, Langsdorff could only wonder that "Seventy years ago, the
excellent Steller wished to turn the attention of his countrymen to this subject,
but it remains in just the same state as at that time."[14]

Shortly after the voyage, Langsdorff submitted to the state a long memorandum on Kamchatka outlining its environmental problems, and some potential solutions. The ecological component of Russian colonization in Kamchatka resembled that in the Aleutians. Like Aleuts, Kamchadals were required to spend much of their time collecting food for their Russian conquerors. Compared to the Kamchadals' pre-contact state, which consisted of hunting bears, seals, wild sheep, and reindeer, "the abundance of which provided them with clothing and healthy food," life had become "very depressing." [15] Langsdorff mixed a celebration of primitivism with a concern that declining access to the natural world threatened to undermine that happy state. His prescriptions showed a growing faith in the power of natural history. To better exploit the peninsula's natural abundance, a full-time naturalist should be stationed there in order to identify useful medicinal plants. This expert could also research new animals to be hunted (Langsdorff suggested that the Kamchadals kill more puffins for food), help the Kamchadals construct better canoes in imitation of the Aleuts, and brew spirits and vinegar. Langsdorff also dragged out, one more time, the old hopes for a whale fishery for export to China.[16]

Naturalists had grown more influential by the time Langsdorff wrote his critique. Largely ornaments of the court in the middle of the eighteenth century, after Pallas foreign-born technocrats enjoyed ready access to the levers of power. Langsdorff's most important contact was N. P. Rumiantsev, the Minister of Commerce. While still in Siberia, Langsdorff sent Rumiantsev a copy of his plan for Kamchatka, requesting that it be forwarded to the emperor, Alexander I. At nearly the same time, the returning naturalist met the current Siberian governor, I. B. Pestel, who also took an interest in his plan, promising to withdraw soldiers from Kamchatka, per Langsdorff's prescription.[17] There was even talk of sending Langsdorff to Kamchatka as governor, along with a suite of "German scientists and craftsmen."[18] Langsdorff never returned to Kamchatka, but new settlers outfitted with seeds and cattle were eventually sent. A surgeon was even ordered to Kamchatka, though mostly to try to cure the rampant syphilis, rather than conduct botanical research. Though this was not exactly Langsdorff's plan, elements of it were visible. Like most such ideas in the North Pacific, its implementation proved far more difficult than its conception. The new settlers immediately sold their animals, began stealing from the Kamchadals, and, like all others before them, gave up agriculture in favor of fishing.[19]

Langsdorff's critical, reformist writings about the North Pacific did not go unchallenged. Characteristic of the chaotic, argumentative Krusenstern voyage, a chorus of Russian voices tried to shout down Langsdorff's criticisms. Lisiansky's account of the voyage directly questioned the German's command of the Russian language, his observational abilities, and even his truthfulness.[20] One of the most interesting defenses of the Russian Empire's civility focused, *à la* d'Auteroche, on the quality of the environment. Unlike nearly every other European at the time, Fedor Shemelin, who sailed as the RAC's representative, found that North Pacific nature was far superior to that of the tropical Pacific.[21] "Besides a lot of mice," Shemelin wrote, the South Pacific Islanders

> ...don't have any animals whose skin would be worth even a kopek... and while they may eat pigs on holidays, the rest of the time they feed themselves on seeds, mollusks, and fish. And the fish are not even the tasty kind; just bonitos, mackerel, etc.

In Alaska, on the other hand, there was an "amazing abundance" of salmon, which, according to Shemelin, were far tastier than the tropical fish he mentioned. Sea otters and sea lions abounded too, providing useful material for boat-building and making a nice meal in a pinch.[22] Shemelin's sardonic statement reversed the common opposition between abundant tropical nature and the dismal North Pacific articulated by Cook, Pennant, and many others. It also revived the trope of animal abundance threatened under the scrutiny of Russophobic natural historians.

Several historians have identified this first Russian circumnavigation as a turning point for Russian cultures of exploration and science, abandoning Siberia as Alaska's main point of reference and entrenching a more competent image of Russia in European minds.[23] In fact, the Billings Expedition had already initiated these processes a decade earlier, due in part to its cosmopolitan crew and the wide dissemination of its results throughout Europe. However, from an environmental standpoint, the Krusenstern expedition does stand out. Despite Langsdorff's fierce accusations of environmental mismanagement, others such as Lisiansky, Shemelin, and Rezanov increasingly portrayed the North Pacific as a place of abundance and good order. In part, this was because Russian administrators had instituted crucial changes, such as the beginning of fur seal conservation, but it was also due to an increasingly skilled handling of information about Alaska and Kamchatka. In contrast to foreign press reports about the Billings Expedition, Europeans were full of praise for Krusenstern. In the 1820s, after Krusenstern had compiled an atlas of the North Pacific, Britain's Royal Geographical Society had to dolefully admit that the Russians had surpassed the Royal Navy's knowledge of the region.[24] Krusenstern's voyage marked the moment when Russians began successfully co-opting the concerns and language of European observers to recast their Pacific empire. A new imperial attitude toward environmental concerns was apparent in the way administrators listened even to someone like Langsdorff's complaints.

One way in which Russians adopted European language was in an increasing concern with the animals themselves. Animals were present everywhere in the nineteenth-century accounts of the North Pacific, in a more intimate and sentimental manner than they had been in the eighteenth century. Steller, a notable early exception, had once opined that he would have liked to have taken some sea otters home with him and kept them as pets. The lonely doctor, who had been married only a few months before leaving on the expedition, was also deeply affected by the animals' conjugal fidelity. According to his observations, sea otters and sea cows both remained true to their mates for lives. Proof of the sea cows' "marital love" came from the struggle between sea cows and men in which Steller took part:

> The husband sea cow tries with all its might to help his wife when she is fastened with a hook and dragged to shore. He ignores all the blows that he receives from us, even coming on to the shore. However, it is all in vain...[25]

Sea otters manifested similar familial emotions, though this recognition seemed to mean little to the men who killed these animals without pause after 1741. In fact, there were few who repeated Steller's sentiments in those decades.

In the early nineteenth century, when the importance of sentiment (toward humans as well as animals) was gaining increased emphasis,[26] those serving the Russian Empire could express their feelings toward animals more directly.[27] Hermann Ludwig von Löwenstern, a Baltic-German officer on Krusenstern's ship, described several such examples on board which featured animals, both domestic and wild. Early in the voyage, a wagtail found refuge from a storm on the ship. Over time it became tame, living in the back of the ship where it "whistled, totally unafraid, its innocent song." To Löwenstern's great sorrow, one of the Japanese on board "like a predatory animal, grabbed our darling and squeezed it to death."[28] Löwenstern also chastised his Russian shipmate Golovachev for torturing every animal with which he came into contact. The French-German naturalist Adelbert von Chamisso, who sailed with Otto von Kotzebue into Alaskan waters in 1816, forged relationships with fur seals nearly as intimate as the animals' killers did. On the beach of St. George in the Pribylof Islands, Chamisso "observed and stroked a...newborn [fur seal]; he opened his eyes and as he was gazing at me put himself in a defensive posture by raising himself on his rear flippers and showing me some very beautiful teeth." The seal pup's father put an end to the sentimental scene when it angrily charged the naturalist.[29] Caring for and even cuddling wild animals (while sometimes still killing them in the name of science)—this was a new breed of naturalist in the North Pacific.

Cultured Russian travelers throughout the nineteenth century experienced sadness and regret at the killing of marine mammals. In the 1820s, the explorer

Frederic Litke called the killing of fur seals on the Pribylofs and the subsequent wasting of their furs "700,000 pointless murders." Furthermore, he remarked,

> There is something revolting in this cold blooded carnage of thousands of defenseless animals. The hunters themselves, hardened as they are to this form of murder, confess that often they can hardly raise their clubs to strike this innocent creature which, lying on its back with its paw in the air and crying plaintively like a baby, seems to be imploring mercy.[30]

Ivan Veniaminov, the learned priest who spent many years in the colonies, used emotion to advocate for stricter conservation measures of fur seals. "It is not easy," he reported the hunters as saying, "for everyone to raise a hand to kill such innocent creatures which are guilty only of having a fine down [undercoat]."[31] Here Veniaminov gave religious accent to his more practical concerns with good management. There was a powerful strain in Russian orthodoxy imagining the end of conflict between humans and animals, the species united in a peaceable kingdom resembling the Garden of Eden.[32] The monk Father Herman, who found refuge from colonial wickedness on Spruce Island (near Kodiak Island) from 1808 to 1836, earned renown and respect for his kindness to both downtrodden Aleuts and animals. Russian clergy in the colonies in general provided a steady stream of criticism toward the RAC, though there were few other than Veniaminov and Herman who dwelled on the treatment of animals.

Lisiansky's sorrow over the sea otters' cruel deaths at the hands of the Alaskan natives, who did not possess the emotional capabilities of Europeans, demonstrates how sentiment could affect empire-building in the North Pacific. Later during the circumnavigation, Lisiansky again accused the Aleuts of "dreadful depredations," blaming them for the decline in sea otters from Prince William Sound to Sitka, and emphasizing their cultural inferiority to the Russian colonizers.[33] In 1818, Captain V. M. Golovnin reported particularly damaging behavior by Aleuts, "a people who have no greater pleasure in life than to search for sea otters."[34] On a trip to the Spanish possessions in California, the Aleuts brought along went mad with desire to kill the sea otters in Monterey Bay, so numerous were the animals in comparison with the then-depleted herds in Alaska. Because the hunters were within sight of Spanish officials, Golovnin forbade the Aleuts to hunt, but the Aleuts "could not constrain themselves." They killed seventy-two otters in two weeks and took one male onboard as a pet for several days. Golovnin's description of Aleut hunting indicates the mingling of respect and disgust he had for them:

> After sighting one of these animals on the water, an Aleut cannot take his eyes off it and trembles all over like a hunting dog in sight of

prey.... An Aleut in his boat cannot refrain from throwing his spear at anything he sees in the water: a marine animal, a fish, a bird, or just a piece of floating vegetation.[35]

In the wake of European condemnation of Russian colonial environmental practices, the discourse of native environmental savagery and unfavorable comparison with Russians' own restraint was comforting, and would prove effective in reinterpreting the havoc in the North Pacific.

Part of the critique's effectiveness can be explained by the fact that it had caught up with the broader sentiments of colonial Europeans, who tended to blame their indigenous trading partners or colonized subjects for their own environmental troubles. Fur traders such as the Canadian Richard Thompson held Native Americans accountable for their lack of beavers and degraded environment. For Thompson, the greed and manipulation of the colonizer never came into play. The Scot John Richardson's 1829 *Fauna Boreali-Americana* offered a slightly more nuanced view, claiming that some Native Americans "destroy, as far as they are able, both young and old, and the numbers of Beaver are consequently now very much reduced." The Iroquois, on the other hand, had devised some conservation measures. Elsewhere even the Iroquois were guilty of indiscriminately setting traps. Richardson considered the possibility of disease having reduced beaver numbers, but wasted no ink in examining the British contribution to the animal's decline.[36] While some nineteenth-century commentators examined the link between colonization and environmental destruction,[37] it was still far more common to blame indigenous peoples. In this regard, Russians had begun to claim parity with, if not superiority to, other European empires in their environmental values.

The new sentimental relationship with animals contained the potential to lead in several different directions. While some thought that feeling for animals might mean that they should not be hunted—this was never stated very forcibly—others perceived in their own sentiment another source of cultural superiority over Aleuts and Creoles (the children of Aleut-Russian unions), and therefore contributed one more argument for Russian control over colonial wild animal resources. To sentimental preferences, the RAC added growing fiscal concerns. By the middle of the nineteenth century, the conservation measures coming from these sources served as new markers of Russian civility, reversing the late-eighteenth-century association of empire and extinction.

Fur Seal Conservation

Despite the recent creation of the Russian American Company, when the Krusenstern Expedition came to the colonies it was clear that the fur trade was in serious jeopardy. Rezanov wrote to the company directors that, "in view of the continually diminishing number of fur-bearing animals" the Company would not be able to survive without expansion into Southeast Alaska.[38] It was in this context that, in 1804, Rezanov proposed shutting down the Pribylof fur-seal hunt for several years. About the same time, most of the Russians and Aleuts moved to one of the Pribylof Islands, leaving the other "solely for the reproduction of the animals." [39] Areas under protection were called *zapusks* (set aside). Despite these initial measures, little was done to institutionalize conservation in the colonies. After 1808, fur seals were again hunted, with a theoretical maximum catch of forty thousand per year allowed (but never adhered to). The numbers had already gotten so low that hunting could only take place on one of the two Pribylofs—St. George Island.[40] Despite some early successes, the company under chief manager Aleksandr Baranov (1799–1818) was not notable for conservation successes.

After 1818, RAC governors began to take further precautions in the fur seal hunt. An order from that year instructed employees on St. Paul Island to "establish orderly fur hunting so as not to frighten off the animals."[41] These somewhat vague orders may have indicated merely that hunters should not shoot at the seals as they approached the shores, but as "frightening off" was the main concern about declining animal populations, it may in fact have been an exhortation to restrain the numbers killed. In the 1820s, a sort of ad-hoc, year-by-year determination of the harvest took place. Company directors would establish a goal for the number of seals to be killed in the Pribylofs, and then leave it to the local manager to determine what constituted a sustainable hunt. In 1829, for example, company directors hoped for thirty-one thousand seals to be killed, but, "if this proved to be impossible without harming the hunt in future years," the local manager was allowed take only twenty-six thousand.[42] When the animals seemed to be decreasing too quickly, governors could also close one of the Pribylof Islands for hunting, such as Matvei Muravev did in 1822.[43] These measures, it seems, did little to stem the decline in fur seals, and many of the veteran fur traders thought that closed seasons did more harm than good.[44]

Alaskan administrators were likely pursuing a flawed ecological strategy, at least in part. In the late 1810s, according to observers, hunters preferentially killed females and spared the males, as female skins fetched better prices in China.[45] Because the females were essential to the herd's reproduction, however, such measures spelled disaster. By the late 1820s, the RAC had begun to shift toward the opposite strategy. The hunters would first divide the fur seals by sex, and then age, leaving the female seals and killing a set number of younger, "bachelor" seals.[46] The key to this measure's effectiveness lay in the polygamous nature of fur seals—one older male (a *sicatch*) controlled a large harem of females, thus keeping many younger or smaller males from breeding. Theoretically, these "excess" seals could be killed without doing any long-term damage to the herd. Sea lions were hunted in the same manner. While the sex-selection method was more reliable than the quota system, its effects on the herd in actuality depended on a vast number of unknowable variables, including oceanic productivity over huge swaths of the North Pacific, as some Creole observers would point out.[47] The Russian and Aleut hunters never could be sure of the size of the returning herd, nor whether the bachelors they were taking would have produced healthier offspring. Some Russians urged that stricter measures be taken—Litke wondered whether it was sufficient to separate the large, breeding males from the non-breeding bachelors. "From where will come more large males?" he asked.[48] Most in the colonies, though, found the method satisfactory, and by the 1860s they claimed with confidence that the fur-seal hunt proceeded in as orderly and sustainable a fashion as "the slaughter of domestic cattle."[49]

Conservation practices were by then not limited to the all-important fur-bearers, but seem to have penetrated the North Pacific colonies generally. Friedrich Heinrich von Kittlitz, a German naturalist who took part in Litke's circumnavigation, spent several months in Kamchatka in the 1820s. Traveling up the Kamchatka River, he found the measures taken to conserve migrating salmon resources impressive (see Figure 6.1). Fish traps were designed "so that the [juvenile] fish which are coming downstream are not taken…because

Figure 6.1 Kittlitz's drawing of a fish dam on the Kamchatka River. The dam was constructed to let salmon fry pass unharmed downstream, but to catch the large fish, such as the gigantic specimens pictured along the shore. From Sammlung Prof Engländer Universitätsbibliothek Köln.

otherwise too many could be caught... but instead only the largest are taken."[50] The Kamchadals seem to have taken conservation practices seriously, or even to have enacted the measures themselves. When Kittlitz shot a king salmon, the local *toion* (tribal leader) scolded him and informed the scientist there could be a serious penalty for such reckless behavior. The use of guns everywhere in the North Pacific was discouraged, as it was thought to unduly frighten the prey. With great relief Kittlitz learned a year later that no one had turned him in to the authorities.[51] By the late nineteenth century, Russians of all ranks would be integrated into policing the Far East's fur- and fish-resources.[52]

Sea Otter Conservation

In comparison with fur-seal conservation, measures to preserve the remaining sea otters in the North Pacific lagged, both because the situation at times seemed hopeless and because the animals did not exhibit the predictable behavior and convenient polygamy of the fur seal. Despite these limitations, sea-otter hunting had become a far more regularized affair under the control of the RAC. Instead of groups of *promyshlenniki* alighting on an island and demanding that the inhabitants turn over their furs and hunt for more, now large numbers of Aleuts assembled on Kodiak Island at the beginning of each summer and from there departed on Russian ships or in their own baidarkas to the best hunting grounds. The Kodiak hunters would commonly search for the small number of sea otters still inhabiting the island's coast, and then sail northward to the Alaskan coast and Cook Inlet. An Unalaska detachment would hunt the Eastern Aleutian Islands, proceeding up the Alaskan peninsula, making sure to hit the legendary sea otter grounds of Sannakh Island. One other Aleutian party, from Atka, would scour the meager pickings of the formerly rich Andreanof Islands.

Company directors in the nineteenth century were aware that their predecessors "in previous times" had "rested" sea otter populations.[53] Early attempts were sporadic, and probably carried out at the initiation of local employees. Around 1804, Maxim Lazarez, a RAC *promyshlennik*, moved all eighty-five of Amchitka's residents several hundred miles eastward to Atka in the Andreanof group, probably with an aim to letting the sea otters in the Rat Islands gain a reprieve (the Amchitkans did not enjoy the move, and were returned to their home island six or seven years later).[54] In 1952, the Aleut Cedor Snigaroff recalled that the Russians used to limit the number of sea otters killed to three hundred per year, but it is difficult to pinpoint the period to which he referred.[55]

In the early nineteenth century, Baranov seems to have looked to continued expansion, rather than husbandry, to continue the Company's profits. Historian P.A. Tikhmenev, with access to sources since lost (but with a bias toward the Company), wrote that Baranov pushed his fur traders to "pay no heed to conservation," but rather to kill as many animals as quickly as possible.[56] Instructions from the time emphasize the need to obtain large catches of sea otters, with no mention of conservation.[57] However, such plans soon demonstrated their insufficiency. Though Baranov increasingly contracted with Americans to take his Aleut hunters to California to catch sea otters, those waters began to fail, just as had the Aleutians. "Even the sea otters themselves," wrote Kodiak manager and amateur naturalist, Kirill T. Khlebnikov in 1835, "which had earlier inhabited the [Californian] bays and inlets in such large herds, were now noticeably disappearing...the peace loving animals had sought shelter in some quieter place."[58] By 1812, apparently, the entirety of Russian possessions in the North Pacific had become "denuded of sea otters."[59]

Documents from around 1815 demonstrate that the Company decided at that point (or had decided a few years earlier) to make most of the Alexander Archipelago off limits, though some sources say that a limited hunt continued into the 1820s.[60] Several hunting camps in the Aleutian Islands were closed at around the same time, and the men moved elsewhere.[61] Three years later, however, the company still acknowledged that "the catch is diminishing everywhere."[62] In 1821, as the company's charter was being renewed, RAC directors conducted a comprehensive overview of sea-otter hunting from the Kuriles to the Northwest Coast. According to the still-prevailing wisdom concerning sea-otter behavior, the ever-scarcer animals were thought to be fleeing Russian hunting, rather than diminishing. Hunters were ordered heretofore to observe "the principles of good economic management," or the sea otters would become completely extinct. The methods used to ensure the survival of the species, though, seems to have been left vague.[63] In 1825, the Board of Directors again ordered an end to hunting around Alaska's Alexander Archipelago, though the primary motivation was not conservation, but rather the resentment this hunting engendered in the feared Tlingits.[64]

These hesitant policies seem to have given Aleutian sea otters a small respite. In 1820, the animals "appeared in various places," and hunting was increased around Attu and Semichi Island that decade. Russian administrators explained this pleasant surprise as a result of in-migration from other islands, rather than a natural increase through reproduction. Khlebnikov even thought that the Aleutian increase was directly due to foreigners hunting in Southeast Alaska, which frightened the sea otters back to their original homeland.[65] With this small taste of success, the RAC began to believe that more sea otters could be coaxed out of depleted areas. In the long-exhausted Andreanof Islands, Company directors felt that it "would be easy to increase the sea-otter catch," except that the Aleuts were not offered enough incentive to hunt.[66] Thus, through the 1820s, while fur-seal conservation was becoming firmly entrenched, sea-otter policy

still veered between grudging halts and eager resumptions of the hunt when-
ever and wherever more animals appeared. Despite a quarter-century of concern
over the possibility of extinction, the RAC still possessed no consistent sea-otter
conservation policy, as scholar Katherine Arndt has noted.[67]

The situation began to permanently change in the 1830s. In 1834 the
Company's St. Petersburg Board of Directors approved Governor Etolin's proposal to close the most important sea-otter hunting grounds, some for as long as
twelve years.[68] In August 1839, the Board of Directors advised him that,

> It would be more useful to send fewer hunting parties, but with greater
> numbers of *baidarka*s to known sea-otter locations, with the result that
> each of the locations would go unhunted for 3 or 4 years (or however
> many seems appropriate), in order that the sea otters can breathe easily
> and reproduce, while they wait their turn.[69]

While it was not much, this single order constituted the company's first sustained program of sea otter conservation. Subsequently, Russian parties began
alternating their hunting grounds yearly. One year the fleet of forty-five baidars,
filled with Aleuts and Russians, would disperse from Kodiak and hunt around
the islands to the north; the next year, they would sail to the south.[70] These policies took some time to implement, or were implemented only as the local situation seem to dictate. For example, in the Atka District in May 1840, company
leaders responded to the Aleut chief Nikolai Dedokhin's pleas to decrease the
demand for sea otters in view of the poor health and declining numbers of hunters. The company responded by cutting the number of hunting parties in half,
since in any case the hunters had been "scaring the sea otters away." In fact, the
previous year Dedokhin had, of his own accord, sent out only one hunting party,
achieving the same result as with two. "As a result," wrote Etolin, "we may suppose that this new arrangement will be more beneficial to the company than it
was previously with two parties."[71]

Sometimes disagreements between the Board of Directors and the Alaskan
governors over proper conservation measures arose. In 1832, Governor
Wrangel, after carefully securing the assent of the Yakutat Tlingits, decided to
send a hunting party to Yakutat and Lituya Bays, located on the Gulf of Alaska
between Sitka and the Copper River. These locations had already showed very
thin sea otter populations at the beginning of the RAC's existence, some thirty
years previously. When the Board of Directors learned of his decision, it was
furious. "Why have you sent hunters," the directors wrote, "to collect the crumbs
left in these old hunting grounds, which will never leave the hands of the company?" Furthermore, from St. Petersburg's point of view, Wrangell had endan-
gered the company's entire conservation strategy: "the longer these places are

rested (*dano budet otdikha*), the more benefit we can expect from them in the future." Wrangel's response demonstrated that the company's monopoly did not always exempt it from the kind of ecologically ruinous competition that had plagued the private companies of the eighteenth century, though now the threat came from foreigners instead of rival Russian traders:

> Why did the sea otters of the straits [the Alexander Archipelago] escape the companies' hands and into foreigners'? Is it not because we gave them a 17-year rest in the anticipation of future benefits, which have now been lost forever? [because foreigners bought them from the Tlingits].... From now on I will conform to the intentions of the Board of Directors and leave the Yakutat and Lituya sea otters for the benefit of the Tlingits.

"In 1832," Wrangel added sarcastically, "I was still so naïve that I fancied I was providing the company some benefit by having our Aleuts kill 138 sea otters in our colonial territories, that is, twice as much as the Kodiak department was able to attain."[72]

Besides demonstrating the international pressures that complicated attempts at conservation, Wrangel's response also sheds some light on the problem of interdepartmental competition. Despite the fact that the RAC was supposed to be able to take a long-term view of its colonies (something that its defenders stressed), pressures to increase the company's dividends were often paramount.[73] As Wrangel wrote another time, "The directors only have ears and hearts when we write about the furs we have sent, but when we write about improving life here they are dumb and without feeling, like idols or blockheads."[74]

By the 1860s the company had worked out fairly specific regulations for the sea-otter hunt. According to an American ship captain who visited the Aleutian Islands in the 1890s and talked with the Aleuts, the RAC would allocate to the various districts different quantities of sea otters to be caught every year. If the Aleuts killed too many sea otters in one year, they would have a smaller quota the next. The method of hunting also came under control, with extra precautions taken not to frighten the sea otters reserved for hunting in future years. No firearms were to be used, and fires had to be lit far away from the sea otter herds, smoke being considered one of the chief culprits in driving away the animals. Females, too, were spared, as far as this was possible considering that the animals were killed at sea. Young Aleuts were taught to distinguish the sexes by noticing the "color and shape of its head and neck."[75] Whether this was longstanding Aleut practice or a Company innovation is not clear.

Despite the range of conservation measures the RAC had implemented since 1804—and most of them would have been unthinkable a century before—there were many in the colonies who thought them misguided, or at best insufficient. Testimony by Veniaminov reveals that the rotational policies of the 1830s brought limited success, at least in the Aleutians. Veniaminov lived at Unalaska and traveled extensively throughout the area from 1824 to 1834. He probably had the most expansive, as well as intimate, knowledge of the region of any literate person of his era. Everywhere he saw formerly rich sea-otter habitats, especially near shore, now practically empty. Where once Russians had caught hundreds (Veniaminov even claimed thousands) of sea otters per year, in some years only a dozen would be caught, and in some places the animals were entirely extinct. Where sea otters still persisted, they had moved far offshore and hauled out much less frequently than before.[76] To remedy the situation, Veniaminov proposed many of the same solutions that company directors had tried to implement earlier. Firstly, females should not be killed—this, in fact, repeated a law originally proclaimed by Empress Elizabeth, in 1748, apparently still not honored. As Veniaminov himself explained, "True, an order [he does not specify which one] had been issued not to kill the young, but this order remained meaningless, because if the young is not killed, but the mother is, it will soon die by itself, totally uselessly."[77] Expressing a more sophisticated understanding of sea-otter biology than his predecessors, Veniaminov noted that it was especially crucial for young sea otters to have several peaceful years in which to grow to maturity before being subjected to the hunt.

In the 1860s, the Creole Aleksandr Kashevarov felt the Company's latest solution to declining otters—limiting the number of hunting parties sent out every year—also had inherent problems. A hunting party could find that it was unusually successful, and in the process decimate a large proportion of the remaining otters. On the other hand, if the hunting parties had bad luck, there was no possibility of catching a sufficient number of otters for the year. Instead, Kashevarov suggested that the Company limit the number of animals caught each year.[78]

Other observers thought the Company's measures more successful. In the late 1820s Litke reported that, though sea otters continued to decline in some places, they "have multiplied afresh in a remarkable manner in those areas where they have been left in peace for some time."[79] Litke pointed in particular to the Kurile Islands, in which the company was then placing great hope as a new source of sea otters. By about 1817 hunting there had completely ceased due to a lack of animals, but in 1827 the new Russian settlement was killing up to one thousand of these animals per year. "Let us hope," wrote Litke, "that for [the Company's] own good this renewed hunting will be conducted with more economy than previously."[80] And yet, consistent with the air of mystery that still surrounded the animals, others thought that Company policies had nothing to do with the sea otter's reappearance. Kashevarov wrote that the animal's reappearance—and its disappearance—owed more to cataclysms endemic to the North Pacific than to human hunting. Frequent earthquakes, and the "suffocating, stinking smoke and soot" of live volcanoes which often spread far offshore either killed the animals or forced them on one of their migrations which many Russians thought the small animals capable.[81] In fact, volcanic activity has been shown to have significantly affected sea otter distribution and abundance; for example, the 1964 Good Friday earthquake in the Gulf of Alaska displaced many sea otters.[82]

The RAC provided its own, somewhat more hesitant statement about sea otters in 1862, which mixed boasts of success with an admission that the empire's overall ecological toll was still profoundly negative:

> Isn't it so, that out of thousands of sea otters only a few have remained, and that this animal, especially such a lover of cleanliness and rest, has decreased not only because of hunting, but also because it does not breed when confronted with the least disturbance, and of course, it could be that it is destroyed from its continual pursuit, as is proved by the poverty of sables,..., and squirrels in Siberia and Kamchatka, and the complete destruction of sea otters in the straits and especially in California, where they were found in huge numbers?"[83]

Thus, the RAC, in the last years of its existence, seemed to accept a combination of explanations for animal extermination, including reduced breeding success and outright overhunting, with evidence gleaned from the entire North Pacific rim (see Figure 6.2). Sometimes, however, Russian comprehension of sea otter behavior remained surprisingly ill-informed. "As is well known," wrote Kashevarov, "sea otters eat seaweed."[84] Still, it should be remembered that sea otter ecology retains enough mystery that causes of the animals' declines or gains are rarely easy to discern in the twenty-first century.[85]

Extinction and Aleuts

By the middle of the nineteenth century, most colonial administrators not only recognized the need for conservation, but also readily admitted the possibility of extinction, and had a number of explanations at hand. Khlebnikov pinpointed the sea otters' low rate of reproduction as the reason it "is subject to rapid extinction if hunted indiscriminately." He also quoted an anonymous observer, "zealous for the benefit of the fatherland," who noted that,

> they kill all the sea otters, just like at the town of Arkhangelsk, when they caught all the cod. 'Codfish spawn roe, but sea otters give birth to

only one or two young ones, and because of this inequality the sea otter could be extinguished altogether."[86]

Veniaminov was even more precise, noting that the *promyshlenniki*'s erroneous belief that female fur seals gave birth for the first time in their third year (when in fact it was the fourth) meant that the three-year closed seasons still did not give the seals time to reach sexual maturity.[87] In an apparent attempt to place such visible decrease within a loose cosmology, Khlebnikov also noted that "Time does not alter the quality of organic produce, but it can decrease the quantity due to physical reasons. I do not apply this to the plant kingdom... but refer to the animals." [88] Thus Khlebnikov attempted to keep intact the inalterability of species, while admitting that their abundance could change fundamentally.

Veniaminov came to a similar, if slightly more radical conclusion: "it is not possible for any species of wild or domestic animals to become extinct by themselves."[89] Here he stood the eighteenth-century notion of the impossibility of extinction on its head. Whereas Buffon, Cuvier, and others had posited that extinction might take place from natural causes (usually long ago cataclysms), but never by human hands, Veniaminov's experience taught him the opposite— in fact, only humans could cause the extinction of god's creatures. As a cleric, Veniaminov held a vision of a fallen world, which perhaps helped ease this conceptual leap, but the principal influence seems to have been the declining marine life of the North Pacific.

Veniaminov's further observations of sea otter behavior show that Russians, even after eight decades of hunting the animals, retained their firm belief in sea otters' migratory capabilities. The reason sea otters had grown scarce, the priest insisted, were "not because they were hunted out, but because... they do not like to live where they are disturbed. The sea otters are as much exterminated as frightened away."[90]

While there were Russian (especially Siberian) precedents for the migration theory, other evidence indicates that the RAC may have picked up some of its ecological thinking from the Aleuts. Veniaminnov related a story that suggests several points of convergence. Sometime in the late eighteenth or early nineteenth century, on St. George Island in the Pribylofs, hunters conducting their usual summer drive of seals found the sun fast setting without time to separate males from females. The hunters decided to pause for the night, and in the darkness the seals escaped and threw themselves into the sea. Because the cliffs at that part of the island are so high, all the animals perished. Though the number of seals lost was not particularly great, thereafter the hunt on St. George began a precipitous decline, much faster even than on neighboring St. Paul, though hunting methods did not differ.[91] This story implies that the fur seals exacted revenge for their careless handling (not separating males from females) and that

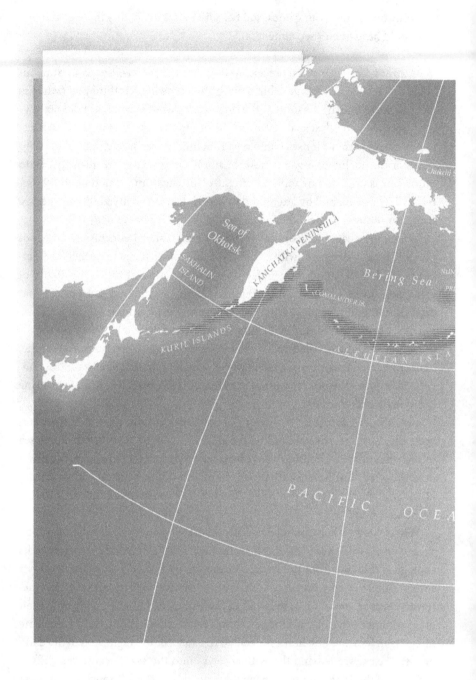

Figure 6.2 Known Aleut and Russian sea-otter hunting grounds in the nineteenth-century North Pacific along with important Russian settlements. New Arkhangelsk was established in 1804 to move Russians closer to the abundant sea otters of Southeast Alaska. Fort Ross was settled in California in 1812 as an agricultural colony.

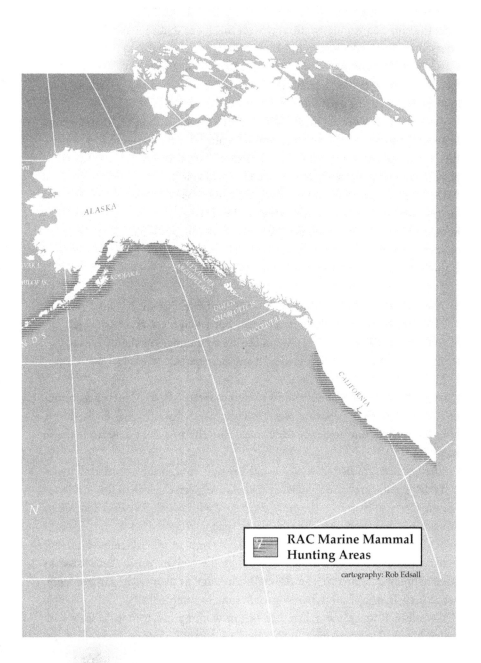

ALASKA

CALIFORNIA

RAC Marine Mammal
Hunting Areas

cartography: Rob Edsall

the numbers hunted alone could explain the animals' decline. The fur seals' fall from the cliff also resonates strongly with the Aleut tradition ascribing the sea otters' creation to two incestuous lovers' plunge over a cliff into the ocean (the fur seals in Veniaminov's story were also both male and female).[92] While this may represent a garbled version of Aleut beliefs, cross-cultural encounters are known for producing such mistranslations.

Several earlier pieces of evidence strengthen the suspicion that Russians took many of their ideas about marine mammal biology from the Aleuts. In 1813, the RAC's Main Administration wrote, regarding the fur-seal hunt, that the company "had to issue a prohibition against hunting fur seals...lest the seals become aware of the decimation and begin to avoid these islands because of the terrible slaughter."[93] The company's focus on the seals' awareness and judgment of human action strongly resembles Aleut belief, and suggests that Aleut ideas penetrated to the top levels of the RAC. Four years later, in 1817, Chamisso stopped at the Pribylof Islands. "Only thirty years ago," he wrote,

> sea otters were here in such abundance, that man could catch from two to three hundred of them in an hour; but when these animals, which are accounted by the Aleutians as the most cunning, saw themselves so pursued, they suddenly vanished from these parts.[94]

Chamisso's story, like Veniaminov's, demonstrates that Aleut conceptions of marine mammal behavior were well known. His account, furthermore, links together in one sentence Aleut ideas and the prevalent Russian belief in migration.

The relationship between Aleut and Russian conceptions of marine mammal ecology must remain somewhat speculative given the lack of firm evidence joining the two. However, the close proximity with which Russians and Aleuts hunted together for over a century makes such a transfer of ideas very likely. It is also known that Russian fur traders and government officials relied on native information and native collaborators to map the North Pacific. And, Russians often expressed admiration for Aleuts' knowledge of their home environment, particularly in regards to their navigational and hunting skills.[95]

Certainly, Russian naturalists had begun working much more closely with native North Pacific peoples in the early nineteenth century. Langsdorff, for example, took much of his information directly from Aleut and Kamchadal informants. Chamisso, using similar methods, produced the best natural history of North Pacific whales to that point, a serious revision of Pallas's cetaceous information in the ZRA. His 1824 essay, "Cetaceorum maris Kamtschatici imagines, ab Aleutis e lingo fictas" ("Models of Whales from the Kamchatkan Sea, Made from Wood by the Aleuts"), not only used Aleut conceptions of whale

Figure 6.3 Wooden Aleut models of whales commissioned and collected by Adelbert von Chamisso on Unalaska in 1816 and 1817. Chamisso gave the Aleut names for these two species—*Aliomoch* (humpback whale?) and *Agidagich* (sperm whale), as well as including Linnaeus' Physeter Linnaeus for the sperm whale. Photographs by Carola Radke, Courtesy of Museum für Naturkunde Berlin Historische Bild- u. Schriftgutsammlungen (Sigel: MfN, HBSB). Bestand: Zool. Mus. Signatur: B XII/248 and 249.

speciation and Aleut names for young and old whales, but also provided draw-ings of Aleut wooden models that Chamisso had commissioned while in Alaska (these can be seen in Figure 6.3). Chamisso had "the most experienced Aleuts prepare and explain the whale models," through which he learned something of the ecology of each species. Such reliance on indigenous knowledge repre-sented a radical challenge to prevailing European conceptions of species and demonstrated a significant shift from the days when Steller imperiously ordered Kamchadals to turn over every beached whale for the naturalist's inspection.[96]

Despite later Russian claims that conservation was a mark of their enlight-ened empire derived entirely from national virtues, in fact, the conception and practice of preserving fur seals and sea otters owed much to Aleut ideas. Russian protests notwithstanding, such readiness to adopt aspects of indigenous environ-mental ideas would seem a mark of the empire's productive flexibility. Evidence from Lake Baikal reveals that such interpenetration of ecological conceptions occurred frequently across the vast spread of peoples and ecosystems between St. Petersburg and Sitka. Elsewhere, however, the outcome of such shared learn-ing seems to have been the more effective destruction of natural resources.[97]

While coerced and cooperative sea-otter decimation characterized the beginning of Russian impact in the North Pacific, by the 1840s Russians and Aleuts had, through a process of mutual accommodation, forged one of the colonial world's most effective conservation regimes. Naturalists did not play the leading role here, but the outcomes fulfilled the hopes they had forcefully expressed in the 1790s and early 1800s.

RAC and HBC

Whatever the inconsistency of their methods, Russians in the nineteenth century had some reason to feel pride in their legacy of conservation. A comparison with the Hudson's Bay Company (HBC), which faced similar (if mainly terrestrial) concerns in the Pacific Northwest at the same time, demonstrates both the advances and limitations of the RAC's methods. Like the RAC officials, Hudson's Bay traders had a keen awareness of the problems of overhunting. Beavers—their main prey—have an ecology similar to that of Siberian sables, but the British and French traders managed to much more effectively organize the beavers' extermination, achieving this mainly through trade rather than direct hunting. Beavers are also similar to sea otters in that they only slowly recolonize denuded areas, though their superior rates of reproduction and terrestrial habitat means that their populations are not quite as tenuous as that of the sea otter.[98] As early as the 1630s, Europeans in Canada were attempting to stave off beaver extirpation by better regulating the hunt,[99] and by at least the 1740s they were becoming worried about the survival of the species. In 1749 Peter Kalm, a student of Linnaeus studying North America's natural history, described declining beaver populations everywhere from Delaware to Canada.[100]

By the 1820s and 1830s, roughly contemporaneous with the first major thrusts of RAC conservation, HBC officials had grown very worried about the beaver supply. Chief trader John McLoughlin complained that, "Furs are already becoming scarce & at the present supply is obtained by an almost exterminating system of hunting." Company Executive George Simpson feared that it would not be long before "the fur-bearing race becomes extinct." As a result, in 1821, Simpson instituted the company's first systematic conservation attempts on the Pacific. He limited hunts in troubled areas, ordered that sexually immature animals be spared, advocated shifting hunting toward more prolific species, banned steel traps and castorum baits, imposed a quota system, and tried to do away with summer hunting. Simpson even hoped to establish a "Beaver Park" in the territories, where no hunting would be allowed, though this plan was never put into effect.[101] Simpson's initial suite of reforms failed in large part, it was alleged, because their Native American trade partners refused to cooperate, both because they had become dependent on the trade and because they did not share the HBC's belief in the effectiveness of conservation.[102] Furthermore, the Company did not revise its employees' incentives in line with conservation goals, still basing pay on the number of furs delivered. A deep-rooted culture of frontier machismo may also have encouraged continued excess killing.[103] Another reason for the reforms' failure (and one which paints the HBC's program in a different light) was competition from American fur traders along the company's southern territories. In those areas the HBC carried out a "fur-desert" policy, in which it attempted to exterminate the beaver to the greatest extent possible in order to discourage American expansion. The measures taken in the Snake River country and elsewhere were devastating. "This day a Beaver 1 Otter we have now ruined this quarter we may prepare to Start" reads an HBC journal entry from 1826.[104] The idea for the fur deserts came from the same George Simpson who had formulated the HBC's conservation program, and it makes clear that whatever attempts to save beavers the Company did make were not done out of any concern for the animal's well being.

One area in which the HBC excelled was its sensitivity to animal ecologies. By the 1820s, company traders had recognized that marten, lynx, and other fur-bearing populations tended to fluctuate on three-year cycles. Chief factors accordingly ordered limited harvests during those times when the animals were already likely to be in decline based on other factors. As an 1847 report stated,

> it is feared that we are on the eve of one of those fluctuations to which the Marten trade independently of hunting is almost periodically subject, and if so there will be a further decline in the returns of that fur next year and for some years later, until from some unknown cause they again multiply and reappear in their native forests in the utmost abundance.[105]

If the causes of fluctuation remained mysterious (and the HBC, like the RAC, was inclined to suspect migration),[106] nonetheless, the HBC's attention to its dynamic environment set it off from RAC managers. The Russian company's lack of ecological perception would soon emerge as a strong argument in favor of its liquidation.

In comparison with the problems the HBC faced in conserving fur-bearers, the RAC did enjoy some advantages. Most importantly, the RAC had much greater control over its hunters; while Tlingits continued to operate much on their own accord, Aleuts and Creoles both worked under fairly strict supervision. Their access to Company and even native goods could be controlled and used to direct their hunting activities. In the Aleutians and Southwest Alaska, at least, the RAC's preponderance of power gave it a unique possibility to pursue long-range conservation. Additionally, the Aleuts, despite a long history of overhunting, had an environmental ethos that could be—and was—used to encourage cooperation with Russian administrators. The Russian belief that animals fled instead of diminishing made sense in an Aleut context, or perhaps came from the Aleuts directly. In contrast, in the HBC's western districts, it was only after years of trials that the Indian trading partners began to believe in the efficacy of restraining the hunt.[107] Against such advantages must be stacked the disadvantage of dealing with marine mammals that spend most of their lives underwater and were essentially unobservable to eighteenth- and nineteenth-century humans. The RAC's continued economic difficulties, especially with the expenses involved in supplying the colonies, also made it difficult to trade short- for long-term boons.

However, with the clear advances in conservation theory and practice made in the nineteenth-century North Pacific, it is easy to wonder why the RAC did not accomplish more. A case in point is the lack of conservation undertaken in Californian waters, an increasingly important hunting region after 1803. The RAC actually faced little foreign competition there, with neither the Spanish nor the Americans ever doing much hunting north of San Francisco Bay. After 1821 the Russians even contracted with the Spanish to hunt legally as far south as San Diego.[108] As Governor Wrangel once wrote to the Board of Directors: "Everywhere sea otters are rare, except California. There lies our only hope."[109] Yet, there is no evidence of any attempt to conserve this last remaining consistent supply of the company's most valuable export, and the foundation of Russian imperial power in the North Pacific. This highlights the fact that the RAC's conservation policy remained strictly reactive, an attempt to breathe some flicker of life back into badly depleted areas.

Empire of Conservation

By the middle of the nineteenth century, a new conception of the Russian colonies had emerged, at least among Russian commentators. In place of the profligate, despotic environmental despoilers of the eighteenth century, Russians in the North Pacific now saw themselves as uniquely good stewards of their environment. Tikhmenev, for example, congratulated the RAC, for "had it not been for strict and necessary conservation measures taken by the company, many kinds of fur-bearing animals which are now found in the colonies would only be a memory."[110] Increasingly, the rhetorical battlefield witnessed a reverse, with foreigners, especially Americans, being denounced as environmental mismanagers. These ideas were embedded in a larger comparison of European colonialisms, much as they had been in the eighteenth century, though now the environment began to play a more central role.

Certainly, criticism from naturalists continued, especially those on the numerous round-the-world voyages of the period. But the criticism became distinctly milder. Chamisso discussed Aleut "slavery" in 1818, but also noted that "the Russians...are here themselves oppressed." Environmental degradation also appears in Chamisso's account. He noted that, "The sea otter appears not to extend north beyond the Aleutian Islands, and has begun even there to become rare, after causing the decline of the native inhabitants."[111] In the tradition of Sauer and Langsdorff, Chamisso here accused the Russians of destroying both animals and humans, but elliptically, without making a clear connection between the two processes. Later, he claimed that the fur seal hunt provided the RAC with a "dependable and substantial profit," evidence that heedless destruction had been relegated to the past.[112] Several years later, Kittlitz related that in Southeast Alaska, "In our time the sea otters were already rare...forcing the Kalosches [Tlingit] to become accustomed to seeking their wealth in other fur-bearing animals."[113] Kittlitz put the stress not on the threat environmental change posed to Tlingit primitivism, but rather the commercial hardships they faced. Others, like Eschscholtz and the Dane Marten Wormskiold (who botanized in Kamchatka in 1817 and 1818), left no records of complaints. Russian travelers like Litke wrote their sentimental laments about otter murders, but stressed that those days were in the past. The naval officer Golovnin provided the strongest statement about the colony's improvements. He admitted abuses had taken place in Alaska, but now (1819), the "Chief Administrator of all the Company's colonies has taken strong and efficient measures to eliminate the evils in various Company practices that existed in spite of the good intentions of the Company itself."[114] No longer was the Russian Empire profligate and destructive in the North Pacific—and in addition, it had never even meant to be.

These more positive responses were due in part to the company's takeover by naval officers in 1818. A series of cultured navy men serving as company managers maintained close links with St. Petersburg, encouraged the creation of a Creole population loyal to the empire, and made very favorable impressions on foreign visitors. Their management was, in many ways, more regular and less violent, though it did not release Aleuts and Alutiit from intense hunting obligations.

Just as importantly, Russians also found better ways to describe their North Pacific empire. Whereas, in the eighteenth century, unflattering comparisons between Russian and Spanish New World colonization appealed to travelers in the North Pacific, these were now largely discarded. As Russians grew more accustomed to running an overseas colony, they began to lose their earlier fascination with British and French imperialism, finding that these enterprises were at least as flawed as their own. As Khlebnikov wrote, "any who criticize [depopulation in the North Pacific] should recall that in none of the European colonies in the New World has the original population increased or remained intact and unharmed."[115] Depopulation, which had seemed to threaten the legitimacy of Catherine's overseas empire, could now be attractively situated within the global replacement of indigenous peoples by Europeans: "Perhaps through the unseen paths of Providence," Khlebnikov continued, "all the indigenous peoples of the New World will gradually disappear or mix with the new arrivals, but the places where they lived will not remain empty."[116] Governor Wrangell added in 1839 that,

> it must be understood that the inhabitants of the whole of America suffered no better fate than that of the Aleuts.... I would merely call to mind the first English occupation of North America, the continual struggle of many Indian tribes and their final confinement behind narrow frontiers...the epidemics brought by Europeans.... The impact of civilization on these wild children of wood and wilderness has taken a frightful toll.[117]

Despite this dreadful picture of imperial impact, Russian commentators did not draw depressing conclusions about their own exploits. Instead, the imperial pessimism of the late eighteenth century gave way to a sense that Russian overseas rule was natural and inevitable.

Naturalists played a crucial role in this reconceptualization. Karl Ernst von Baer, a Baltic German professor at the University of Dorpat (today Tartu, Estonia) and arguably the Russian empire's greatest nineteenth-century naturalist, portrayed the Russian-America colonies as the inescapable domination of advanced civilization over people determined by history and nature to decline.[118] Writing in the 1830s, he claimed that Russian colonization had in fact been more benevolent than that of other European empires, contrasting Spain's "extermination" of humans with Russia's more benevolent treatment of its conquered peoples. Reversing the eighteenth century's linking of autocracy and imperial misrule, von Baer claimed that the Russian autocracy was actually better prepared to defend the welfare of the "natives," as it stood above private interests. Many of the outrages that Russian fur traders had perpetrated were the "unavoidable result of the injurious climate and the newness of the settlements." In contrast to these earlier excesses, the RAC had managed to rein in "those who were exterminating animals, and to introduce systematic protection of the people." [119] Finally, von Baer provided the bittersweet coda that summed up well many nineteenth-century naturalists' reconciliation with empire:

> Could we see [imperial expansion] as moving, and arranging the pieces provided by Providence or, from the point of [view of] natural history,

regard men as working contrary to a higher purpose, we must understand that recent history is a struggle between civilization and the natural state, a struggle from which the former proceeds victorious. The
overthrow of the natural state can, and should, pierce our hearts, but it
is unavoidable.[120]

Here, we see the ways in which nineteenth-century natural history, instead of cataloging resources (*pace* Krasheninnikov) or providing a poetics of empire (*pace*
Pallas), directly naturalized the process of Russian domination and situated it
confidently within the flow of world history. Von Baer wrote as a world-weary
Buffon might have, no longer so sure that imperial expansion could proceed
without pain, but with renewed confidence that the "natural state" had to recede.

A significant part of the argument for the supposed benevolence of Russian
imperialism involved the empire's superior environmental practices, especially
when compared with those of other imperial powers. Outrage at European
incursion into the North Pacific had long brought protest from both the state
and traders, but in the nineteenth century an appealing contrast with the free-
wheeling fur-traders was coming into focus. British, French, and American
traders continued to barter for sea otters with the Tlingit. American whalers,
who had moved to the North Pacific in great numbers in the 1840s, killed seals
and whales with no thought for preservation, slaughtering young and old alike,
even dispatching the nursing mothers that Russians were now supposed to
spare. Such examples of Yankee "liberty" appalled the Russians, in no small part
because the Americans were taking animals that Russians considered their own.
As Litke put it, at the founding of New Arkhangelsk, "Otters still existed in large
numbers in the vicinity and their furs would have realized a preferential income,"
except that "foreigners carried on their shameful trading" and "as a result, the
otters were exterminated."[121] With the steps taken in the early nineteenth century to curb the worst of the overhunting, the RAC could point with pride to its
record: "Were it not for [our] systematic management of the harvesting of animals," officials wrote in the 1860s, "they would have long ago been exterminated
by the [American] whalers."[122] Foreigners also brought less direct forms of ecological mayhem. In 1816, the RAC Director, M. M. Buldakov, ruefully sent the
Academy of Sciences a piece of wood "almost completely devoured by marine
worms." The wood had belonged to a RAC ship, but ever since the arrival of a
foreign ship around 1803, the worms had proliferated in Sitka harbor, forcing
the Russians to copperplate the ships' hulls.[123]

Native Americans, too, could be used to make a similar point about enlightened Russian environmental practices. Lisiansky and Golovnin had depicted
Aleut hunters as insensate killers, whose "depredations" accounted for the
decline in sea otters. After conservation measures were in place, RAC officials

suspected that Aleuts were flouting them, paddling their *baidaras* out in bad weather to find hauled-out sea otters and using firearms to kill them.[124] Similarly, the Tlingits were blamed for putting profit ahead of conservation and leaving the sea otters with no refuge.[125] Nor did company directors think that its native workers were capable of their own accord to preserve *zapusks* (places where hunting was at least temporarily forbidden). The same held for Creoles, who were thought to flout the orderly hunting procedures for which the company strived.[126] Elsewhere, however, the company could help tutor the unenlightened natives in conservation. Demonstrating an arrogance developed over sixty years of nearly autocratic rule in the colonies, the RAC thought that it could inspire in Alaska's natives a better sense of protecting fur resources. By paying non-subject Alaskan low prices, or refusing to buy any furs procured during an animal's breeding season, the "savages will accustom themselves to the necessity of following the general order."[127] Of course, the worst possible scenario was the combined irregularity of the Aleuts and the rapacity of the Americans. If the Aleuts were allowed to do as they pleased, they would falter under the temptation of vodka proffered by the Americans, and both Aleut and Creole alike would "forget the laws for the development of their own well-being and the development of the region, hunting would be done with all available means at all times, and therefore in a few years they will have little to eat and nothing to hunt."[128] Though the Aleuts likely provided the inspiration for much of the RAC's conservation practices, the patronizing attitude demonstrated here may give some clue why such inspiration was rarely acknowledged.

A. F. Kashevarov and the Last Debate about Conservation

At the beginning of the 1860s, the last decade of Russian occupation in Alaska, reformers began advocating for the dissolution of the Company's monopoly on fur-bearing animals, hoping to release the creative energy of Russian subjects and develop Alaska's economic potential more thoroughly. Some foretold dire consequences if this were to take place, with questions of marine mammal conservation at the center of the argument. Into this debate stepped an Aleut-Russian Creole, Aleksandr Filippovich Kashevarov, who opposed some of the company's conservation measures. Kashevarov was an immensely talented and well-educated man. Born on Kodiak Island to a Russian father and Creole mother, he entered company service and played an important role in the exploration of northern Alaska. He also spent much of his life in Russia and would become a Naval Corps General-Major in 1865.[129] Writing from St. Petersburg in the socially progressive journal *Morskoi Sbornik* (Naval Collection) in 1862, Kashevarov contributed his pen to the reformers' cause, raising several environmental arguments against the RAC's continued monopoly on marine mammal hunting. This article, the RAC's response, and Kashevarov's final rebuttal later that year demonstrate several directions that the environmental history of the Russian North Pacific could have taken, had the colony not been sold to the United States five years later.

Kashevarov began his attack on company privileges conventionally enough, reminding readers of the era before company control, when unrestrained private Russian hunting had nearly exterminated Alaska's sea otters and fur seals. The RAC deserved the acclaim it had received for heading off the extinction of valuable fur-bearing animals—especially fur seals—rendering Russia real benefits. Liberalization could indeed "lead to the deadly effects of the distant past, to the possibility of its repetition in the future—how terrible."[130] This was an argument that company directors, too, were making in defense of their monopoly. Based on his privileged, indigenous knowledge of the North Pacific, however, Kashevarov felt that, if it were done right, the end of monopoly might not lead to a new environmental catastrophe.

Kashevarov's prescription rested on two precepts. First, the RAC's conservation of sea otters and land animals had not in fact succeeded, as opposed to the effective management of fur seals. In fact, according to Kashevarov, a "real" conservation policy for sea otters was impossible. In essence, sea-otter ecology was too complex for Russians to manage. Sea otters could not be counted on to be present at the same places every year. If sea otter food was scarce the animals might not return for several years, frustrating any attempt to determine whether their numbers were increasing or decreasing. Experienced hunters could, by observing local food sources, foretell when sea otters would be scarce and predict where they would be in abundance. However, it was impossible to determine whether the sea otters appearing in locations of abundant food were the same that had abandoned the denuded bays. In fact, Kashevarov reopened the entire question of sea otter migration that had preoccupied earlier observers, though his discussion was at least marked by an attempt to systematically interrogate the animal's behavior. Whereas earlier observers had postulated merely that sea otters fled persecution, Kashevarov pondered whether sea otters, like fur seals, regularly migrated. After considering several options, he could only conclude that, "the question is unanswered."[131] Such migrations could potentially present terrible problems for the Russian colonies. Again, foreigners were the bogey. What if American ships, which roved throughout the North Pacific, were to stumble upon the winter sea otter grounds? They surely would not show any moderation in the hunt, cutting into their numbers just as they were taking whales elsewhere.[132]

The second part of Kashevarov's plan involved a more radical suggestion: handing over the fur trade to the Aleuts and Creoles. While the formation of the RAC and its control by naval officers may have ended some of the
worst abuses against the Aleuts, Alutiit, and Tlingit, the company's charters also
strengthened and codified native dispossession of the most important products
in their lives. All fur-bearing animals became property of the RAC; any animal
caught had to either be turned over to the company (if the hunter was on salary), or sold to it. Marine mammal products, such as *baidarka* covers or sea-otter
clothing, could be bought from the company, though in practice hardly anyone could afford the latter. In order to save the colony from "the possibility of
exterminating the precious fur-bearing animals," Kashevarov thought the time
had come to entrust their hunting to those who knew them best: the Aleuts. As
Kashevarov noted, "*hundreds* of sea otters are found exclusively in those places
where they are hunted *only* by Aleuts—conscientious (*dobrosovetsnye*) masters
of their trade."[133] In fact, he asserted, Aleuts possessed unique insights into the
North Pacific environment, and—contrary claims notwithstanding—they were
excellent conservationists. "Creating *zapusk*s at the right time, when necessary—this is the specialty of Native hunters,"[134] Kashevarov claimed.

The Company disagreed. It thought that Aleuts and Creoles lacked the ratio-
nality to manage marine mammals, and it never tired of pointing out their willingness to evade all laws that stood in the way of killing as many animals as possible.
The Company's answer to Kashevarov made clear that it alone could compe-
tently manage the fur trade. The Pribylof Islands provided a point in case. With
curiously twisted logic, the Company argued that the Aleuts really had no vested
interest in the islands (since it was the Company that had brought them there in
the first place): "For the natives, who do not possess sailing vessels, the islands
are worthless, and it follows that they would give up their possession to the first
who wanted it, who, of course, would be none other than foreign whalers."[135] On
this point, at least, the Company agreed with Kashevarov; the profligate, treacherous Americans could be counted on to introduce environmental havoc.

Kashevarov's advocacy for native hunting incorporated another, equally radical claim. Like the members of the Billings and Krusenstern expeditions, he
noted that the Aleuts had been deprived of their traditional means of subsistence. In contrast to those voyagers, Kashevarov turned this observation into a
direct plea for environmental justice. "It is somehow strange," he wrote with feeling, "to keep from the inhabitants of this maritime colony the right to freely use
the products of their home sea, given to them by God for their well-being!"[136]
Ever since the beginning of Russian occupation of the Aleutian Islands, the
natives had been denied ownership of the animals. First, *yasak* demands took sea
otters and fur seals out of their hands. After the *yasak*'s abolishment, the Russian
American Company was given ownership of all marine mammals. Reformers

who wanted to liberalize trade still wanted to place restrictions on the numbers of animals caught. Kashevarov felt such measures would only perpetuate the longstanding injustice; Aleuts still depended on these animals for almost all of their daily needs and finally had a chance to regain some autonomy in the most important facet of their lives. He finished with an anguished plea:

> We [Creoles and Aleuts] are people just like everyone else. If we don't know foreign ways, we know our own very well, and understand that, for the perfection of our own lives, we had to see much, learn and imitate new, useful things from others. Just let it be that others can be fair with us... [137]

As Russians prepared to leave the North Pacific after 120 years of occupation, Kashevarov's final statement spoke of the colony's impossible future, a future that might have engaged seriously with the question of environmental justice. Just when Aleuts sensed the possibility of adding their voices to Russian America's history, that history came to an end. They would wait a very long time for another chance under American rule.

Extinction in Nineteenth-Century Europe

As Russians debated the efficacy of conservation in the nineteenth century and considered again their place among the circle of European colonizers, those animals already gone did not disappear from sight. Instead, they entered more prominently into European ideas about extinction. The contentious Krusenstern expedition first pushed forward the European debate about extinction, putting the sea cow squarely in the middle of it. Langsdorff wrote definitively of the sea cow's extinction in his published account of the voyage. While *en route* he had also kept up a lively correspondence with one of his mentors, Johan Friedrich Blumenbach. Langsdorff's reports demonstrate his developing conviction that the sea cow had really gone extinct. "From Steller's sea cow," he wrote from Kamchatka, "which you have requested that I keep an eye out for, I have unfortunately heard that for many years it has retreated to the North up into the Bering Strait." [138] After his trip to the Russian colonies, including the Pribylof Islands in the north, Langsdorff began to doubt that the sea cow would be found anywhere. He still wondered if the animal might be found further north, but it was becoming increasingly likely that it was "a new example of a species entirely gone from the present creation." [139] When Langsdorff's polished version of the expedition reached the public, reviews prominently mentioned the fact that the naturalist believed the animal entirely extinct. [140]

Blumenbach was the most important conduit for disseminating information about the sea cow's extinction, as well as the most important influence
on Langsdorff's conception of natural history. In the early nineteenth century,
Blumenbach was a rising star at the University of Göttingen, a place that, like
Steller's Halle, had been founded as a nursery for Prussian public servants.
His *Handbuch der Naturgeschichte* (Handbook of Natural History), which first
appeared in 1788, went through more than ten editions through the first decade
of the nineteenth century and was widely read. Blumenbach is also remembered
as popularizing the study of skull size to classify different human races, and
Langsdorff dutifully brought him back a Marquesan head. Blumenbach was one
of the few in his field to reject the impossibility of extinction:

> Nature...will not go to pieces even if one species of creature dies out,
> or another is newly created, seeing no threat to the order of the world
> even if one species of creature dies out, or another is newly created—
> and it is more than merely probable, that both cases have happened
> before now—and all this without the slightest danger to order, either in
> the physical or in the moral world, or for religion in general.

Blumenbach presented a wealth of evidence to support his claim, from the dodo,
"in the time of our fathers," to the wolves of England and Scotland somewhat
earlier.[141] Such ideas encouraged Langsdorff in his confident proclamation that
the sea cow was extinct.

As late as the 1830s, however, many Russians were still not convinced that
Steller's sea cow had completely disappeared. Khlebnikov wrote that, "Mr.
Langsdorff thinks that they have disappeared from the animal kingdom like
other primitive animals...I do not believe it."[142] Chamisso was more ambivalent,
reporting that in Unalaska, we "heard only corrupted traditions...which seemed
to refer to the *Manatus borealis*."[143] A zoology he worked on, but never published,
described *Le Grand Lamatin du Kamtschatka* (great manatee of Kamchatka)
without mentioning its extinction.[144] Confusing the issue, Tilesius (one of the
naturalists on the Krusenstern Expedition) made preposterous claims of the sea
cow's continued existence in waters from which it had disappeared many millennia before. He wrote in 1835 in a German newspaper that "Travelers who come
back from California and Sitka confirm that [sea cows] are also found there."[145]
Tilesius also revived Pennant's outdated lumping of sirens around the world into
one species, conflating again tropical manatees of all sizes with Steller's sea cow.
Tilesius's unhelpful contribution to sirenian studies looks even more perverse
when one considers that he had helped edit Pallas's ZRA, which had seemingly
cleared up the taxonomic confusion surrounding the sea cow. In all events, the
claims of sea cows suddenly appearing throughout the North Pacific—without

naming the travelers who transmitted these reports, thirty years after Tilesius's last trip to the region—produced a new round of headaches for St. Petersburg academicians. Others began making an increasingly popular argument that, though terrestrial extinction was possible, ocean animals were hardly likely to suffer such persecution from humans.

Meanwhile, more reliable zoological knowledge from the North Pacific was making its way throughout European circles. Cuvier, the popularizer of extinction, kept up to date with Alaskan and Siberian developments, corresponding with the Livonian zoologist Eschscholtz about the "fossil remains of animals."[146] Cuvier even provided detailed descriptions of Ludwig Choris's drawings, which had been made on Kotzebue's first voyage (see Figure 6.4). He remarked, as many did, on the Aleuts' close understanding of the marine world they inhabited. An Aleut hunting visor which Choris had drawn was populated with "very recognizable animals, and show that these savages have examined them with great care." Noting the great size of the squid depicted on the visor, Cuvier also mused that this might represent evidence of the semi-legendary kraken; in the North Pacific, then, he was resurrecting species instead of consigning them to eternal rest.[147]

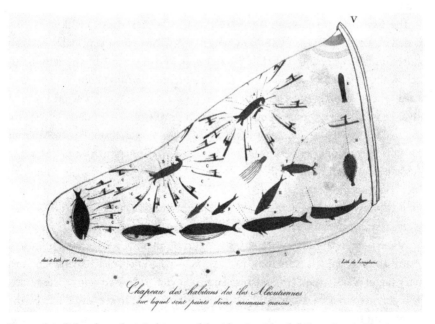

Figure 6.4 "A hat from the inhabitants of the Aleutian Islands." From Louis Choris, *Voyage pittoresque autor du monde: Avec des Portraits de Sauvages d'Amérique, d'Asie, d'Afrique* (Paris, 1822), Plate V. The Aleut wooden hat which Choris collected and for which the eminent scientist Georges Cuvier provided commentary. Courtesy of the Huntington Library, Rare Books Collection.

In part as a response to Tilesius's misinformation in the late 1830s, the Academy of Sciences again became interested in the sea cow. Through its intermediaries in the Russian American Company, it organized an all-out search for any remnants of the creature that could be found in the Commander or the Aleutian Islands, offering cash prizes to any hunter who could come back with a skull (while strictly warning against forgeries). Aleuts, too, were asked to help the company. The Academy expressed a guarded certainty that the animal was extinct: "the last specimen of this extraordinary animal was killed in 1768, and from that time, according to all the travelers who have been in the region, and even the inhabitants of the Aleutian Islands and the Northwest Coast of America, it has not been seen again."[148] That same year (1839), Johann Brandt, a German scientist working for the St. Petersburg Academy of Sciences, asked the Russian naturalist Ilya Vosnesenskii to procure a live specimen of a sea cow for the zoological museum. Only after Vosnesenskii had searched tirelessly for the better part of a decade, uncovering only one rib fragment, could Brandt be "certain that the creature is absolutely extinct."[149] In 1840, von Baer finally made the (almost) definitive statement on the sea cow's extinction. Surveying much of the literature, as well as noting conspicuous silences in other travelers' reports, von Baer dismissed claims that the sea cow might be found in Californian waters, or anywhere else for that matter.

The Russo-German scientists were put in an interesting position, having to defend the extinction of sea cow without pointing to an especially Russian shortcoming in causing it. While Brandt supplied the meat of the counterattack against extinction doubters (pointing out, among other things, that other sea-dwellers, such as the Great Auk, had gone extinct), von Baer did more to advance a careful argument about the Russian Empire in the process. The zoologist held outspoken opinions about the problems of imperialism. He wrote about the evils of missionaries who went out to change native cultures, and described Russian colonization in the North Pacific as "robbery." At the same time, von Baer had become a staunch defender of Russia's American colonies, and was at pains to show that they were equally well, if not better, managed than European overseas possessions.

When writing about the sea cow's extinction, then, von Baer was interested in stressing colonial factors that did not exclusively involve Russians. His primary target was Steller. "The relationship of Steller to [the sea cow]," he wrote, "is highly remarkable. He is not only the only naturalist to see and describe the animal, but he also to some extent contributed to its extinction, inasmuch as he counseled the greedy fur hunters to provision themselves with sea cow meat on Bering Island."[150] Von Baer's claims that Steller had directly advised the fur traders was pure speculation, but it served his claim that non-Russians had actively contributed to the sea cow's extinction. He noted sarcastically that, far from an inconvenience, Steller had found his shipwreck on Bering Island to be "a pleas-ant memory," from which he gained a "very nice capital" of three hundred sea otter pelts. Von Baer also claimed that the Russian government had very little to do with the subsequent fur trade that developed in the Aleutian Islands, and thus could not be implicated in the general environmental havoc that took place.[151] By blaming Steller and absolving the Russian government for the sea cow's extinction, von Baer shifted the blame from Russians in particular to humans at large. "The *Rhytina*," von Baer concluded, "gives us a noteworthy example of how quickly some species can be destroyed by the persecutions of man."[152] Whether this was an intentional whitewashing of the Russian colonial legacy or not, von Baer's expansive conclusion indicated how greatly the nineteenth-century conception of extinction and its causes had changed. While extinction in the eighteenth century was a useful cudgel against Russian imperial claims, it had become, in the nineteenth century, an indictment of all of humanity.

Von Baer and Brandt's influential writings on the sea cow established the creature as one of the icons of anthropogenic extinction. In 1866, the editors of Britain's *National Encyclopedia* still doubted the extinction of the dodo and the great auk, but wrote that the sea cow's loss was proof that humans could kill off an entire species. Elsewhere, the dodo was the best recognized example of extinction, but the sea cow often appeared shortly down the list.[153] Yet, into the 1860s, some prominent naturalists continued to doubt that the sea cow was gone. Darwin's great opponent, Richard Owen, speculated that there were likely undiscovered sea cow colonies in the Arctic Ocean, along the shores of both Siberia and Alaska. Even if the animal were extinct, then humans were hardly to blame. Instead, longer-term natural changes also responsible for the extinc-tion of the mammoth had brought about the sea cow's demise.[154] Owen's opin-ions found an enthusiastic second from the Livonian naturalist Carl Edouard Eichwald, who worked at the St. Petersburg School of Mines in the middle of the nineteenth century. Eichwald opined that sea mammals were harder to kill than land mammals as they could flee into the open ocean, and thus were unlikely to go extinct. While philosophical opposition to extinction may have been dead, the seductive notion of long-distance migration found new life, even though all accounts of the sea cow described it as a creature of the shallow waters.[155] Additionally, Eichwald pointed to one further persecutor of the sea cow: the Aleuts, who had, according to his account, been hunting the animals with har-poons for centuries and largely driven them out of the Aleutian Islands.[156]

Eichwald's accusations brought the afterlife of the sea cow to a strangely modern conclusion. Twenty-first-century archaeologists largely agree with him about the Aleuts' role in sea cow extinction, finding the animals' remains to be common in ancient Aleut middens but largely absent in more recent dig sites. Yet Eichwald's suspicion of the Aleuts was not free of the prejudices Lisiansky displayed when blaming the same people for the savage destruction of the sea otter. Eichwald, for example, claimed entirely without evidence that Aleuts were still hunting the sea cow, which had fled to the Arctic Ocean to "hide and rest from Aleut pursuit."[157] He also entirely ignored the long history of brutal colonial exploitation that had in part forced Aleuts to denude their own environment. Modern conceptions of extinction have numerous genealogies, not all of which would pass contemporary muster.

As Russia's American colony itself faced extinction, the extinction of animal species had become a central part of its history. The optimistic beginnings, when Steller and others claimed the North Pacific's endless animals would finally open the door to Japan and China, had faded and disappeared the same way the sea cow had and the sea otter nearly had. Looking back, commentators like von Baer could see the seeds of the colony's demise in Steller's own actions. And yet, the history of Russia's North Pacific colonies cannot be summed up quite so easily in the twinned stories of imperial and beastly extinction. In the process of alighting upon a foreign, volatile environment and attempting to redirect its humans and animals, Russians in the North Pacific had made signal contributions to humanity's understanding of historical ecology. Naturalists, uniquely present from the beginning, had chronicled and described the region's ecological changes. They had been the first to note the sea cow's extinction and realize the impact it should have on Enlightenment conceptions of natural order. They had also linked ecological change to imperial mismanagement. By the mid-nineteenth century, however, Russia's naturalists had become strangely docile. One way of understanding this change is to point toward their increasing influence on imperial power, as they became integrated into the cultures of management and study of the North Pacific, and to see in that the naturalists' domestication. Another way of understanding Lisiansky, Litke, and von Baer's generally positive impressions of the Russian North Pacific is to realize that the Russian colonizers had, in fact, absorbed many of the naturalists' earlier concerns, implementing sensible conservation measures and making their successes widely known. Problems remained, especially around the issue of ecological justice for the Aleuts. However, in the end, extinction did not kill the Russian Empire in the North Pacific.

Conclusion

Empire and Extinction

> The conquerors of our days, peoples or princes, want their empire to possess a united surface over which the superb eye of power can wander without encountering any inequality which hurts or limits its view. The same code of law, the same measures, the same rules, and if we could gradually get there, the same language; that is what is proclaimed as the perfection of the social organization... The great slogan of the day is *uniformity*.
>
> —Benjamin Constant, *De l'esprit de conquete*

Empire of Extinction has shown how the European imperial experience—especially the Russian experience—was instrumental in smashing old ideas about the impossibility of species disappearing from the face of the earth. It has also described the ways that species extinction impacted Russia's North Pacific empire by eroding the lifeways of the Aleuts and Alutiit, and the independence of the common Russian fur traders; harming the empire's reputation; and ultimately provoking changes in imperial policy and image. In the book, extinction has served as both event and metaphor. Much the same can be said about empire. Both words describe the facts on the ground—sea cows disappeared and Russians gained control over the labor of many formerly independent people. Both terms also describe conceptions, aspirations, and fears—the possibility of extinction, for example, was used sometimes to capture the entire range of bad imperial Russian results.

Such conclusions indicate the close historical relationship between empire and extinction. After all, imperial expansion has as one of its goals the remaking of colonial space to serve metropolitan interests. Preindustrial empires in particular reshaped local cultures and ecologies into forms more useful and familiar to themselves. Even where empires try to maintain difference, for example attempting to repress economic development on the periphery, the ultimate consequence is often the eradication of the local, the extinction of cultures and living organisms.[1] As numerous studies have shown, imperial expansion has almost always been accompanied by a loss of biodiversity in newly assimilated ecosystems. Continents and islands previously isolated from more densely populated regions have been especially vulnerable.[2]

Viewed from this level, the Russian imperial experience in the North Pacific had much in common with colonial locations in the rest of the world. Especially during the half-century from around 1760 to 1810, it is possible to discern a global conjuncture between declining colonial ecological diversity and an intensification of natural history study.[3] This conjuncture was crucial for producing the first widespread European awareness of species extinction. In Russia, this period saw, after several decades of relative inactivity, the transformative Academy Expeditions to Siberia (led by Pallas), and Billings and Krusenstern's fruitful expeditions to Kamchatka and Alaska. European scientific study of the North Pacific peaked in the decade around Billings (1790–1800), with major exploratory expeditions launched by the Spanish (Malaspina), French (La Perouse), and British (Vancouver). In the British Empire at this time, the naturalist Joseph Banks rose to prominence as an administrator, and his activities helped instill in the new colony of Australia an interest in natural history from its outset. By 1800, decades before Darwin's explorations, both corners of the Pacific had become sites of rich ethnographical, geographical, botanical, and zoological description.

Similar patterns emerged in the Atlantic, and in the Spanish, Dutch, and Portuguese empires. Spain's Bourbon monarchy initiated a major reform of its empire after 1759, placing increased stress on the economic potential of natural history. Between that time and 1808, Emperor Charles III sent more than sixty scientific expeditions to study the Spanish colonies, many of which were just as cosmopolitan as those of the Russians.[4] The Spanish, in fact, pursued botany's links with empire more thoroughly and systematically than even the British had, enlisting and in some cases demanding environmental research from all overseas crown officials. A standard questionnaire, termed a *Relación Geográfica*, was distributed to officials to be filled out with natural historical data and returned to the crown.[5] Such tasks required enormous manpower, bringing "into collaboration traveling European naturalists, colonial *criollo* naturalists, mestizo and indigenous collaborators, and administrators and institutions across the empire (in the Atlantic and in the Pacific)."[6] Expeditions throughout South America, even the many that ended in failure, resulted in an avalanche of data piling up in Madrid. A few decades later, the Dutch too began to train naturalists to systematically study the East Indies and report back to the University of Leiden.[7] Lisbon had already begun something similar. In 1783, Portugal's top center of learning, the University of Coimbra, revised its courses in natural history, placing new emphasis on observation and the potential economic benefits of colonial products. It also developed its first systematic instructions to be given out to naturalists heading to overseas colonies.[8]

The parallels and links with the Russian experience are striking. Just three years after the Coimbra standardization (1786), Pallas wrote up his detailed instructions for the French (later German) naturalist on the Billings Expedition. A decade later, Langsdorff left Portugal to join the first Russian circumnavigation, and later went to Brazil to conduct scientific explorations of the Amazon. As these multiple intellectual and personal crossings between empires show, intellectual and personal connections throughout Europe, Russia, and the colonial Atlantic and Pacific worlds thickened noticeably at the end of the eighteenth century.

Natural history's success in this period came partly from being in vogue, but it also served a real need for European empires. The discipline had gained increased relevance with Linnaeus's labors to make all nature commensurate across the globe, rendering complex ecologies into easily compared lists through the language of species. What was lost in comprehension (and his ideas were often derided for their "unnatural" quality) was made up for in utility. Just at the moment when natural history received its greatest challenge in the nearly inconceivably complex task of describing a rapidly enlarging world for Europeans, it found the necessary language. The bizarre flora and fauna of Australia may have had no analogs in Europe (or anywhere else), but the Linnaean style of systematizing could nonetheless locate each species according to rigid criteria legible to naturalists, philosophers, and—equally importantly—colonial administrators. Krasheninnikov undertook these Linnaean-like labors in his *History of Kamchatka*. The work was lambasted for its dry technicality and overly thorough topographical description, however, Krasheninnikov was merely ahead of his time (preceding Linnaeus's crucial tenth edition of *Systema Naturae* by two years). He had, in fact, made the peninsula legible to St. Petersburg and amenable to military, economic, and ecological maneuvers in ways none of his nonscientific predecessors had been able to. Natural history was "*the* colonial science *par excellence*."[9]

In the North Pacific, as in many other colonial locations, naturalists had to deal not only with exotic natures, but also changing natures. This is a point too often missed by scholars concerned with understanding the creation and transfer of natural historical knowledge in the colonial world. Bruno Latour, in particular, with his model of immutable mobiles, sees the task of the colonial scientist as revealing a fixed world to those at home.[10] That world, though, was often a snarling beast on the move, or a painting washing away before the naturalist's eyes. Its vagaries profoundly influenced the production and uses of natural history. Many attempts at transcribing nature ended in bitter failure, as bad weather, bad luck, or wild beasts themselves ended naturalists' quests. Steller and Sauer both bitterly turned back toward Asia after brief stays in America, when their ship captains weighed safety over science. Linnaeus's student Falck committed suicide in Central Asia rather than continue to bear the psychic and physical terrors of the journey. In Brazil, the Jesuit Joseph de Jussieu dreamed of exploring the fabled "Land of Cinnamon," but encountered only dangerous animals and impenetrable forests once he got there. Even the plants he managed to collect went to ruin.[11] More subtly, but perhaps more importantly, changing natures frustrated even those safely back in metropolitan capitals. Peter Simon Pallas, writing from his St. Petersburg home, devoted nearly half his life to the *Zoographia Rosso-Asiatica*. Intended to be a complete description of the empire's animals, his masterpiece included at least one that had already vanished. Pallas's illustrator, Tilesius, further multiplied the sea cow's specter and described for Europeans a wholly imaginary North Pacific fauna.

This evidence points to a second convergence of global colonial history—rapid ecological change—which natural history had more difficulty describing. Echoing Buffon, a popular natural history book among late-eighteenth-century travelers called humankind "a microcosm of the Universe...master of the earth, the facilitator of Nature and often also its destroyer."[12] Evidence—and reports—of this destruction was everywhere. By the last decade of the eighteenth century, colonial observers had begun to fear for the total destruction of some animal populations. In May 1790, the colonial commandant of newly settled Norfolk Island (located roughly between Australia and New Zealand) put limits on the numbers of Mount Pitt birds the convict settlers could kill, because "If every body was at liberty to kill them when they thought proper, ther [sic] would Soon not be a pidgeon left on the Island." The "great havoc and destruction" threatened both the convicts' future food supply and marked them as cruel barbarians.[13] Ten years later, on the south coast of Australia, the French explorer Nicolas Baudin warned that the seals would soon be exterminated if nothing were done to stop their rampant exploitation. In 1802, the *Sydney Gazette* called for action: "A well-wisher to POSTERITY" lamented the seals' "general massacre" which could be "a constant source of enterprise and emolument" if "properly managed."[14] In that same year, a Spanish colonial reported that in Paraguay, "the population of this province has so shrunk the number of Jaguars that those who remain are only on the coasts, and they take refuge in the impenetrable forests."[15] Similar concerns surrounded kangaroos in Tasmania in 1806.[16]

Not all naturalists put down the decrease to human causes; Alexander Humboldt claimed that in South America a somewhat mysterious "accidental, long-continued, and gradually increasing conflict among the animals" was to blame.[17] However, most viewed European imperial expansion as the chief cause of environmental change, and some began contemplating the extinction of entire species. In Pennsylvania in 1806, Benjamin Barton prophesied (entirely erroneously) that the opossum was doomed to extinction with the westward movement of American settlers. "Future naturalists," he wrote, "will only know these animals by their histories and pictures."[18] In 1785, on the Newfoundland

Grand Banks, a conjunction of island ecosystem and imperial expansion strikingly similar to that of the eighteenth-century North Pacific occurred. English Captain George Cartwright wrote of the imperiled great auk:

> ...it has been customary in later years for several crews of men to live all summer on that island for the sole purpose of killing the birds for the sake of their feathers; the destruction they have made is incredible. If a stop is not soon put to that practice, the whole breed will be diminished to nothing, particularly the penguins [great auks], for this is now the only island they have left to breed upon...[19]

Thomas Hallock has deemed 1788 to 1801 a crucial transition period for American conceptions of frontier ecological decline, an era of profound "social and ecological change."[20] Set against such examples, Sauer's, Merck's, and Langsdorff's particularly impassioned distress at "havock" in the Russian Empire puts them at the crest of a gathering wave of concern over colonial extinction.

Undoubtedly, many of the same developments that had encouraged natural history's explosion had also hastened the destruction of the plants and (especially) animals coming under consideration. Over the entire early modern period, imperial expansion into lightly peopled landscapes, large-scale human population growth, and advances in organization technologies (such as more powerful states) increased pressure on colonial environments.[21] In the late eighteenth century, Atlantic colonial commerce, rebounding from the reduced flows of the Seven Years' War and not yet dampened by the Napoleonic Wars, was enjoying a boom.[22] The global hunt for marine mammals, especially in the Pacific, was just entering its heyday.[23] Between 1793 and 1907, off the coast of South America, an estimated 3.5 million Juan Fernandez seals would be killed.[24] Russians would manage to kill similar numbers in the North Pacific. The resulting decline of some marine mammals was exceptionally visible. The late eighteenth century was not the first era of dramatic colonial environmental change. Monk seals in the Azores were extinct by the seventeenth century, while the early eighteenth century had witnessed the local extinction of humpback whales in the Atlantic and the near total depletion of bowheads and walrus around Greenland.[25] Still, these earlier depletions received little published attention. Only in the decades around 1800 did the increasing number of naturalists begin to mount a sustained attack on colonial environmental degradation.

Several themes run through global colonial reactions to animal declines. First, as the *Sydney Gazette* writer demonstrated, economic concerns—a conservationist ethic—motivated some observers. Similar ideas spurred Rezanov's decision to shut down the Pribylof seal hunt. However, strictly conservationist concerns were not always most important. The French zoologist François

Péron condemned the Australian sealing trade not only for its wastefulness, but also for "the cruelty with which English crews killed these 'gentle and peaceful' animals."[26] Sentiment also motivated conservation on Norfolk Island, and is an underrated factor in colonial environmentalism. In the 1770s, the American naturalist William Bartram and his hunters killed a bear in Florida, and then witnessed its cub weeping over its dead mother. Bartram related that

> The continual cries of this afflicted child, bereft of its parent, affected me very sensibly; I was moved with compassion, and charging myself as if accessary to what now appeared to be a cruel murder, endeavoured to prevail on the hunter to save its life, but to no effect! for by habit he had become insensible to compassion towards the brute creation: being now within a few yards of the harmless devoted victim, he fired, and laid it dead upon the body of the dam.

This distressing event helped convince Bartram of the wondrous complexity of divine creation as well as animals' capability for "premeditation, perseverance, resolution, and consummate artifice," as opposed to Cartesian notions of brute mechanism.[27] That Bartram blamed his hunters' dulled sentiment also connects him with Yuri Lisiansky's and Fedor Litke's condemnations of Aleut hunters' brutality. Sentiment functioned throughout Europe's colonies as a marker of class difference as well as an occasional reason to preserve nature.

Religion, as with Steller and Veniaminov, could also encourage a less rapacious attitude toward colonial environments. A remarkable sermon preached in colonial Tasmania in 1804 asked colonists to "give God thanks for the grass of the field…let us take notice of the great variety of those creatures which are made for our use…at the same time let us remember that our right in these creatures is not absolute, we hold them for God."[28] Here, the idea of plenitude—that God had created species to fulfill all possibilities of life—which was often used to reject the idea of extinction, provided a caution. Steller's firebrand Pietism, pitted against Orthodoxy's more formal structures, also showed the disruptive force religion could become when misaligned with imperial practices. Religion gave no sure guide to animal preservation though, as it was often closely implicated in the greater imperial projects. Veniaminov, while deeply concerned with the effects ecological degradation was having on the Aleuts, was also a fierce proponent of Russian interests in the North Pacific.

Another underrated factor in the origins of this global concern over colonial environments was an erupting anti-imperialism, which tied questions of empire and environment together in new ways. Many eighteenth-century Europeans responded to their new encounters with exotic environments by empathetically (if not always accurately) celebrating these edenic human and natural worlds. Backlash against the colonial despoliation of island paradises occurred in St. Helena, Mauritius, and some Caribbean Islands in the eighteenth century. However, the promise of colonial wealth often washed away philosophical pre-occupations with unsullied nature. Many colonists responded to environmental change ruefully, got on with the business of making empire, and managed to combine a feeling of crisis with a keen sense of opportunity. Along the North American frontier, "elegies for things disappeared" became a standard trope celebrating a pre-European world irrevocably lost, while also emphasizing that new ecologies meant new possibilities. In other words, loss—and the possibility for renewal in different forms—set the stage for American empire. As the territorial seal for the Northwest Territory of the trans-Appalachian West had it, *meliorem lapsa locavit*—"a better one has replaced it." [29]

In some locations, though, concern for environmental justice made for a radical critique of colonialism, and naturalists in the Russian North Pacific played a leading role in formulating these ideas. Similar ideas echoed, decades later, on the American Western frontier. In 1847, Lieutenant James Abert lamented that

> This winter, the buffalo have almost deserted the river, there is no grass for them; and the poor Indian, forced by the cold season to take refuge in the timber that alone grows on the streams, must now travel far away from the village to get meat for his subsistence. There should be a law to protect these noble pasture grounds. [30]

Such concern for the ecological consequences of colonialism on subjected peoples contrasted sharply with earlier denunciations of indigenous peoples' environmental irrationality. Abert's suggestions, which cut against the grain of American colonialism, showed the same sensitivity to human ecology as did the ideas of Steller, Sauer, Langsdorff, Chamisso, and Veniaminov. They observed the close linkages between humans and animals in Kamchatka and Alaska, and perceived at an early stage the threat colonial extraction posed to happiness of imperial subjects. Perhaps most surprisingly, they cared about the future of both colonized humans and animals.

Those in the Russian North Pacific understood this conjuncture of empire and extinction in idiosyncratic ways, which was their signal contribution to the assessment of colonial environmental change. Russians, and those who observed the Russian Empire, rarely found the same confidence that Americans, Australians, and others achieved about their resource frontiers. The perilously overstretched and perennially undermanned Russian empire had to employ naturalists from all around Europe to try to describe and understand the North Pacific. The diverse nationalities of the empire's scientists certainly played a role in encouraging unusually biting criticism about the waste and cruelty involved in the fur trade. Indigenous Russian practices and conceptions contributed as well to creating new environmental practices. Russia's long history of imperial flexibility allowed for foreign contributions to expansion, encouraged close interaction with indigenous peoples such as the Aleuts, and helped foster an ethos of diversity expressed in such works as Peter Simon Pallas's ZRA. By the mid-nineteenth century, the Russian empire was even moving toward a kind of environmental hubris, as it found excuses for the eradication of its colonial subjects and celebrated its magnificent management of nature. These boasts rested on real (if imperfect) conservation successes crafted from careful reactions to self-produced criticism, Aleut notions of animal behavior, and the strong influence of naturalists and scientifically minded colonial bureaucrats.

Here, explanations for Russian responses also have to move beyond human actors in ways that histories of science do not account for. The animals of the North Pacific proved extremely vulnerable to imperial expansion, and their massive declines were exceptionally visible. The colder weather of the 1750s helped doom the sea cow, while likely pushing up pinniped and sea otter numbers before the latter's near-extinction throughout the Aleutians in the 1790s. The Russian colonizers could do nothing to affect changing oceanic regimes, nor did they control the rate of animal extraction very well. Russians did not mean to eradicate the sea cow, and for much of the eighteenth century they wielded blunt, clumsy force at the North Pacific's fur-bearers, working through terrorized Aleuts and Alutiit, and basing their expectations on an incommensurable Siberian experience. Even the humble conservation successes achieved after the 1820s were poorly understood, as sea otters seemed to reappear mysteriously, or just as puzzlingly, fail to reappear. Until the colony's end, in 1867, Russians had not gained a firm grasp on sea-otter ecology.

Taking into account the unpredictable ecosystems and the developing Russian ethos of conservation, empire in the North Pacific could also encourage diversity. In these ways, empire and extinction remained far apart, even at odds. A thread of resistance to flattening human and animal worlds runs from Steller through unheralded eighteenth-century state servitors, blossoms in the sharp protests of Sauer and Langsdorff, and is expressed more practically by Russian naval officers, priests, and colonial administrators in the nineteenth century. Kamchadals, Aleuts, and Alutiit, too, likely raised a similar lament (the few records surviving suggest they did). Of course, indigenous North Pacific peoples, and men like Steller and Sauer, also contributed to the environmental change they criticized. Empire exacted a terrible human and environmental toll, even as it offered rich rewards for entrepreneurs, collaborators, and naturalists.

Russia's Alaskan empire experienced its own extinction 1867, and another fur rush—this time led by Americans—descended upon the region. Ignoring the Russian experience, only after an excruciatingly long time did Americans too learn to better manage sea otters and fur seals. The animals finally rebounded after the international Fur Seal Treaty of 1911 and the respite provided by the Second World War. Meanwhile, Alaska's native peoples were further dislocated and exploited, while Russian influences were overlain by American, Scandinavian, and Filipino immigrants. Now, Russians rarely trammel those seas, but sea otters and fur seals proliferate. Aleuts and Alutiit are reclaiming their precontact heritage, even as they largely retain their Russian Orthodox religion. Besides the occasional church, and a few pockets of Russian speakers, it can seem that Russia left little lasting impact in the region. The Russian Empire surged into the Pacific and then quietly drained away. But some things empires do are forever. The sea cow will never return.

Appendix A

CHAPTER 2 SOURCES

For no other portion of this book is the question of sources as crucial or as difficult as it is for Chapter 2. Records of catches, essential for determining the extent of environmental change, are available, but they are fragmentary and sometimes of doubtful veracity. Though Russian merchants were instructed to leave accounts of their voyages with local authorities, many of the reports were either never filed, or were subsequently lost over two and a half centuries of neglect and accidents. The archives in Okhotsk and Yakutsk, both repositories of *promyshlenniki* reports, burned down in the nineteenth century, but before the fires occurred, several scholars collected materials relating to Russian voyages to the North Pacific. The first of these collectors was the academician Gerhard Friedrich Müller, who took part in the Second Kamchatka Expedition. While in Siberia, Müller searched the Siberian archives for materials on Siberian history, and he naturally developed an interest in the North Pacific fur trade and its documentation. Müller perused and copied many of the *promyshlenniki* reports that made it into the Moscow Archive of Foreign Affairs, and after 1770 he also started an intensive letter exchange with Captain Timofei Shmalev, who was stationed in Kamchatka. Shmalev sent him the most recent *promyshlenniki* reports until Müller died in 1783. Although he intended to publish the Shmalev and archival reports, before his death Müller succeeded only in writing a history of Bering's second voyage, printed as "Nachrichten von Seereisen" in 1758. The materials Müller collected, however, remain in the so-called "Fondi Millera" (Müller folios) in the Russian State Archive of Ancient Acts. They constitute only a fragmentary record of *promyshlennik* voyages, but in many cases they are the sole direct accounts still extant.

Peter Simon Pallas took up Müller's work after the latter's death, and succeeded in publishing many of his friend's reports in his series *Neue Nordische Beyträge zur physikalischen und geographischen Erd–und Völkerbeschreibung, Naturgeschichte und Oekonomie* (New Northern Contributions to Earth Sciences, Geography, Anthropology, Natural History, and Economy), which appeared from 1781 to 1796 in both St. Petersburg and Leipzig. Pallas himself added new materials that he had collected in the last part of the eighteenth century, including a valuable report on Mednyi Island which he had asked the Cossack Dmitri Bragin to collect in 1772. With an array of correspondents, including the Kamchatka governor Magnus Behm, Pallas had the best grasp in St. Petersburg of North Pacific events in the last quarter of the eighteenth century.

Nonetheless, neither Müller nor Pallas possessed a comprehensive view of Russian voyages to the Aleutians. They did not have access to Siberian archives, nor to the papers of the Russian American Company, which was founded in 1799 and took possession of the reports of many of the private fur trading companies. In the nineteenth century, two tsarist officers used the RAC papers and other documents to compile valuable chronologies of eighteenth–century *promyshlennik* voyages, including information on their hunting grounds and cargoes. The first officer to do so, Vasilii Berkh, took part in the first Russian round–the–world voyage from 1803 to 1806, serving on the ship of Yuri Lisiansky.[1] When the expedition stopped at the RAC's stations on Kodiak Island and Sitka, Berkh looked through the company's archives and spoke with many of the "old voyagers" still alive who had been active during the early years of the fur trade. In 1823, Berkh published a *Chronological History of the Discovery of the Aleutian Islands*, in which he listed all the voyages known to him, together with cargo information.[2]

Berkh's information was unique, with voyage details found nowhere else. Still, the *Chronological History* is incomplete. Some of the gaps were filled in by A. S. Polonskii, a tsarist official who, in the early nineteenth century, served for approximately twenty years in Petropavlovsk, Okhotsk, and Yakutsk.[3] Polonskii had unique access to local archives, which held reports of several unknown North Pacific voyages. With these materials, supplemented with some figures from Berkh's *Chronological History*, Polonskii produced two manuscript works: a "List of Russian *Promyshlennik* Voyages to the Eastern Ocean from 1743 to 1800," and "*Promyshlenniki* in the Aleutian Islands (1743–1800)," both currently in the Archive of the Russian Geographical Society in St. Petersburg.[4] Polonskii's voyage descriptions are much more detailed than Berkh's, and he uncovered several voyages that Berkh missed altogether. Some scholars (particularly Soviet scholars) have suggested that he exaggerated the *promyshlenniki*'s crimes against the Aleuts, and that he did not adequately document some of his claims. These possible failures aside, his statistical information is the most complete of any available, and there would seem to be little motivation to have altered this type of data.

As most of the materials with which Berkh and Polonskii worked have been lost, later scholars have treated their works as primary sources. The Soviet scholar Raisa Makarova has to date published the most comprehensive history of the eighteenth–century North Pacific fur trade: *Russians in the Pacific Ocean in the Second Half of the Eighteenth Century* (1968). In the book, Makarova listed all known eighteenth–17century voyages, mostly relying on Berkh's account, though supplemented with some data from Polonskii. In her ethnohistory of Atkha Island, Lydia Black published a similar list of voyages, this time appending a recently uncovered document from the fur trader Grigorii Shelikhov, along with his own list of preceding voyages.[5]

A full reckoning of the eighteenth–century voyages is essential in order to tabulate the numbers of each animal caught, and to determine where local populations were reduced or extirpated. Black, writing during a period when the Geographical Society Archives were closed to foreign researchers, did not have access to the Polonskii materials. At the time, she stated that

> Until there is a thorough statistical analysis of the reported catches, with attention paid to the extent of the geographic area hunted and the exact times in which particular catches obtained, no statement can be made of how heavily overhunted, if at all, the Aleutians were.[6]

With the reopening of Russian Archives—and particularly with renewed access to Polonskii's research—such work is now possible. The pages below list catches of sea otters, fur seals, blue (polar) foxes, and other foxes on Russian voyages from 1742 to 1799, using data from Polonskii, Berkh, and the Fondi Millera.[7]

LIST OF HUNTING EXPEDITIONS IN THE NORTH PACIFIC FROM 1742 TO 1800

Year	Company	Hunting Location	Sea Otters	Fur Seals	Blue Foxes	Other Foxes	Profit
1. 1742	Bering, Steller	Bering Island	900				
2. 1743–17-45	Basov	Bering Island	1,200		4,000		64,000 rubles
3. 1745–1746	Trapeznikov	Bering Island	1,670	1,990	2,240		112,200
4. 1745–1747	Chabaevskii Trapeznikov	Attu, Agatu, Semichi Near Aleutians	743				19,200
5. 1747–1748	Trapeznikov, Basov Tolstikh	Mednyi Island	970	2,000	1,520		50,020
6. 1747–1748	Kholodilov Trapeznikov	Bering Island	321	40	1,421		52,590
7. 1747–1749	Rybinski Trapeznikov	Mednyi Island	460	100	2,110		23,024
8. 1747–1749	Vsevidov	??					5,990

(*Continued*)

Year	Company	Hunting Location	Sea Otters	Fur Seals	Blue Foxes	Other Foxes	Profit
9. 1748–1749	Bakhov, Shalaurov	Bering Island	58	650			4,780
10. 1749–1750	Trapeznikov, Basov	Mednyi Island	522	1,300	1,080		39,376
11. 1749–1750	Trapeznikov	Bering Island Near Aleutian Islands					3,127
12. 1749–1752	Kholodilov Trapeznikov	Bering Island Attu	1,607				95,690
13. 1750–1752	Trapeznikov	Attu (shipwrecked)					–
14. 1750–1752	Rybinskaya Trapeznikov	Mednyi Island	1,520	7,010	1,900	224	61,520
15. 1750–1753	Trapeznikov	Near Aleutian Islands					105,730
16. 1750–1754	Yugov	Bering, Mednyi	825	2,224	2,698		65,429
17. 1751–1752	Trapeznikov	Aleutian Islands	1,935				11,650
18. 1752–1757	Trapeznikov	Bering Island	218	2,500	3,851		3,473
19. 1753–1755	Rybinskaya Serebrennikov	Bering Eastern Near Aleutians	1,260				65,060
20. 1753–1755	Kholodilov Trapeznikov	Bering, Near Aleutians Attu	1,813		75		109,355
21. 1754–1757	Trapeznikov	Attu	3,117	10	720		187,268
22. 1754–1758	Krasil'nikov Trapeznikov	Commander Islands	169		1,400	300	14,438

23. 1755–1758	Protasov	??	1,824	840	720		unknown
24. 1756–1758	Serebrennikov Rybinskii	Aleutians, Kikigalask	1,120				50,355
25. 1756–1759	Kholodilov	Bering, Attu, Agatu	5,463		1,040		317,541
26. 1757–1761	Zhilkin	Bering, Far Aleutians Avada, Near Aleutians	202	4			17,330
27. 1758–1762	Nikiforov, Snigirev Trapeznikov	Fox Islands, Umnak Unalashka	1,564		1,263	1,100	130,450
28. 1758–1763	Chabaevskii	Attu	1,857		109		104,218
29. 1758–1763	Trapeznikov	Near Aleutians, Kiska	881				58,170
30. 1758–1763	Krasil'nikov	Aleutians, Unimak	1,485				78,304
31. 1759–1761	Rybinskaya Serebrennikov	Near Aleutians	3,097		336		150,270
32. 1759–1762	Kulakov	Near Aleutians	1,550		530		101,430
33. 1760–1762	Bechevin	Umnak, Alaska	1,320		408	2	52,570
34. 1760–1763	Chabaevskii, Popov	Avadak, Amchitka, Buldir, Kvasnik, Attu Kiska	567	67			5,409
35. 1760–1764	Kholodilov	Andreanof Islands Adak, Amlya, Atkha Kanaga, Tanaga	3,365		532		120,000

(Continued)

Year	Company	Hunting Location	Sea Otters	Fur Seals	Blue Foxes	Other Foxes	Profit
36. 1762–1763	Rybinskaya Serebrennikov	Near Aleutians	305		9		17,040
37. 1762–1764	Trapeznikov	Unalashka	145			188	"small cargo"
38. 1764–1766	Panovs	Umnak, Unalashka	532			2,437	42,280
39. 1764–1768	Chabaevskii, Popov	Near Aleutians, Fox	1,327			735	98,840
40. 1765–1768	Trapeznikov	Commander Islands	378	3,350	1733		32,547
41. 1765–1769	Krasil'nikov	Attu	1,524	1,845	1,045		83,387
42. 1765–1770	Shilov, Lapin	Fox	623			2,076	68,520
43. 1767–1770	Panov	Andreanof	5,855		1,098		284,868
44. 1767–1772	Popov, Lapin	Fox	1,121		700	3,083	109,943
45. 1768–1773	Mukhin, Zasilkin	Near and Andreanof	2,718		1,127		140,670
46. 1770–1774	Serebrennikov Arkashev, Shaposh.	Andreanof	2,574		1,130		136,050
47. 1770–1775	Shilov, Orekhov Lapin	Fox, Alaska	1,993			5,019	137,455
48. 1772–1779	Orekhov Peloponesov	Unimak, Kodiak	4,680		1,104	2,939	300,416
49. 1772–1778	Kholodilnikov	Fox, Kodiak, Bering	3721	1430		702	166,056
50. 1773–1779	Burenin	Fox	951	540		1,008	52,520

51. 1774	Osokin, Shvetsov	Ship wrecked in Sea of Okhotsk					-------
52. 1774–1778	Shubin	Commander Islands	310	39,500		990	98,840
53. 1776–1777	Panovs	Commander Islands					unknown
54. 1776–1781	Lapin, Orekhov Shilov	Fox	2,720	11,910		2,701	172,020
55. 1777–1779	Alin, Shelikhov	Commander Islands	936	33,840	1,584		74,240
56. 1777–1781	Panov	Amchitka	733	8,000	1,106		41,948
57. 1777–1781	Savelev, Shelikhov	Andreanof	491	11,500		1,600	57,860
58. 1777–1782	Golikov, Shelikhov	Attu, Amchitka	955	4,716		609	133,150
59. 1777–1781	Kiselevs	Commander, Atkha	483	6,160		1,116	49,215
60. 1778–1785	Panovs	Fox, Kodiak	1,218	61		1,848	89,160
61. 1778–1785	Panovs	Fox, Kodiak	2,663			3,744	127,834
62. 1779–1785	Golikov, Shelikhov Panovs	Near, Andreanofskie	1,321	640		724	63,417
63. 1780–1786	Shelikhov	Near Aleutians	1,000	18,500		931	93,827
64. 1780–1786	Panovs	Amlya, Unimak	1,144	1,395		3,004	71,746
65. 1780–1786	Kholodilov	Umnak, Chugach Bay	shipwrecked				-------
66. 1780	Zhuravlev, Krivorotov	-------	shipwrecked				-------

(*Continued*)

Year	Company	Hunting Location	Sea Otters	Fur Seals	Blue Foxes	Other Foxes	Profit
67. 1781–1789	Lebedev–Lastochkin	Pribylof Islands, Fox	2,730	31,151		6,794	253,018
68. 1781–1787	Alin.	Mednyi, Amchitka	398	7,600		56	35,219
69. 1781–1786	Panovs	Unalashka, Chugach Bay, Akun, Unga	882	3,352		2,116	63,367
70. 1781–1791	Orekhov	Unalashka, Alaska,	2,223	37,712		6,822	238,700
71. 1782–1791	Protasov	Andreanofs, Fox Pribylofs	2,146	72,000	4,850	150	171,914
72. 1782–1791	Panov	Fox	2,459	290		2,224	109,733
73. 1783–1786	Shelikhov, Golikov	Kodiak, Afognak	1,111	266		1,061	56,000
74. 1783–1789	Shelikhov, Golikov	Kodiak, Afognak	5,005			4,727	300,000
75. 1783–1790	Lebedev–Lastochkin	Kenai Gulf					102,108

	Operator	Location					
76. 1783–1793	Shelikhov, Golikov	Northwest Coast Aleutians	64,000	128,000			
77. 1783–1795	Kozitsyn	Commander Islands	45			88	unknown
78. 1785–1793	Panov	Commander Islands	1,388			183	73,000
79. 1790	Golikov, Shelikhov	Pribylofs	shipwrecked				
80. 1790–1792	Golikov, Shelikhov	Northwest Coast	4,502			4,969	376,000
81. 1790–1797	Lebedev–Last.	Unalashka, Kenai Gulf	1,189	66,860		1,655	183,200
82. 1792–1797	Kiselov	Unalashka	88	10,000		500	38,860
83. 1795	Golikov, Shelikhov	NW Coast	3,468			4,789	321,138
84. 1795	Golikov, Shelikhov	NW Coast	1,095	75,000	600		276,500
85. 1797	Golikov, Shelikhov	NW Coast	467	5		21,912	
86. 1797	Shirokikh	NW Coast	402	45,000		804	51,000

NOTES

Introduction

1. Daryl P. Domning, *Sirenian Evolution in the North Pacific Ocean*. Vol. 18, University of California Publications in Geological Sciences (Berkeley: University of California Press, 1977).
2. Rudyard Kipling, *The Jungle Book* (New York: Penguin, 1987), 110–112.
3. Kipling, *The Jungle Book*, 98.
4. John McBratney, "Imperial Subjects, Imperial Space in Kipling's 'Jungle Book,'" *Victorian Studies* 35, no. 3 (Spring 1992): 277–293.
5. Richard Ellis, *No Turning Back: The Life and Death of Animal Species* (New York: Harper Collins, 2004), xix.
6. Ellis, *No Turning Back*, part II.
7. Dean Littlepage, *Steller's Island: Adventures of a Pioneer Naturalist in Alaska* (Seattle: Mountaineers Books, 2006); Corey Ford, *Where the Sea Breaks its Back: The Epic Story of a Pioneer Naturalist and the Discovery of Alaska* (Boston: Little, Brown, 1996).
8. Callum Roberts, *The Unnatural History of the Sea* (Washington, DC: Island Press/Shearwater Books, 2007), 11–15.
9. John F. Richards, *The Unending Frontier: An Environmental History of the Early Modern World* (Berkeley: University of California Press, 2003), 544–545.
10. Ellis, *No Turning Back*, 11. Mark Barrow has recently written the fullest history of Europeans' and Americans' struggles with the idea of extinction. See Mark Barrow, *Nature's Ghosts: Confronting Extinction from the Age of Jefferson to the Age of Ecology* (Chicago: University of Chicago Press, 2009).
11. Georg H. von Langsdorff, *Bemerkung auf einer Reise um die Welt in den Jahren 1803 bis 1807*, vol. 1 (Frankfurt am Mayn: Im Verlag bei Friedrich Wilmans, 1812), 23.
12. Martin Sauer, *An Account of a Geographical and Astronomical Expedition to the Northern Parts of Russia* (London: T. Cadell, 1802), 181.
13. Victor Scheffer, "The Last Days of the Sea Cow," *Smithsonian* 3, no. 10 (1973): 64–66.
14. Scheffer, "The Last Days of the Sea Cow," 66.
15. Alexander Etkind, *Internal Colonization: Russia's Imperial Experience* (Cambridge: Polity Press, 2011), 13; Homi Bhabha, *The Location of Culture* (London: Routledge, 1994).
16. Georges Louis Leclerc Buffon, *Buffon's Natural History*, vol. 5, trans. William Smellie, (London: C. and G. Kearsley, 1792), 92, 93.
17. Adelbert von Chamisso, "Remarks and Opinions of the Naturalist of the Expedition, Aldelbert von Chamisso." In Otto von Kotzebue, *A Voyage of Discovery into the South Sea and Beering's Straits*, vol. 2 (London: Longman, Hurst, Rees, Orme, and Brown, 1821), 294.
18. Nootka was a settlement on Vancouver Island contested by the Nuu-cha-nulth, Spanish, and British; Baranov's verse was overly optimistic in predicting its incorporation into the Russian Empire.

19. Richard Grove, *Green Imperialism: Colonial Expansion, Tropical Island Edens and the Origins of Environmentalism, 1600–1860* (Cambridge: Cambridge University Press, 1995).

20. John Muir, *The Cruise of the Corwin* (San Francisco: Sierra Club Books, 1993), 7.

21. C. R. Harrington, "The Evolution of Arctic Marine Mammals," *Ecological Applications* 18 (2008): 23–40.

22. Jim Lichatowitz, *Salmon without Rivers: A History of the Pacific Salmon Crisis* (Washington: Island Press, 1999), 13.

23. Lydia Black, "Volcanism as a Factor in Human Ecology: The Aleutian Case," *Ethnohistory* 28, no. 4 (Autumn 1981): 313–340.

24. One example is the massive, still unexplained decline in sea otters during the 1990s. The work of James Estes and his students is particularly noteworthy on this topic. See Angela M. Doroff, et al., "Sea Otter Population Declines in the Aleutian Archipelago," *Journal of Mammlogy* 84, no. 1 (February 2003): 55–64; J. A. Estes, et al., "Killer Whale Predation on Sea Otters Linking Oceanic and Nearshore Ecosystems," *Sciences* New Series 282, no. 5388 (October 16, 1998): 473–476; Thomas Gelatt, Donald Siniff, and James Estes, "Activity Patterns and Time Budgets of the Declining Sea Otter Population at Amchitka Island, Alaska," *The Journal of Wildlife Management* 66, no. 1 (January 2002): 29–39.

25. Herbert Maschner, et al., "Biocomplexity of Sanak Island," *Pacific Science* 63 (2009): 673–709; David Yesner, "Effects of Prehistoric Human Exploitation on Aleutian Sea Mammal Populations," *Arctic Anthropology* 25 (1988): 28–43.

26. Charlotte Coté, *Spirit of Our Whaling Ancestors* (Seattle: University of Washington Press, 2010).

27. Jonathan Raban, *Passage to Juneau: A Sea and its Meanings* (New York: Vintage, 2000), 24–25.

28. Library of Congress, Manuscript Division. Yudin Collection, Archive of the Holy Synod, Box 643, 53–58.

29. Adelbert von Chamisso, *The Alaska Diary of Adelbert von Chamisso, Naturalist on the Kotzebue Voyage, 1815–1818*, trans. Robert Fortuine (Anchorage: Cook Inlet Historical Society, 1986), 29.

30. For a contemporary look at the region's environment, see Terry Johnson, *The Bering Sea and Aleutian Islands: Region of Wonders* (Fairbanks: Alaska Sea Grant College Program, University of Alaska Fairbanks, 2003), 27.

31. G. W. Steller, *Journal of a Voyage with Bering*, ed. O. W. Frost, trans. Margritt Engel and O.W. Frost (Stanford, CA: Stanford University Press, 1988), 66–67.

32. Peter Simon Pallas, *Betrachtungen über die Beschaffenheit der Gebürge...* (Frankfurt und Leipzig, 1778), 42; Adelbert von Chamisso, *Discovery in the South Sea*, vol. 3 (London: Printed for Sir Richard Phillips and Co., 1821), 283.

33. Ferdinand von Wrangel, *Russian America: Statistical and Ethnographical Information*, trans. Mary Sadouski (Kingston, Ontario: The Limestone Press, 1980), 86.

34. Aron Crowell, Amy Steffian, and Gordon Pullar, eds., *Looking Both Ways: Heritage and Identity of the Alutiiq People* (Fairbanks: University of Alaska Press, 2001), 26; S. A. Arutiunov and W. W. Fitzhugh, "Prehistory of Siberia and the Bering Sea." In W. W. Fitzhugh and A. L. Crowell, eds., *Crossroads of Continents: Cultures of Siberia and Alaska* (Washington, DC: Smithsonian Institution Press, 1988), 117–129.

35. The question of who counted as a natural historian in the eighteenth century is far from straightforward. In that era, for the first time in Europe, there were many who made their living entirely through the study of the natural world. Academies of Science, including the branch in St. Petersburg (founded 1725), enjoyed imperial patronage and allowed their members a great degree of specialization. Though the modern fields of biology, botany, and geology still blended together into one discipline, natural history had nonetheless become largely distinct from mathematics, physics, and social history. Still, the amateur pursuit of natural history was far from dead, especially in the colonies. Any man with literary interests who traveled to the North Pacific wrote profusely about the environment, and was assured of an interested audience of both amateurs and professionals. For the purpose of this study, all those who wrote about natural history are considered natural historians, though of course the difference between amateur and professional sometimes impacted the writer's viewpoint, and receives discussion where merited.

36. For knowledge-production as a mode of making imperial claims, see Patricia Seed, *Ceremonies of Possession in Europe's Conquest of the New World, 1492–1640* (Cambridge: Cambridge University Press, 1995) and James Delbourgo and Nicholas Drew, eds., *Science and Empire in the Atlantic World* (New York: Routledge, 2008).

37. Willard Sunderland, *Taming the Wild Field: Colonization and Empire on the Russian Steppe* (Ithaca, NY: Cornell University Press, 2004), 79.

38. See Joyce Chaplin, "The Curious Case of Science and Empire," *Reviews in American History* 34, no. 4 (2006): 434–440.

39. See Mary Louise Pratt, *Imperial Eyes: Travel Writing and Transculturation* (New York: Routledge, 1992); John Gascoigne, *Joseph Banks and the English Enlightenment: Useful Knowledge and Polite Culture* (Cambridge: Cambridge University Press, 1994) and *Science in the Service of Empire: Joseph Banks, the British State and the Uses of Science in the Age of Revolution* (Cambridge: Cambridge University Press, 1998); Richard Drayton, *Nature's Government: Science, Imperial Britain, and the Improvement of the World* (New Haven: Yale University Press, 2000); David MacKay, *In the Wake of Cook: Exploration, Science, and Empire, 1780–1801* (New York: St. Martin's Press, 1985); Margarette Lincoln, *Science and Exploration in the Pacific: European Voyages to the Southern Oceans in the Eighteenth Century* (Woodbridge, Suffolk, UK: Boydell Press, 1998); for a dissenting viewpoint see Susan Scott Parrish, *American Curiosity: Cultures of Natural History in the Colonial British Atlantic World* (Chapel Hill: University of North Carolina Press, 2006).

40. Drayton, *Nature's Government*, xv.

41. Simon Schaffer, "Afterword." In David Philip Miller and Peter Hanns Reill, eds., *Visions of Empire: Voyages, Botany, and Representations of Nature* (Cambridge: Cambridge University Press, 1996), 336.

42. Bruno Latour, *Science in Action: How to Follow Scientists and Engineers through Society* (Cambridge, MA: Harvard University Press, 1987).

43. Patricia Para, *Sex, Empire & Botany: The Story of Carl Linnaeus and Joseph Banks* (New York: Columbia University Press, 2003); Lisbet Koerner, *Linnaeus: Nature and Nation* (Cambridge, MA: Harvard University Press, 1999); Carolyn Merchant, *The Death of Nature: Women, Ecology, and the Scientific Revolution* (San Francisco: Harper & Row, 1973).

44. See Neil Safier, *Measuring the New World: Enlightenment Science and South America* (Chicago: University of Chicago Press, 2008), and "Global Knowledge on the Move: Itineraries, Amerindian Narratives and Deep Histories of Science," *Isis* 101, no. 1 (March 2010): 133–145; Julie Cruikshank, *Do Glaciers Listen? Local Knowledge, Colonial Encounters, and Social Imagination* (Vancouver: UBC Press, 2005); Alan Bewell, "Romanticism and Colonial Natural History," *Studies in Romanticism* 43, no. 1 (Spring 2004): 5–34.

45. For a notable exception, see Barbara Sweetland Smith, ed., *Science under Sail: Russia's Great Voyages to America, 1728–1867* (Anchorage: Anchorage Museum of History and Art, 2000).

46. For examples, see Andreas Kappeler, *Russland als Vielvölkerreich: Entstehung, Geschichte, Zerfall* (München: Beck, 1992); Dominic Lieven, *Empire: The Russian Empire and its Rivals* (New Haven, CT: Yale University Press, 2000); Geoffrey Hosking, *Russia: People and Empire, 1552–1917* (Cambridge, MA: Harvard University Press, 1998); Willard Sunderland, *Taming the Wild Field: Colonization and Empire on the Russian Steppe* (Ithaca, NY: Cornell University Press, 2004); Jane Burbank, Mark von Hagen, and Anatolyi Remnev, eds., *Russian Empire: Space, People, Power, 1700–1930* (Bloomington: Indiana University Press, 2007). Also see the international journal dedicated to the study of the Russian Empire, *Ab Imperio*, founded in 2000.

47. Mark Bassin, "Russia between Europe and Asia: The Ideological Construction of Geographical Space," *Slavic Review* 50, no. 1 (1990): 6–8.

48. Michael Khodarkovsky, *Russia's Steppe Frontier: The Making of a Colonial Empire, 1500–1800* (Bloomington: Indiana University Press, 2002), 6.

49. Anatolyi Remnev, "Siberia and the Russian Far East in the Imperial Geography of Power." In Burbank, et al, eds, *Russian Empire*, 436; Denis J. B. Shaw, "Geographical Practice and its Significance in Peter the Great's Russia," *Journal of Historical Geography* 22, no. 2 (1996): 176.

50. See A. Yu. Petrov, *Obrazovanie Russkoi-Amerikanskoi Kompanii* [The Formation of the Russian American Company] (Moscow: Nauka, 2000).

51. Beginning with Hubert Howe Bancroft, *History of Alaska* (San Francisco: A. L. Bancroft, 1886). See also Stephen Haycox, *Alaska: An American Colony* (Seattle: University of Washington Press, 2002). Haycox's view of Alaskan history during the Russian period stresses the continuities with post-1867 history.

52. Anthony Pagden, *Lords of All the World: Ideologies of Empire in Spain, Britain and France c. 1500–c. 1800* (New Haven: Yale University Press, 1995), 4; Dominic Lieven, *Empire: The Russian Empire and its Rivals* (New Haven: Yale University Press, 2000), 224.

53. Andrei Grinev, "A Brief Survey of the Russian Historiography of Russian America of Recent Years," *Pacific Historical Review* 79, no. 2 (May 2010): 265–278; Grinev, "Nekotorye Tendentsii v Otechestvennoi Istoriografii Rossiiskoi Kolonizatsii Alyaski," *Voprosy Istorii* (1994).

54. Ilya Vinkovetsky, "Circumnavigation, Empire, Modernity, Race: The Impact of Round-the-World Voyages on Russia's Imperial Consciousness," *Ab Imperio* 1, no. 2 (2001): 191–209; Ilya Vinkovetsky, *Russian America: An Overseas Colony of a Continental Empire, 1804–1867* (Oxford: Oxford University Press, 2011). See also Richard Wortman, "Texts of Exploration and Russia's Western Identity." In Cynthia Hyla Whittaker, ed., *Russia Engages the World, 1453–1825* (Cambridge, MA: Harvard University Press, 2003). For an opposite viewpoint see Martina Winkler, "Another America: Russian Mental Discoveries of the North-west Pacific Region in the Eighteenth and Early Nineteenth Centuries," *Journal of Global History* 7, no. 1 (March 2012): 27–51.

55. For some of the differences faced by Russians in colonizing the North Pacific, see James Gibson, "Russian Expansion in Siberia and America," *The Geographical Review* 70 (1980): 127–136.

56. See Jeffrey H. Solomon, "Unsettling the Nation: Anti-Colonial Nationalism and Narratives of the Non-Western World in U.S. Literature and Culture, 1783–1860." PhD diss., University of Southern California, 2011.

57. Lev Gumilev, *Etnosfera: Istoriia liudei i istoriia prirody* (Moscow: AST, 2010). For an explanation of Gumilev's ideas, see Mark Bassin, "Nurture Is Nature: Lev Gumilev and the Ecology of Ethnicity," *Slavic Review* 68, no. 4 (Winter 2009): 872–897. On Eurasianism, see Mark Bassin, "Nationhood, Natural Region, *Mestorazvitie*: Environmentalist Discourses in Classical Eurasianism." In Mark Bassin, Christopher Ely, and Melissa K. Stockdale, eds., *Space, Place, and Power in Modern Russia* (DeKalb: Northern Illinois University Press, 2010); Thomas Barrett, *At the Edge of Empire: The Terek Cossacks and the North Caucasus Frontier, 1700–1860* (Boulder: Westview press,1999); Maya Peterson, "'Native' Rice, American Cotton, and the Struggle for Water in Central Asia." In Nick Breyfogle, ed, *Eurasian Environments* (forthcoming); David Moon, "The Environmental History of the Russian Steppes: Vasilii Dokuchaev and the Harvest Failure of 1891," *Transactions of the RHS* 15 (2005): 149–174; Sunderland, *Taming the Wild Field*, David Moon, "Peasant Migration and the Settlement of Russia's Frontiers, 1500–1897," *The Historical Journal* 40, no. 4 (December 1997): 876–878.

58. See Richards, *The Unending Frontier*, 463–616.

59. See Amy R. W. Myers, "Picturing a World in Flux: Mark Catesby's Response to Environmental Interchange and Colonial Expansion." In Amy R. W. Meyers and Margaret Beck Pritchard, eds., *Empire's Nature: Mark Catesby's New World Vision* (Chapel Hill: University of North Carolina Press, 1998); J. A. Padua, "'Annihilating Natural Productions': Nature's Economy, Colonial Crisis and the Origins of Brazilian Political Environmentalism (1786–1810)," *Environment and History*, 6, no. 3 (August 2000); Richard W. Judd, "A 'wonderfull order and balance': Natural History and the Beginning of Forest Conservation in America, 1730–1810," *Environmental History* 11, no. 1 (January 2006); Richard W. Judd, *The Untilled Garden: Natural History and the Spirit of Conservation in America, 1740–1840* (Cambridge: Cambridge University Press, 2009).

60. Roderick Nash, *Wilderness and the American Mind* (New Haven, CT: Yale University Press, 1967); Donald Worster, *Nature's Economy: A History of Ecological Ideas* (New York: Cambridge University Press, 1985); Ramachandra Guha, *Environmentalism: A Global History* (New York: Longman, 2000). Another proponent of widening the search for

environmentalism's antecedents is Aaron Sachs, *The Humboldt Current: Nineteenth-Century Exploration and the Roots of American Environmentalism* (New York: Viking, 2006).

61. Grove, *Green Imperialism*, X.

62. For the dodo, and island extinctions in general, see David Quammen, *The Song of the Dodo: Island Biogeography in an Age of Extinction* (New York: Scribner, 1996).

63. Peter Coates, *Nature: Western Attitudes since Ancient Times* (Berkeley: University of California Press, 1988),136.

Chapter 1

1. Leonhard Stejneger, *Georg Wilhelm Steller, the Pioneer of Alaskan Natural History* (Cambridge, MA: Harvard University Press, 1936), 352.

2. Stejneger, *Georg Wilhelm Steller*, 18.

3. Steller's biographical details can be found in Stejneger, *Georg Wilhelm Steller*, and Wieland Hintzsche and Thomas Nickol, eds., *Die Grosse Nordische Expedition. Georg Wilhelm Steller: Ein Lutheraner Erforscht Siberien und Alaska* (Gotha: Justus Perthes Verlag, 1996).

4. For more details on Russian colonization in Siberia, see George V. Lantzeff and Richard A. Pierce, *Eastward to Empire: Exploitation and Conquest on the Russian Open Frontier, to 1750* (Montreal: McGill-Queen's University Press, 1973); Alan Wood, *Russia's Frozen Frontier: A History of Siberia and the Russian Far East, 1581–1991* (London: Bloomsbury Academic, 2011).

5. See J. L. Black, *G. F. Müller and the Imperial Russian Academy* (Kingston, Ontario: McGill-Queen's University Press, 1986), 101–102.

6. See James Gibson, "Paradoxical Perceptions of Siberia." In Galya Diment and Yuri Slezkine, eds., *Between Heaven and Hell: The Myth of Siberia in Russian Culture* (New York: St. Martin's Press, 1993).

7. See especially Jorge Cañizares-Esguerra, *Puritan Conquistadors: Iberianizing the Atlantic, 1550–1700* (Stanford, CA: Stanford University Press, 2006).

8. Terrence Armstrong, ed., *Yermak's Campaign in Siberia: A Selection of Documents* Translated from the Russian by Tatiana Minorsky and David Wileman (London: The Hakluyt Society, 1975).

9. James H. Billington, *The Icon and the Axe: An Interpretive History of Russian Culture* (New York: Knopf, 1966), 129. A previous press had been established in 1564, but was burned down by a mob the following year. See Billington, *Icon and the Axe*, 101.

10. See Konstantin A. Bogdanov, *O Krokodilakh v Rossii: Ocherki iz Istorii Zaimstsvovanii i Ekzotikov* (Moscow: Novoe literaturnoe obozrenie, 2006).

11. Stejneger, *Georg Wilhelm Steller*, 67.

12. Avvakum Petrovich, "Archpriest Avvakum: The Life Written by Himself," trans. Kenneth N. Brostrom. In Serge A. Zenkovsky, ed., *Medieval Russia's Epics, Chronicles, and Tales* (New York: Dutton, 1963), 413.

13. Bruce T. Holl, "Avvakum in the Genesis of Siberian Literature." In Diment and Slezkine, eds., *Between Heaven and Hell*.

14. Roy Robson, *Solovki: The Story of Russia Told through its Most Remarkable Islands* (New Haven, CT: Yale University Press, 2004), 7.

15. Richard Pierce, ed., *The Russian Orthodox Religious Mission in America, 1794–1837* (Kingston, Ontario: Limestone Press, 1978), 30.

16. Biographies of Father Herman, who is still venerated by the Alaskan Orthodox population, include A. S. Korsun, *Prepodobnyi German Alyaskinskiy: Valamskiy Podvizhnik v Amerike* (Moscow: Pravoslavnyi Sviato-tikhonovskii Gumanitarnyi Universitet, 2005), and Frank Golder, *Father Herman: Alaska's Saint* (Platina, CA: St. Herman of Alaska Brotherhood, 2005).

17. Valerie Kivelson, *Cartographies of Tsardom: The Land and its Meanings in Seventeenth-Century Russia* (Ithaca, NY: Cornell University Press, 2006), 118. For more on Russian ecclesiastical views of North Pacific nature, see Ryan Jones, "Lisiansky's Mountain: Changing Views of Nature in Russian Alaska," *Alaska History* 25, no. 1 (Spring 2010): 1–22.

18. Kivelson, *Cartographies of Tsardom*, chapter 6.

19. Quoted in Kivelson, *Cartographies of Tsardom*, 165.

20. Quoted in Kivelson, *Cartographies of Tsardom*, 159.

21. S.P. Krasheninnikov's Report to G. W. Steller, October 28, 1740, Archive of the St. Petersburg Branch of the Russian Academy of Sciences (RAN), f. 3, op. 1, d. 800, p 252.

22. N. I. Prokofev and L. I. Alekhina, eds., *Zapiski Russkikh Puteshestvennikov XVI-XVII vv* (Moscow: Sovetskaia Rossia, 1988), 423.

23. "An Account by the Cossack Piatidesiatnik Vladimir Atlasov, Concerning his Expedition to Kamchatka in 1707." In Basil Dmytryshyn, E. A. P. Crownhart-Vaughan, and Thomas Vaughan, eds., *Russia's Conquest of Siberia, 1558–1700: A Documentary Record* (Portland, OR: Oregon Historical Society Press, 1985), 11.

24. A. L. Narochnitskii, et al., eds., *Russkie Ekspeditsii po Izucheniu Severnoi Chasti Tikhogo Okeana v Pervoi Polovine XVIII v.: Sbornik Dokumentov, v I* (Moscow: Nauka, 1984), 30.

25. For more on the motives for this expedition see Raymond Fisher, *Bering's Voyages: Whither and Why* (Seattle: University of Washington Press, 1977), and Evgenii Kushnarev, *V Poiskakh Proliva: Pervaia Kamchatskaia Ekspeditsiia, 1725–1730* (Leningrad: Gidrometeoizdat, 1976).

26. "February 3, 1725, Instructions of the Admiralty-College to Vitus Bering about the Organization of the First Kamchatka Expedition." In Narochnitskii, et al., *Russkie Ekspeditsii*, 37.

27. Thus Steller became in two senses Messerschmidt's successor. For more on Messerschmidt, see Folkwart Wendland, "Daniel Gottlieb Messerschmidt (1685–1735)." In Hintzsche and Nickol, eds., *Die Grosse Nordische Expedition*. 68–69.

28. For an English history of the Academy see Alexander Vucinich, *Science in Russian Culture: A History to 1860* (Stanford, CA: Stanford University Press, 1963).

29. For the Academy's ornamental function, see Michael Gordin, "An Arduous and Delicate Task: Princess Dashkova, the Academy of Sciences, and the Taming of Natural Philosophy." In Sue Anne Prince, ed., *The Princess and the Patriot: Ekaterina Dashkova, Benjamin Franklin, and the Age of Enlightenment* (Philadelphia: American Philosophical Society, 2006).

30. Willard Sunderland, "Imperial Space: Territorial Thought and Practice in the Eighteenth Century." In Jane Burbank, Mark von Hagen, and Anatolyi Remnev, eds., *Russian Empire: Space, People, Power: 1700–1930* (Bloomington: Indiana University Press, 2007).

31. See Anonymous (Gerhard Friedrich Müller), trans. Arthur Dobbs, *A Letter from a Russian Sea-Officer to a Person of Distinction at the Court of St. Petersburgh* (London: A. Linde, 1754), 2.

32. Fisher, *Bering's Voyages*, 126.

33. *Polnoe Sobranie Russkikh Zakonov* (PSZ), vol. VIII (St. Petersburg, 1820), no. 6023, p 749.

34. *PSZ*, vol. VIII, no. 6291, p. 1006.

35. Fisher, *Bering's Voyages*, 127.

36. "A *Gramota* from Tsar Mikhail Fedorovich to the Voevoda of Tobolsk, Prince Andrei Khovanskii, Concerning Exploration for Iron Ore, October 3, 1625." In Basil Dmytryshyn, E. A. P. Statehart-Vaughan, and Thomas Vaughan, eds., *Russia's Conquest of Siberia, 1558–1700: A Documentary Record* (Portland, OR: Oregon Historical Society Press, 1988), 120.

37. Russian State Archive for Ancient Acts (RGADA), f. Gosarkhiva, r. XXIV, d. 8, ll. 6–9. Translation in Fisher, *Bering's Voyages*, 131.

38. Martina Winkler argues that Russians did not conceive of the Alaskan coast as part of the "New World." That may be true, especially for common Russians, but officials did perceive parallels with other European maritime empires in the old world and new. Martina Winkler, "Another America: Russian Mental Discoveries of the North-west Pacific Region in the Eighteenth and Early Nineteenth Centuries," *Journal of Global History* 7 (2012): 27 – 51, 34.

39. Hans Sloane, *A Voyage to the Islands Madera, Barbados, Nieves, S. Christophes and Jamaica, with the Natural History of the Herbs and Trees, Four-footed Beasts, Fishes, Birds, Insects, Reptiles, &c* (London, 1707).

40. Alton S. Donnelly, "Peter the Great and Central Asia," *Canadian Slavonic Papers / Revue Canadienne des Slavistes* 17, no. 2/3 (Summer and Fall 1975): 210–211.

41. Dittmar Dahlmann "Introduction to Johann Georg Gmelin," *Expedition ins unbekannte Sibirien* (Sigmaringen: Thorbecke, 1999), 76.

42. See George V. Lantzeff, *Siberia in the Seventeenth Century: A Study of the Colonial Administration* (New York: Octagon Books, 1972), ch. 4. and A. A. Amenev, *Voevodskoye Upravlenie v. Sibiri v XVIII-om Veke* (Novosibirsk: Sova, 2005).

43. Raporti i Putevye Opisanie S. P. Krasheninnikova, RAN, f. 21, op. 5 no. 34 l. 54 ob.

44. RAN, f. 21, op. 5, l. 64 ob.

45. Order from Georg Wilhelm Steller to Stepan Krasheninnikov, October, 27, 1740, RAN, r. 1, op. 13, d. 11, p 153. Steller was perfectly within his rights to demand his inferior's notes. Charges by Soviet historians that Steller subsequently plagiarized Krasheninnikov's work seem unfounded.

46. Instructions from Georg Wilhelm Steller to Andrei Furman, December 13, 1740, RAN, f. 3, op. 1, d. 800, p 305 ob.

47. See for example Sarychev, v II, p 41.

48. Georg Wilhelm Steller, *Journal of a Voyage with Bering, 1741–1742*, ed. O. W. Frost (Stanford, CA: Stanford University Press, 1988), 64.

49. The causes of Bering's death are still a matter of dispute. A Russian-Danish archaeological expedition exhumed Bering's grave in 1991 and concluded that he actually died of a pre-existing ailment compounded by fatigue and malnutrition. Most crew members undoubt-edly died of the latter two factors. Svend E. Albrethsen, "Vitus Bering's Second Kamchatka Expedition—The Journey to America and Archaeological Excavations on Bering Island." In N. Kingo Jacobsen, ed., *Vitus Bering, 1741–1991* (Copenhagen: Reitzel, 1993); V. D. Len'kov, G. L. Silant'ev, and A. K. Staniukovich, *The Komandorskii Camp of the Bering Expedition (An Experiment in Complex Study)*, trans. Katherine L. Arndt, ed. O.W. Frost (Anchorage: The Alaska Historical Society, 1992).

50. This time on Bering Island is evocatively described by several authors, including Corey Ford, *Where the Sea Breaks its Back: The Epic Story of a Pioneer Naturalist and the Discovery of Alaska* (Boston: Little, Brown, and Co., 1996); Dean Littlepage, *Steller's Island: Adventures of a Pioneer Naturalist in Alaska* (Seattle: The Mountaineer Books, 2006); and Ann Arnold, *Sea Cows, Shamans, and Scurvy: Alaska's First Naturalist: Georg Wilhelm Steller* (New York: Farrar, Straus and Giroux, 2008). Steller has also inspired at least two books of poetry, one in Russian, and one in German. Andrei Bronnikov, *Ischezayushchii Vid: Species Evanescens* (Self published, 2009); W. G. Sebald, *Nach der Natur* (Frankfurt: Fisher Verlag, 1995), translated as *After Nature*.

51. See Orcutt Frost, "Adam Olearius, the Greenland Eskimos, and the First Slaughter of Bering Island Sea Cows, 1742: An Elucidation of a Statement in Steller's Journal." In Richard Pierce, ed., *Russia in North America: Proceedings of the 2nd International Conference on Russian America, Sitka, Alaska August 19–22, 1987* (Kingston, Ontario: Limestone Press, 1990). Lydia Black, however, finds no evidence to support Frost's contention. See Lydia Black, *Russians in Alaska, 1732–1867* (Fairbanks: University of Alaska-Fairbanks, 2004), 56.

52. Georg Wilhelm Steller, "Letter to Gmelin." In Frank Golder, *Bering's Voyages: An Account of the Efforts of the Russians to Determine the Relationship of America and Asia* (New York: American Geographical Society, 1922–1925), 245.

53. Georg Wilhelm Steller, *Ausführliche Beschreibung von Sonderbaren Meerthieren* (Halle, 1753), 48.

54. K. E. von Baer, "Untersuchungen Über die Ehemalige Verbreitung und die Gänzliche Vertilgung der von Steller Beobachteten Nordischen Seekuh (Rytina M.)," *Memoires Scientifiques* (St. Petersburg, 1840), 78.

55. Steller probably earned at least four and a half times his yearly salary (660 rubles) from the Academy of Sciences. For salary, see P. P. Pekarskii, *Materiali dlia Istorii Imperatskoi Akademii Nauk*, vol. VII (St. Petersburg, 1895), 225.

56. Russian State Naval Archive (RGAVMF), f. 216 (Beringa), d. 48, l. 744. Reprinted in Dmytryshyn, *Russian Penetration*, 192–198 and V. A. Dvinin, ed., *Russkaia tikhookeanskaia epopeia* (Khabarovsk, 1979), 300–303. Chirikov also recommended that the government collect a tax of two-thirds of the catch, a measure which surely would have bankrupted the trade.

57. RGAVMF, f. 216 (Beringa), d. 28, l. 1.

58. Joseph von Sonnenfels, *Grundsätze der Polizey, Handlung, und Finanz*, Bd. I, 5th. ed (Vienna, 1787), 20–21.

59. Sunderland, "Imperial Space," 36.

60. Gerhard Friedrich Müller, "Introduction to S. P. Krasheninnikov." In *Opisanie Zemli Kamchatka*, vol. 2 (St. Petersburg, 1755), ii. Translation in James Grieve, *The History of Kamtschatka, and the Kurile Islands, with the Countries Adjacent* (Glocester, 1754), i, ii.

61. See for example Rudolf Vierhaus, *Germany in the Age of Absolutism* (Cambridge: Cambridge University Press, 1988), 82.

62. Margery Rowel, "Linnaeus and Botanists in Eighteenth-Century Russia," *Taxon* 29, no. 1 (February 1980), 22.

63. For another interpretation of Krasheninnikov's scientific work, see Rachel D. Koroloff, "The Beginnings of a Russian Natural History: The Life and Work of Stepan Petrovich Krasheninnikov (1711–1755)." Master's thesis, Oregon State University, 2007.

64. S. P. Krasheninnikov, "'Rech' o Pol'ze Nauk i Khudozhestv, Chitannaya Stepanom Krasheninnikovym, Botanikom i Istorii Natural'noi Professorom v Publichnom Akademicheskom Sobranii Sentyabrya 6 Dnya, 1750 Godu." In N. N. Stepanova, ed., *S. P. Krasheninnikov v Sibiri: Neopublikovannye Materialy* (Moscow: Nauka, 1966), 227.

65. Krasheninnikov, "Rech," 231.

66. Krasheninnikov, "Rech," 230.

67. Krasheninnikov, "Rech," 229.

68. Krasheninnikov, "Rech," 228.

69. Krasheninnikov, "Rech," 230.

70. Gorlanoff's description can be found in RAN, f. 21, op. 5, no. 65.

71. James Grieve, "Introduction." In *The History of Kamtschatka*, i, ii.

72. Krasheninnikov, *Opisanie Zemli Kamchatki*, 86.

73. Steller, *Journal of a Voyage with Bering*, 89.

74. F. Ernest Stoeffler, "Introduction." In Peter C. Erb, ed., *Pietists: Selected Writings* (New York: Paulist Press, 1983).

75. Orcutt Frost, "Introduction." In Steller, *Journal of a Voyage with Bering*, 9.

76. Orcutt Frost, *Bering: The Russian Discovery of America* (New Haven, CT: Yale University Press, 2003), 207.

77. See August Hermann Francke, "Admonition to the Twelve Students Traveling to Lapland." In Erb, *Pietists*, 165.

78. For more on Steller's difficult relationship with Pietism, see my "Steller and the Strange Beasts of the Sea." In A. E. Ryzantsev, *Kamchatskie Ekspeditsii v Istoricheskoi Retrospektive* (Petropavlovsk-Kamchatskii: Izdatel'stvo KamGU im. Vitusa Beringa, 2007).

79. Georg Wilhelm Steller, *History of Kamchatka*, trans. Margritt Engel and Karen Willmore, ed. Marvin Falk (Fairbanks: University of Alaska Press, 2003), 103.

80. Krasheninnikov, "Rech," 231.

81. Mary Fulbrook, *Piety and Politics: Religion and the Rise of Absolutism in England, Wurttemberg, and Prussia* (Cambridge: Cambridge University Press, 1984).

82. Steller, *Journal of a Voyage with Bering*, 144.

83. Steller, *Journal of a Voyage with Bering*, 146. Steller considered sea otter meat to be an antiscorbutic.

84. Steller, *Von Sonderbaren Meerthieren*, 42.

85. Steller, *Von Sonderbaren Meerthieren*, 54.

86. Keith Thomas, *Man and the Natural World: Changing Attitudes in England 1500–1800* (London: Allen Lane, 1983).

87. Quoted in Jacques Roger, *Buffon: A Life in Natural History* (Ithaca, NY: Cornell University Press, 1997), 232–233.

88. Krasheninnikov, *Opisanie Zemli Kamchatka*, 86.

89. Steller, *Von Sonderbaren Meerthieren*, 53.

90. Steller, *Von Sonderbaren Meerthieren*, 41.

91. Steller, *History of Kamchatka*, 251.

92. Steller, *History of Kamchatka*, 173.

93. James Forsyth, *A History of the Peoples of Siberia: Russia's North Asian Colony* (Cambridge, MA: Cambridge University Press, 1992), 136–138; Sgibnev, "Istoricheskii Ocherk Glavneischikh Sobitii v Kamchatke s 1650 po 1865 gg." *Morskoi Sbornik 105.* (St. Petersburg: Vtipografii Morskago ministerstva, 1869).

94. Steller, *History of Kamchatka,* 174.

95. Steller, *History of Kamchatka,* 177.

96. Steller, *History of Kamchatka,* 231.

97. Steller, *History of Kamchatka,* 283–284.

98. Krasheninnikov, *Opisanie Zemli Kamchatka,* 321.

99. Krasheninnikov, *Opisanie Zemli Kamchatka,* 321.

100. Georg Wilhelm Steller, Reisejournal von Irkuck nach Ochock und Kamchatka, 4. March 1740 bis 16. September 1740, RAN, f. 21, op. 5, d. 113, p 64 ob.

101. Steller, *History of Kamchatka,* 206.

102. Steller, *History of Kamchatka,* 213.

103. Anonymous (Gerhard Friedrich Müller), *Leben Herrn Georg Wilhelm Steller, gewesnen Adiuncti der Kaiserl.* Academie der Wissenschafften zu St. Petersburg (Frankfurt, 1748), 28.

104. Steller, *Journal of a Voyage with Bering,* 65.

105. Academy Proceedings, April 9, 1746, in Pekarskii, ed., *Materialy,* vol. VIII, p 78.

106. Briefe von Euler an Wettstein vom 16.7 und 10.12.1746, in A.P. Juskevic and E. Winter, eds., *Die Berliner und die Petersburger Akademie der Wissenschaften in Briefwechsel Leonhard Eulers.* Teil 3 (Berlin: Akademie-Verlag, 1976), 259–261.

107. "Request from the Professors to the Empress Elizabeth Petrovna from October 25, 1743." In Pekarskii, ed., *Materialy,* vol. V, 927–929. For the state of the Academy at this time see Black, *G.F. Müller* and Lothar Maier, "Die Krise der St. Petersburger Akademie der Wissenschaften nach der Thronbesteigung Elisabeth Petrovnas und die 'Afäre Gmelin,' " in *Jahrbücher für die Geschichte Osteuropas* 27 (1978): 353–373.

108. Quoted in Johann Georg Gmelin, *Reise ins Unbekannte Sibirien,* 71–72.

109. See Stejneger, *Georg Wilhelm Steller,* 492.

110. Müller, *Leben Herrn Georg Wilhelm Steller,* 8.

111. Müller, *Leben Herrn Georg Wilhelm Steller,* 28.

112. Müller, *Leben Herrn Georg Wilhelm Steller,* 8.

113. Though officially anonymous, Müller's authorship is proved by a note from the President of the Academy of Sciences ordering him to write such a letter. See Pekarskii, *Materialy,* vol. I, 143.

114. For more on this controversy, and the Russian policy of secrecy in general, see Carol Urness, "Russian Mapping of the North Pacific." In Stephen Haycox, James K. Barnett, and Caedmon Liburd, eds., *Enlightenment and Exploration in the North Pacific, 1741–1805* (Seattle: University of Washington Press, 1997).

115. Müller, *Letter from a Russian Sea-Officer,* 4, 11.

116. Müller, *Letter from a Russian Sea-Officer,* 30.

117. Arthur Dobbs, *Observations upon the Russian Discoveries, &c,* (London, 1754), 37.

118. Read 29 Jan, 1760. L&P 111 412 Krash. *Archive of the Imperial Society,* p 1.

119. "Advertisement." In S. P. Krasheninnikov, *The History of Kamtschatka, and the Kurilski Islands,* i, ii.

120. Quoted in Rowel, 19.

121. The publishers despaired that "hope wanes for the publication of the rest of Steller's long-awaited works." Anonymous, "Introduction." In G.W. Steller, *Ausführliche Beschreibung,* 2.

122. Pallas, *NNB,* vol. II, 225.

123. J. B. Scherer, "Leben des Herrn Stellers (introduction)." In G. W. Steller, *Beschreibung von dem Lande Kamtschatka* (Halle, 1774), 5.

124. Peter Simon Pallas, "Zuverlässige Nachrichten von den letzten Schicksalen des Herrn Georg Wilhelm Steller." In *Physikalisch-ökonomische Bibliothek...von Johann Beckmann,* vol. 8 (Göttingen: im Verlag der Wittwe Bandenhoeck, 1777), 459.

125. Claudine Cohen, *The Fate of the Mammoth: Fossils, Myth, and History,* trans. William Rodarmor (Chicago: University of Chicago Press, 2002), 94–96.

Chapter 2

1. A. S. Polonskii, "Perechen' puteschestvii russkikh promyshlennikh v Vostochnom Okeane s 1743 po 1800 god," (Enumeration of the Voyages of Russian *Promyshlenniks* in the Eastern Ocean from 1743 to 1800) Archive of the Russian Geographical Society, razryad 60 op. 1, no. 2, pp 6–8.

2. Lydia Black, "The Nature of Evil: Of Whales and Sea Otters," in Shepard Krech, ed., *Indians, Animals, and the Fur Trade: A Critique of Keepers of the Game* (Athens, GA: University of Georgia Press, 1981): 109–147, 121.

3. Daniel Mann, Aron Crowell, Thomas Hamilton, and Bruce Finney, "Holocene Geologic and Climatic History around the Gulf of Alaska," *Arctic Anthropology* 25, no. 1 (1998): 112– 131.

4. A. P. McCartney and D. W. Veltre, "Aleutian Island Prehistory: Living in Insular Extremes," *World Archaeology* 30, no. 3 (February 1999): 513; Nicole Misarti, Bruce Finney, Herbert Maschner, and Matthew J. Wooller, "Changes in Northeast Pacific Marine Ecosystems over the Last 4500 Years: Evidence form Stable Isotope Analysis of Bone Collagen form Archaeological Middens," *The Holocene* 19, no. 8 (2009): 1141.

5. Debra Corbett, Christine Lefevre, and Douglas Siegel-Causey, "The Western Aleutians: Cultural Isolation and Environmental Change," *Human Ecology* 25, no. 3 (September 1997): 460.

6. William S. Laughlin, "Ecology and Population Structure in the Arctic." In G. A. Harrison and A. J. Boyce, eds., *The Structure of Human Populations* (Oxford: Oxford University Press, 1972).

7. George L. Hunt, Jr., and Phyllis J. Stabeno, "Oceanography and Ecology of the Aleutian Archipelago: Spatial and Temporal Variation," *Fisheries Oceanography* 14, Suppl. 1 (2005): 292.

8. The Aleuts' westward migration enjoys scholarly consensus, though not unanimity. See Dixie West, Michael Crawford, and Arkady Savinetsky, "Genetics, Prehistory, and the Colonisation of the Aleutian Islands," *Earth and Environmental Science Transactions of the Royal Society of Edinburgh*, 98 (2007): 47; D. H. O'Rourke, D. L. West, and M. H. Crawford, "Unangan Past and Present: The Contrasts between Observed and Inferred Histories," *Human Biology* 82, nos. 5–6 (October–December 2010): 759.

9. West, et al., "Genetics, Prehistory, and the Colonisation of the Aleutian Islands," 53.

10. Daniel Mann, Aron Crowell, Thomas Hamilton, and Bruce Finney, "Holocene Geologic and Climatic History around the Gulf of Alaska," 114.

11. Douglas Causey, Debra G. Corbett, Christine LeFevre, et al., "The Paleoenvironment of Humans and Marine Birds of the Aleutian Islands: Three Millennia of Change," *Fisheries Oceanography* 14, Suppl. 1 (2005): 259–276.

12. Causey, et al., "The Paleoenvironment of Humans and Marine Birds of the Aleutian Islands," 259.

13. West, et al., "Genetics, Prehistory, and the Colonisation of the Aleutian Islands," 349.

14. West, et al., "Genetics, Prehistory, and the Colonisation of the Aleutian Islands," 52.

15. Phillip R. Mundy, ed., *The Gulf of Alaska: Biology and Oceanography* (Fairbanks: University of Alaska-Fairbanks, 2005).

16. Mundy, *The Gulf of Alaska*, 20.

17. Franco Biondi, Alexander Gershunov, and Daniel Cayan, "North Pacific Decadal Climate Variability since 1661," *Journal of Climate* 14, (January 2001): 8.

18. Mann, et al., "Holocene Geologic and Climatic History around the Gulf of Alaska," 114.

19. Mann, et al., "Holocene Geologic and Climatic History around the Gulf of Alaska," 122; N. G. Razzhigaeva, et al., "Pleistocene Sedimentation in the Bering Island Coastal Zone (Komandorskie Islands)," *Geology of the Pacific Ocean* 14 (1999): 381–403.

20. Corbett, et al., "The Western Aleutians," 468; D. M. Hopkins, "Landscape and Climate in Beringia during Late Pleistocene and Holocene Times." In W. S. Laughlin and A. B. Harper, eds., *The First Americans: Origins, Affinities, and Adaptations* (New York: G. Fischer, 1979).

21. See Jeff Wheelwright, *Degrees of Disaster: Prince William Sound: How Nature Reels and Rebounds* (New Haven, CT: Yale University Press, 1996).

22. See, for example, C. H. Ainsworth, T. J. Pitcher, J. J. Heymans, and M. Vasconcellos, "Reconstructing Historical Marine Ecosystems Using Food Web Models: Northern British Columbia from Pre-European Contact to Present," *Ecological Modeling* 216 (2008): 354–368.

23. Misarti, et al., "Changes in Northeast Pacific Marine Ecosystems over the Last 4500 Years," 1148.

24. West, et al., "Genetics, Prehistory, and the Colonisation of the Aleutian Islands," 345; David Yesner, "Effects of Prehistoric Human Exploitation on Aleutian Sea Mammal Populations," *Arctic Anthropology* 25, no. 1 (1988): 39.

25. Herbert Maschner, et al., "Biocomplexity of Sanak Island," *Pacific Science* 63 (2009): 673–709.

26. Polonskii, "Perechen' ", 3.

27. Andrei Grinev, "The Watchful Eye of the Empire: Passports and Passport Controls in Russian America," *Alaska History* 23, nos. 1 / 2 (Spring/Fall 2008): 21–34.

28. For Russian property rights, see Richard Pipes, *Russia under the Old Regime* (New York: Scribner, 1974), xxi–xxii.

29. S. P. Krasheninnikov, "Raporty i Putevye opisanie," in RAN, F. 21, op. 5, no. 34, 54 ob.

30. Garrett Hardin, "The Tragedy of the Commons," *Science* 162 (1968): 1243–1248.

31. Lydia Black, et al., *The History and Ethnohistory of the Aleutians East Borough* (Kingston, Ontario: The Limestone Press, 1999), 9.

32. S. I. Kornev and S. I. Korneva, "Some Criteria for Assessing the State and Dynamics of Sea Otter (*Enhydra lutris*) Populations in the Russian Part of the Species Range," *Russian Journal of Ecology* 27, no. 3 (2006): 172–179, 176. The authors of the census (2005) from which I have taken these numbers consider the population to be above an optimum level and expect that it will decrease as prey species decline.

33. Georg Wilhelm Steller, *Journal of a Voyage with Bering, 1741–1742*, ed. O. W. Frost (Stanford, CA: Stanford University Press, 1988), 172.

34. Polonskii, "Perechen'," 6.

35. "From the inquiry of the Bolsheretsk Chancellery on the voyage of Sergeant E. S. Basov on the boat *Sv. Petr* to the Commander Islands in 1743–1746 and the Discovery of Copper Island," in A. I. Andreev, ed., *Russkie otkrytiya v tikhom okeane i severnoi Amerike v XVII–XIX vekah* (Moscow: Ogiz, 1948), 33; Polonskii, "Perechen'," 6.

36. Polonskii, "Perechen'," 8–9.

37. Polonskii, "Perechen'," 12.

38. Karl Kenyon, *The Sea Otter in the Eastern Pacific Ocean* (New York: Dover Publications, 1975), 66–67.

39. S. V. Zagrebel'ny, V. V. Fomin, and A. M. Burdin, "Dynamics of Abundance and Population Structure of Sea Otters, *Enhydra Lutris*, on the Commander Archipelago and Activity of their Migrations between Islands," *Russian Journal of Ecology* 39, no. 1 (2008): 41.

40. Law of February 12, 1748, in *PSZ*, vol. XII, no. 9480, pp 830–831.

41. James L. Bodkin and Brenda E. Ballachey, "Modeling Effects of Mortality on Sea Otter Populations," *Scientific Investigations Report 2010–5096* (Reston, Virginia: U.S. Geological Survey, 2010), 3.

42. RGADA, f. 25, op 22, d. 485a, 11, 436–441 ob.

43. See Fedor Soimonov, "Prodolzhenie Drevnaya Poslovitsa: Sibir Zolotoe Dno," *Ezhemesiachnye Sochineniia* (February 1764), 52–53.

44. Soimonov, "Prodolzhenie," 52.

45. Russian State Archive for Ancient Acts (RGADA), f. 199 d. 539, ch. 1, notebook. 16, p. 4.

46. "Protocol of the Seventeenth Working Group Meeting under Project 02.05-61, 'Marine Mammals,' under Area V of the U.S.-Russia Agreement on Cooperation in the Field of Environmental Protection. Listviyanka Settlement, Irkutsk Region, Russia. September 15–19, 2002." http://nmml.afsc.noaa.gov/alaskaecosystems/sslhome/protocolUSRus.htm. Accessed December 5, 2013. Also see James Bodkin, Ronald Jameson, and James Estes, "Sea Otters in the North Pacific Ocean," http://biology.usgs.gov/s+t/noframe/s043.htm. Accessed December 5, 2013. See similar numbers for 2006 in Zagrebel'ny, et al., "Dynamics of Abundance and Population Structure of Sea Otters, *Enhydra Lutris*, on the Commander Archipelago and Activity of their Migrations between Islands," 41.

47. Ivan Veniaminov, *Notes on the Islands of the Unalashka District*, Richard A. Pierce, ed. and Lydia T. Black and R. H. Geoghegan, trans. (Kingston, Ontario: The Limestone Press, 1984), 333.

48. That is, 1,380 out of an estimated 2881 remaining sea otters (47.7%). Sea Otter Populations determined by the formula: $X = aX - bX2 - H$, where: X is the annual change in population, H is the harvest, a is the maximum proportional growth rate (17–20 % [from Estes, "Growth and Equilibrium"]), and $b = a/X$.

49. Polonskii, "Perechen," 31.

50. "Not earlier than December 7, 1758, From the Report of the Nizhnekamchatskoi Izba to the Bolsheretskuyu Chanellery on the Voyage of P. Bashmakova on the boat *St. Peter and St. Paul* from 1756–1758 to the Aleutian Islands and the Discovery of Islands to the east of the Near Aleutians," in A. L. Narochnitskii, et al., eds., *Russkie Ekspeditsii po Izucheniu Severnoi Chasti Tikhogo Okeana v Pervoi Polovine XVIII v.: Sbornik Dokumentov*, v I (Moscow: Nauka, 1984), 50.

51. Christian Bering, Unpublished Journal, RGAVMF, f. 913, op. 11, l. 287, p 70, ob.

52. K. T. Khlebnikov, R. G. Liapunova, S. G. Fedorova, and Richard A. Pierce, *Notes on Russian America*, parts II–V (Kingston, Ontario: The Limestone Press, 1994), 214.

53. Bodkin and Ballachey, "Modeling Effects of Mortality on Sea Otter Populations," 9.

54. See for example the report of Grigorii Shelikhov, 1790, Translation in Lydia Black, *Atka: An Ethnohistory of the Western Aleutians* (Kingston, Ont.: Limestone Press, 1984), 148.

55. Polonskii, "Perechen," 6–7.

56. Pallas, *NNB*, vol. II, 305.

57. Polonskii, "Perechen," 38.

58. See E. P. Orlova, *Itel'meny* (Saint Petersburg: Nauka, 1999); N. K. Starkova, *Itel'meny Material'naya Kul'tura XVII—60-e Gody XX Veka* (Moscow: Nauka, 1976).

59. See Alexander I. Lebedintsev, et al., "Maritime Cultures of the North Coast of the Sea of Okhotsk," *Arctic Anthropology* 35, no. 1 (1998): 296–320; A. K. Ponomarenko, *Drevniaia Kul'tura Itel'menov Vostochnoi Kamchatki* (Moscow: Nauka, 1985).

60. Pallas, *NNB*, v. I, pt 2, p 292.

61. Georg Wilhelm Steller, *History of Kamchatka*, trans. Margritt Engel and Karen Willmore, ed. Marvin Falk (Fairbanks: University of Alaska Press, 2003), p 90.

62. Aron Crowell, *Archaeology and the World System: A Study from Russian America* (New York: Plenum Press, 1997), 152.

63. See, for example, company contracts found in the Russian State Historical Archive (RGIA), F. 1374, Op. 2, No. 1672.

64. Andrei Grinev, *Kto Est' Kto v Istorii Russkoi Ameriki* (MoscowAcademia, 2009), 328; Polonskii, "Perechen," 28.

65. Gavriil Davydov, *Two Voyages to Russian America, 1802–1807* (Kingston, Ont.: Limestone Press, 1977), 80.

66. Dean Stoddard Worth, *Kamchadal Texts Collected by W. Jochelson* ('S-Gravenhage: Mouton & Co., 1961), 43.

67. Jean-Baptiste Barthémy De Lesseps, *Travels in Kamtschatka, during the Years 1787 and 1788* (London: Printed for J. Johnson, 1790), 105; David Koester, "When the Fat Raven Sings: Mimesis and Environmental Alterity in Kamchatka's Environmentalist Age." In Erich Kasten, ed., *People and the Land: Pathways to Reform in Post-Soviet Siberia* (Berlin: Dietrich Reimer Verlag, 2002), 50.

68. Steller, *History of Kamchatka*, 98.

69. Otto von Kotzebue, *Neue Reise um die Welt, in den Jahren 1823, 24, 25 und 26...* (Weimar: Verlag von Wilhelm Hoffman, 1830), 7–8.

70. For example, see the contract drawn up by Natalia Shelikhova in 1794, in RGIA, F. 1374, Op. 2, No. 1672, p 38 ob.

71. De Lesseps, vol. I, 183.

72. Pavlov, P. N. *K Istorii Rossiisko-Amerikanskoi Kompanii (Sbornik Dokumental'nykh Materialov)* (Krasnoyarsk: Krasnoiarskii gosudarstvennyi arkhiv, Krasnoiarskii gosudarstvennyi pedagogicheskii institut, 1957), 72.

73. Mikhail Levashev, Unpublished Journal, RGAVMF, F. 913, Op. 1, D. 130, p 164.

74. Gavriil Sarychev, *Account of a Voyage of Discovery to the North-East of Siberia, the Frozen Ocean and the North-East Sea* (London: Printed for Richard Phillips...by J. G. Bernard, 1806), v. I, 57.

75. Polonskii, "Perechen," 17.

76. David Hopkins, "Landscape and Climate of Beringia during Late Pleistocene and Holocene Time." In William S. Laughlin and Albert B. Harper, eds., *The First Americans: Origins, Affinities, and Adaptations* (New York: Axel Springer Verlag, 1979), 20.

77. Bruno Frohlich, "Aleutian Settlement Distribution on Adak, Kagalaska, Buldir and Attu Islands. Aleutian Islands, Alaska," in Bruno Frohlich, Albert B. Harper, and Rolf Gilberg, eds., *To the Aleutians and Beyond: The Anthropology of William S. Laughlin* (Copenhagen: Department of Ethnography, the National Museum of Denmark, 2002), 66.

78. Polonskii, "Perechen," 21.

79. Lucien Turner, *An Aleutian Ethnography*, ed. Raymond Hudson (Fairbanks: University of Alaska Press, 2008), 106–107.

80. C. L. Hooper, *A Report on the Sea-Otter Banks of Alaska* (Washington, DC: Government Printing Office, 1897), 5.

81. Polonskii, "Perechen," 21.

82. Berkh, "Khronologicheskaya Istoriya," in *Voprosy Istorii Kamchatki*, vol. 2 (2006), 126.

83. Compare Berkh, "Khronologicheskaya Istoriya," 126 and Polonskii, " 'Perechen," 20.

84. Polonskii, "Perechen," 20–22.

85. Polonskii, "Perechen," 36.

86. Polonskii, "Perechen," 40. Also see Lydia Black, *Atka*, p 75.

87. Black, *Atka*, 76.

88. Polonskii, "Perechen," 109.

89. Polonskii, "Perechen," 61.

90. Polonskii, "Perechen," 63.

91. For 1960s estimates, see "Aleutians West Coastal Resource Service Area, Volume II: Resource Inventory and Analysis," Revised August 2006, http://www.alaskacoast.state.ak.us/Explore/AWCRSA_04_07/pdf/pdf%20from%20word/volume%20II/vol2aug06.pdf. Also James Estes, "The Sea Otter (*Enhydra Lutris*): Behavior, Ecology, and Natural History," *Biological Report* 90, no. 14 (September, 1990), For current population estimates, see J. A. Estes et al, "Continuing Sea Otter Population Declines in the Aleutian Archipelago," *Marine Mammal Science* 21, no. 1 (January, 2005): 169–17 and U.S. Fish & Wildlife Service, "Draft Revised Northern Sea Otter (*Enhydra lutris kenyoni*): Southwest Alaska Stock," April 2013. http://www.fws.gov/alaska/fisheries/mmm/seaotters/pdf/Draft%20Southwest%20Alaska%20Sea%20Otter%20April%202013.For%20Surname.pdf; Angela M. Doroff, et al, "Sea Otter Declines in the Aleutian Archipelago," *Journal of Mammology* 84, no. 1 (2003): 55–64.

92. See Carol Ladd, et al., "Marine Environment of the Eastern and Central Aleutian Islands," *Fisheries Oceanography* 14, Supplement 1 (2005): 22–38.

93. P. Krenitsyn, "Ekstrakt Zhurnalova." In V.A. Divin, *Russkaya Tikhookeanskaya Epopeya* (Khabarovsk: Khabarovskoe knizhnoe izdatel'stvo, 1979), 357, 360.

94. See Grinev, "The Russian Colonies in Alaska on the Threshold of the Nineteenth Century," in N. N. Bolkhovitinov, ed., *Istoriya Russkoi Ameriki, 1732–1867*, Tom II (Moscow: Mezhdunarodnye otnosheniia, 1999).

95. Berkh, *Chronological History*, 133.

96. See R. G. Liapunova, "Relations with the Natives of Russian America," in S. Frederick Starr, ed., *Russia's American Colony* (Durham, NC: Duke University Press, 1987), 111.

97. William S. Laughlin, *Aleuts: Survivors of the Bering Land Bridge* (Fort Worth: Holt, Reinhart and Winston, Inc., 1980), 130; Margaret Lantis, "The Aleut Social System, 1750 to 1810, from Early Historical Sources." In Margaret Lantis, *Ethnohistory in Southwestern Alaska and the Southern Yukon: Method and Content* (Lexington: University of Kentucky Press): 161–184, 179.

98. Berkh, *Chronological History*, 41.

99. The Soviet approach is best typified by A. A. Andreev, *Russkie Otkrytiia v Tikhom Okeane i Severnoi Amerike v XVIII-XIX (Sbornik Materialov)* (Moscow: Izdatelstvo Akademii Nauk SSSR, 1944). More recently, Michael Oleksa, Lydia Black, and Yuri Petrov have presented a

modified version, with Black in particular emphasizing the benefits of Russian Orthodoxy as well as literacy.

100. Black, "Nature of Evil," 126; Veniaminov, *Notes*, 223.
101. *Unangam Uniikangis Ama Tunuzangis*, 707.
102. George Vancouver, *A Voyage of Discovery to the North Pacific Ocean and Round the World*, vol. III (London: Printed for G.G. and J. Robinson, Paternoster-Row, and J. Edwards, Pall-Mall, 1798), 227.
103. Veniaminov, *Notes*, 184.
104. Veniaminov, *Notes*, 215.
105. Kashevarov, "Otvet," 162.
106. von Wrangell, *Russian America*, 18.
107. See, for example, "Russian-American Company, Main Office to Governor General Matvei Muraviev," July 15, 1824, Alaska State Library, MS 4, Box 2 #13, f. 181.
108. Liapunova, "Relations with the Natives of Russian America," 114.
109. Hooper, *A Report on the Sea-Otter Banks of Alaska*, 5.
110. Shepard Krech, *The Ecological Indian: Myth and History* (New York: Norton, 2002).
111. Black, "Nature of Evil," 135.
112. Andreev, 117–18, translation by Black, "Nature of Evil," 136.
113. "Letter from Veniaminov to Archbishop Michael of Irkutsk, written June 1828," in Alaska State Library, MS 4, Box 2, #3, Item 4, pp 1–3.
114. Veniaminov, *Notes*, 227.
115. James W. Vanstone, "An Early Nineteenth-Century Artist in Alaska: Louis Choris and the First Kotzebue Expedition," *The Pacific Northwest Quarterly* 51, no. 4 (October 1960): 145–158.
116. David Yesner, "Effects of Prehistoric Human Exploitation on Aleutian Sea Mammal Populations," *Arctic Anthropology* 25, no. 1 (1988), 28–43.
117. Turner, *Aleutian Ethnography*, p 153.
118. Letter, Baranov to Larionov, March 22, 1801, in P. A. Tikhmenev, *History of the Russian American Company*, vol 2, Documents (Kingston, Ontario: The Limestone Press, 1979), 123.
119. Letter, Larionov to Baranov, August 5, 1801, in Tikhmenev, *Russian American Company*, vol. II, 130.
120. "Instructions, Colonel G. K. Ugrenin, Commandant of Okhotsk oblast, to Company Personnel and to Inhabitants of the Aleutian Islands and their Chiefs, June 15, 1787." In P. A. Tikhmenev, *History of the Russian American Company*, vol. 2, Documents (Kingston, Ontario: The Limestone Press, 1979), 16.
121. See Khlebnikov, *Baranov*, pp 123, 124.
122. See Ann M. Carlos and Frank D. Lewis, "Indians, the Beaver, and the Bay: The Economics of Depletion in the Lands of the Hudson's Bay Company, 1700–1763," *The Journal of Economic History* 55, no. 3 (September 1993): 465–494.
123. Though when European trade goods came to be considered a necessity, price signals would lose some of their meaning.
124. A population of 13,526 around Kodiak alone in 1991 and 11,005 in 2004. These numbers are likely to have been higher in the eighteenth century. See "Draft Revised Northern Sea Otter (*Enhydra lutris kenyoni*), 5.
125. Mary Wheeler, "The Russian-American Company and the Imperial Government: Early Phase." In Starr, ed., *Russia's American Colony*, 45.
126. Lydia Black, "Warriors of Kodiak: Military Traditions of Kodiak Islanders," *Arctic Anthropology* 41, no. 2 (2004): 140–152.
127. See chapter 1 in Katerina G. Solovjoa and Aleksandra A. Vovnyanko, *The Fur Rush* (Anchorage: Phenix Press, 2002).
128. See Valovoy Kontrakt, 1797, in RGIA, F. 1374, Op. 1, No. 1672, pp 5, 6.
129. Bering, Unpublished Journal, 64.
130. Bering, Unpublished Journal, 64.
131. Tikhmenev, *History of the Russian American Company*, vol. II, 91.
132. It must be kept in mind that the catch-per-year totals of some of Shelikhov's ships cannot be directly compared to earlier voyages. His ships were making only short summer sailings

from Kodiak to the nearby Alaskan coast, while the others could count on at least two years of voyage time from Kamchatka or Okhotsk to the Aleutian Islands and back. Getting the quickly captured furs to market would mean adding another year or two to Shelikhov's voyages.

133. Letter, Baranov to Shelikhov, from Chugach Bay, July 24, 1793, in Tikhmenev, *History of the Russian American Company*, vol. 2, 32.

134. These factors are still debated. See A. Yu. Petrov, *Obrazovanie Rossisko-Amerikanskoi Kompanii* (Moscow: Nauka, 2000).

135. *PSZ*, vol. XXIV, no. 18.067, 670.

136. A. J. von Krusenstern, *Reise um die Welt in den Jahren 1803, 1804, 1805 und 1806…* (St. Petersburg, 1810), XI.

137. Letter, Shelikhov to Delarov, from Okhotsk, August 30, 1789, in Tikhmenev, *History of the Russian American Company*, vol. 2, 20.

138. Veniaminov, *Notes on the Islands of the Unalashka District*, 70.

139. Polonskii, "Perechen," 157.

140. Roger L. Gentry, *Behavior and Ecology of the Northern Fur Seal* (Princeton, NJ: Princeton University Press, 1998), 16.

141. See Leonhard Stejneger, "The Asiatic Islands and Fur Seal Industry." In David Starr Jordan and George Archibald Clark, eds., *The Fur Seals and Fur Seal Islands of the North Pacific Ocean* (Washington, DC, 1898), 114; Tikhmenev, *History of the Russian American Company*, vol. 1, 60.

142. Veniaminov, *Notes*, 144.

143. "Description of St. George Island by the Creole Zachar Chichenev, 1832–1833" copy in Alaska State Library—Juneau, Ms. 4, box 2, #9.

144. Veniaminov, *Notes*, 144.

145. Khlebnikov, *Notes on Russian America*, Parts II—V, 288.

146. Veniaminov, *Notes*, 344.

147. Veniaminov, *Notes*, 345–346.

148. Basil Dmytryshyn, E. A. P. Crownhart-Vaughan, and Thomas Vaughan, eds., *Russian Penetration of the North Pacific Ocean: A Documentary Record, 1700–1797* (Portland, OR: Oregon Historical Society Press, 1988), 502.

149. See Douglas Veltre, "Gardening in Colonial Russian America," *Ethnoarchaeology* 3, no. 2 (September 2011): 119–138.

150. NARA-RRAC, CR, roll 6, folio 195.

151. A. B. Savinetsky, et al., "Dynamics of Sea Mammal and Bird Populations of the Region over the Last Several Millenia," *Palaeogeography, Palaeoclimatology, Palaeoecology* 209 (2004): 342.

152. Robert G. Anthony, et al., "Bald Eagles and Sea Otters in the Aleutian Archipelago: Indirect Effects of Trophic Cascades," *Ecology* 89, no. 10 (2008): 2725–2735; S. E. Reisewitz, J. A. Estes, and S. A. Simensted, "Indirect Food Web Interactions: Sea Otters and Kelp Forest Fishes in the Aleutian Archipelago," *Oecologia*, 146, no. 4 (January, 2006): 623–31; J. A. Estes and D. O. Duggins, "Sea Otters and Kelp Forsets in Alaska: Generality and Variation in a Community Ecological Paradigm," *Ecological Monographs* 65, no. 1 (February, 1995): 75–100.

153. See Gwenn Miller, *Kodiak Kreol: Communities of Empire in Early Russian America* (Ithaca, NY: Cornell University Press, 2010), 46.

154. Since the 1990s, marine biologists have charted one of the most surprising and mysterious ecological changes of recent times: the reduction of 90% of the sea otter population throughout its Aleutian range (and an attendant decline in sea lion numbers). In this case, the direct culprit is surely not human predation. Instead, researchers have pointed to declining fish stocks due to commercial fishing, genetic bottlenecks caused by the small relict population surviving the Russian assault, and—most convincingly—increased predation by killer whales. Killer whales are supposed to have turned to eating sea otters after the removal of larger prey during the era of industrial whaling, a proposition supported by a number of sightings of killer whale attacks on sea otters in the Aleutian Islands in recent years. This last explanation (which has encountered skepticism) in particular should introduce some caution into ascribing eighteenth-century declines simply to overhunting. The killer whale

explanation relies on an extremely complex series of events spread out over huge expanses of the Pacific Ocean, and warns against overly local explanations.

155. Constantine Grewingk, *Grewingk's Geology of Alaska and the Northwest Coast of America*, ed. Marvin Falk, trans. Fritz Jaensch (Fairbanks: University of Alaska Press, 2003), 242.

156. Black, "Volcanism," 314.

157. John f. Richards, *The Unending Frontier: An Environmental History of the Early Modern World* (Berkeley: University of California Press, 2003), Part IV.

158. See Briton Cooper Busch, *The War against the Seals: A History of the North American Seal Fishery* (Kingston: McGill-Queen's University Press, 1985).

159. Domning, *Sirenian Evolution in the North Pacific Ocean* (Berkeley: University of California Press, 1978), 140.

160. A. B. Savinetsky, "Ancient Population Dynamics of the Sea Cow (*Hydromalis Gigas*, Zimm. 1780) in the Late Holocene," *Doklady Biological Sciences* 320, nos. 1–6 (1995): 403.

161. See Leonhard Stejneger, "On the Extermination of the Great Northern Sea-Cow (Rytina): A Reply to Professor A.E. Nordenskiold," *Bulletin of the American Geographical Society* 18, no. 4 (1886): 1053; and S. T. Turvey and C. L. Risley, "Modelling the Extinction of Steller's Sea Cow," *Biology Letters* 2 (2006): 95.

162. D. L. West, C. Lefevre, and D. Corbett, "Radiocarbon Dates for the Near Islands, Aleutian Islands, Alaska," *Current Research in the Pleistocene* 16 (1999): 83–85; Corbett, et al., "Aleut Hunters, Sea Otters, and Sea Cows," 62.

163. David Quammen, *Song of the Dodo: Island Biogeography in an Age of Extinctions* (New York: Scribner, 2004), Chapter 4.

164. Georg Wilhelm Steller, *Ausführliche Beschreibing von Sonderbaren Meerthieren* (Halle: In Verlag, Carl Christian Kümmel, 1753), 98.

165. Corbett, et al., "Aleut Hunters, Sea Otters, and Sea Cows," 69.

166. Steller, *Von Sonderbaren Meerthieren*, 103.

167. P. Pekarskii, "O Rechi v Pamyat' Lomonosova proiznesennoi v Akademii nauk doktorom LeKlerkom," *Zapiski Imperatorskoi akademii nauk* 10, no. 2 (1866): 178–187, 185.

168. Stejneger, "On the Extermination of the Great Northern Sea-Cow," 1053, Pekarskii, "O Rechi v Pamyat' Lomonosova," 185.

169. Pekarskii, "O Rechi v Pamyat' Lomonosovo," 186.

170. Pekarskii, "O Rechi v Pamyat' Lomonosovo," 185.

171. "Account of the Totma Merchant, Stepan Cherepanov, concerning his stay in the Aleutian Islands, 1759–1762." In A. I. Andreev, ed., *Russkie Otkrytiia v Tikhom Okeane i Severnoi Amerike v XVIII Veke* (Moscow, 1948), 113. Original in RGADA, Portfeli Millera, no. 534, ch. 1, 11. 21–27 ob. "Podannoe Prokop'em Lisenkovym opisanie nakhodqshimsya po akiqnu/moryu to Kamchatki osrovam..." In V. A. Divin, *Russkaya Tikhookeanskaya Epopeya* (Khabarovsk: Khabarovskoe Knizhnoe Izdatel'stvo, 1979), 344.

172. Grigorii Shelikhov, *A Voyage to America, 1783–1786*, trans. Marina Ramsay, ed. Richard A. Pierce (Kingston, Ontario: The Limestone Press, 1981), 36.

173. Martin Sauer, *Account of a Geographical and Astronomical Expedition to the Northern Parts of Russia* (London: Printed by A. Strahan, Printers Street: For T. Cadell, Jun. and W. Davies, in the Strand, 1802), 181.

174. Karl Ernst von Baer, "Untersuchungen über die Ehelmalige Verbreitung der von Steller beobachteten nordischen Seekuh (*Rytina Ill.*)," *Mém. Acad. Sci. St.-Pétersbourg* 6 (October, 1840): 53–80, 74.

175. Stejneger, "How the Great Northern Sea-Cow (Rytina) Became Exterminated," 1050–1053.

176. Paul Anderson, "Competition, Predation and the Evolution and Extinction of Steller's Sea Cow, *Hydromalis gigas*," *Marine Mammal Science* 11, no. 3 (1995), 391–394.

177. Turvey and Risley, "Modelling the Extinction of Steller's Sea Cow," 94.

178. James Gibson, "*De Bestiis Marinis*: Steller's Sea Cow and Russian Expansion from Siberia to America, 1741–1768." In N. N. Bolkhovitinov, ed., *Russkaia Amerika, 1799–1867* (Moscow: Akademii Nauk, Inst. Vseobshchei Istorii, Tsentr Severoamerikanskikh Issledovanii, 1999), 43.

Chapter 3

1. Folkwart Wendland, *Peter Simon Pallas (1741–1811): Materialien einer Biographie* (Berlin: W. de Gruyter, 1992), 160.
2. His notes, entitled "Kurzgefasste Anweisung zur Forstwirtschaft für das Russische Reich," and "Über das Fortwesen im Russischen Reich," can be found in RAN, R.1, op. 121, no. 1. The former has recently been published in translation: P. S. Pallas, "Kratkie polozheniia, kotorye pri ustroistve lesov preimushchestvenno dolzhny byt' prinyaty ov vnimanie," trans. V.F. Gnucheva, *Studies in the History of Biology* 3, no. 3 (2011): 88–93.
3. See Wendland, *Peter Simon Pallas*, 631.
4. Peter Simon Pallas, Letters to G. F. Müller, March 24, 1781, November 2, 1781, in RAN, F. 21, Op. 3, No. 22a, p 186.
5. Peter Simon Pallas, *Travels through the Southern Provinces of the Russian Empire in the Years 1793 and 1794* (London: Printed for John Stockdale, Piccadilly, 1812), 33–34.
6. V. K. Teplyakov, Ye. P. Kuzmichev, D. M. Baumgartner, and R. L. Everett, *A History of Russian Forestry and its Leaders* (unknown publisher, 1998), 5; see also Stephen Brain, *Song of the Forest: Russian Forestry and Soviet Environmentalism, 1905–1953* (Pittsburgh: University of Pittsburgh Press, 2011).
7. Stepan Petrovich Krasheninnikov, *Opisanie Zemli Kamchatka* (St. Petersburg, 1755), 169.
8. Georg Wilhelm Steller, *History of Kamchatka*, trans. Margritt Engel and Karen Willmore, ed. Marvin Falk (Fairbanks: University of Alaska Press, 2003), 89.
9. Krasheninnikov, *Opisanie Zemli Kamchatka*, 120.
10. Callum Roberts has pointed out that these descriptions may not be exaggerations, such were the immense numbers of animals in the New World before the European invasion; Callum Roberts, *The Unnatural History of the Sea* (Washington, DC: Island Press/Shearwater Books, 2007), xv.
11. Georg Wilhelm Steller, *Ausführliche Beschreibung von Sonderbaren Meerthieren* (Halle, 1753), 58.
12. Quoted in Shepard Krech, *The Ecological Indian: Myth and History* (New York: Norton, 1999), 73–74.
13. Peter Martyr's first account of Sebastian Cabot's voyage, 1516. Quoted in J. A. Williamson, ed., *The Cabot Voyages and Bristol Discovery under Henry VII* (Cambridge: Cambridge University Press, 1962), 35.
14. Richard H. Grove, *Green Imperialism: Colonial Expansion, Tropical Island Edens and the Origins of Environmentalism, 1600–1860* (Cambridge: Cambridge University Press, 1996), p 11.
15. Jean Baptiste-Barthelemy de Lesseps, *Travels in Kamtschatka, during the Years 1787 and 1788* (London, 1790), 6, 230.
16. Georg Forster, *A Voyage around the World in His Britannic Majesty's Sloop Resolution, Commanded by Capt. James Cook, during the Years 1772, 3, 4, and 5* (London, 1777) 37.
17. Steller, *History of Kamchatka*, 141–142.
18. Fedor Soimonov, "Drevnyaya Poslovitsa Sibir' Zolotoe Dno. Opisanie Soobschennoe iz Sibiri," *Ezhemesiachnye Sochineniia i Perevody, k Pol'ze i Uveseleniiu Sluzhaschiia* (December 1761), 450.
19. Soimonov, "Drevnaya Poslovitsa," 464.
20. L. A. Goldenberg, *Fedor Ivanovich Soimonov (1692–1780)* (Moscow: Nauka, 1966), 145–152.
21. Soimonov, "Drevnaya Poslovitsa," 466.
22. Soimonov, "Drevnaya Poslovitsa," 466–467.
23. Raymond Henry Fisher, *The Russian Fur Trade, 1550–1700* (Berkeley: University of California Press, 1943), 79.
24. See S. P. Krasheninnikov, "O Sobolnom Promisle," in RAN, f. 21, op 5, no. 51, p 1 ob.
25. Krasheninnikov, *Opisanie Zemli Kamchatka*, 91.
26. See for example, Gerhard Friedrich Müller, "Izvestie o Torgokh Sibirskikh," *Ezhemesiachnye Sochineniia k Pol'ze i Uveseleniiu Sluzhatsiia* (October 1755), 196.
27. Steller, *History of Kamchatka*, 89.

28. Krasheninnikov, *Opisanie Zemli Kamchatka*, 121.
29. Abbé Jean Chappe d'Auteroche, *Voyage en Siberie*, 2 vols. (Paris, 1768). Translated as *A Journey into Siberia, Made by the Order of the King of France by M. L'abbe Chappe D'Auteroche, Of the Imperial Academy of Sciences at Paris in 1761. Containing an Account of the MANNERS and CUSTOMS of the RUSSIANS, the Present State of their EMPIRE; with the Natural History, and Geographical Description of their Country, and Level of the Road from PARIS to TOBOLSKY* (London, 1770).
30. Marcus C. Levitt, "An Antidote to Nervous Justice: Catherine the Great's Debate with Chappe d'Auteroche over Russian Culture," *Eighteenth Century Studies* 32, no. 1 (1998): 50.
31. D'Auteroche, *A Journey into Siberia*, 62.
32. Anonymous (Catherine II), *Antidote, ou Examen du mauvais livre superbement imprime intitule Voyage en Siberie* (St. Petersburg, 1770). Translated into English as *The Antidote: Or An Enquiry into the Merits of a Book, Entitled A Journey into Siberia* (London, 1772).
33. Catherine II, *Antidote*, 4.
34. Catherine II, *Antidote*, 8.
35. See Clarence J. Glacken, *Traces on the Rhodian Shore: Nature and Culture in Western Thought from Ancient Times to the End of the Eighteenth Century* (Berkeley: University of California Press, 1967), 10.
36. Larry Wolff, *Inventing Eastern Europe: The Map of Civilization on the Mind of the Enlightenment* (Stanford, CA: Stanford University Press, 1994), 363.
37. G. E. Pavlova and A. S. Fedorov, *Mikhail Vasilevich Lomonosov, 1711–1765* (Moscow, 1986), 119.
38. J. L. Black, *G. F. Müller and the Imperial Russian Academy* (Kingston, Ontario: McGill-Queen's University Press, 1986), Part III.
39. Peter Simon Pallas, *Reise durch Verschiedene Provinzen des Russischen Reichs* vol. III (St. Petersburg, 1770), 221.
40. Peter Simon Pallas, "Letter to Gerhard Friedrich Müller," November 17, 1770, in RAN, f. 21, op. 3, no. 22, p 95.
41. Peter Simon Pallas, "Letter to Gerhard Friedrich Müller," August, 1772, in RAN, f. 21, op. 3, no. 222, p 140 ob.
42. Peter Simon Pallas, "Letter to Gerhard Friedrich Müller," November 16, 1770, in RAN, f. 21, op. 3, no. 222, p 90 ob.
43. Timofei Shmalev, "Report to G.F. Müller on the Discovery of New Islands near America," University of Washington Special Collections, Frank Golder Photostat Collection, vol. 11.
44. Many of Shmalev's reports are found in the Portfeli Millera in RGADA, f. 199, no. 539. See also Frank Golder Photostat Collection, University of Washington Special Collections, vol. 11, p 1.
45. Black, *G. F. Müller and the Imperial Russian Academy*, 178.
46. See Freidrich Plenisner, "Letter to Gerhard Friedrich Müller," November, 29, 1762 in RGADA, f. 199, no. 258, ch. 1, 5, p 1.
47. More of Plenisner's letters are found in RGADA, f. 199, no. 546, ch. 8.
48. Friedrich Plenisner, "Letter to Gerhard Friedrich Müller," December 8, 1767, in RGADA, f. 199, no. 528, ch. 1, 5, p 7 ob.
49. Peter Simon Pallas, "Letter to Gerhard Friedrich Müller," July 29, 1778, in RAN, f. 21, op. 3, no. 222a, p 60 ob.
50. Richard Pierce, *Russian America: A Biographical Dictionary* (Kingston, Ontario: The Limeston Press, 1990), 400.
51. Pierce, *Russian America: A Biographical Dictionary*, 288.
52. See Harry Liebersohn, *The Traveler's World: Europe to the Pacific* (Cambridge, MA: Harvard University Press, 2006), 32–57.
53. Quoted in Frieder Sondermann, "Tilesius und Japan. Teil 1: Tagebuchauszüge über Ankunft und Aufenthalt in Nagasaki 1804/5," *TohokuGakuin Research Journal* 154 (2009–12): 105–147.
54. G. W. Steller, "Report," March, 29, 1747, in RAN, F. 3, Op. 1, No. 813, p 194.
55. Letter, Voznesenskii to Fedor Fedorovich, June 24, 1840. Leonid Shur Collection, University of Alaska Fairbanks, Roll 22, No. 150, p 11 ob.

56. NARS-RRAC, CS, roll 4, folios 325, 241.
57. Michael D. Gordin, "Arduous and Delicate Task: Princess Dashkova, the Academy of Sciences, and the Taming of Natural Philosophy." In Sue Anne Prince, ed., *The Princess and the Patriot: Ekaterina Dashkova, Benjamin Franklin, and the Age of Enlightenment* (Philadelphia: American Philosophical Society, 2006), 17.
58. V. I. Osipov, ed., *Nauchnoe Nasledie P.S. Pallas: Pis'ma, 1768–1771 gg* (St. Petersburg: Tialid, 1993),55.
59. Letter, from Euler to Pallas, August, 27, 1772, "Materialy o Pallase, from the archival collections of the Academy of Sciences, collected by Keppen," p. 13.
60. Peter Simon Pallas, Letter to G.F. Müeller, May 17, 1773, in RAN, F 21, Op. 3, No. 222, p. 172.
61. Peter Simon Pallas, Letter to Joseph Banks, March 26/April 6th, 1782, in the British Library Manuscript Department, Add MSS 8095, pp 105, 105 op.
62. For more on the tensions naturalists felt while serving the Russian empire, see Ryan Jones, "Peter Simon Pallas, Siberia, and the European Republic of Letters," *Studies in the History of Biology* 3, no. 3 (September 2011): 55–67.
63. Pallas to Müller, March 28, 1777 in RAN, f. 21, op 3, no. 222a, p 24 ob.
64. Georg Wilhelm Steller, Letter to Gmelin, December, 4, 1742, in Deutsche Staatsbibliothek zu Berlin, Handschriftsabteilung, MS. germ. fol 788, p 19.
65. Peter Simon Pallas, "Immergrün," in the Deutsche Staatsbibliothek zu Berlin, Handschriftsabteilung, MS. germ. fol. 788. A copy can also be found in RAN, r. 1, op. 121, no. 24.
66. See Grove, *Green Imperialism*, 11.
67. Glacken, *Traces on the Rhodian Shore*, 665.
68. Quoted in Glacken, *Traces on the Rhodian Shore*, 663.
69. Pallas, *NNB*, vol. VII, p 147.
70. Pallas to Müller, March 2, 1773, in RAN, f. 21 op. 3 no. 222, p 160 op.
71. Pallas, *Travels through the Southern Provinces of the Russian Empire in the Years 1793 and 1794*, vol. I, 14.
72. Pallas to Müller, September 13, 1773, in RAN, f. 21, op. 3, no. 222, p 185.
73. Douglas Cole and Maria Tippett, "Pleasing Diversity and Sublime Desolation: The 18th-Century British Perception of the Northwest Coast," *Pacific Northwest Quarterly* 65, no. 1 (January, 1974).
74. "An Account by the Cossack Piatidesiatnik Vladimir Atlasov." In Basil Dmytryshyn, E. A. P. Crownhart-Vaughan, and Thomas Vaughan, eds., *Russian Penetration of the North Pacific Ocean: A Documentary Record, 1700–1797* (Portland, OR: Oregon Historical Society Press, 1988), 5.
75. Krasheninnikov, *Opisanie Zemli Kamchatki*, 92.
76. Magnus Behm, "Pribavlenie: O Kamchatskom Zemledelii, ot Byvshago v Kamchatke Komandanta Maiora Bema," *Trudy Volnogo Ekonomicheskogo Obschestva*, Part XXXIII (1783), 47.
77. Peter Simon Pallas, "News of the Animal Husbandry and Agriculture Introduced into Kamchatka and around Okhotsk, under the Commmand of the Udskom fortress lying around the Sea of Okhotsk," in *Trudy Volnogo Ekonomicheskogo Obschestva*, Part XXXIII (1783), 32.
78. "A report dictated in St. Petersburg by Fedor Afansevich Kukov concerning his 1762 voyage to the Aleutian Islands," in Dmytryshyn et al., eds., *Russian Penetration of the North Pacific*, 228.
79. Sven Larsson Waxell, *The American Expedition*, trans. M.A. Michael (London: W. Hodge, 1952), 61.
80. O. Solomina, et al., "Multiproxy Records of Climate Variability for Kamchatka for the Past 400 Years," *Climate of the Past* 3 (2007): http://www.clim-past.net/3/119/2007/cp-3-119-2007.pdf. Accessed December 6, 2013.
81. Krasheninnikov, *Opisanie Zemli Kamchatki*, 10.
82. "Raporti Krashennikova," RAN, f. 21, op. 5, l. 79 ob.
83. James Gibson, *Feeding the Fur Trade: Provisionment of the Okhotsk Seaboard and the Kamchatka Peninsula* (Madison: University of Wisconsin Press, 1969), 79, 136.

84. Dmytryshyn et al., eds., *Russian Penetration of the North Pacific Ocean*, 11.
85. Steller, *History of Kamchatka*, 174.
86. I. Bulychev, "Ob opytakh zemledeliya v Kamchatke," *Vestnik Imperatorskavo russkavo geograficheskavo obshchestva*, Part 8 (1853), 78–79.
87. Krasheninnikov, *Opisanie Zemli Kamchatki*, 86.
88. Law of January 2, 1742. PSZ, vol. XI, no. 8507, p 578.
89. Steller, *History of Kamchatka*, 35.
90. See Alfred Crosby, *Ecological Imperialism: The Biological Expansion of Europe, 900–1900* (Cambridge, MA: Harvard University Press, 1986).
91. See Stephen Baehr, *The Paradise Myth in Eighteenth-Century Russia: Utopian Patterns in Early Secular Russian Literature and Culture* (Stanford, CA: Stanford University Press, 1991), and Willard Sunderland, *Taming the Wild Field: Colonization and Empire on the Russian Steppe* (Ithaca, NY: Cornell University Press, 2004).
92. Quoted in Sunderland, *Taming the Wild Field*, 94.
93. Sunderland, *Taming the Wild Field*, 95.
94. Steller, *History of Kamchatka*, 37.
95. Krasheninnikov, *Opisanie Zemli Kamchatki*, 89.
96. Waxell, *The American Expedition*, 185.
97. Quoted in A. Sokolov, "Severnaya ekspeditsiya 1733–43 godu," *Zapiski Gidrograficheskavo Departamenta* 9 (1851): 424–425.
98. PSZ, vol. I, no. 46, p. 214.
99. Timofei Shmalev, "Kratkoye opisanie o Kamchatke," *Opyt trudov Volnavo rossiiskavo sobraniya pri Imperatorskom moskovskom universitete*, Part 1 (1774), 209, 211.
100. Joseph Bradley, "Subjects into Citizens: Societies, Civil Society, and Autocracy in Tsarist Russia," *The American Historical Review* 107, no. 4. (October, 2002): 1094–1123.
101. See V. V. Oreshkin, *Vol'noe Ekonomicheskoe Obshchestvo v Rossii, 1765–1917* (Moscow, 1963); James Arthur Prescott, "The Russian Free Economic Society: Foundation Years," *Agricultural History* 51, no. 3 (July 1977): 503–512; Colum Leckey, *Patrons of Enlightenment: The Free Economic Society in Eighteenth-Century Society* (Newark: University of Delaware Press, 2011).
102. *Trudy Vol'nogo Ekonomicheskogo Obshchestva* I (1765), 180–193.
103. Wendland, *Peter Simon Pallas*, 732.
104. Pallas, "News," 29.
105. List of Pallas's works in Wendland, *Peter Simon Pallas*, vol. II, 870.
106. P. S. Pallas, "Izvestiya o vvedennom skotovodstve i zemlepashestve v Kamchatke i okolo Okhotska, pri Udskom ostroge lezhashchem podle Okhotskavo morya," *Prodolzhenie trudov Volnavo ekonomicheskavo obshchestva ...*, pt. 3 (1783): 26–40, 40.
107. Pallas, "Izvestiya," 40.
108. A. S. Sgibnev, "Istoricheskii Ocherk Glavneischikh Sobitii v Kamchatke s 1650 po 1865 gg," in *Morskoi Sbornik* 105 (1869): 37.
109. Pallas, "Izvestiya," 49.
110. Magnus Behm, "Pribavlenie: O Kamchatskom zemledelii, ot byvshago v Kamchatke Komendanta Maiora fon Behma," *Trudy Volnavo ekonomicheskavo obshchestva*, pt 33 (1783)," 49.
111. See Gibson, *Feeding the Fur Trade*, 167.
112. Grigorii Shelikhov, *A Voyage to America 1783–1786*, trans. Marina Ramsay, ed. Richard Pierce (Kingston, Ontario: The Limestone Press, 1981), 52.
113. Katerina G. Solovjova and Aleksandra A. Vovnyanko, *The Fur Rush*, 62; taken from *K istorii Rossiisko-amerikanskoi kompanii*, 64.
114. Dmytryshyn et al., *Russian Penetration of the North Pacific Ocean*, 357.
115. Langsdorff, *Bemerkung auf einer Reise*, v II p 161.
116. Yuri Lisiankii, *Puteshestvie vokrug Sveta na Korable* "Neva" (Moscow, 1947), p 177.
117. Steller, *History of Kamchatka*, 99.
118. Pallas, "Izvestiya," p 41.
119. John Rickman, ed., *Journal of Captain Cook's last voyage to the Pacific Ocean, on Discovery; in the years 1776, 1777, 1778, 1779* (London, 1781), 354–356.

120. See Gibson, *Feeding the Fur Trade*, 183. Such a dramatic drop in cattle can only be explained by the British visit.

121. Pallas, "Izvestiya," 41.

122. Behm did finally gain a government post in Riga.

123. "O Torgovle v Redutakh s Dikami," in the Archive of the Russian Geographical Society, p 7 ob.

124. Gavriil Sarychev, *Account of a Voyage of Discovery to the North-East of Siberia, the Frozen Ocean, and the North-East Sea* (London: Printed for Richard Phillips, 1806), v. I, 69.

125. Quoted in Raymond Fisher, *Bering's Voyages: Whither and Why* (Seattle: University of Washington Press, 1977),113.

126. Tatiana Fyodorova, et al., *Martin Spangsberg: A Danish Explorer in Russian Service* (Esbjerg, Denmark: *Fiskeri- og Søfartsmuseet*, 1999), 116.

127. Steller, *History of Kamchatka*, 288.

128. Steller, *History of Kamchatka*, 288

129. Polonskii, "Perechen'', 47. Berkh gives the figure as 22 puds. See Vasilii Berkh, *A Chronological History of the Discovery of the Aleutian Islands*, Dmitri Krenov, trans. (Kingston, Ontario: The Limestone Press, 1974), 101.

130. Berkh, *Chronological History*, 107.

131. See Clifford Foust, *Muscovite and Mandarin: Russia's Trade with China and its Setting, 1727–1805* (Chapel Hill: University of North Carolina Press, 1969), 46–47.

132. Foust, *Muscovite and Mandarin*, 277.

133. G. F. Müller, "Istoriia o Stranakh, pri Reke Amure Lezhashchikh, Kogda Onyia Sostoiali pod Rossiiskim Vladeniem," in *Ezemesachnye Sochineniia*, (October, 1757), 328.

134. See J. L. Black, *G. F. Müller and the Imperial Russian Academy*, 148–149.

135. See Pallas, "Letter to Müller," November 4, 1778, RAN, f. 21, op. 3, no. 22a, p 63 op.

136. Pallas, *Reise Durch Verschiedene Provinzen*, vol. III, 281.

137. Pallas, "Letter to Pennant," November 25/December 5th, 1779, in Carol Urness, ed., *A Naturalist in Russia: Letters from Peter Simon Pallas to Thomas Pennant* (Minneapolis: University of Minneapolis, 1967), 113.

138. See Lisbet Koerner, *Linnaeus: Nature and Nation* (Cambridge, MA: Harvard University Press, 1999).

139. See Foust, *Muscovite and Mandarin*, 368.

140. Steller, *History of Kamchatka*, 17.

141. Pallas, *Reise Durch Verschiedene Provinzen*, Part III, 207.

142. See R. V. Makarova, *Russkie na Tikhom Okeane vo Vtoroi Polovine XVIII v.* (Moscow, 1968), 112, and A. Corsak, *Istoriko-Statisticheskoe Obozrenie Torgovykh Snoshenii Rossii s Kitaem* (Kazan, 1957), 81.

143. Müller, "Izvestiia o Torgakh Sibirskikh," 213.

144. Pallas, "Letter to Pennant," November 25/December 5, in Urness, ed., *A Naturalist in Russia*, 113.

145. Chikashi Takahashi, "Inter-Asian Competition in the Fur Market in the Eighteenth and Nineteenth Centuries," in A. J. H. Latham and Heita Kawakatsu, eds., *Intra-Asian Trade and the World Market* (London: Routledge, 2006), 40. For an excellent discussion of the sea otter trade in the Western Pacific, see Richard Ravalli, "Soft Gold and the Pacific Frontier: Geopolitics and Environment in the Sea Otter Trade," PhD. diss., University of California, Merced, 2009.

146. Takahashi, "Inter-Asian Competition in the Fur Market in the Eighteenth and Nineteenth Centuries," 41.

147. Brett L. Walker, *The Conquest of Ainu Lands: Ecology and Culture in Japanese Expansion, 1590-1800* (Berkeley : University of California Press, 2001), 157.

148. de Lesseps, *Travels in Kamtschatka*, vol. I, 209.

149. Katherine Plummer, *The Shogun's Reluctant Ambassadors: Japanese Sea Drifters in the North Pacific* (Portland: Oregon Historical Society Press, 1991), 43–51.

150. Pallas, *NNB*, vol. VI (1793), 253.

151. Donald Keene, *The Japanese Discovery of Europe, 1720–1830* (Stanford, CA: Stanford University Press, 1969), p 57.

152. Data from Makarova, *Russkie na Tikhom Okeane*‿ "'Perechen' Polonskogo,'" and Lydia Black, *Atka: An Ethnohistory of the Western Aleutians* (Kingston, Ontario: The Limestone Press, 1984).

153. Quoted in James Gibson, "Sitka-Kyakhta versus Sitka-Canton: Russian America and the China Market," *Pacifica* 2 (November 1990): 43.

154. Tatiana Fyodorova, et al., *Martin Spangsberg: A Danish Explorer in Russian Service* (Esbjerg, Denmark: Fiskeri- og Søfartsmuseet, 1999).

155. Pallas, "Letter to Müller," Deember 5, 1772, RAN

156. NARS-RRAC, CS, roll 4, folio 228.

157. Warren Dean, *With Broadaxe and Firebrand: The Destruction of the Brazilian Atlantic Coastal Forest* (Berkeley: University of California Press, 1995).

158. A. S. Korsun, "Iz Istorii Postupleniya Severoamerkanskikh Kolletskii MAE v XVII Stoletii," in A.D. Dribzo and G. I. Dzeniskevich, eds., *Otkritie Ameriki Prodolzhaetsya* (St. Petersburg, 2001), 123.

159. Krasheninnikov, *Opisanie Zemli Kamchatki*, 33.

160. Steller, *Journal of a Voyage with Bering*, 105.

161. Steller, *History of Kamchatka*, 10.

162. Pallas, *NNB*, vol. I, part 2, p 275.

163. Martin Sauer, *Account of a Geographical and Astronomical Expedition to the Northern Parts of Russia* (London: Printed by A. Strahan, Printers Street: For T. Cadell, Jun. and W. Davies, in the Strand, 1802), xiv.

164. Pallas, *Reise Durch Verschiedene Prozinven*, vol. III, p 21.

165. For more on this process see Steven Shapin and Simon Schaffer, *Leviathan and the Air Pump: Hobbes, Boyle, and the Experimental Life* (Princeton, NJ: Princeton University Press, 1989).

166. Krasheninnikov, *Opisanie Zemli Kamchatki*, 100.

167. A. A. Andreev, *Russkie Otkrytiia v Tikhom Okeane i Severnoi Amerike v XVIII–XIX (Sbornik Materialov)* (Moscow: Izdatelstvo Akademii Nauk SSSR, 1944), 80.

168. Pallas, *NNB*, v I, part 2, p 275.

169. James R. Masterson, ed., *Bering's Successors, 1745–1780: Contributions of Peter Simon Pallas to the History of Russian Exploration toward Alaska* (Seattle: University of Washington Press, 1948), 72.

170. Pallas, *NNB*, vol. I, part 2, p 296.

Chapter 4

1. Martin Sauer, *Account of a Geographical and Astronomical Expedition to the Northern Parts of Russia* (London: Printed by A. Strahan, Printers Street: For T. Cadell, Jun. and W. Davies, in the Strand, 1802), 332.

2. See Richard Pierce, *Biographical Dictionary of Russian America* (Kingston, Ontario: The Limeston Press, 1990), 444.

3. RGAVMF, R. 212, O. II, d. 890; Printed in M. I. Belov, *Russians in the Bering Strait, 1648–1791*, Katerina Solovjova, trans. (Anchorage: White Stone Press, 2000), 51.

4. *Allgemeine Literatur-Zeitung*, v. IV, October 11, 1804 (Halle, 1804), 89.

5. Quoted in James Gibson, *Otter Skins, Boston Ships, and China Goods: The Maritime Fur Trade of the Northwest Coast, 1785–1841* (Seattle: University of Washington Press, 1992), 19.

6. William Beloe, and Thomas Rennel, *The Sexegenarian: Or, the Recollections of a Literary Life* (London, 1817), 55–56.

7. Arthur Aitkin, ed., *The Annual Review and History of Literature* I, Issue 1 (1802): 9.

8. *The Anti-Jacobin Review and Magazine or Monthly Political and Literary Censor* 13 (September–December 1802): 241.

9. *The British Critic* XIX (June 1802): 3.

10. Aitkin, *The Annual Review*, 12, 17.

11. *The Monthly Magazine, or, British Register 14*, Part II (1802): 3.

12. *The Monthly Review* XLI (May 1803): 21.
13. John Rickman, ed., *Journal of Capt. Cook's Last Voyage to the Pacific Ocean*... (London: Printed for E. Newberry, 1781), 383.
14. Rickman, ed., *Journal of Capt. Cook's Last Voyage*, 371.
15. J. C. Beaglehole, *Cook and the Russians: An Addendum to the Hakluyt Society's Edition of The Voyage of the Resolution and Discovery, 1776–1780* (London: Kakluyt Society, 1973) 3.
16. Peter Simon Pallas, Letters to G. F. Müller, October 28, 1779, December 12, 1779, January 2, 1780, April 16, 1780, RAN, f. 21, op. 3 no. 22a, pp 98–110 ob.
17. Barry Gough, *Distant Dominion: Britain and the Northwest Coast of North America, 1579–1809* (Vancouver: University of British Columbia Press, 1980) and David McKay, *In the Wake of Cook: Exploration, Science and Empire 1780–1801* (New York: St. Martin's Press, 1985).
18. James Strange, *James Strange's Journal and Narrative of the Commercial Expedition from Bombay to the North West Coast of America* (Fairfield, WA: Ye Galleon Press, 1982), 113.
19. Lydia Black, *Russians in Alaska 1732–1867* (Fairbanks: University of Alaska Fairbanks, 2004), 92.
20. Folkwart Wendland, *Peter Simon Pallas (1741–1811): Materialien einer Biographie* (Berlin: W. de Gruyter, 1992), 642.
21. Peter Simon Pallas, Letter to Thomas Pennant, 1779, in Carol L.Urness, ed., *A Naturalist in Russia: Letters* (Minneapolis: University of Minnesota Press, 1967), 119. Sensitivity about Krenitsyn's remarks by no means died with time. The latest publication of his journals, published in the last years of the Soviet Union, omits his criticisms of Russian behavior toward the Aleuts.
22. William Coxe, *Account of the Russian Discoveries between Asia and America to which Are Added, the Conquest of Siberia and the History of the Transactions and Commerce between Russia and China* (London: Printed by J. Nichols for T. Cadell, 1780), x.
23. Coxe, *Account of the Russian Discoveries between Asia and America*, viii.
24. Coxe, *Account of the Russian Discoveries between Asia and America*, 19.
25. J.L. Black, *G. F. Müller and the Imperial Russian Academy* (Kingston, Ontario: McGill-Queen's University Press, 1986), 102.
26. Coxe, *Account of the Russian Discoveries between Asia and America*, 5, 259.
27. Narochnitskii, et al., *Russkie Ekspeditsii*, vol. II, document no. 65.
28. For an opposing view that does not see a strong link between Cook's and Billings's voyages, see Simon Werrett, "Russian Responses to the Voyages of Captain Cook." In Glyndwr Williams, ed., *Captain Cook: Explorations and Reassessments* (Rochester, NY: Boydell Press, 2004).
29. James Gibson, "The Abortive First Russian Circumnavigation: Captain Mulovsky's 1787 Expedition to the North Pacific," *Terrae Incognitae* 31 (1999): 49–60.
30. Joseph Banks, Letter to Peter Simon Pallas, September 22, 1785, in Deutsche Staatsbibliothek zu Berlin, Handschriftabteilung, MS. germ. fol 788, p 58.
31. Joseph Billings, Letters to Peter Simon Pallas, November 17, 1789, November 9, 1790, May 8, 1791, in Deutsche Staatsbibliothek zu Berlin, Handschriftabteilung, MS germ. fol 788.
32. Vasilii Divin, *Russkie Moreplavaniia na Tikhom Okeane v XVIII Veke* (Moscow, 1971), 259.
33. Joseph Billings, Letter to Peter Simon Pallas, March 20, 1795, in Deutsche Staatsbibliothek zu Berlin, Handschriftsabteilung, MS germ. fol 788, p 70.
34. Sauer, *Account of a Geographical and Astronomical Expedition*, 64.
35. Peter Simon Pallas, Letter to Joseph Banks, June 2/13, 1785, in British Library Manuscript Department, Add MSS 8096, p 148.
36. Letter from Luka Voronin to the Vice President of Admiralty, September 5, 1785, in V. A. Dvinin, *Russkaya Tikhookeanskaya Epopeya* (Khabarovsk, 1979), 369.
37. Matthias Christian Sprenger, *Bibliothek der Neusten und Wichtigsten Reisebeschreibungen* vol. 8 (Weimar, 1803), iv.
38. Pallas to Banks, June 2/13, Add MSS 8096, p 149.
39. Pallas to Banks, January 8/19, in British Library Manuscript Department, Add MSS 8095, p 37 op.; Peter Simon Pallas, letter to Gerhard Friedrich Müller, November 7, 1779, in RAN, f. 21, op. 3, no. 22a, p 100 ob.

40. Wendland, *Peter Simon Pallas*, 672.
41. Billings to Pallas, May 9, 1786, MS. germ. fol. 788, p 79.
42. Gavriil Sarychev, *Account of a Voyage of Discovery to the North-East of Siberia, the Frozen Ocean, and the North-East Sea* (London: Printed for Richard Phillips, 1806), v. I, I. 80.
43. Sauer, *Account of a Geographical and Astronomical Expedition*, 9.
44. Sarychev, *Puteshestvie*, 7.
45. See Galya Diment and Yuri Slezkine, eds., *Between Heaven and Hell: The Myth of Siberia in Russian Culture* (New York: St. Martin's Press, 1993), Introduction.
46. Pallas, *NNB*, vol. VII, p 147.
47. Sauer, *Account of a Geographical and Astronomical Expedition*, 54, 58.
48. Sauer, *Account of a Geographical and Astronomical Expedition*, 66.
49. John Ledyard, Letter to Thomas Jefferson, in Stephen Watrous, ed., *John Ledyard's Journey through Russia and Siberia, 1787–1788. The Journal and Selected Letters* (Madison: University of Wisconsin Press, 1966), 123.
50. Catherine II, Letter to Baron von Grimm, November 26, 1787, in "Pis'ma Imperatritsy," in *Sbornik imperatorskago russkago istoricheskago obshchestva* 23 (St. Petersburg, 1878), 424.
51. "A Report from Ivan V. Iakobi, Governor General of Siberia, to Aleksandr A. Bezborodko, College of Foreign Affairs, Concerning the Travels of John Ledyard," in Dmytryshyn, et al., *Russian Penetration of the North Pacific Ocean*, 342.
52. Grigorii Shelikhov, "Notes on Conversations with John Ledyard," Irkutsk, August 18/29, 1787, in Grigorii Shelikhov, *A Voyage to America 1783–1786*, trans. Marina Ramsay, ed. Richard Pierce (Kingston, Ontario: The Limestone Press, 1981), 118.
53. Watrous, ed., *John Ledyard's Journey through Russia and Siberia*, 50–51, and Eufrosena Dvoichenko-Markov, "John Ledyard and the Russians," *Russian Review* 11 (1952): 220–221. Pallas claimed—probably incorrectly—that Billings had cast suspicions on him. See Edward D. Clarke, *Travels to Russia, Tartary, and Turkey* vol. 1, sec. 1 (Philadelphia, 1811), 10. Parts of this letter were found in Pallas's personal collection in St. Petersburg, and published in James Zug, ed., *The Last Voyage of Captain Cook: The Collected Writings of John Ledyard* (Washington, DC: National Geographic Society, 2005). However, the portions quoted here were excised—probably by Pallas due to their sensitivity—and put in his private collection, which his daughter inherited upon his death in Berlin. This letter is now found in the Deutsche Staatsbibliothek zu Berlin, Handschriftsabteilung, MS. germ. fol. 788.
54. John Ledyard, Letter to Peter Simon Pallas, December, 1787 in Deutsche Staatsbibliothek zu Berlin, Handschriftsabteilung, MS. germ. fol. 788, pp 79, 79 op.
55. Ledyard, Letter to Pallas, MS. germ. fol. 788, p 80.
56. Watrous, *John Ledyard's Journey through Russia and Siberia*, 60.
57. Sauer, *Account of a Geographical and Astronomical Expedition*, 100.
58. Joseph Billings, Unpublished Journal, RGAVMF, f. 913, op. 1, d. 160, p 270.
59. "Confidential Report of Acting Governor-General of Irkutsk and Kolyvan, Ivan Peel, to the Ruling Senate, Irkutsk, September 19, 1789," in Shelikhov, *A Voyage to America 1783–1786*, 125–126.
60. "Complaints made by Natives of the Unalaska District to Russian Government Inspectors About Treatment by Russian Promyshlenniks and Seamen; Responses to these Charges from those Named by the Natives," Library of Congress, Manuscript Division. Yudin Collection, Box 2, Folder 23; see also Veniaminov, *Notes*, p 254, where he repeats the story once more.
61. Sauer, *Account of a Geographical and Astronomical Expedition*, 101.
62. Report of Ivan V. Iakobi to Catherine II, November 30, 1787. RGADA, f. Senata, no. 4383/812, 11. Translation in Dmytryshyn, et al., *Russian Penetration of the North Pacific*, 351–352.
63. I. S. Bak, ch. 14, "M.V. Lomonosov and the Struggle to Develop the Productive Forces of Russia," in John Letiche, ed., *The History of Russian Economic Thought* (Berkeley: University of California Press, 1964), 370–396.
64. Report of Ivan V. Iakobi to Catherine II, November 30, 1787, RGADA, f. Senata, no. 4383/812, p 351.
65. Report of G.I. Shelikhov to I. V. Iakobi, April 19, 1787, in N. N. Bolkhovitinov, ed., *Istoriya Russkoi Ameriki, 1732–1867* vol. II (Moscow: Nauka, 1999), 243.

66. Report of Ivan V. Iakobi, RGADA, f. Senata, p 355.

67. Bolkhovitinov, ed., *Istoriya Russkoi Ameriki* vol. I, 238.

68. "A Report from Ivan A. Pil, Governing General of Irkutsk and Kolyvan, to Empress Catherine II, October 7, 1791, in Aleksandr Andreev, ed., *Russkie Otkrytiia v Tikhom Okeane i Servernoi Amerike v XVIII-XIX Vekakh* (Moscow: Izdatelstvo Akademii Nauk SSSR, 1944), 305.

69. See Glynn Barratt, *Russia in Pacific Waters, 1715–1825 : A Survey of the Origins of Russia's Naval Presence in the North and South Pacific* (Vancouver : University of British Columbia Press, 1981), 80.

70. Andreev, ed., *Russkie Otkritiye*, 98–102.

71. Sauer, *Account of a Geographical and Astronomical Expedition*, 145–146.

72. Sarychev, *Puteshestvie* vol. II, 66.

73. Coxe, *Account of the Russian Discoveries between Asia and America*, 21.

74. Sauer, *Account of a Geographical and Astronomical Expedition*, 158.

75. Billings, Unpublished Journal, 270.

76. Sarychev, *Puteshestvie* vol. II, 11.

77. Sauer, *Account of a Geographical and Astronomical Expedition*, 181.

78. Sauer, *Account of a Geographical and Astronomical Expedition*, 267.

79. Karl Heinrich Merck, *Siberia and Northwest America 1788–1792: The Journal of Carl Heinrich Merck, Naturalist with the Russian Scientific Expedition led by Captains Joseph Billings and Gavriil Sarychev*, Fritz Jaensch, trans. (Kingston, Ontario: The Limestone Press, 1980), 96.

80. Sarychev, *Puteshestvie*, 211.

81. Christian Bering, Unpublished Journal, RGAVMF, f. 913, op. 1, pp 64, 72 ob.

82. As the traveler Edward Clarke reported from a conversation with Pallas in 1800. See Clarke, *Travels to Russia, Tartary and Turkey*, part I, p 12.

83. Sauer, *Account of a Geographical and Astronomical Expedition*, 181.

84. See Leonhard Stejneger, "On the Extermination of the Great Northern Sea-Cow (Rytina): A Reply to Professor A.E. Nordenskiold," *Bulletin of the American Geographical Society* 18, no. 4 (1886): 10.

85. Merck, *Siberia and Northwestern America*, 87.

86. Vasilii Berkh reported this to Dr. K. E. von Baer in 1830. K.E. von Baer, "Untersuchungen Über die Ehemalige Verbreitung und die Gänzliche Vertilgung der von Steller Beobachteten Nordischen Seekuh (Rytina M.)," *Memoires Scientifiques* (St. Petersburg, 1840), 73–74.

87. See Richard H. Grove, *Green Imperialism: Colonial Expansion, Tropical Island Edens and the Origins of Environmentalism, 1600–1860* (Cambridge: Cambridge University Press, 1996), Grove refers to European concerns about extinction somewhat cryptically. He mentions only that in the late eighteenth century the "full significance of [the dodo's] extinction start[ed] to enter a wider scientific consciousness." See Grove, 44, 93, 146-148

88. Quoted in Roberts, *The Unnatural History of the Sea*, 65.

89. Sarychev, *Puteshestvie*, 30.

90. Sarychev, *Puteshestvie*, 58.

91. Merck, *Journal of Carl Heinrich Merck*, 80, 102, Sarychev, Puteshestvie, 102.

92. "A confidential report to the Governing Senate from Ivan Alferevich Pil, Acting Governor General of Irkutsk and Kolyvan, transmitting information on conditions in Russian possessions in Alaska and the Aleutian Islands." Library of Congress, Manuscript Division. Golder Collection. Transcripts, Box 3.

93. Sauer, *Account of a Geographical and Astronomical Expedition*, 272.

94. Joseph Billings, Unpublished Journal. RGAVMF, f. 913, op. 1, d. 160, 243, 258, p. 279.

95. Merck, *Journal of Carl Heinrich Merck*, p 80, Sarytchev, v II, p 72.

96. Christian Bering, Unpublished Journal, RGAVFM, p 64.

97. Bak, "P.I. Rychkov, Inquirer into the Economy of Russia." In *The History of Russian Economic Thought*, 442–451.

98. See, for example, William Tooke, "Public Institutions for the Preservation and Increase of the Population," in Tooke, *View of the Russian Empire During the Reign of Catherine the Second, and to the Close of the Eighteenth Century* vol. I (London, 1800), Section II.

99. Aitkin, *The Annual Review*, 17.

100. See Willard Sunderland, *Taming the Wild Field: Colonization and Empire on the Russian Steppe* (Ithaca, NY: Cornell University Press, 2004), 72, and Sarychev, *Puteshestvie*, 5.

101. John Forsyth, *A History of the Peoples of Siberia: Russia's North Asian Colony, 1581–1990* (Cambridge: Cambridge University Press, 1994), 146.

102. Quoted in Khlebnikov, *Notes on Russian America*, parts II–V, 181.

103. As the English privateer Cox supposedly hoped to do in 1790. See Makarova, *Russkie na Tikhom Okeane*, 153.

104. Quoted in Sauer, *Account of a Geographical and Astronomical Expedition*, 43.

105. Bering, Unpublished Journal, 68.

106. Sauer, *Account of a Geographical and Astronomical Expedition*, 213.

107. See Richard Wortman, *Visual Texts, Ceremonial Texts, Texts of Exploration: Collected Articles on the Representation of Russian Monarchy* (Brighton, MA: Academic Studies Press, 2014), for the difficulties Russian naval officers had in replicating Cook's standards.

108. The literature on this subject is vast. See Ter Ellingson, *The Myth of the Noble Savage* (Berkeley: University of California Press, 2001), who argues that the idea of the noble savage originated in early-seventeenth-century Canada.

109. Sauer, *Account of a Geographical and Astronomical Expedition*, 46.

110. Quoted in Yuri Slezkine, *Arctic Mirrors: Russia and the Little People of the North* (Ithaca, NY: Cornell University Press, 1994), 66.

111. Sauer, *Account of a Geographical and Astronomical Expedition*, 273–274.

112. Merck, *Journal of Carl Heinrich Merck*, 80.

113. Sankar Muthu, *Enlightenment against Empire* (Princeton, NJ: Princeton University Press, 2003), chs. 1, 2.

114. Sarychev, *Puteshestvie*, 218.

115. Muthu, *Enlightenment against Empire*, ch. 1.

116. Thomas Barren, *Russia Reads Rousseau, 1762–1825* (Evanston, IL: Northwestern University Press, 2002), 55.

117. Douglas Cole and Maria Tippett, "Pleasing Diversity and Sublime Desolation: The 18th-Century British Perception of the Northwest Coast," *The Pacific Northwest Quarterly* 65, no. 1 (January, 1974): 1–7, 5.

118. Billings, Unpublished Journal, RGAVMF, p 92 ob.

119. Sarychev, *Puteshestvie*, 42.

120. Georg Heinrich von Langsdorff, *Voyages and Travels in Various Parts of the World* (London: Printed for Henry Colburn, 1814), v. II, p 70.

121. Sauer, *Account of a Geographical and Astronomical Expedition*, 213.

122. Sauer, *Account of a Geographical and Astronomical Expedition*, 261.

123. See Larry Wolff, *Inventing Eastern Europe: The Map of Civilization on the Mind of the Enlightenment* (Stanford, CA: Stanford University Press, 1994).

124. Sauer, *Account of a Geographical and Astronomical Expedition*, 274.

125. Sauer, *Account of a Geographical and Astronomical Expedition*, 279.

126. See Martin Sauer, Voyage Faite par Ordre de l'Imperatrice de Russie Catherine II, J. Castera, trans. (Paris, 1802); Martin Sauer, Viaggio Fatto per Ordire dell' Imperatrice di Russia Caterina II…, Conte Cav. Luigi Bossi, trans. (Milan, 1816).

127. No author, *The Monthly Review*, 17.

128. Sarychev, *Puteshestvie*, 11.

129. Billings, Unpublished Journal, RGAVMF, p 4.

130. "Information Concerning Mr. Billings Expedition to the North East Part of the Russian Empire and the coast of America," National Library of Scotland, MS. 1075, p 212.

131. Quoted in Shepard Krech, *The Ecological Indian: Myth and History* (New York: Norton 1999), 183.

132. David Thompson, *David Thompson's Narrative of his Explorations in Western America: 1784–1812* (Berkeley: University of California Press, 1916), 77, 113, 206. See also Calvin Martin, *Keepers of the Game: Indian-Animal Relationships and the Fur Trade* (Berkeley: University of California Press, 1978).

133. Peter Kalm, *Travels into North America*, John Reinhold Forster, trans. (Barre, MA: The Imprint Society, 1972), 231, xxiv.

134. See Fara, *Sex, Botany & Empire: The Story of Carl Linnaeus and Joseph Banks* (New York: Columbia University Press, 2003); James Delbourgo and Nicholas Dew, eds., *Science and Empire in the Atlantic World* (New York: Routledge, 2008); Richard Harry Drayton, *Nature's Government: Science, Imperial Britain, and the "Improvement" of the World* (New Haven, CT: Yale University Press, 2000); and Mary Louise Pratt, *Imperial Eyes: Travel Writing and Transculturation* (New York: Routledge, 1992).

135. See, for example, David Elliston Allen, *Naturalists and Society: The Culture of Natural History in Britain, 1700–1900* (Aldershot, UK: Ashgate, 2001); Drayton, *Nature's Government*; Grove, *Green Imperialism*; and Clarence J. Glacken, *Traces on the Rhodian Shore: Nature and Culture in Western Thought from Ancient Times to the End of the Eighteenth Century* (Berkeley: University of California Press, 1967).

136. For this point of view, see John F. Richards, *The Unending Frontier: An Environmental History of the Early Modern World* (Berkeley: University of California Press, 2003); and Richard Ellis, *The Empty Ocean: Plundering the World's Marine Life* (Washington, DC: Island Press/Shearwater Books, 2003).

Chapter 5

1. Thomas Pennant, *Arctic Zoology* vol. 3 (London: Printed for Robert Faulder, 1792), 1–2.

2. See *Histoire Naturelle des Indes: The Drake Manuscript in the Pierpont Morgan Library* (New York: Norton, 1996).

3. See Ray Desmond, *Great Natural History Books and their Creators* (London: British Library, 2003), 38.

4. Alix Cooper, *Inventing the Indigenous: Local Knowledge and Natural History in Early Modern Europe* (Cambridge: Cambridge University Press, 2007).

5. See for example, John Ray, *Catalogus Plantarum circa Cantabrigiam Nascentium* (London, 1660).

6. Georges-Louis LeClerc, Comte de Buffon, *Histoire Naturelle* 36 vols. (Paris, 1749–1788).

7. Thomas Pennant, *Synopsis of Quadrupeds* (London, 1771).

8. Quoted in Wilfrid Blunt, *The Compleat Naturalist: A Life of Linnaeus* (New York: Viking, 1971), 149.

9. Lisbet Koerner, *Linnaeus: Nature and Nation* (Cambridge, MA: Harvard University Press, 1999), 77.

10. Thomas Pennant, *British Zoology* 2d ed., 3 vols. (London, 1768–1770), vol. I, i.

11. Pennant, *British Zoology* vol. I, xi.

12. Mark V. Barrow, *Nature's Ghosts: Confronting Extinction from the Age of Jefferson to the Age of Ecology* (Chicago: University of Chicago Press, 2009), 33.

13. Erich Donnert, *Russia in the Age of Enlightenment* (Leipzig: Edition Leipzig, 1986), 110.

14. Peter Simon Pallas, *Zoographia Rosso Asiatica Sistens Omnium Animalium in Extenso Imperio Rossico et Adjacentibus Maribus Observatorum Rescensionem, Domicilia, Mores et Descriptiones, Anatomen Atque Icones Plurimorum* (Hereafter ZRA) 2 vols. (St. Petersburg, 1811), vol. I, v.

15. William Coxe, "Travels in Poland, Russia, Sweden, and Denmark, 1689–1812." In Peter Putnam, ed., *Seven Britons in Russia, 1698–1812* (Princeton, NJ: Princeton University Press, 1952), 270.

16. P.S. Pallas, *Betrachtungen über die Beschaffenheit der Gebürge und Veränderungen der Erdkugel, besonders in Beziehung auf das Rußische Reich* (Frankfurt und Leipzig: np, 1778),4, 8.

17. See "Materialy o Pallase," in Archive of the Russian Academy of Sciences (RAN), f. 92, op. 1, no. 103, p 19.

18. RAN, r. 1, op. 121, no. 13, p. 3.

19. Pallas, Letter to Thomas Pennant, October 24th / November 4th, 1777, in Carol L.Urness, ed., *A Naturalist in Russia: Letters* (Minneapolis: University of Minnesota Press, 1967), 15.

20. See Pallas, Undated Letter to Lovitz, in RAN, r. 1, op. 121, no. 6.

21. RAN, f. 92, op. 1, no. 103, p 19 ob.

22. Pallas, *ZRA* vol. I, IX, XVIII.

23. See Hans Rogger, *National Consciousness in Eighteenth-Century Russia* (Cambridge, MA: Harvard University Press, 1960), 259.

24. See for example, "Plan d'un ouvrage geographique et topographiqe sur l'Empire Russe," in RAN, r. I, op. 121, no. 13. The terms most commonly used were *vaste* (French) or *weitläufig* (German).

25. Martin Sauer, *Account of a Geographical and Astronomical Expedition to the Northern Parts of Russia* (London: Printed by A. Strahan, Printers Street: For T. Cadell, Jun. and W. Davies, in the Strand, 1802), viii.

26. Harsha Ram, *The Imperial Sublime: A Russian Poetics of Empire* (Madison: University of Wisconsin Press, 2003).

27. Catherine's "Nakaz to the Legislative Assembly," in L. Jay Oliva, ed., *Catherine the Great* (Englewood Cliffs, NJ: Prentice-Hall, 1968), 53–54.

28. Rogger, *National Consciousness in Eighteenth-Century Russia*, 258.

29. Gerhard Friedrich Müller, *Bering's Voyages: The Reports from Russia*, Lydia Black, trans. (Fairbanks: University of Alaska Press, 1986), 139.

30. Johann Gottlieb Georgi, *Russland: Beschreibung aller Nationen des Russischen Reiches; ihrer Lebensart, Religion, Gebräuche, Wohnungen, Kleidungen und übrigen Merkwürdigkeiten* vol. I. (St. Petersburg, 1776), I.

31. Pallas, *ZRA* vol. I, IX.

32. See E. I. Kolchinskii, A. K. Sytin, and G. I. Smagina, *Estestvennaya Istoriya v Rossii (Ocherki Razvitiya Estestvoznaniya v Rossii v XVIII veke)* (St. Petersburg: Nestor Istoriya, 2004), 119.

33. Mikhail Lomonosov, "Kratkoe opysanie raznykh puteshestvi," quoted in Rogger, *National Consciousness in Eighteenth-Century Russia*, 259.

34. "Ankündigung einer auf Allerhochsten Befehl Ihro Rußisch-Kaiserlichen Majestät Katharina der II herauszugebenden botanisch-ökonomischen Beschreibung und Abbildung aller inländischen Bäume, Strauben, und Pflanzen," in RAN, r. I, op. 121, no. 3, pp 1, 2.

35. RAN, r. I, op. 121, no. 13 ("Plan d'un ouvrage géographique et topographique sur l'Empire Russe), p. 1 ob.

36. Recently published in Yu. E. Berezkin, ed., *The Alutiit/Sugpiat: A Catalog of the Collections of the Kunstkamera* (Fairbanks: University of Alaska Press, 2012).

37. Peter Simon Pallas, Letter to Joseph Banks, March 2/10, 1779, in the British Library Manuscript Department, Add MS 8094, pp 237, 237 op.

38. Folkwart Wendland, *Peter Simon Pallas (1741–1811): Materialien einer Biographie* (Berlin: W. de Gruyter, 1992), 648.

39. Mairin Mitchell, *The Maritime History of Russia, 848–1948* (London: Sidgwick and Jackson, 1949), 112.

40. Quoted in James Cracraft, *The Revolution of Peter the Great* (Cambridge, MA: Harvard University Press, 2003), 234.

41. See Richard Wortman, *Visual Texts, Ceremonial Texts, Texts of Exploration: Collected Articles on the Representation of Russian Monarchy* (Brighton, MA: Academic Studies Press, 2014), 99.

42. J. A. von Krusenstern, *Reise um die Welt in den Jahren 1803, 1804, 1805 und 1806…* (St. Petersburg, 1810), v.

43. von Krusenstern, *Reise um die Welt in den Jahren 1803, 1804, 1805 und 1806…*, XIV.

44. See Donald Worster, *Nature's Economy: A History of Ecological Ideas* (Cambridge: Cambridge University Press, 1994), 34.

45. Quoted in Worster, *Nature's Economy*, 36.

46. George, le Comte de Buffon, "Les Animaus Carnassiers," quoted in Jacques Roger, *Buffon: A Life in Natural History* (Ithaca, NY: Cornell University Press, 1997), 233.

47. John Bruckner, A Philosophical Survey of the Animal Creation (London, 1768), 83.

48. M. Morel, *Observations sur la Physique por l'an, 1778*, tom xii., p. 154. Notes.

49. Jean Bory de St. Vincent, *Voyage dans les quatre principales lies des Mers d'Afrique (1801)* ; and Charles Grant Vaux, *History of Mauritius* (1801).

50. George Edwards, *Gleanings of Natural History* (London, 1770), 175.

51. Janet Browne, *The Secular Ark: Studies in the History of Biogeography* (New Haven, CT: Yale University Press, 1983), 65.

52. Martin J. S. Rudwick, *The Meaning of Fossils: Episodes in the History of Palaeontology* (Chicago: University of Chicago Press, 1985); Stephen Jay Gould, *The Lying Stones of Marrakech: Penultimate Reflections in Natural History* (New York: Harmony, 2000).

53. Quoted in John Gascoigne, *Joseph Banks and the English Enlightenment: Useful Knowledge and Polite Culture* (Cambridge: Cambridge University Press, 1994), 48–49. I am indebted to Nigel Chambers for pointing out this passage.

54. Quoted in Barrow, *Nature's Ghosts*, 29.

55. Georges Cuvier, "Mémoire sur les espèces d'élephans tant vivantes que fossils," *Magasin Encyclopédique* 3 (1795): 440–445.

56. See Martin J. S. Rudwick, *Georges Cuvier, Fossil Bones, and Geological Catastrophes: New Translations & Interpretations of the Primary Texts* (Chicago: University of Chicago Press, 1997).

57. In a letter to Müller in May 1777, Pallas reported that Linneaus was going insane, and wondered "who will assume the mantle of botanical Dictator?" RAN, f. 21, op. 3, no. 222a, p 28 ob.

58. Ivan Lepekhin, "Reflexions sur la necessité d'etudier la vertû des plantes indigenes," *Nova Acta* I (1783): 83–84.

59. Pallas, *ZRA*, vol. I, p 53.

60. Urness, *A Naturalist in Russia*, 4.

61. Pennant, *Arctic Zoology* 2d ed., vol. III, 1.

62. Pennant, *Arctic Zoology* 2d edi., vol. III, 1–2.

63. Browne, *The Secular Ark*, 61.

64. As opposed to the wilder theoretical speculations of Buffon and Linnaeus, which attempted to reconstruct the entire history of post-deluvial dissemination without first accumulating the necessary data to comprehend contemporary biogeography. See James Larson, "Not Without a Plan: Geography and Natural History in the Late Eighteenth Century," *Journal of the History of Biology* 19, no. 3 (Fall 1998): 454.

65. Pennant, *Arctic Zoology* 2d ed., vol. III, 5.

66. David Quammen, *The Song of the Dodo: Island Biogeography in an Age of Extinctions* (New York: Scribner, 1996), ch. 1.

67. Pennant, *Arctic Zoology* 2d ed., vol. I, 25.

68. Pennant, *Arctic Zoology* 2d ed., vol. I, 103.

69. Sauer, *Account of a Geographical and Astronomical Expedition*, 265.

70. Sauer, *Account of a Geographical and Astronomical Expedition*, 181.

71. Pennant, *Arctic Zoology* 1st ed., vol. I, CXXI.

72. Steller, *Von Sonderbaren Meerthieren*, 102.

73. Pallas, *ZRA* vol. I, 269.

74. Pallas, Reise Durch Verschiedene Provinzen, 311–321.

75. James Larson, "Not Without a Plan: Geography and Natural History in the Late Eighteenth Century," *Journal of the History of Biology* 19, no. 3 (Fall, 1998): 447–488, 461–462.

76. Pallas, *NNB* vol. VII, 42.

77. Steller, *Von Sonderbaren Meerthieren*, 102.

78. Pallas, *ZRA* vol. I, 273.

79. Stejneger, "On the Extermination of the Great Northern Sea Cow (Rytina): A Reply to Professor A.E. Nordenskiold," *Bulletin of the American Geographical Society* 18, no. 4 (1886): 317–328, 325–326.

80. Langsdorff, *Bemerkung auf einer Reise* vol. II, 23.

81. Wendland, *Peter Simon Pallas*, 541.

Chapter 6

1. Yuri Lisiansky, *Voyage Round the World* (London: S. Hamilton, Weybridge, Surrey, 1814), 203.

2. See Ryan Jones, "Lisiansky's Mountain: Changing Views of Nature in Russian Alaska," *Alaska History* 25, no. 1 (Spring 2010).

3. "Letter from Tilesius von Tillenau to Krusenstern," April 22, 1803, in RAN, F. 31, Op. 1, No. 19, p 1.

4. Adam J. von Krusenstern, *Voyage Round the World in the Years 1803, 1804, 1805, and 1806*, vol. I (London: For John Murray, 1813), 29.

5. Rudolf Mumenthaler, "Johann Kaspar Horner als Astronom auf Krusensterns Weltumseglung." In Eva Maeder Niederhäuser and Peter Niederhäuser, eds., *Von Zürich nach Kamtschata: Schweiyer im Russischen Reich* (Zürich: Chronos Verlag, 2008).

6. Lisiansky, *Voyage*, 25.

7. Krusenstern, *Voyage*, 38.

8. Lydia Black, *Russians in Alaska, 1732–1867* (Fairbanks: University of Alaska-Fairbanks, 2004), 170.

9. Lorenz von Oken *Isis, oder enzyclopädische Zeitung* (1817), 1511.

10. G. I. Davydov, *Two Voyages in Russian America, 1802–1807* (Kingston, Ontario: The Limestone Press, 1977), 100, 112, 155, 159, 161.

11. Georg Heinrich von Langsdorff, *Bemerkungen auf einer Reise um die Welt in den Jahren 1803 bis 1807*, vol. II (Frankfurt am Mayn: Im Verlag des Friedrich Wilmans), 66.

12. "Letter from G. H. Langsdorff to I. F. Krusenstern," December 20, 1807, RAN, F. 31, Op. 1, No. 11, p 1.

13. "Letter from G. H. Langsdorff to I. F. Krusenstern," January 21, 1809, RAN, F. 31, Op. 1, No. 11, p 5.

14. Langsdorff, *Voyage*, vol. II, 264.

15. Georg Heinrich von Langsdorff, "Darstellung," in B.N. Komissarov and T.K. Shafranovskaya, "Neizvestnaya Rukopis' Akademika G.I. Langsdorfa o Kamchatke," *Stran i narody Vostoka* 17 (1975), 100.

16. Langsdorff, "Darstellung," 113–114.

17. B. N. Komissarov and T. K. Shafranovskaya, "Neizvestnaya Rukopis' Akademika G. I. Langsdorfa o Kamchatke," *Strany i narody Vostoka* 17 (1975), 93.

18. Estonian State Archive, F. 1414, Op. 3, d. 22, pp 91-92.

19. A. S. Sgibnev, "Istoricheskii Ocherk Glavneishikh Sobitii v Kamchatke s 1650 po 1865 gg." *Morskoi Sbornik 105*. (1869), 69.

20. Lisiansky, *Voyage*, 215.

21. For preference for the tropical Pacific, see James R. Gibson, *Otter Skins, Boston Ships, and China Goods: The Maritime Fur Trade of the Northwest Coast, 1785–1841* (Seattle: University of Washington Press, 1992), 50.

22. Fedor Shemelin, *Zhurnal Pervogo Puteshestviia Rossiian vokrug Zemnogo Shara…* vol. II (St. Petersburg, 1816), 235–236.

23. Ilya Vinkovetsky, "Circumnavigation, Race, and Empire," *The Russian Review* 70 (July 2011): 380–396; and Simon Werrett, "Technology on Display: Instruments and Identities on Russian Voyages of Exploration," *The Russian Review* 70 (July 2011): 396.

24. No author or title, *The Journal of the Royal Geographical Society* 7 (1837), 406.

25. Georg Wilhelm Steller, *Ausführliche Beschreibung von Sonderbaren Meerthieren* (Halle, 1753), 101, 202.

26. Kathleen Kete, "Introduction: Animals and Human Empire," in Kathleen Kete, ed., *A Cultural History of Animals in the Age of Empire* (Oxford: Oxford University Press, 2007), 6–7.

27. See for example, Jane Costlow and Amy Nelson, eds., *Other Animals: Beyond the Human in Russian Culture and History* (Pittsburgh: University of Pittsburgh Press, 2010); Leonid Heller, ed., *Utopiia zverinosti: Reprezentatsii Zhivotnykh v Russkoi Kulture* (Lausanne: Universite de Lausanne, 2007); Arja Rosenholm and Sari Autio-Sarasmo, eds., *Understanding Russian Nature: Representations, Values and Concepts* (Helsinki: University of Helsinki, Aleksanteri Institute, 2005).

28. Hermann Ludwig von Löwenstern, *The First Russian Voyage around the World*, Victoria Moessner, trans. (Fairbanks: University of Alaska Press, 2003), 19, 65. Löwenstern himself, despite his best intentions, also killed innocent animals. He had taken on board a parakeet that had grown progressively less tame. "To make it behave, I hit the bird several times. The little bird misunderstood and wanted to fly away. In my hurry, I grabbed it somewhat too

harshly. My little parrot's eyes began to roll and, so that I did not have to watch the misery any longer, I threw it overboard" (65).

29. Adelbert von Chamisso, *The Alaska Diary of Adelbert von Chamisso, Naturalist on the Kotzebue Voyage, 1815–1818*, Robert Fortune, trans. (Anchorage: Cook Inlet Historical Society, 1986), 50.

30. Frederic Litke, *A Voyage around the World 1826–1829* (Kingston, Ontario: The Limestone Press, 1987), 111, 113.

31. Ivan Veniaminov, *Notes on the Islands of the Unalashka District*, Lydia T. Black and R. H. Geoghegan, eds. and trans. (Kingston, Ontario: The Limestone Press, 1984), 341.

32. See Jane Costlow and Amy Nelson, "Introduction: Integrating the Animal," in Jane Costlow and Amy Nelson, eds., *Other Animals: Beyond the Human in Russian Culture and History* (Pittsburgh: University of Pittsburgh Press, 2010), 8.

33. Lisiansky, *Voyage*, 242.

34. V. M. Golovnin, *Around the World on the Kamchatka, 1817–1819*, Ella Wiswell, trans. (Honolulu: University of Hawaii Press, 1979), 154.

35. Golovnin, *Around the World on the* Kamchatka, 154.

36. John Richardson, *Fauna Boreali-Americana, or the Zoology of the Northern Parts of British America* (London: John Murray, Albermarle-Street, 1829), 108.

37. For example see George Simpson, *An Overland Journey Round the World During the Years 1841 and 1842* (Philadelphia: Lea and Blanchard, 1847), 99.

38. P.A. Tikhmenev, *A History of the Russian-American Company* (Seattle: University of Washington Press, 1978) vol. I, 91.

39. K. T. Khlebnikov, R. G. Liapunova, S. G. Fedorova, and Richard A. Pierce, *Notes on Russian America*, parts II–V (Kingston, Ontario: The Limestone Press, 1994), 136.

40. Veniaminov, *Notes*, 344; Tikhmenev, vol. I, 152–153.

41. "Instruction to company employee Cherkashchenin…June, 1818." In Richard Pierce, ed., *The Russian-American Company: Correspondence of the Governors Communications Sent: 1818* (Kingston, ON: The Limestone Press, 1984), 114.

42. "Letter from P. E. Chistiakov to K. T. Khlebnikov," May 28, 1829. In N. N. Bolkhovitinov, *Rossiisko-Amerikanskaia Kompaniia i Izuchenie Tikhookeanskogo Severa* (Moscow: Nauka, 2005), 229.

43. K. T. Khlebnikov, R. G. Liapunova, S. G. Fedorova, and Richard A. Pierce, *Notes on Russian America*, parts II–V (Kingston, ON: The Limestone Press, 1994), 291.

44. Veniaminov, *Notes*, 346.

45. See James W. Vanstone, "An Early-Nineteenth-Century Artist in Alaska: Louis Choris and the First Kotzebue Expedition," *The Pacific Northwest Quarterly* 51, no. 4 (October 1960): 157.

46. "Report of Zakhar Chichinov," in Alaska State Library—Juneau, Manuscript Division, p 6. This manuscript, found only in translation, was produced by the infamous Ivan Petrov, who is known to have forged several documents. Its accuracy is therefore not assured, although it is clear that Russians moved at some time to killing non-breeding males.

47. Kashevarov, "Otvet na Zamechaniya Glavnogo Pravleniya," *Morskoi Sbornik* 62, no. 9 (September, 1862): 151–168, 158.

48. Fedor Petrovich Litke, *A Voyage around the World, 1826–1829*, Richard Pierce, ed., Renée Marshall, trans. (Kingston, Ontario: The Limestone Press, 1987), 113.

49. (V. Kashevarov), "O Torgovle v Redutakh s Dikami," in the Archive of the Russian Geographical Society, p 2 ob.

50. Friedrich Heinrich von Kittlitz, *Denkwürdigkeiten einer Reise nach den russischen Amerika, nach Mikronesien und durch Kamtschatka* (Gotha, 1858), 2, 190.

51. Kittlitz, *Denkwürdigkeiten einer Reise nach den russischen Amerika, nach Mikronesien und durch Kamtschatka*, 2, 107; see also Lisa Strecker, "Friedrich Heinrich Freiherr von Kittlitz: Ein Deutscher Adeliger Erforscht im Dienste der Kaiserlich Russischen Akademie der Wissenschaften die Halbinsel Kamcatka." In Friedrich Heinrich von Kittlitz, *Denkwürdigkeiten einer Reise nach den russischen Amerika, nach mikronesien und durch Kamtschatka*, ed. Erich Kasten (Norderstedt: Kulturstiftung Sibirien, 2011), 190. http://www.siberian-studies.org/publications/PDF/kittlitz.pdf. Accessed December 12, 2013.

52. "Perepiska ob okhrane bobrovykh lezhbishch v primorskoi oblasti, 25 noiabria 1892–29 ian-varia 1896," f. 702.2.83, Russian State Archive of the Far East, Vladivostok, Russia.

53. NARS-RRAC, CS, roll 12, No. 50 (25 May, 1842), folio 402.

54. Khlebnikov, *Notes on Russian America*, parts II–V, 212, 218.

55. Cedor Snigaroff, *Niigugis Maqaxtazaqngis: Atkan Historical Traditions Told in 1952 by Cedor L. Snigaroff* (Fairbanks: University of Alaska Press, 1979), 34.

56. Tikhmenev, vol. II, 153.

57. See, for example, "Instructions to commander of company vessels… May, 1818," In Richard Pierce, ed., *The Russian-American Company: Correspondence of the Governors Communications Sent: 1818* (Kingston, ON: The Limestone Press, 1984), 96.

58. Kiril Khlebnikov, *Baranov: Chief Manager of the Russian Colonies in America*, trans. Colin Bearne (Kingston, ON: The Limestone Press, 1973), 75.

59. Khlebnikov, *Baranov*, 84.

60. "F.P. Wrangel's Report to the RAC Board of Directors, April 10, 1834," in *RAC i Izuchenie Tikhookeanskogo Severa*, 290. Khlebnikov says that forty-seven sea otters were caught in the "Straits and Chastykh Islands" in 1821; see Khlebnikov, *Notes on Russian America*, part I, 94.

61. Pierce, *The Russian-American Company*, 166.

62. Pierce, *The Russian-American Company*, 39.

63. Tikhmenev, vol. I, 152; also Tikhmenev, *Istoricheskoe Obozrenie*, 237.

64. RVAMF, f. 1375, op. 1, d. 4, l. 512, also quoted in A. V. Grinev, *The Tlingit Indians in Russian America, 1741–1867* (Lincoln: University of Nebraska Press, 2005), 161.

65. Khlebnikov, *Notes on Russian America*, parts II–V, 249.

66. NARS-RRAC, CR, roll 4, No. 509, folio 181.

67. Katherine Arndt, "Preserving the Future Hunt: The Russian-American Company and Marine Mammal Conservation Policies," *Fort Ross-Salt Point Newsletter* (Fall 2007): 4–6.

68. Tikhmenev, vol. I, 235.

69. NARS-RRAC, CR roll 4, No. 481 (August 18, 1839), folio 402.

70. (V. Kashevarov), "O Torgovle," 15.

71. *Records of the Russian-American Company*, Correspondence Received, v. 12, No. 50, p 401 ob.

72. "F. P. Wrangel's Report to the RAC Board of Directors, April 10, 1834." In Bolkhovitinov, *RAC i Izuchenie Tikhookeanskogo Severa*, 290.

73. Katherine Arndt has made this same point. See Arndt, "Preserving the Future Hunt," 6.

74. "Letter, F.P. Wrangel to F.P. Litke, December 2, 1832–March 23, 1833," in *RAC i Izuchenie Tikhookeanskogo Severa*, p. 269.

75. C. L. Hooper, *A Report on the Sea-Otter Banks of Alaska* (Washington, DC: Government Printing Office, 1897), 3.

76. Veniaminov, *Notes*, 39, 329–333.

77. Veniaminov, *Notes*, 334.

78. Kashevarov, "Otvet," 162.

79. Litke, *Atlas Lithographié d'aprés les dessins originaux d'A. Postels*, 80.

80. Litke, *Atlas Lithographié d'aprés les dessins originaux d'A. Postels*, 81.

81. Kashevarov, "Otvet," 156.

82. Lydia Black, "Volcanism as a Factor in Human Ecology: The Aleutian Case," *Ethnohistory* 28, no. 4 (Autumn 1981): 313–340, see p. 323.

83. Board of Directors, "Zamechanie glavnogo pravleniia Russkisko-Amerikanskoi Kompanii," *Morskoi Sbornik* 59, no. 6 (1862): 1 – 8, 7.

84. Kashevarov, "Otvet," 158.

85. Peter Fimrite, "Sea Otter Numbers Take a Turn for the Worse," *San Francisco Chronicle*, August 16, 2010.

86. Khlebnikov, *Notes on Russian America*, part I, 62.

87. Veniaminov, *Notes*, 346.

88. Khlebnikov, *Notes on Russian America*, parts II–V, 147, 306; Khlebnikov, *Russkaia Amerika v Neopublikovannykh Zapiskakh* (Leningrad: Nauka, 1979), 113, 216.

89. Veniaminov, *Notes*, 346.

90. Veniaminov, *Notes*, 332.

91. Veniaminov, *Notes*, 147.

92. Margaret Lantis, "The Aleut Social System, 1750 to 1810, from Early Historical Sources." In Margaret Lantis, *Ethnohistory in Southwestern Alaska and the Southern Yukon: Method and Content* (Lexington: University of Kentucky Press): 161–184, 155.

93. A Report from the Main Administration of the Russian American Company to Osip P. Kozodavlev...September 30, 1813," in Basil Dmytryshyn, E. A. P. Crownhart-Vaughan, and Thomas Vaughan, eds., *Russia's Conquest of Siberia, 1558–1700: A Documentary Record* (Portland, OR: Oregon Historical Society Press, 1985), 210..

94. Otto von Kotzebue, *Discovery into the South Sea and Beering's Straits, v. II: Remarks and Opinions of the Naturalist of the Expedition, Adelbert von Chamisso* (London, 1821), 177.

95. Aleksei V. Postnikov, "Learning from Each Other: On a History of Russian-Native Contacts in Exploration and Mapping of Alaska and the Aleutian Islands (Late Eighteenth—Early Nineteenth Centuries) http://www.loc.gov/rr/european/mofc/postnikov.html. Accessed December 12, 2013.

96. Adelbert von Chamisso, "Cetaceorum maris Kamtschatici imagines, ab Aleutis e lingo fictas, adumbravit recensuitque Albertus de Chamisso," *Nova Acta Academiae Caesarae Leopoldino-Carolinae Germanicae naturae Curiosorum* 12, no. 1 (1824); Marie-Theres Federhofer, *Chamisso und die Wale* (Norderstedt: Kulturstiftung Sibirien, 2012).

97. Nicholas Breyfogle, "The Fate of Fishing in Russia: The Human-Fish Nexus in Lake Baikal," *Sibirica: Interdisciplinary Journal of Siberian Studies* 12, no. 2 (Summer 2013): 1–29.

98. John F. Richards, *The Unending Frontier: An Environmental History of the Early Modern World* (Berkeley: University of California Press, 2003), 513.

99. Bruce G. Trigger, "Ontario Native People and the Epidemics of 1634–1640," in Shepard Krech, edi., *Indians, Animals and the Fur Trade: A Critique of Keepers of the Game* (Athens: University of Georgia Press, 1981), 27.

100. See Peter Kalm, *Travels into North America*, trans. John Reinhold Forster (Barre, MA: The Imprint Society, 1972), 231.

101. Richard Somerset Mackie, *Trading Beyond the Mountains: The British Fur Trade on the Pacific, 1793–1843* (Vancouver, BC: UBC Press, 1997), 246; Arthur Ray, "Some Conservation Schemes of the Hudson's Bay Company, 1821–1850: An Examination of the Problems of Resource Management in the Fur Trade," *Journal of Historical Geography* 1, no. 1 (1975): 49–68.

102. Ray, "Some Conservation Schemes," 57–58.

103. Lorne Hammond, "Marketing Wildlife: The Hudson's Bay Company and the Pacific Northwest, 1821–49," *Forest & Conservation History* 37, no. 1 (January 1993): 14–25, see p. 20.

104. Jennifer Ott, "'Ruining' the Rivers in the Snake Country: The Hudson's Bay Company's Fur Desert Policy," *Oregon Historical Quarterly* 104, no. 2 (Summer 2003); 166–195.

105. Quoted in Hammond, "Marketing Wildlife," 22.

106. Hammond, "Marketing Wildlife," 22.

107. Ray, "Some Conservation Schemes," 66.

108. See Adele Ogden, *The California Sea Otter Trade, 1784–1848* (Berkeley: University of California Press, 1941), chs. V, VI.

109. "F. P. Wrangel's report to the RAC Board of Directors," April 10, 1834, in *RAC i Issledovanie Tikhookeanskogo Severa*, 290.

110. Tikhmenev, vol. I, 359–360.

111. Adelbert von Chamisso, *Werke* (Leipzig, 1896), 446–447.

112. Adelbert von Chamisso, *The Alaska Diary of Adelbert von Chamisso, Naturalist on the Kotzebue Voyage, 1815–1818*, ed. Robert Fortuine and Eva R. Trautmann (Anchorage, AL: Cook Inlet Historical Society, 1986), 46.

113. Kittlitz, "Extract from Friedrich Heinrich Baron von Kittlitz. In *Denkwürdigkeiten einer Reise nach den russischen Amerika*, (Gotha, 1858), in Litke, *A Voyage Around the World*, 153.

114. Vasilii Golovnin, *Around the World on the Kamchatka, 1817–1819*, trans. Elie Wiswell (Honolulu: University of Hawaii Press, 1979), 117.

115. Khlebnikov, *Notes on Russian America*, Parts II–V, 103.

116. Khlebnikov, *Notes on Russian America*, Parts II–V, 105.

117. Ferdinand von Wrangel, *Russian America: Statistical and Ethnographic Information*, trans. Mary Sadouski (Kingston, ON: The Limestone Press, 1980), 16.

118. For more on Baer, see Boris Evgenevich Raikov, *Karl Ernst von Baer, 1792–1867: Sein Leben und Sein Werk* (Leipzig, 1968); Jane Oppenheimer, "Science and Nationality: The Case of Karl Ernst von Baer (1792–1867)," *Proceedings of the American Philosophical Society* 134, no. 2 (June 1990): 75–82.

119. Karl Ernst von Baer, "Introduction." In Ferdinand von Wrangel, *Russian America: Statistical and Ethnographic Information*, trans. Mary Sadouski (Kingston, ON: The Limestone Press, 1980), xv, xvii.

120. Von Baer, "Introduction," xx.

121. Fedor Litke, *A Voyage Around the World, 1826–1829* (Kingston, ON: The Limestone Press, 1987), 56.

122. "Zamechaniya Glavnogo Pravleniya Rossiisko-Amerikanskoi Kompoanii," *Morskoi Sbornik* 59, no. 6 (June, 1862), 5.

123. Report from RAC Director M. M. Buldakov to the St. Petersburg Academy of Sciences, November 26, 1816, in T. S. Fedorova and L. I. Spiridonova, eds., *Rossiisko-Amerikanskaq Kompania i Izuchenie Tikhookeanskogo Severa, 1815–1841* (Moscow, 2005), 24.

124. Kashevarov, "Otvet," 162.

125. Khlebnikov, *Notes on Russian America*, part I, 62.

126. "Zamechanie," 7.

127. "Zamechanie," 6.

128. "Zamechanie," 8.

129. James Vanstone, ed., *A. F. Kasehvarov's Coastal Explorations in Northwest Alaska, 1838* (Chicago: Field Museum of Natural History, 1977); A.V. Grinev, *Kto Est' Kto v Istorii Russkoi Ameriki* (Moscow: Academia, 2009), 218.

130. Kashevarov, "Shto Takoe Zapusk," *Morskoi Sbornik* 59, no. 4 (1862), 91.

131. Kashevarov, "Shto Takoe Zapusk," 89.

132. Kashevarov, "Shto Takoe Zapusk," 89–90.

133. Kashevarov, "Otvet," 163. (Italics in the original.)

134. Kashevarov, "Shto Takoe Zapusk," 91.

135. "Zamechaniya Glavnogo Pravleniya Rossiisko-Amerikanskoi Kompoanii," 2.

136. Kashevarov, "Shto Takoe Zapusk," 91.

137. Kasehvarov, "Otvet," 167.

138. Georg Heinrich von Langsdorff, "Fernere Reisenachrichten vom Herrn Langsdorff aus einem Breife desselben am Hrn. Hofr. Blumenbach," *Magazin für den neuesten Zustand der Naturkunde...*XI, no. 4 (April 1806), 298.

139. Georg Heinrich von Langsdorff, "Auszug eines Briefes des Hrn. Langsdorfs, an Hrn. Hofrath BLUMENBACH zu Göttingen," *Magazin für den neuesten Zustand der Naturkunde...*XXV, no. 4 (April 1808), 479.

140. See, for example, *Allgemeine Geographische Ephemeriden* vol. 40 (1813), 297; *Allgemeine Literatur-Zeitung* (December 1815), 890.

141. J. F. Blumenbach, *Beyträge zur Naturgeschichte* vol. I (Göttingen: bey Heinrich Dieterich, 1806), 26; translation in J. F. Blumenbach, *Anthropological Treatises of Blumenbach and Hunter* (London: Longman, Green, Longman, Roberts, & Green, 1865), 282, 289.

142. Khlebnikov, *Notes on Russian America*, parts II–V, 381.

143. Adelbert von Chamisso, *Werke* (Leipzig, 1896), 447; von Kotzebue, *Discovery into the South Sea and Beering's Straits, v. II*, 307.

144. Nachl. Adelbert von Chamisso, K. 10, Nr. 8, "Zoologische Systeme," *Staatsbibliothek zu Berlin Handschritenabteilung.*

145. Tilesius von Tilenau, "Die Wallfische," *Isis von Oken* 28 (Jena, 1835), 719–720.

146. Letter from Johann Friedrich Eschscholtz to Adelbert Chamisso, April 8, 1830, in Tatiana Lukina, *Johann Friedrich Eschscholtz*, trans. Wilma C. Follette (Leningrad, 1975), 155.

147. Georges Cuvier, "Chapeau de Bois." In Louis Choris, *Voyage Pittoresque autor due Monde...*(Paris, 1822), 21.

148. "Order given by I.A. Kureianov to the Atkha department, May 10, 1839." In *RAC i Issledovanie Tikhookeanskogo Severa*, 385.

149. J. F. Brandt, "Bemerkungen über die Verbreitung und Vertilgung der *Rytina*." *Melanges Biol. Bull. Acad. Sci. St.-Petersburg* (1862), 4, 259–268.

150. Von Baer, "Untersuchungen Über die Ehemalige Verbreitung und die Gänzliche Vertilgung der von Steller Beobachteten Nordischen Seekuh (Rytina M.)," *Memoires Scientifiques* (St. Petersburg, 1840), 20.

151. Von Baer, "Untersuchungen," 65–66.

152. Von Baer, "Untersuchungen," 78.

153. See *The National Encylopedia: A Dictionary of Universal Knowledge by Writers of Eminence in Literature, Science, and Art* (London: William MacKenzie, 1866–1867), 157.

154. Richard Owen, *Paleontology* (Edinburgh: Adam and Charles Black, 1860), 400.

155. J. F. Brandt, "Nochmaliger Nachweis der Vertilgung der Nordischen oder Steller'schen Seekuh (Rhytina Borealis)," *No. 2 Bulletin de la Societe Imperiale* (Moscow, 1862).

156. Carl Edouard d'Eichwald, *Lethaea ou Palaeontologie de la Russie* vol. 3 (Stuttgart: Libraire et Imprimerie de E. Schweizebart, 1853), 343.

157. d'Eichwald, Lethaea ou Palaeontologie de la Russie vol. 3, 343.

Chapter 7

1. For the importance empires at times attribute to maintaining difference see Jane Burbank and Frederick Cooper, *Empires in World History: Power and the Politics of Difference* (Princeton: Princeton University Press, 2010).

2. See Alfred W. Crosby, *Ecological Imperialism: The Biological Expansion of Europe, 900–1900* (Cambridge: Cambridge University Press, 1986).

3. Alan Bewell, " Romanticism and Colonial Natural History," *Studies in Romanticism* 43, no. 1 (2004): 5–34 (see pages 21, 31).

4. Antonio Lafuente and Nuria Valverde, "Linnaean Botany and Spanish Imperial Biopolitics." In Londa Schiebinger and Claudia Swan, eds., *Colonial Botany; Science, Commerce, and Politics* (Philadelphia: University of Pennsylvania Press, 2004), 136; Daniela Bleichmar, *Visible Empire: Botanical Expeditions & Visual Culture in the Hispanic Enlightenment* (Chicago: The University of Chicago Press, 2012), 20.

5. Paula deVos, "Pursuit of Empire in Eighteenth-Century Spain," *Eighteenth-Century Studies* 40, no. 2 (2007): 214.

6. Daniela Bleichmar, "Atlantic Competitions: Botanical Trajectories in the Eighteenth-Century Spanish Empire," in *Science and Empire in the Atlantic World*, ed. Nicholas Dew and James Delbourgo (New York: Routledge, 2008), 229.

7. Eulalia Gasso Miracle, "The Significance of Temminck's Work on Biogeography: Early Nineteenth Century Natural History in Leiden, The Netherlands," *Journal of the History of Biology* 41, no. 4 (Winter 2008): 677–716 (see page 680).

8. Neil Safier, " 'Every Day that I Travel...Is A Page that I turn,': Reading and Observing in Eighteenth-Century Amazonia," *Huntington Library Quarterly* 70, no. 1 (March 2007): 103–128 (see page 115).

9. Alan Bewell, "Romanticism and Colonial Natural History," *Studies in Romanticism* 43, no. 1 (Spring 2004): 5–34 (see page 11).

10. Bruno Latour, *Science in Action: How to Follow Scientists and Engineers through Society* (Cambridge, MA: Harvard University Press, 1988), Chapter 2.

11. Neil Safier, "Fruitless Botany: Joseph de Jussieu's South American Odyssey." In *Science and Empire in the Atlantic World*, 216.

12. *Cours d'histoire*, v. Quoted in Safier, "Every day that I travel..." 112.

13. Tim Bonyhady, *The Colonial Earth* (Carlton, Vic.: Miegunyah Press, 2000), 27, 30, 34.

14. Quoted in Bonyhady, *The Colonial Earth*, 6.

15. Quoted in Anita Cavagnaro Been, *Animals and Authors in the Eighteenth-Century Americas: A Hemispheric Look at the Writing of Natural History* (Providence, RI: The John Carter Brown Library, 2004), 111.

16. James Boyce, *Van Diemen's Land* (Collingwood, VIC: Black, Inc,, 2011), 54.

17. Alexander Humboldt, *Views of Nature: Or Contemplations on the Sublime Phenomena of Creation* (London: Henry G. Bohn, 1850), 199.

18. Quoted in Richard William Judd, *The Untilled Garden: Natural History and the Spirit of Conservation in America, 1740–1840* (New York: Cambridge University Press, 2009), 208.

19. G. Cartwright and C. W. Townsend, *Captain Cartwright and His Labrador Journal* (Boston: Dana Estes & Co., 1911), 318–319.

20. Thomas Hallock, *From the Fallen Tree: Frontier Narratives, Environmental Politics, and the Roots of a National Pastoral, 1749–1826* (Chapel Hill: University of North Carolina Press, 2003), 6.

21. John F. Richards, *The Unending Frontier: An Environmental History of the Early Modern World* (Berkeley: University of California Press, 2003).

22. Jacob Price, "The Imperial Economy," in P. J. Marshall, ed., *The Oxford History of the British Empire. Volume II: The Eighteenth Century* (New York: Oxford University Press, 1998).

23. Briton Cooper Busch, *The War against the Seals: A History of the North American Seal Fishery* (Montreal: McGill-Queens University Press, 1987).

24. Quoted in Steve Nicholls, *Paradise Found: Nature in America at the Time of Discovery* (Chicago: University of Chicago Press, 2009), 35.

25. Monica A. Silva, et al., "Historic and Recent Occurrences of Pinnipeds in the Archipelago of the Azores," *Mammalia* 73 (2009): 60–62; Richards, *The Unending Frontier*, 617–618, Chapter 16.

26. Bonyhady, *The Colonial Earth*, 6.

27. William Bartram, *Travels through North and South Carolina, Georgia, East and West Florida* (Philadelphia: Printed by James and Johnson, 1791), xviii, xix; see also Judd, *The Untilled Garden*, 204.

28. Quoted in Boyce, *Van Diemen's Land*, 35.

29. Hallock, *From the Fallen Tree*, 7, 9.

30. Quoted in Aaron Sachs, *The Humboldt Current: Nineteenth-Century Exploration and the Roots of American Environmentalism* (New York: Viking, 2006), 19.

Appendix A

1. Raisa Makarova, *Russkie na Tikhom Okeane* (Moscow: Nauka, 1968), 17.

2. Vasilii Berkh, *A Chronological History of the Discovery of the Aleutian Islands*, Dmitri Krenov, trans. (Kingston, Ontario: The Limestone Press, 1974), 41.

3. Makarova, *Russkie na Tikhom Okeane*, 18.

4. A. S. Polonskii, "Perechen' puteschestvii russkikh promyshlennikh v Vostochnom Okeane s 1743 po 1800 god," RGO r. 60 op. 1, no. 2, pp 6–8. "A. S. Polonskii, "Promyshlenniki v Aleutskikh Ostrovakh, 1743–171800," RGO, r. 60, op. 1, no. 1.

5. Lydia Black, *Atka: An Ethnohistory of the Western Aleutians* (Kingston, Ontario: The Limestone Press, 1984), 34.

6. Lydia Black, "The Nature of Evil: Of Whales and Sea Otters," in Shepard Krech, ed., *Indians, Animals, and the Fur Trade: A Critique of Keepers of the Game* (Athens, GA: University of Georgia Press, 1981): 109–147, 119.

7. Data in the list cannot be considered complete, as catch records for every voyage are not available. Additionally, some voyages may have never been recorded. Ship captains certainly had ample fiscal motivation for not reporting their voyages and avoiding the 10% taxation that each ship faced upon making port. Still, it seems that most ships did report their cargo, for there were few safe landing places away from the government ports, and there are no firm records of ships having avoided taxation. Another caution to bear in mind regarding the data is that some catch figures from different sources contradict each other. Where they contradict, I have chosen Polonskii's numbers, which are usually more thorough than Berkh's, on the assumption that catches were unlikely to have been exaggerated or fabricated altogether.

INDEX

Printed in the USA
CPSIA information can be obtained
at www.ICGtesting.com
CBHW020837241223
2846CB00013B/53

9 780190 670818